LM

Amsterdam

written and researched by

Martin Dunford, Jack Holland and Phil Lee

with additional contributions by

Karoline Densley and Malijn Maat

ROUGH GUIDES

www.roughguides.com

Introduction to

Amsterdam

Amsterdam is a compact, instantly likeable city. It's appealing to look at and pleasing to walk around, an intriguing mix of the parochial and the international; it also has a welcoming attitude towards visitors and a uniquely youthful orientation, shaped by the liberal counterculture of the last four decades. It's hard not to feel drawn by the buzz of open-air summer events, by the cheery intimacy of the city's clubs and bars, and by the Dutch facility with languages: just about everyone you meet in Amsterdam will be able to speak good-to-fluent English, on top of their own native tongue, and often more than a smattering of French and German too.

The city's layout is determined by a web of canals radiating out from an historical core to loop right round the centre. These planned, seventeenth-century extensions to the medieval town make for a uniquely elegant urban environment, with tall gabled houses reflected in their black-green waters. This is the city at its most beguiling, a world away from the traffic and noise of many other European city centres, and it has made Amsterdam one of the continent's most popular short-haul destinations. These charms are supplemented by a string of first-rate attractions, most notably the Anne Frankhuis, where the young Jewish diarist hid away during the German occupation of World War II, the Rijksmuseum, with its wonderful collection of Dutch

paintings, including several of Rembrandt's finest works, and the peerless Vincent van Gogh Museum, with the world's largest collection of the artist's work.

However, it's Amsterdam's population and politics that constitute its most enduring characteristics. Celebrated during the 1960s and 1970s for its radical permissiveness, the city mellowed only marginally during the 1980s, and, despite the gentrification of the last twenty years, it retains a laid-back feel. That said, it is far from being as cosmopolitan a city as, say, London or Paris: despite the huge numbers of immigrants from the former colonies in Surinam and Indonesia, as well as Morocco and Turkey – to name but a few – almost all live and work outside the centre and can seem almost invisible to the casual visitor. Indeed, there is an ethnic and social homogeneity in the city centre that seems to run counter to everything you may have heard of Dutch integration.

The apparent contradiction embodies much of the spirit of Amsterdam. The city is world famous as a place where the possession and sale of cannabis are

effectively legal – or at least decriminalized – and yet, for the most part, Amsterdammers themselves can't really be bothered with the stuff. And while Amsterdam is renowned for its tolerance towards all styles of behaviour and dress, a primmer, more correct-thinking big city, with a more mainstream dress sense, would be hard to find. Behind the cosy cafés and dreamy canals lurks the suspicion that Amsterdammers' hearts lie squarely in their wallets, and while newcomers might see the city as a liberal haven, locals can seem just as indifferent to this as well.

In recent years, a string of hardline city mayors have taken this conservatism on board and seem to have embarked on a generally successful − if often unspoken − policy of squashing Amsterdam's image as a counterculture icon and depicting it instead as a centre for business and international high finance. Almost all the inner-city squats − which once well-nigh defined local people-power − are gone or legalized, and coffeeshops have been forced to choose between selling dope or alcohol, and, if only for economic reasons, many have switched to the latter. Such shifts in attitude, combined with alterations to the cityscape, in the form of large-scale urban development on the outskirts and regeneration within, combine to create an unmistakeable feeling that Amsterdam and its people are busy reinventing themselves, writing off their hippyfied history to return to earlier, more stolid days.

Nevertheless, Amsterdam remains a casual and intimate place, and Amsterdammers themselves make much of their city and its attractions being *gezellig*, a rather overused Dutch word roughly corresponding to a combination of "cosy", "lived-in" and "warmly convivial". Nowhere is this more applicable than in the city's unparalleled selection of drinking places, whether you choose a traditional brown bar or one of a raft of newer, designer cafés, or grand cafés. The city boasts dozens of great restaurants too, with its Indonesian cuisine second-to-none, and is at the forefront of contemporary European film, dance, drama and music. The city has several top-rank jazz venues and the Concertgebouw concert hall is home to one of the world's leading orchestras. The club scene is restrained by the standard of other main cities, although the city's many gay bars and clubs partly justify Amsterdam's claim to be the "Gay Capital of Europe".

Where to go

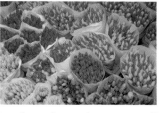

Confined by the circuitous sweep of the Singelgracht canal, **Amsterdam**'s **compact centre** contains most of the city's leading attractions and only takes about forty minutes to stroll from one end to the other. **Centraal Station**, where you're likely to arrive, lies on the centre's northern edge, its back to the River IJ, and from the station the city fans south in a web of concentric canals, surrounded by expanding suburbs.

Butting up to the River IJ, the **Old Centre** spreads south from Centraal Station bisected by Damrak and its continuation, Rokin, long the city's main drag; en route is the Dam, the main square. The Old Centre remains Amsterdam's commercial heart, with the best of its bustling street life. It also holds myriad shops, bars and restaurants, includes the **Red Light District**, just to the east of Damrak, and contains dozens of fine old buildings, most memorably the Oude Kerk, the Amstelkring and the Koninklijk Paleis. The Old Centre is bordered by the first of the major canals, the Singel, which is followed closely by the Herengracht, Keizersgracht and Prinsengracht – collectively known as the **Grachtengordel**, or "Girdle of Canals". These canals were part of a major seventeenth-century urban extension and, with the interconnecting radial streets, form the city's distinctive web shape. This is Amsterdam's most delightful area and the one you see on all the brochures – handsome seventeenth- and eighteenth-century canal houses, with their distinctive gables, overlooking narrow, dreamy canals: a familiar image perhaps, but

one that is still entirely authentic. It's here you'll also find the city's most celebrated attraction, the **Anne Frankhuis**, a poignant reminder of the Holocaust.

Immediately to the west of the Grachtengordel lies the **Jordaan**, one-time industrial slum and the traditional heart of working-class Amsterdam, though in recent years the district has experienced a measure of gentrification. The same applies to the adjacent **Westerdok**, though the origins of this district are very different. The artificial islands of the Westerdok were dredged out of the river to create extra wharves and shipbuilding space during the city's Golden Age and only in the last few decades has the shipping industry moved out. On the other side of the centre is the **Old Jewish Quarter**, which was once home to a thriving Jewish community until the German occupation of World War II. Post-war development has laid a heavy hand on the quarter, but nonetheless there are a couple of poignant survivors, principally the Portuguese syn-

**A uniquely elegant urban environment,
with tall gabled houses reflected in black-green waters**

agogue and the Jewish Historical Museum. The adjacent **Plantagebuurt** is greener and more suburban, but it does possess one excellent museum, the Verzetsmuseum (Resistance Museum) – as does the neighbouring **Oosterdok**, another area of former dockland that is undergoing a rapid process of renewal and revival.

Amsterdam's **Museum Quarter** contains, as you might expect, the city's premier art museums, principally the **Rijksmuseum** and the **Van Gogh Museum**. Each has a superb collection and both lie just a stone's throw from the city's finest park, the **Vondelpark**. Finally, the residential suburbs – or **Outer Districts** – spreading beyond Singelgracht are relatively short of attractions, one notable exception being the wooded parkland of the Amsterdamse Bos.

Talk to Amsterdammers about visiting other parts of their country and you may well be met with looks of amazement: ignore them. The Dutch have an outstanding public transport system, an integrated network of trains and buses that puts the city within easy grasp of a large and varied slice of the country. Consequently, the choice of possible **day-trips** is extensive: the towns of **Haarlem** and **Alkmaar**, the old Zuider Zee ports of **Marken** and **Volendam**, and two villages, pretty **Edam** and the recreated seventeenth-century Dutch hamlet of **De Zaanse Schans**, are all worth a visit.

When to go

A msterdam enjoys a fairly standard temperate climate, with warm, if characteristically mild, **summers**, and moderately cold and wet **winters**. The climate is certainly not severe enough to make very much difference to the city's routines, which makes the city an ideal all-year destination. That said, high summer – roughly late June to August – sees the city's parks packed to the gunnels and parts of the centre almost overwhelmed by the tourist throng, whereas **spring** and **autumn** are not too crowded and can be especially beautiful, with mist hanging over the canals and low sunlight beaming through the cloud cover. In the summer mosquitoes can be bothersome, and at any time of the year, but particularly in summer, try to book your accommodation ahead of time.

Average daily temperatures (°C) and monthly rainfall (mm)

	Jan	Feb	Mar	Apr	May	June	July	Aug	Sept	Oct	Nov	Dec
Min °C	−0.2	−0.5	1.5	3.8	7.5	10.5	12.5	12.5	10.5	7.3	3.8	1.1
Max °C	4.3	4.9	8.1	11.6	16	19.1	20.5	20.5	18.3	14	8.8	5.7
mm	79.1	43.6	89.3	39.3	50.2	60.1	73.4	60	80.1	103.7	76.4	72.3

23

things not to miss

It's not possible to see everything Amsterdam has to offer on a short trip – and we don't suggest you try. What follows is a subjective selection of the city's highlights, from elegant canalside architecture and vibrant markets to outstanding art collections and traditional bars – all arranged in colour-coded categories to help you find the very best things to see, do and experience. All entries have a page reference to take you straight into the guide, where you can find out more.

01 Trams Page **25** • Rattling across the city, Amsterdam's fast and efficient trams are an enjoyable way to reach all of the most interesting attractions.

03 Haarlem Page **122** ● Just a few minutes by train from Amsterdam, Haarlem is a lovely little town and home to the outstanding Frans Hals Museum.

02 Tuschinski cinema Page **74** ● Opened in 1921, the Tuschinski cinema has a superb Art Deco interior.

04

Albert Cuyp market Page **112** ● Shop for clothes or sample delicacies at this excellent open-air market.

05

Begijnhof Page **57** ● The antique Begijnhof is one of the quietest and prettiest corners of the city centre.

06 **Flea and antique markets** Page **207** • With every justification, Amsterdam is famous for its flea and antiques markets.

07 **The Golden Bend** Page **71** • Herengracht's De Gouden Bocht – the Golden Bend – boasts some of Amsterdam's most elegant Neo-classical mansions.

08 **Queen's Day** Page **230** • Amsterdammers let their tresses down on Queen's Day, the city's biggest and wildest municipal knees-up.

xi

09 Brouwersgracht Page **62** • With its houseboats and spout gables, Brouwersgracht is an especially charming canal.

10 Indonesian restaurants Pages **171**, **173**, **175**, **177** & **178** • Amsterdam's Indonesian restaurants – a legacy of Dutch colonialism – are second-to-none.

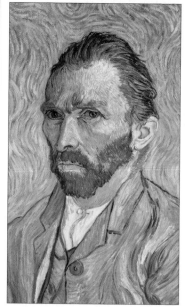

11 Van Gogh Museum Page **103** • The Van Gogh Museum holds the world's most comprehensive collection of the artist's work. Simply unmissable.

12 Museum Amstelkring Page 51 • Once a clandestine church for the city's Catholics, the seventeenth-century Amstelkring is Amsterdam's most distinctive historic site.

13 Bric-a-brac shops Page 80 • The Jordaan holds many of the city's most diverting secondhand and bric-a-brac shops.

14 Brown cafés Page 161 • Amsterdam is famous for its brown cafés – dark, cosy and very traditional.

15 Rijksmuseum Page **98** • The Rijksmuseum has an impressive collection of Dutch paintings, including Rembrandt's famous *The Night Watch*.

16
Kadinsky coffee shop Page **167** • Chocolate chip cookies, jazz and dope – one idea of nirvana?

17 Van Loon Museum Page **73** • The Van Loon Museum occupies a handsome canal house complete with Rococo stucco work and Romantic murals.

18

Vondel-park Page **107** • Leafy Vondelpark, with its ponds, footpaths and colony of parrots, is the city's most attractive park.

19

Esnoga synagogue Page **90** • The Esnoga synagogue of 1675 is a fascinating reminder of the once numerous Jewish community.

20

Jenever Page **158** • Served ice-cold, jenever, the Dutch version of gin, is the nation's favourite spirit.

21

Rembrandt-huis Page **87** •
Now a museum, this was the house where Rembrandt spent his happiest and most prosperous years.

22

Westerkerk
Page **63** •
Amsterdam is celebrated for its soaring church spires – the Westerkerk's is the most striking.

23 **Anne Frankhuis**
Page **63** •
During the German occupation, Anne Frank and her family hid away in a secret annexe, its entrance camouflaged by a bookcase.

Contents

Using this Rough Guide

We've tried to make this Rough Guide a good read and easy to use. The book is divided into eight main sections, and you should be able to find whatever you want in one of them.

Colour section

The front **colour section** offers a quick tour of Amsterdam. The **introduction** aims to give you a feel for the place, with tips on where to head for and when to go. Next, our authors round up their favourite aspects of Amsterdam in the **things not to miss** section – whether it's great food, amazing sights or a special hotel. After this comes a full **contents** list.

Basics

The Basics section covers all the **pre-departure** nitty-gritty to help you plan your trip and the practicalities you'll want to know once there. This is where to find out how to get there, about money and costs, Internet access, transport and local media – in fact just about every piece of **general practical information** you might need.

The City

This is the heart of the Rough Guide, divided into user-friendly chapters, each of which covers a city district or nearby day-trip destinations. Every chapter starts with an **introduction** that helps you to decide where to go, followed by an extensive tour of the sights.

Listings

This section contains all the consumer information needed to make the most of your stay, with chapters on **accommodation**, places to **eat** and **drink**, **nightlife**, **shopping** and **festivals**.

Contexts

Read Contexts to get a deeper understanding of what makes Amsterdam tick. We include a brief **history**, a piece on **Dutch art**, and a further reading section reviewing dozens of **books** relating to the city.

Language

The **language** section offers useful guidance for speaking Dutch and includes a comprehensive **menu reader**. Here you'll also find a **glossary** of art and architecture terms.

Index + small print

Apart from a **full index**, which includes maps as well as places, this section covers publishing information, credits and acknowledgements, and also has our contact details in case you want to send us updates, corrections or suggestions for improving the book.

Colour maps

The back colour section contains ten detailed **maps and plans** to help you explore the city up close and locate every place recommended in the guide.

Map and chapter list

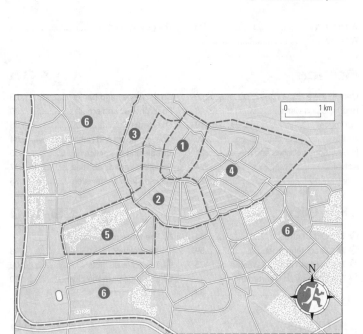

Contents

Contexts

Language

Index + small print

Colour maps

Amsterdam
Amsterdam city centre
The Old Centre
Grachtengordel West
Grachtengordel South

Jordaan
Old Jewish Quarter
Museum Quarter
Trams, Buses & Metro
De Pijp

Map symbols

maps are listed in the full index using coloured text

——	Road	⊠	Post office
▬▬	Pedestrianized road	Ⓜ	Metro station
------	Tunnel	▬	Building
- - -	Footpath	⊞	Church
▬▬	Waterway	◯	Stadium
━━	Railway	✡	Synagogue
----	Chapter division boundary	⊙	Statue/memorial
≍	Bridge	⍫	Gardens
✈	Airport	⊥	Cemetery
ⓘ	Information office	▦	Park/National park

Basics

Basics

Getting there

UK travellers are spoilt for choice in deciding how to get to Amsterdam. There are flights to Amsterdam from London and a string of regional airports; Eurostar trains from London to Brussels, from where it's a little under three hours onwards by train; and ferries from Harwich to the Hook of Holland, Hull to Rotterdam and Newcastle (North Shields) to Ijmuiden, with all three Dutch ports within easy striking distance of the city. Two further options are Eurotunnel from Folkestone to Calais, a 400-kilometre drive from Amsterdam, and a regular international bus service from London.

For **North American** travellers, the main decision is whether to fly direct to Amsterdam – easy enough as Schiphol airport is a major European hub – or fly via another European city, probably London. From **Australia** and **New Zealand**, every flight to Amsterdam requires one or two stops on the way. Note also if your visit to Amsterdam is part of a wider journey around Europe by train, that many **train passes** have to be purchased before you leave home (see p.15).

Airfares from North America, Australia and New Zealand to Amsterdam depend on the **season**, with the highest prices applying from around late June to early September, the peak tourist season; you'll get the best prices during the low season, mid-November through to April (excluding Christmas and New Year when prices are hiked up and seats are at a premium). Note also that flying at the weekend is generally more expensive. If you're flying from the UK or Ireland, the same general strictures apply, though the market is more haphazard with the airlines constantly moving their prices up and down – a reflection of the intensity of the competition.

Special deals aside, you can often cut airfare costs by going through a **specialist flight agent** rather than an airline. These agents come in two main forms: there are **consolidators**, who buy up blocks of tickets from the airlines and sell them at a discount, and **discount agents**, who in addition to dealing with discounted flights may also offer special student and youth fares and a range of other travel-related services such as travel insurance, rail passes, car rentals and the like. Some agents specialize in **charter**

flights, which may be cheaper than anything available on a scheduled flight, though be aware that departure dates are fixed and withdrawal penalties high.

A further possibility **from North America** is to see if you can arrange a **courier flight**, although you'll need a flexible schedule, and preferably you'll be travelling alone with very little luggage. In return for shepherding a parcel through customs, you can expect to get a deeply discounted ticket, though you'll probably be restricted in the duration of your stay.

Package deals from **tour operators** are rarely going to save you money, but several of the best provide special-interest tours that will put you in touch with other like-minded souls, from cyclists to canal lovers.

Booking flights online

Many airlines and travel websites offer you the opportunity to **book tickets online**, cutting out the costs of middlemen. Good deals can often be found through discount or auction sites, as well as through the airlines' own websites.

Online booking agents and general travel sites

ⓦ **www.cheapflights.com** Bookings from the UK and Ireland only. Flight deals, travel agents, plus links to other travel sites.

ⓦ **www.cheaptickets.com** Discount flight specialists.

ⓦ **www.etn.nl/discount.htm** A hub of consolidator and discount agent web links, maintained by the non-profit European Travel Network.

ⓦ **www.expedia.com** Discount airfares, all-airline search engine and daily deals.

Ⓑ

ⓦ **www.flyaow.com** Online air travel information and reservations site.

ⓦ **www.gaytravel.com** Gay online travel agent, concentrating mostly on accommodation.

ⓦ **www.hotwire.com** Bookings from the US only. Last-minute savings of up to forty percent on regular published fares. Travellers must be at least 18 and there are no refunds, transfers or changes allowed. Log-in required.

ⓦ **www.lastminute.com** Offers good last-minute holiday package and flight-only deals.

ⓦ **www.priceline.com** Name-your-own-price website that offers deals at around forty percent off standard fares. You cannot specify flight times (although you do specify dates) and the tickets are non-refundable, non-transferable and non-change-able.

ⓦ **www.skyauction.com** Bookings from the US only. Auctions tickets and travel packages using a "second bid" scheme. The best strategy is to bid the maximum you're willing to pay, since if you win you'll pay just enough to beat the runner-up regardless of your maximum bid.

ⓦ **www.skydeals.co.uk** Discount flight-only specialists for worldwide destinations.

ⓦ **www.smilinjack.com/airlines.htm** Lists an up-to-date compilation of airline website addresses.

ⓦ **www.travelocity.com** Destination guides, hot Web fares and best deals for car rental, accommodation and lodging as well as fares. Provides access to the travel agent system SABRE, the most comprehensive central reservations system in the US.

ⓦ **www.travel.com.au** Comprehensive online travel company for travel from Australia and New Zealand.

ⓦ **www.travelshop.com.au** Australian website offering discounted flights, packages, insurance and online bookings.

ⓦ **travel.yahoo.com** Incorporates a lot of Rough Guide material in its coverage of destination countries and cities across the world, with information about places to eat, sleep etc.

Flights from the UK

Amsterdam is one of the UK's most popular short-haul destinations, and you'll find lots of choice in carriers, flight times and departure airports. Aside from the major full-service carriers (KLM and British Airways), there is a hat-full of no-frills airlines operating to Amsterdam, including easyJet, BMIbaby and MyTravelLite. Bear in mind also that competition is intense, so new routings appear and existing ones are abandoned on a regular basis.

Fares with a no-frills airline such as easyJet range from £35 return to £100 or more, though the cheapest tickets usually need to be booked weeks in advance and entail midweek travel at unsociable hours. The cheapest tickets are usually non-exchangeable and/or non-refundable too. Booking at the last minute can often, but not always, mean shelling out a lot more – say £300–400. For weekend travel and more reasonable departure and arrival times, no-frills flights can often be matched by the full-service airlines, with KLM's prices starting at £59 return, and rising, with improved flexibility, to around £280. For BA, fares start around £79 for a non-flexible, non-refundable return economy flight, and rise to almost £400, without the restrictions and closer to the date of departure. All carriers offer their lowest prices online.

UK airlines and routings

BMI British Midland ☎0870/607 0555, ⓦ www.flybmi.com. London Heathrow to Amsterdam Schiphol.

bmibaby ☎0870/264 2229, ⓦ www.bmibaby.com. East Midlands Airport to Amsterdam Schiphol.

British Airways ☎0845/773 3377, ⓦ www.ba.com. Birmingham International, London Gatwick, London Heathrow & Manchester to Amsterdam Schiphol.

easyJet ☎0870/600 0000, ⓦ www.easyjet.com. Belfast, Edinburgh, Glasgow, Liverpool, London Gatwick and Luton to Amsterdam Schiphol.

KLM ☎0870/507 4074, ⓦ www.klmuk.com. Aberdeen, Birmingham International, Bristol, Cardiff, Edinburgh, Glasgow, Humberside, Leeds/Bradford, London City, London Heathrow, Manchester, Newcastle, Norwich & Teesside to Amsterdam Schiphol. Also London Heathrow to Rotterdam, London Stansted to Eindhoven and Maastricht.

MyTravelLite ☎0870/156 4564, ⓦ www .mytravellite.com. Birmingham International to Amsterdam Schiphol.

Ryanair ☎0871/246 0000, ⓦ www.ryanair.com. London Stansted to Eindhoven, Maastricht and Groningen, all in the Netherlands. Ryanair bought rival no-frills carrier Buzz in early 2003 and may – or may not – resuscitate Buzz's London Stansted to Amsterdam Schiphol service.

Scotairways ☎0870/606 0707, ⓦ www .scotairways.co.uk. Southampton to Amsterdam Schiphol.

VLM London ☎020/7476 6677, Manchester
☎0161/493 3232, Jersey ☎01534/783 283;
🖳www.vlm-airlines.com. Manchester and London
City to Rotterdam.

Specialist flight agents in the UK

Bridge the World ☎0870/444 7474,
🖳www.bridgetheworld.com. Good Dutch deals
aimed at the backpacker market.
Co-op Travel Care Belfast ☎0870/112 0099,
🖳www.travelcareonline.com. Flights and holidays
to Amsterdam.
Destination Group ☎020/7400 7045,
🖳www.destination-group.com. Good discount
flights to Amsterdam, part of the lastminute.com
online booking service.
Flightbookers ☎0870/010 7000, 🖳www.ebookers
.com. Low fares on an extensive selection of scheduled
flights.
Flight Centre ☎0870/890 8099, 🖳www
.flightcentre.co.uk. Good discounts on scheduled
flights.
Flynow ☎0870/444 0045, 🖳www.flynow.com.
Large range of discounted tickets.
North South Travel ☎01245/608 291, 🖳www
.northsouthtravel.co.uk. Friendly, competitive travel
agency offering discounted fares worldwide – profits
are used to support projects in the developing world,
especially the promotion of sustainable tourism.
Rosetta Travel Belfast ☎028/9064 4996,
🖳www.rosettatravel.com. Flight and holiday agent.
STA Travel ☎0870/160 0599,
🖳www.statravel.co.uk. Worldwide specialists in
low-cost flights and tours for students and under-
26s, though other customers welcome.
Top Deck ☎020/7244 8000, 🖳www.topdecktravel
.co.uk. Long-established agent dealing in discount
flights.
Trailfinders ☎020/7628 7628, 🖳www.trailfinders
.co.uk. One of the best-informed and most efficient
agents for independent travellers.
Travel Cuts ☎020/7255 2082, 🖳www.travelcuts
.co.uk. Specialists in budget, student and youth travel.

Tour operators in the UK

Most high-street travel agents can fix you up
a city break to Amsterdam with one of the
many large-scale **tour operators**. The list
below includes details of some of the more
individual companies.

Bridge Travel ☎0870/191 7117, 🖳www
.bridge-travel.co.uk. Tour operator offering city
breaks to Amsterdam, The Hague, Rotterdam and
Maastricht as well as smaller towns such as Arnhem
and Delft. Will also tailor-make packages for cycling
holidays and excursions to the bulbfields.
Brightwater Holidays ☎01334/657 155,
🖳www.brightwaterholidays.com. Fife-based tour
operator running trips to the Dutch bulbfields,
departing from London and Dover.
Cresta Holidays ☎0870/238 7711,
🖳www.crestaholidays.co.uk. Part of the Mytravel
Group, offering city breaks to Amsterdam.
Martin Randall Travel ☎020/8742 3355,
🖳www.martinrandall.com. Small-group, five-day
"Dutch Painting" tours, led by an expert on seventeenth-century Dutch art.
Prospect Music and Art Tours ☎020/7486
5704, 🖳www.prospecttours.com. Springtime river
cruises through the bulbfields, exploring towns on
foot with a local guide.
Saddle Skedaddle ☎0191/265 1110,
🖳www.skedaddle.co.uk. Organizes four- or five-
week-long cycling tours of the Netherlands each
year, beginning and ending in Amsterdam, and visiting Alkmaar, Zaanse Schans and Enkhuizen on the
way.
Thomas Cook Holidays ☎01733/563 200,
🖳www.thomascook.com. City breaks in
Amsterdam, The Hague and Rotterdam, with good
deals on flights and accommodation.
Travelscene ☎0870/777 9987, 🖳www
.travelscene.co.uk. City breaks to Amsterdam.
Travelscope ☎01453/821 210, 🖳www
.travelscope.co.uk. Tour operator offering a variety
of family-friendly packages to the Netherlands
including city breaks, cycling holidays, river cruises
and trips to the flower festivals.

Flights from Ireland

From the Republic of Ireland, Aer Lingus flies
six times daily to Amsterdam out of Dublin
and twice daily from Cork, for a minimum
€175–200 return, though, depending on the
season, this can rise to €450 or more.
Skynet flies from Shannon six times a week,
from €195 (requiring 2 days' minimum stay)
to €445. The upper-end tickets are fully flexible and fully refundable within a twelve-
month period.

Airlines in Ireland

Aer Lingus ☎0818/365 000, 🖳www.aerlingus.ie.
BMI British Midland ☎01/407 3036,
🖳www.flybmi.com.
British Airways ☎1800/626 747,
🖳www.ba.com.

Ryanair ☎0818/303 030, ⊛www.ryanair.com.
Skynet ☎061/234 455, ⊛www.skynetair.net.

Flight and travel agents in Ireland

Aran Travel International ☎091/562 595,
⊛homepages.iol.ie/~arantvl/aranmain.htm. Good-value flights.
CIE Tours ☎01/703 1888, ⊛www.cietours.ie.
General flight and tour agent.
Go Holidays ☎01/874 4126,
⊛www.goholidays.ie. Offers package tours, especially city breaks to Amsterdam.
Joe Walsh Tours ☎01/676 0991, ⊛www
.joewalshtours.ie. General budget fares agent.
Lee Travel ☎021/427 7111, ⊛www.leetravel.ie.
Flights and holidays worldwide.
McCarthy's Travel ☎021/427 0127,
⊛www.mccarthystravel.ie. General flight agent.
Neenan Travel ☎01/607 9900,
⊛www.neenantrav.ie. Specialists in European city breaks, including Amsterdam.
Student & Group Travel ☎01/677 7834. Student and group specialists.
Trailfinders ☎01/677 7888,
⊛www.trailfinders.ie. One of the best-informed and most efficient agents for independent travellers.

Flights from the US and Canada

Amsterdam's Schiphol airport is among the most popular and least expensive gateways to Europe from North America, and getting a convenient and good-value flight is rarely a problem. Virtually every region of the US and Canada is well served by the major airlines, and KLM/Northwest, Continental, Singapore Airways and Delta all offer **nonstop flights**. Many more fly via London and other European centres – and are nearly always cheaper because of it.

In the US, KLM and Northwest, which operate a joint service, offer the widest range of flights, with direct or one-stop flights to Amsterdam from eleven US cities, and connections from dozens more. An average high-season round-trip fare from New York (flight time 8hr 10min) comes in at $585; from Chicago $750 (11hr 15min); and from Los Angeles $755 (10hr 30min). Of the other carriers, Singapore Airlines offers the least expensive fares from New York at $600 for a high-season return, followed by United Airlines, Continental and topped off

by Delta at a pricey $840. From elsewhere in the US, the Dutch charter firm Martinair flies year round from Miami and Orlando direct to Amsterdam, with fares from both cities averaging $600. Singapore Airlines and United also fly direct to Amsterdam from Chicago, while Delta operates from Atlanta (direct) and Salt Lake City (with one stop); Continental flies nonstop from Houston for around $790.

From Canada, KLM flies year-round direct to Amsterdam from Vancouver (9hr 45min) with a round-trip fare for roughly C$1600, and from Toronto (7hr 30min) for C$1310. Flying from Montréal involves a stopover, and costs about C$1360. In summer (April–Oct), Martinair flies from Toronto, Vancouver, Edmonton and Calgary; sample fares for a high-season round trip are C$1015 from Toronto, and C$1170 from Vancouver.

As with any long-distance flight, it is nearly always less expensive to fly non-direct. Many European carriers fly from major US and Canadian cities to Amsterdam Schiphol via their own capitals, for example Air France from New York and Los Angeles via Paris, from $640 return fare.

Airlines in North America

Air Canada ☎1-888/247-2262,
⊛www.aircanada.ca.
Air France US ☎1-800/237-2747,
⊛www.airfrance.com; Canada ☎1-800/667-2747; ⊛www.airfrance.ca.
American Airlines ☎1-800/433-7300,
⊛www.aa.com.
British Airways ☎1-800/247-9297,
⊛www.british-airways.com.
Continental Airlines ☎1-800/231-0856,
⊛www.continental.com.
Delta ☎1-800/241-4141, ⊛www.delta.com.
Martinair Holland ☎1-800/627-8462,
⊛www.martinairusa.com.
Northwest/KLM ☎1-800/447-4747,
⊛www.nwa.com.
Singapore Airlines ☎1-800/742-3333,
⊛www.singaporeair.com.
United ☎1-800/538-2929, ⊛www.ual.com.

Courier flights from North America

Air Courier Association ☎1-800/282-1202,
⊛www.aircourier.org. Courier flight broker.

Membership ($29/yr) also entitles you to twenty percent discount on travel insurance and name-your-own-price non-courier flights.

International Association of Air Travel Couriers ☎308/632-3273, ⓦwww.courier.org. Courier flight broker with membership fee of $45/yr.

Discount travel companies in North America

Air Brokers International ☎1-800/883-3273, ⓦwww.airbrokers.com. Consolidator and specialist in round-the-world tickets.

Airtech ☎212/219-7000, ⓦwww.airtech.com. Standby seat broker; also deals in consolidator fares and courier flights.

Airtreks.com ☎1-877-AIRTREKS or 415/912-5600, ⓦwww.airtreks.com. Round-the-world tickets. The website lets you build and price your own RTW itinerary.

Council Travel ☎1-800/2COUNCIL, ⓦwww.counciltravel.com. Mostly specializes in student/budget travel.

Educational Travel Center ☎1-800/747-5551 or 608/256-5551, ⓦwww.edtrav.com. Student/youth discount agent.

New Frontiers ☎1-800/677-0720 or 310/670-7318, ⓦwww.newfrontiers.com. Discount travel firm.

SkyLink US ☎1-800/AIR-ONLY or 212/573-8980, Canada ☎1-800/SKY-LINK, ⓦwww.skylinkus.com. Consolidator.

STA Travel US ☎1-800/781-4040, Canada 1-888/427-5639, ⓦwww.sta-travel.com. Worldwide specialists in independent travel; also student IDs, travel insurance, car rental, rail passes, etc.

Student Flights ☎1-800/255-8000 or 480/951-1177, ⓦwww.isecard.com. Student/youth fares, student IDs.

TFI Tours ☎1-800/745-8000 or 212/736-1140, ⓦwww.lowestairprice.com. Consolidator.

Travac ☎1-800/TRAV-800, ⓦwww.thetravelsite.com. Consolidator and charter broker.

Travelers Advantage ☎1-877/259-2691, ⓦwww.travelersadvantage.com. Discount travel club, with membership fee.

Travel Avenue ☎1-800/333-3335, ⓦwww.travelavenue.com. Full-service travel agent that offers discounts in the form of rebates.

Travel Cuts Canada ☎1-800/667-2887, US ☎1-866/246-9762, ⓦwww.travelcuts.com. Student travel organization.

Worldtek Travel ☎1-800/243-1723, ⓦwww.worldtek.com. Discount travel agency for worldwide travel.

Tour operators in North America

Abercrombie & Kent ☎1-800/323-7308 or 630/954-2944, ⓦwww.abercrombiekent.com. Upmarket tours taking in Amsterdam and its surroundings.

CBT Tours ☎1-800/736-2453 or 312/475-0625, ⓦwww.cbttours.com. Bicycle tours from Amsterdam to Brussels following the North Sea Coast. Springtime tours to the bulbfields and Keukenhof Gardens.

Cosmos ☎1-800/276-1241, ⓦwww.cosmosvacations.com. Plans vacation packages in Amsterdam with an independent focus.

Pack and Pedal Europe ☎1-570/965-2064, ⓦwww.tripsite.com. Offers eleven guided and self-guided cycling tours of the Netherlands, including Amsterdam, and Belgium; accommodation usually in two- or three-star hotels.

Venture Out ☎1-888/431-6789, ⓦwww.venture-out.com. Cycling and cultural small-group tours for gay travellers; optional add-on for Amsterdam's Gay Pride.

Flights from Australia and New Zealand

There's no shortage of flights to Amsterdam from Australia and New Zealand, though all of them involve **at least one stop**. Singapore Airways and Malaysian offer the most direct routes out of Sydney (stopping in Singapore and Kuala Lumpur respectively). Thai, Austrian and Qantas all have two stops (Bangkok/Frankfurt, Kuala Lumpur/Vienna and Singapore/Frankfurt). One further option is to pick up a cheap ticket to London, and then continue your journey to Amsterdam with one of the no-frills budget airlines (see p.10).

Tickets purchased direct from the airlines tend to be expensive, with published fares ranging from A$2000/NZ$2500 in low season to A$2500–3000/NZ$3000–3600 in high season. **Travel agents** can offer better deals, and have the latest information on special promotions, such as free stopovers en route and fly-drive-accommodation packages. Flight Centre and STA generally offer the best discounts, especially for students and those under 26. For a discounted ticket from Sydney, Melbourne or Auckland, expect to pay A$1600–2500/NZ$2000–2700.

For extended trips, a **round-the-world** (RTW) ticket, valid for up to a year, can be good value. Fares are based either on the number of continents you visit, or the number of miles you travel, and tickets are usually cheapest through travel agents. The lowest-priced tickets usually involve three to four stopovers, with prices rising the further you travel or the more stops you add. Those that take in Amsterdam include the "Star Alliance" (Air Canada, Air NZ, Lufthansa, SAS, Singapore, Thai and United) which starts at A$2800/NZ$3350, and the One World Alliance "Global Explorer" (American, British Airways, Canadian, Cathay, Finnair, Iberia and Qantas) which starts at A$2400–2900/NZ$2900–3400.

Airlines in Australia and New Zealand

Air New Zealand Australia ☏ 13 24 76, ⊛ www.airnz.com.au; NZ ☏ 0800/737 000, ⊛ www.airnz.co.nz.
British Airways Australia ☏ 1300/767 177; NZ ☏ 0800/274 847, ⊛ www.ba.com.
Cathay Pacific Australia ☏ 13 17 47, NZ ☏ 09/379 0861; ⊛ www.cathaypacific.com.
KLM/Northwest Australia ☏ 1300/303 747, NZ ☏ 09/309 1782; ⊛ www.klm.com.
Malaysia Airlines Australia ☏ 13 26 27, NZ ☏ 0800/777 747;
⊛ www.malaysiaairlines.com.my.
Qantas Australia ☏ 13 13 13,
⊛ www.qantas.com.au; NZ ☏ 0800/808 767, ⊛ www.qantas.co.nz.
Singapore Airlines Australia ☏ 13 10 11, NZ ☏ 0800/808 909; ⊛ www.singaporeair.com.
Thai Airways Australia ☏ 1300/651 960, NZ ☏ 09/377 0268; ⊛ www.thaiair.com.

Travel agents in Australia and New Zealand

Flight Centre Australia ☏ 13 31 33 or 02/9235 3522, ⊛ www.flightcentre.com.au; NZ ☏ 0800/243 544 or 09/358 4310, ⊛ www.flightcentre.co.nz.
Harvey World Travel
⊛ www.harveyworld.com.au.
Holiday Shoppe NZ ☏ 0800/808 480, ⊛ www.holidayshoppe.co.nz.
New Zealand Destinations Unlimited NZ ☏ 09/414 1685, ⊛ www.holiday.co.nz.
Northern Gateway Australia ☏ 800/174 800, ⊛ www.northerngateway.com.au.
STA Travel Australia ☏ 1300/733 035, ⊛ www.statravel.com.au; NZ ☏ 0508/782 872,

⊛ www.statravel.co.nz.
Student Uni Travel Australia ☏ 02/9232 8444, ⊛ www.sut.com.au; NZ ☏ 09/379 4224, ⊛ www.sut.co.nz.
Trailfinders Australia ☏ 02/9247 7666, ⊛ www.trailfinders.com.au.

Tour operators in Australia and New Zealand

Abercrombie and Kent Australia ☏ 03/9536 1800 or 1300/851 800, NZ ☏ 0800/441 638; ⊛ www.abercrombiekent.com.au. Upmarket river-cruise tour of the Netherlands, starting in Amsterdam.
Contiki Australia ☏ 02/9511 2200, NZ ☏ 09/309 8824; ⊛ www.contiki.com. Includes Amsterdam on its European camping country-hopping tours, aimed at 18–35-year-old party animals.
Explore Holidays Australia ☏ 02/9857 6200 or 1300/731 000, ⊛ www.exploreholidays.com.au. Accommodation and sightseeing tours packages in and around Amsterdam.
Kumuka Expeditions Australia ☏ 1800/804 277 or 02/9279 0491, ⊛ www.kumuka.com.au. Independent tour operator, which covers the Netherlands as part of a western and central European overland trip.
Viator Australia ☏ 02/8219 5400, ⊛ www.viator.com. Fly-drive packages in the Netherlands, plus city tours in Amsterdam; bookable online.

By rail from the UK and Ireland

Eurostar trains running through the Channel Tunnel to Brussels put Amsterdam within reasonably easy striking distance of London's Waterloo and Kent's Ashford train stations. The same cannot be said if you're heading off to Amsterdam with Eurostar from much of the rest of the UK, but at least it's possible to keep costs down by through-ticketing from your home station. Alternatively, you can get the train to either Harwich, Hull or Newcastle, from where there are direct car ferries to the Hook of Holland, Rotterdam, and Ijmuiden respectively. All three Dutch ports are a short drive from Amsterdam, but Ijmuiden is the nearest. Travelling to the Netherlands by train **from Ireland** means going via England – a time-consuming journey that is barely worth considering.

Eurostar

There are normally seven or eight **Eurostar** departures from London Waterloo to Brussels (Bruxelles-Midi station) every day, with a journey time of 2 hours 50 minutes. En route, most trains stop at Ashford in Kent; all services stop at Lille in France. From Bruxelles-Midi station, Belgian Railways, Netherlands Railways and Thalys combine to operate a fast and frequent service to Amsterdam's Centraal station; this second train journey takes just under three hours.

The cheapest **fare** from London to Amsterdam is a Leisure Apex 14 for just £90; this requires booking at least 14 days in advance, and requires a stay of at least two nights. Typical add-on prices are around £30 from Edinburgh or Glasgow, £20 from Manchester and £14 from Birmingham. Special deals and bargains are commonplace, especially in the low season; you can also reduce costs by accepting certain ticketing restrictions. A standard return fare to Amsterdam, with more flexibility, is £125, while a fully flexible and refundable ticket for travel any day of the week will set you back no less than £310.

Inter-Rail holders are not entitled to a discount, but there is a youth discount for those under 26.

Rail and ferry via Harwich

A longer, cheaper **rail-and-ferry** route is available through Stena Line (see p.16) in conjunction with several train operators – Scotrail, Anglia, First North Western, First Great Western and Virgin. The journey operates twice daily from London's **Liverpool Street station to Harwich** (1hr 40min) and connects with the rapid ferry crossing to the **Hook of Holland** (Hoek van Holland; 3hr 40min), from where fast trains head on to **Amsterdam** (1hr 35min). Total journey time from London is around eight hours; the afternoon departure doesn't get in until after 2am, though. **Prices** from London start at £60 return for an Apex fare, which must be booked at least a week in advance, with the return journey being made within one month. A standard open return costs £79, or £52.50 with a young person's railcard.

Tickets are available from Anglia Railways and larger mainline stations.

See below for details of Dutch and international train passes.

UK rail contacts

Belgian Railways UK ☎020/7593 2332, ⓦwww.b-rail.be.
Eurostar ☎0870/160 6600, ⓦwww.eurostar.com.
International Rail ☎0870/120 1606, ⓦwww.international-rail.com. Agents for Dutch and Belgian railways.
Rail Europe ☎0870/584 8848, ⓦwww.raileurope.co.uk. Agents for SNCF French Railways. Sells tickets and passes for European train travel.
Trainseurope ☎0900/195 0101, ⓦwww.trainseurope.co.uk. Sells tickets and passes for European train travel.

Dutch Railways

The Dutch train network, operated by **Nederlandse Spoorwegen** or NS (Dutch Railways), is one of the best in Europe: trains are fast, modern, frequent and very punctual, fares are relatively low, and the network of lines comprehensive. NS publishes mounds of information on its various services, passes and fares. Full information is at ⓦwww.ns.nl. Their comprehensive and easy-to-use timetable (*spoorboekje*) is available inexpensively at major stations and in advance from the Netherlands Board of Tourism.

Rail passes

There is a host of **pan-European rail passes**. Some have to be bought before leaving home while others can be bought only in specific countries. **Rail Europe** is the umbrella company for all national and international rail purchases, and its comprehensive website (ⓦwww.raileurope.com) is the most useful source of information on which rail passes are available; it also gives current prices.

An **Inter-Rail pass** (ⓦwww.inter-rail.co.uk) is only available to European residents, and comes in under-26 and over-26 versions. The pass covers 28 European countries (including Turkey and Morocco) grouped together in zones; the Netherlands falls in Zone E, along with France, Belgium and Luxembourg. It's

15

available for 22 days (one zone only) or a month (one or more zones). A twelve-day pass for one zone costs £119/169 for under/over 26s. Online purchase is discounted, as are trains within the UK (including London–Paris by Eurostar) and cross-Channel ferries. If you're coming from Ireland, you must buy a pass for two zones (under/over 26s pay €285/402) in order to cover travel across the UK (Zone A) before you reach Zone E; this also gives reductions on the ferries.

A **Eurailpass** (ⓦ www.raileurope.com) – for non-EU residents only – allows first-class train travel in seventeen countries, including the Netherlands; but it's only an economical option if you're planning to venture further afield. The pass, only available outside Europe, is valid for 15 days (US$588), 21 days (US$762), or one, two or three months. A Eurailpass Youth is valid for second-class travel for under-26s; two to five people travelling together can get a joint Eurail Saverpass. A Eurailpass Flexi is good for ten days' (US$694) or fifteen days' (US$914) first-class travel within a two-month period, and has under-26 (Eurailpass Youth Flexi) and group (Eurailpass Saver Flexi) versions. Finally, the Eurail Selectpass lets you travel in three, four or five adjoining countries for between five and fifteen days within a two-month period; for this plan, Belgium, Luxembourg and the Netherlands count as one country. A five-day pass over three countries costs US$356. It also comes in under-26 (Eurail Selectpass Youth) and group (Eurail Selectpass Saver) versions.

A **Euro-Domino pass** – for those who've lived in the EU for at least six months (ⓦ www.raileurope.co.uk) – is valid on Dutch trains for between three and eight days' travel within a one-month period; a five-day pass, for example, costs £64/84 for under/over-26s. Euro Domino pass holders pay half-price on the ferries between Ireland and the UK, and between the UK and the Netherlands, and also get a 25-percent discount on the train journey across the UK to Harwich (see 15).

By ferry from the UK and Ireland

Some people prefer to go to the Netherlands (and Amsterdam) **from England by ferry**,

feeling that it's a more leisurely and enjoyable journey. It is, however, almost always a comparatively expensive option, though tariffs vary enormously, depending on when you leave, how long you stay, if you're taking a car, what size it is and how many passengers are in it. **Foot passengers** should check that the ferry dock is not miles from the nearest train or bus connection.

Three operators run all-year ferries from the UK direct to the Netherlands. The speediest is **Stena Line**'s ferry from **Harwich in Essex to the Hook of Holland** (daytime 3hr 40min; overnight 6hr 15min). On this route, a weekend fare in high season costs from £233 for a car with four passengers on a daytime crossing, or £426 travelling overnight with basic cabin accommodation. Alternatively, **P&O North Sea Ferries** operates from **Hull to Rotterdam** (11hr) and here, booking well in advance, a car plus four people, with a basic cabin and meals included, costs around £600. The third possibility is the **DFDS Seaways** ferry from **Newcastle (North Shields) to Ijmuiden**, on the coast to the west of Amsterdam. This crossing takes fourteen hours with a bargain Seapex fare, booked at least 21 days ahead, costing from £64 per person return.

There are no direct **ferries from Ireland** to the Dutch coast, leaving travellers with two main options: they can either cross over the Irish Sea by ferry and then head for an English port, or travel with Irish Ferries from Ireland to France and then drive on to the Netherlands from there.

UK and Irish ferry operators

DFDS Seaways ☏ 0870/533 3000, ⓦ www.dfdsseaways.co.uk. Newcastle to Ijmuiden, near Amsterdam.
Irish Ferries ☏ 1890/313 131, ⓦ www .irishferries.com. Dublin to Holyhead; Rosslare to Pembroke; Rosslare to Cherbourg or Roscoff (March–Sept only).
P&O Irish Sea UK ☏ 0870/242 4777, Republic of Ireland ☏ 1800/409 049; ⓦ www.poirishsea.com. Larne to Cairnryan and to Fleetwood; Dublin to Liverpool.
P&O North Sea Ferries ☏ 0870/129 6002, ⓦ www.ponsf.com. Hull to Rotterdam.
Stena Line UK ☏ 0870/570 70 70, ⓦ www .stenaline.co.uk. Harwich to Hook of Holland.

Stena Line Ireland ☎01/204 7777, ⊛www.ste-naline.ie. Dun Laoghaire and Dublin to Holyhead; Rosslare to Fishguard.

By bus from the UK

Given the low cost of air fares, travelling by long-distance **bus from the UK** to Amsterdam may not seem too attractive a proposition, but it is still likely to be the cheapest way of getting there.

Eurolines, a division of the National Express bus company, operates three services daily from London's Victoria Coach Station to Amsterdam's Amstel Station, southeast of the city centre, all using Eurotunnel. The standard fare is £49 return (under-26s and over-60s pay £46), though promotional return fares can be snapped up for just £19. The journey time is ten hours. National Express has connections into London from all round the UK. Eurolines also offers a **Europe-wide pass**, for either 15, 30 or 60 days between 46 European cities, including London, Amsterdam, Barcelona, Berlin, Budapest, Copenhagen, Florence, Madrid, Paris, Prague, Rome, Tallinn and Vienna. A fifteen-day pass costs €117 (under-26s €99), a thirty-day pass €167 (€136), and a sixty-day pass €211 (€167).

The less well-known **Anglia Lines** also operates a bus service between London Victoria and central Amsterdam, which leaves twice daily and costs £35 return if booked seven days in advance.

UK bus operators

Anglia Lines ☎0870/608 8806, ⊛www .anglia-lines.co.uk.
Eurolines ☎0870/514 3219, ⊛www.gobycoach.com. You can also buy tickets from National Express ☎0870/580 8080, ⊛www.nationalexpress.co.uk.

Driving from the UK – Eurotunnel

In addition to the car ferries detailed above, drivers and motorcyclists heading for mainland Europe from the UK have the option of using **Eurotunnel** (UK ☎0870/535 3535, ⊛www.eurotunnel.com), which operates vehicle-carrying trains through the **Channel Tunnel**. Shuttle trains run 24 hours a day

between Folkestone and Coquelles, near Calais, with up to four departures per hour (only 1 hourly midnight–6am) and take around 35 minutes, though you must arrive at least half an hour before departure. Advance booking is advisable, though you can just turn up and buy your **ticket** at the toll booths (after exiting the M20 at junction 11a). From Calais, it's about 400km north to Amsterdam. Note that Eurotunnel only carries cars (including occupants) and motorbikes; cyclists and foot passengers must travel by ferry instead.

Eurotunnel **fares** depend on the time of year, time of day and length of stay (the cheapest ticket is for a day-trip, followed by a five-day return); it's cheaper to travel between 10pm and 6am, while the highest fares are reserved for weekend departures and returns in July and August. Prices are charged per vehicle, with no additions for passengers. Return trips made within five days entitle you to short-stay savers which, for a car, start from £107 (booked 7 days in advance). If you wish to stay more than five days, a long-stay saver costs from £197 (booked 14 days in advance), soaring up to £327 for travelling at weekends in July. To take a motorbike costs from £73, a caravan from £82. Before booking, always ask about special offers. Call ☎0870/535 3535, or, for the lowest rates, book at ⊛www.eurotunnel.com.

Overland to Amsterdam from neighbouring countries

The Netherlands has borders with Belgium and Germany. A veritable raft of **rail lines** runs into the country from its neighbours with many services calling in on, or terminating at, Amsterdam's Centraal Station. Apart from the regular trains, there are also the express trains of **Thalys**, a combined project of the Belgian, Dutch, French and German railways. The hub of the Thalys network is Brussels, from where there are regular trains to Amsterdam.

Mainland Europe rail websites

French Railways (SNCF) ⊛www.sncf.fr.
German Rail ⊛www.bahn.de.
Netherlands Rail ⊛www.hollandrail.com.
Thalys ⊛www.thalys.com.

Red tape and visas

Citizens of the UK, Ireland, Australia, New Zealand, Canada and the US do not need a visa to enter the Netherlands if staying for three months or less. However, citizens of these countries do need to be in possession of a passport valid for at least six months after arrival, as well as a return airline ticket and/or funds deemed to be sufficient to fund their stay.

If you intend to stay beyond three months, you must apply for a **temporary residence permit** (a "VTV") within three days of your arrival in the Netherlands. Go to your local Aliens Police Office (*Vreemdelingenpolitie*) armed with your birth certificate and proof that you have the funds to finance your stay in the Netherlands, a fixed address, and health insurance. For further information, visit the Ministry of Foreign Affairs website at ⍟www.minbuza.nl.

If you intend to work, you will need a **work permit**, for which your employer must apply on your behalf. The exceptions to this rule are the work schemes set up for Australian, New Zealand and Canadian citizens aged 18–30, who can stay for up to twelve months in the Netherlands on a "Working Holiday Scheme", provided you can convince the authorities that your main priority is holidaying, not working. For further information, contact the Dutch embassies in Canberra, Wellington, Ottawa or London.

Dutch embassies abroad

Australia 120 Empire Circuit, Yarralumla, ACT 2600 ☎02/6220 9400, ⍟www.netherlands.org.au.
Canada 350 Albert St #2020, Ottawa, ON, K1R 1A4 ☎613/237 5030, ⍟www.netherlandsembassy.ca.
Ireland 160 Merrion Rd, Dublin 4 ☎01/269 3444, ⍟www.netherlandsembassy.ie.
New Zealand Investment House, Ballance/Featherston St, Wellington ☎04/471 6390, ⍟www.netherlandsembassy.co.nz.
UK 38 Hyde Park Gate, London, SW7 5DP ☎020/7590 3200, ⍟www.netherlands-embassy.org.uk.
USA 4200 Linnean Ave NW, Washington, DC 20008 ☎202/244 5300, ⍟www.netherlands-embassy.org.

Embassies and consulates in the Netherlands

Australia Carniegielaan 4, 2517 KH Den Haag ☎070/310 8200, ⍟www.australian-embassy.nl.
Canada Sophialaan 7, 2514 JP Den Haag ☎070/311 1600, ⍟www.canada.nl.
Ireland Dr Kuijperstraat 9, 2514 BA Den Haag ☎070/363 0993, ⍟www.irishembassy.nl.
New Zealand Carnegielaan 10, 2517 KH Den Haag ☎070/346 9324, ⍟www.nzembassy.com.
UK Lange Voorhout 50, 2514 EG Den Haag ☎070/427 0427, ⍟www.britain.nl. Consulate-General: Koningslaan 44, PO Box 75488, 1070 AL Amsterdam ☎020/676 4343.
USA Lange Voorhout 102, 2514 EJ Den Haag ☎070/310 9209, ⍟www.usemb.nl. Consulate-General: Museumplein 19, 1071 DJ Amsterdam ☎020/575 5309.

Customs restrictions

There are no **customs** restrictions on importing goods (except tobacco) from another EU country, as long as they are not duty-free and you can prove that the goods are for personal use. If you are arriving in the Netherlands from a non-EU country, the following import limits apply: 200g cigarettes or 250g tobacco, 1 litre spirits or 2 litres of wine, 50g perfume. Coffee and tea are also subject to restrictions. If you're caught with more than these amounts, you'll have to pay tax on them, and possibly import duties as well. When you leave the Netherlands, there are no export restrictions on goods if you're travelling on to an EU country, but if you're travelling to a non-EU destination, you will be subject to the import regulations of your destination country. There are no restrictions on the import and export of currency.

Schiphol airport's **"See, Buy, Fly"** scheme is roughly the equivalent of duty-free, which was abolished in Europe in 1999, where the participating shops pay the tax for you. The only catch is that alcohol and tobacco are exempt, and sell at regular retail prices.

Insurance

Prior to travelling, you'd do well to take out an insurance policy to cover against theft, loss and illness or injury. Before paying for a new policy, however, it's worth checking whether you already have some degree of cover: EU health care privileges apply in the Netherlands (see p.20), some all-risks home insurance policies may cover your possessions when overseas, and many private medical schemes include cover when abroad. In Canada, provincial health plans usually provide partial cover for medical mishaps abroad, while holders of official student/teacher/youth cards in Canada and the US are entitled to meagre accident coverage and hospital in-patient benefits. Students will often find that their student health coverage extends during the vacations and for one term beyond the date of last enrolment.

After exhausting the possibilities above, you might want to contact a specialist travel insurance company. A typical travel insurance policy usually provides cover for the loss of baggage, tickets and – up to a certain limit – cash or cheques, as well as cancellation or curtailment of your journey. Most of them exclude so-called **dangerous sports** unless an extra premium is paid. Many policies can be chopped and changed to exclude coverage you don't need – for example, sickness and accident benefits can often be excluded or included at will. If you do take medical coverage,

Rough Guides travel insurance

Rough Guides offers its own travel insurance, customized for our readers by a leading UK broker and backed by a Lloyd's underwriter. It's available for anyone, of any nationality and any age, travelling anywhere in the world.

There are two main Rough Guide insurance plans: **Essential**, for basic, no-frills cover; and **Premier** – with more generous and extensive benefits. Alternatively, you can take out **annual multi-trip insurance**, which covers you for any number of trips throughout the year (with a maximum of 60 days for any one trip). Unlike many policies, the Rough Guides schemes are calculated by the day, so if you're travelling for 27 days rather than a month, that's all you pay for. If you intend to be away for the whole year, the **Adventurer policy** will cover you for 365 days. Each plan can be supplemented with a "Hazardous Activities Premium" if you plan to indulge in sports considered dangerous, such as climbing, scuba-diving or trekking.

For a policy quote, call the Rough Guide Insurance Line on UK freefone ☎0800/015 0906; US toll-free ☎1-866/220-5588, or, if you're calling from elsewhere, ☎+44 1243/621 046. Alternatively, get an online quote or buy online at ⊛www.roughguidesinsurance.com.

ascertain whether benefits will be paid as treatment proceeds or only after your return home, and whether there is a 24-hour medical emergency number. When securing baggage cover, make sure that the per-article limit – typically under £500/$750 – will cover your most valuable possession. If you need to make a claim, you should keep receipts for medicines and medical treatment, and in the event you have anything stolen, you must obtain a crime report statement or number.

Health

Under reciprocal health arrangements involving members of the European Union (EU), nationals of EU countries are entitled to free or discounted medical treatment within the respective public health care systems of every member country. Non-EU nationals should, on the other hand, take out their own medical insurance to travel to Amsterdam and the Netherlands. Indeed this can be handy for EU citizens as well, as it will cover the cost of items not within the EU's scheme, such as dental treatment and repatriation on medical grounds. That said, most private insurance policies don't cover prescription charges – their "excesses" are usually greater than the cost of the medicines. Some policies promise to sort matters out before you pay (rather than after) in the case of major expense; if you do have to pay upfront, keep the receipts. For more on insurance, see p.19. If you're an EU national, you should **complete form E111** before you travel as its possession is proof of your entitlement to treatment under EU arrangements. The form is available from most post offices in the UK (and online at ⓦwww.doh.gov.uk/traveladvice) and from health boards in the Republic of Ireland.

Minor ailments

Minor ailments can be remedied at a **drugstore** (*drogist*). These sell non-prescription drugs as well as toiletries, tampons, condoms and the like. A **pharmacy** or *apotheek* (usually open Mon–Fri 9.30am–6pm, but often closed Mon mornings) is where you go to get a prescription filled. There aren't any 24-hour pharmacies, but the 24-hour Afdeling Inlichtingen Apotheken helpline (ⓟ020/694 8709) will supply addresses of ones that are open late. Most of the better hotels will have these details too.

Seeking medical treatment

Your local pharmacy or hotel as well as the VVV should be able to provide the address of an **English-speaking doctor** or **dentist** if you need one, or try the Hotel and Tourist Doctor, Rapenburg 30 ⓟ020/427 5011. If you're seeking treatment under EU health agreements, double-check that the doctor is working within (and seeing you as) a patient of the public health care system. This being the case, you'll need to pay upfront for treatment and medicines; you'll then be able to reclaim a proportion of the cost by applying to the local Health Service Office (ask the doctor for details) with your E111 form.

You can expect that at least some, if not all, **hospital** staff will speak English. If you know you're going to be admitted to hospital and you're an EU national without a private insurance policy, try to contact the local Health Service Office in advance, producing your E111 form and asking them where to obtain the cheapest treatment. They will give you a certificate confirming they will pay at least part, if not all, of the cost of treatment.

If this is impossible, try to remember to make it clear to the hospital that you are seeking medical treatment under the EU scheme. It's a good idea to hand over a photocopy of your E111 on arrival at hospital to ensure your non-private status is clearly understood. In medical **emergencies**, you can reach the ambulance service by calling ☎112.

AIDS and sexual health matters

The main telephone number for anyone needing confidential advice or information on AIDS and sexually transmitted diseases (Soa) is the **AIDS/Soa Infoline** ☎0900/204 2040, ⍟www.aidsfonds.nl (Mon–Fri 2–10pm).

HIV Vereniging 1e Helmersstraat 17 ☎020/616 0160, ⍟www.hivnet.org; Mon–Fri 8.30am–5pm. The Netherlands HIV Association, which provides the chief point of contact for anyone HIV-positive,

supplies up-to-date information, as well as running an information line (Service point ☎020/689 2577; Mon–Fri 2–10pm). There's also an HIV café and Checkpoint, a walk-in clinic offering HIV testing every Friday 7–9pm (call Service point between 2pm and 6pm for an appointment).
Rutgers Huis Sarphatistraat 620-626 ☎020/626 6222. Infoline ☎0900/9398. A sexual advice bureau with specialized doctors and a good information desk. Mon–Fri 9am–4.30pm Tues & Thurs 7–9pm.
SAD Schorerstichting GG&GD (Municipal Health Department), Groenburgwal 44 (Old Centre) ☎020/555 5822, ⍟www.gggd.amsterdam.nl. Clinic offering STD tests and treatment. Appointments necessary. Mon–Fri 8.30–10.30am & 1.30–3.30pm, Thurs also 7–8.30pm.
Women's Healthcentre Obiplein 14 ☎020/693 4358. Information and advice for women – given by women – on all health matters. Can recommend doctors and therapists. Mon–Fri 10am–1pm (closed for three weeks in July and August).

Information, websites and maps

Information on Amsterdam is easy to get hold of, either from the Netherlands Board of Tourism, via the Internet, or, after arrival, from any of the city's tourist offices, the VVVs.

The Netherlands Board of Tourism

It's not essential, but before you leave for Amsterdam, you might consider contacting the **Netherlands Board of Tourism** (NBT) as they issue (or sell) a number of glossy leaflets on the city in particular and the Netherlands in general. One of their most useful publications is their country-wide *Accommodation* guide, complete with hotel prices, addresses, phone numbers, email addresses and Internet sites, as well as photographs of the hotels and brief (if sometimes rather flattering) descriptions. Amsterdam's three VVVs (see p.22) sell this booklet too. The NBT also has an all-encompassing **website** ⍟www.holland.com, which is particularly strong on practical information.

However, their site is but one of a plethora of websites covering every aspect of visiting the Netherlands, with Amsterdam frequently topping the bill.

Netherlands Board of Tourism offices

Canada PO Box 1078, 25 Adelaide St East, Toronto, Ontario M5C 2K5 ☎416/363 1577, ✉info@goholland.com.
UK PO Box 30783, London WC2B 6DH ☎020/7539 7950, brochures ☎0906/871 7777 (premium line), ✉information@nbt.org.uk.
USA 355 Lexington Ave, 19th Floor, New York, NY 10017 ☎1-888-GOHOLLAND, ✉info@goholland.com.
There are no offices in Australia or New Zealand.

Information offices in central Amsterdam

The Amsterdam Tourist Board runs three **tourist offices** in the city centre: on platform 2, Centraal Station (Mon–Sat 8am–8pm, Sun 9am–5pm); on Stationsplein, across from the entrance to Centraal Station (daily 9am–5pm); on Leidsestraat, just off the Leidseplein (daily 9am–5pm). These three offices share one premium-rate **information line** on ☎0900/400 4040; calls currently cost €0.55 per minute. Their shared website is at ⊛www.visitamsterdam.nl.

These offices, known here as elsewhere in the Netherlands as the **VVV** (pronounced "fay-fay-fay"), offer a wide range of services and sell a competent range of maps and guidebooks as well as tickets and passes for public transport. They are extremely popular, so come early if you want to beat the queues, especially in the summer; note also that the VVV office on Centraal Station's platform 2 is often not as busy as its counterparts. In addition, the VVV takes in-person bookings for **canal cruises** and other organized excursions (see p.27) and operates an extremely efficient **accommodation reservation** service. The latter is especially useful in the height of the season, when accommodation gets mighty tight; the service costs just €3 plus a refundable deposit which is subtracted from your final hotel bill; bear in mind, however, that during peak periods the wait for service can be exhausting. For further details on booking accommodation, see p.143.

As for cultural **events**, the VVV sells a comprehensive, but largely uncritical monthly listings magazine, *Day by Day – What's On in Amsterdam* (€1.50), which details every-thing from theatre and ballet through to rock concerts. They also sell **tickets** for most upcoming performances, from rock and classical concerts through to theatre, as does the Amsterdam Uitburo, or **AUB**, operated by the city council. The latter has a walk-in booking centre tucked away in a corner of the Stadsschouwburg theatre on Leidseplein (daily 10am–6pm, Thurs until 9pm; ☎0900/0191). For more details on entertainment, see Chapter Ten.

There's also a **Holland Tourist Office** (daily 7am–10pm) at Schiphol airport.

Useful websites

Clogs ⊛www.woodenshoes.nl. Provides the (surely unique?) "clog-o-paedia", as well as history and online shopping for the famous wooden shoes.
Digital City ⊛www.dds.nl. De Digital Stad (Digital City) is one of the reasons for the city's high level of Internet access. The site is the result of a plan to create a digital city. A number of themed pages, sharing a geometrical layout, guide the city's "residents" to information on subjects from Books to Education to Technology. Although much of the site is in Dutch, squares (sections) with English content include Sport, Politics, Film and the Gay Scene.
Directory ⊛www.nl-menu.nl. Encyclopedic site crammed with links ranging from province websites to art, computers and philosophy.
Dutch language ⊛www.learndutch.org. Good resource for getting to grips with the Dutch language.
Flowers ⊛www.bbh.nl. The Flower Council of Holland, with listings of flower-related events.
Football ⊛www.ajax.nl. Virtual home of the world-famous Ajax Amsterdam football team – but doesn't sell match tickets.
Listings ⊛www.amsterdamhotspots.nl. City guide emphasizing music and club listings. Also good for the gay scene, coffee shops and the Red Light District.

Tourist passes

The VVV's much touted **Amsterdam Pass** provides free and unlimited use of the city's public transport network, a complimentary canal cruise and free admission to the bulk of the city's museums and attractions. It costs €26 for one day, €36 for two consecutive days and €46 for three, again consecutive days. Altogether it's not a bad deal, but you have to work fairly hard to make it worthwhile. A much more tempting proposition, especially if you're staying for more than a couple of days, is the **Museumjaarkaart** (museum year-card). This pass gives free entry to most museums in the whole of the Netherlands for a year; it costs €35 for anyone over 25 years old, €15 for those 24 years old and under; the pass needs a passport-sized photo to be valid. For details of public transport passes see p.25.

Maps and accommodation ⓦwww
.amsterdam.nl. Excellent site maintained by the
Amsterdam tourist board, with a useful facility
enabling you to print a map for any address in the
city. Also provides a useful accommodation data-
base.

Miscellany ⓦwww.thehollandring.com. Over 300
pages of information on all things Dutch, aimed at
the Dutch expat community.

Museums ⓦwww.hollandmuseums.nl. Slick site
with information on museums in the Netherlands and
links to further information.

Orchestra ⓦwww.concertgebouworkest.nl. Royal
Concertgebouw Orchestra website, providing a listing
of the world-renowned orchestra's concerts, and
enabling online ticket reservation.

Radio Netherlands ⓦwww.rnw.nl. Broadcasting
Dutch news in English, with articles on current
affairs, lifestyle issues, science, health and social
issues.

Royals ⓦwww.koninklijkhuis.nl. The Dutch royal
family.

Tourist Board ⓦwww.holland.com. Excellent, all-
embracing official site of the Netherlands Board of
Tourism.

Van Gogh ⓦwww.vangoghmuseum.nl. Online
guide to the Amsterdam gallery, including essays by
experts on some of Van Gogh's major works.

Maps

Our **maps** are more than adequate for
most purposes, but if you need one on a
larger scale, or with a street index, then
pick up *The Rough Guide Map to
Amsterdam*, which has the added advantage of being waterproof. This map marks
all the key sights as well as many restaurants, bars and hotels, but it does not
extend to the outer suburbs. For this, the
best bet is the Falk map of *Amsterdam*
(1:15,000).

Other options include the city maps sold
by the VVV, which come complete with a
street index, and the handily compact, spi-
ral-bound street atlases produced by Falk

(Suburbs: 1:12,500; centre 1:7500). The
Rough Guide Map is available at most
good bookshops in the UK, but is harder to
get elsewhere, especially in Amsterdam,
but the reverse is true of the Falk maps. For
information on bookshops in Amsterdam,
see p.195.

Map outlets

UK and Ireland

Blackwell's UK ☎01865/793 550, ⓦwww
.blackwell.co.uk.
Easons Dublin ☎01/858 3881, ⓦwww.eason.ie.
Hodges Figgis Dublin ☎01/677 4754,
ⓦwww.hodgesfiggis.com.
Map Shop UK ☎0116/247 1400, ⓦwww
.mapshopleicester.co.uk.
Stanfords UK ☎020/7836 1321, ⓦwww
.stanfords.co.uk.

US and Canada

Adventurous Traveler US ☎1-800/282-3963,
ⓦwww.adventuroustraveler.com.
Elliot Bay Book Co. US ☎1-800/962-5311,
ⓦwww.elliotbaybook.com.
Globe Corner US ☎1-800/358-6013,
ⓦwww.globecorner.com.
Rand McNally US ☎1-800/333-0136,
ⓦwww.randmcnally.com.
World of Maps Canada ☎1-800/214-8524,
ⓦwww.worldofmaps.com.

Australia and New Zealand

Map Shop Australia ☎08/8231 2033,
ⓦwww.mapshop.net.au.
Mapland Australia ☎03/9670 4383,
ⓦwww.mapland.com.au.
Perth Map Centre Australia ☎08/9322 5733,
ⓦwww.perthmap.com.au.
Specialty Maps NZ ☎09/307 2217,
ⓦwww.ubdonline.co.nz/maps.

Arrival

Arriving in Amsterdam by train and plane could hardly be easier. Schiphol, Amsterdam's international airport, is a quick and convenient train ride away from Centraal Station, the city's international train station, which is itself a ten-minute metro ride from Amstel Station, the terminus for long-distance and international buses. Centraal Station is also the hub of an excellent public transport network, whose trams, buses and metro combine to delve into every corner of the city and its suburbs.

By air

Amsterdam's international airport, **Schiphol** (☎0900/7244 7465, ⊛www.schiphol.nl), is located about 18km southwest of the city centre. Arriving passengers are funnelled into a large plaza, which has all the standard facilities, including bureaux de change, car rental outlets, left luggage lockers and ATMs. In addition, there's a Netherlands Railways (NS) ticket office and a **Holland Tourist Office** (daily 7am–10pm), though this has surprisingly little English-language information; the compensation is that they will book accommodation anywhere in the country on your behalf for a modest fee.

From the airport, **trains** run to Amsterdam Centraal Station (Amsterdam C.S.) – a fast service leaving every fifteen minutes during the day, and every hour at night (12.30pm–6am). The journey takes between fifteen and twenty minutes and costs €3.10. There are also trains from Schiphol to most of the suburban stations around Amsterdam as well as direct express services to many other Dutch cities. The main alternative to the train is the **Airport Hotel Shuttle bus** (☎020/653 4975), which departs from the designated bus stop outside the Arrivals hall, though note that the buses themselves bear several different liveries; the newest are marked "Connexxion". Departures are every fifteen minutes or so during peak times (7am–2pm) and every 30min at other times (5–7am & 2–8pm); a single **fare** costs €10.50, return €19. The route followed by the bus is customer-led, which means it varies with the needs of the passengers it picks up at the airport, providing the required destination is one of the fifty hotels on the shuttle list; neither do passengers have to be hotel guests to use it. It takes about thirty minutes for the bus to get from the airport to the Old Centre. The bus follows a prescribed route on the return journey. Finally, the **taxi** fare from Schiphol to the Old Centre is €35–40.

By train

Amsterdam's **Centraal Station** (CS) has regular connections with key cities in Germany, Belgium and France, as well as all the larger towns and cities of the Netherlands. Amsterdam also has several suburban train stations, but these are principally for the convenience of commuters. For all rail enquiries contact NS (Netherlands Railways; international enquiries ☎0900 /9296; domestic enquiries ☎0900/1475; ⊛www.ns.nl).

As you would expect, Centraal Station has a good spread of facilities, including ATMs, a bureau de change and both coin-operated luggage lockers (daily 7am–11pm) and a staffed left-luggage office (daily 7am–11pm). Small coin-operated lockers cost €2.70, the larger ones €4.20 per 24 hours; left luggage costs €5.70 per item. In addition, there's a **VVV tourist office** on platform 2 and a second directly across from the main station entrance on Stationsplein. If you arrive late at night, it's best to take a taxi to your hotel or hostel – and you should certainly avoid wandering aimlessly around the station: it's not a dangerous place by any means, but there are too many shifty characters to make hanging around advisable.

Centraal Station is also the hub of the city's excellent public transport system.

Trams and buses depart from outside on Stationsplein, which is also the location of a metro station and a GVB public transport information office. For more on city transport, see below. There's a taxi rank on Stationsplein too.

By bus

Eurolines (☎020/560 8787, ☺www.eurolines .nl) long-distance, international buses arrive at **Amstel Station**, about 3.5km to the southeast of Centraal Station. The metro journey to Centraal Station takes about ten minutes.

By car

Arriving **by car** on either the A4 (E19) from The Hague or the A2 (E35) from Utrecht, you should experience few traffic problems. The city centre is clearly signposted as soon as you approach Amsterdam's southern reaches. Both the A4 and the A2 lead to the A10 (E22) ring road; on its west side, leave the A10 at either the Osdorp or Geuzenveld exits for the centre. However, be warned that driving in central Amsterdam – never mind parking – is extremely difficult; see p.27 for further details.

City transport

Almost all of Amsterdam's leading attractions are clustered in or near the city centre, within easy walking distance of each other. For longer jaunts, the city has a first-rate public transport system, comprising trams, buses, a pint-sized metro and four passenger ferries across the river IJ to the northern suburbs. Centraal Station is the hub of this transit system, which is operated by a publicly owned company, GVB. GVB's remit does not extend to the city's canals, which are mainly the preserve of cruise boats, but there are still one or two interesting and reasonably economic options for getting round the city by boat.

Trams, buses and the metro

The city centre is crisscrossed by **trams**, which operate on around fifteen different routes and are the mainstay of the transit system. One of the most useful is **Tram #20** (daily 9am–6pm; every 10min), which threads a circuitous route through the centre, passing by most of the leading attractions. For the most part, trams are entered at the rear doors (push the button); if the doors start to close before you've got on, put your foot on the bottom step to keep them open. **Buses**, which are always entered at the front, are mainly useful for going to the outskirts, and the same applies to the **metro**, which has just two downtown stations, Nieuwmarkt and Waterlooplein. The metro is clean, modern and punctual, but at night it attracts too many shifty characters for its own good.

Trams, buses and the metro operate daily between 6am and midnight, supplemented by a limited number of nightbuses (*nachtbussen*). All tram and bus stops display a detailed map of the network. For further details on all services, head for the main **GVB information office** (Mon–Fri 7am–9pm, Sat & Sun 8am–9pm; ☎0900 /9292; ☺www.gvb.nl) on Stationsplein. Their free, English-language *Tourist Guide to Public Transport* is very helpful.

Tickets and passes

The most common type of ticket, used on all forms of GVB transport, is the **strippenkaart** – a piece of card divided into strips. On the city's trams, unless there's a conductor, you insert your *strippenkaart* into the on-board franking machine: fold it over to expose only the last of the strips required for your journey before doing so. One person making a journey within a zone costs two strips – one for the passenger and one for the journey. On the metro, the franking machines are on the station concourse and on the buses the driver does the job. Amsterdam's public transport system is divided into fifteen **zones**. The "Centre" zone covers the city centre and its immediate surroundings (well beyond Singelgracht), but for longer journeys you'll have to dock your *strippenkaart* one additional strip for each zone you cross – thus a journey across two zones requires three strips, and so on. Zones are marked – usually as yellow lozenges – on the transit maps displayed at every tram and bus stop and metro station. More than one person can use a *strippenkaart*, as long as the requisite number of strips is stamped; once this has been done, it can be used to transfer between trams, buses and the metro for up to an hour.

Currently, a two-strip *strippenkaart* **costs** €1.60, three-strip €2.40, fifteen-strip €6.20 and a 45-strip €18.30. The 45-strip is available at a wide variety of outlets including tobacconists, the GVB, the VVV and metro stations. The fifteen-strip is available at the same locations and from some bus drivers, primarily on the longer routes. However, most bus and tram drivers will only issue the two- or three-strip *strippenkaart,* which are also available at metro stations, but not from tobacconists and the VVV. To avoid all this stamping, you can opt instead for a **dagkaart** (day ticket), which gives unlimited access to the GVB system for as many days as you need, up to a maximum of seven. Prices start at €5.50 for one day and €8.80 for two, with seven days costing €21.30; concessions apply to the over-65s and youngsters from 4 to 11 years old. In all cases, children up to 4 travel free. For long-term stays, you might consider a season ticket, valid for a month or a year. For further details and advice visit the GVB office, whose operatives usually speak English. See also the Amsterdam Pass, p.22.

Finally, note that GVB tries hard to keep **fare dodging** down to a minimum and wherever you're travelling, and at whatever time of day, there's a reasonable chance you'll have your ticket checked. If you are caught without a valid ticket, you risk an on-the-spot fine of €29.10.

Canal transport

One good way to get around Amsterdam's waterways is to take the **Canal Bus** (☎020/623 9886; ✆www.canal.nl). This operates on three circular routes, which meet once, at the jetty opposite Centraal Station beside Prins Hendrikkade. Two of the three routes also meet at three other locations – on the Singelgracht (opposite the Rijksmuseum), behind the Leidseplein and beside the Town Hall on Waterlooplein. There are eleven stops in all and together they give easy access to all the major sights. Boats leave from opposite Centraal Station (every 10–20min; 10am–5pm) and at least every half hour from any other jetty. A day ticket for all three routes, allowing you to hop on and off as many times as you like, costs €14 per adult, €10 for children (4–12 years old); it's valid until noon the following day and entitles the bearer to minor discounts at several museums. A similar boat service, the **Museumboot** (☎020/530 1090; ✆www.lovers.nl), calls at seven jetties located at or near many of the city's major attractions. It departs from opposite Centraal Station (every 30–45min; 9.30am–5.30pm) and a come-and-go-as-you-please day ticket costs €14.25.

Finally, **Canal Bike** (☎020/626 5574) has four-seater pedaloes which seem to take a lifetime to get anywhere, but are nevertheless good fun unless – of course – it's raining. They rent their pedaloes out at four central locations: on the Singelgracht opposite the Rijksmuseum; the Prinsengracht outside the Anne Frank House; on Keizersgracht at Leidsestraat; and behind Leidseplein. Rental prices per person per hour are €5.75 (3–4 people) or €7 (1–2 people), plus a refundable deposit of €50. The Canal Bikes can be picked up at one location and left at any of the others; opening times are daily 10am–6.30pm, till 10pm in high summer.

Getting around by bike

One of the most agreeable ways to explore pancake-flat Amsterdam is by **bicycle**. The city has an excellent network of designated bicycle lanes (*fietspaden*) and for once cycling isn't a fringe activity – there are cyclists everywhere. Indeed, much to the chagrin of the city's taxi drivers, the needs of the cyclist often take precedence over those of the motorist and by law if there's a collision it's always the driver's fault. **Bike theft**, however, is a real problem, and you should be sure to lock up your bike whenever it's not in use.

Bike **rental** is straightforward. There are lots of rental companies (*fietsenverhuur*) but **MacBike** (☎020/620 0985, ⊛www.macbike .nl) sets the benchmark, charging €6.50 per day, €16.50 for three days and €30 for a week for a standard bicycle; 21-speed cycles cost twice as much. MacBike have three rental outlets in central Amsterdam, one at the west end of Centraal Station, a second beside Waterlooplein at Mr Visserplein 2, and a third near Leidseplein at Weteringschans 2. For a list of other rental companies, see the Directory on p.233. Before renting, make sure you check the return time and the bike's age and condition. All companies, including MacBike, ask for some type of security, usually in the form of a cash deposit (some will take credit card imprints) and/or passport. Remember that you are legally obliged to have reflector bands on both wheels.

If you want to **buy** a bike, a well-worn bone-shaker will set you back about €50, while €120 should get you quite a decent machine – see p.195 for a list of bike shops. Bicycle locks are sold at all the city's flea markets. For useful cycling terms in Dutch, see p.273.

Cars and taxis

The centre of Amsterdam is geared up for trams and bicycles rather than **cars** as a matter of municipal policy. Pedestrianized zones as such are not extensive, but motorists still have to negotiate a convoluted one-way system, avoid getting boxed onto tram lines and steer round herds of cyclists. **On-street parking** is also very limited – with far too many cars chasing too few spaces – and quite expensive. Every city-centre street where parking is permitted is **metered** with a standard cost of €2.80 for one hour (Mon–Sat 9am–midnight, Sun noon–mid-

night), €16.80 for the day (9am–5pm) and €11.20 for the evening (7pm–midnight). A day's parking (9am–midnight) costs €25.20. If you overrun your ticket, you can expect to be clamped by eager-beaver traffic wardens, and thereafter, if you don't follow the instructions posted on your windscreen promptly, your vehicle will soon be heading off to the municipal pound. The good news is that signs on all the main approach roads to Amsterdam indicate which of the city's **car parks** have spaces and will, in the near future, also detail costs. Car parks in the centre (see p.233 for a list) charge comparable rates to the metered street spaces, but those on the outskirts are a good deal less expensive and are invariably but a short journey from the centre by public transport. Finally, note that some of the better hotels either have their own parking spaces or offer special deals with nearby car parks.

Taxis are plentiful in Amsterdam and taxi ranks are liberally distributed across the city centre; taxis can also be hailed on the street, though some taxi drivers aren't too keen. If all else fails, call the city's central, 24-hour taxi number on ☎020/677 7777. **Fares** are metered and pricey, but distances are small: the trip from Centraal Station to the Leidseplein, for example, costs just €9, and about fifteen percent more late at night.

Organized tours

No one could say the Amsterdam tourist industry doesn't make the most of its canals with a veritable armada of glass-topped **cruise boats** shuttling along the city's inner waterways, offering everything from a quick hour-long excursion to a fully-fledged dinner cruise. There are several major operators and they occupy the prime pitches – the jetties near Centraal Station on Stationsplein, beside the Damrak, and on Prins Hendrikkade. Despite the competition, **prices** are fairly uniform with a one-hour tour costing around €8.50 per adult, €5.50 per child (4–12 years old), and €23 (€15) for a two-hour candlelit cruise. The big companies also offer more specialized boat trips, including the weekly Architecture Cruise run by Lovers (☎020/530 1090; ⊛www.lovers .nl) through to the Red Light District Cruises operated by just about everyone. All these cruises – and especially the shorter and less expensive ones – are extremely popular and long **queues** are commonplace throughout the summer. One way of avoiding much of the crush is to walk down the Damrak from Centraal Station to the jetty at the near end of the Rokin, where the first-rate Reederij P. Kooij (☎020/623 3810) offers all the basic cruises at very competitive prices. Finally, although for many visitors a canal trip is delightful, for others the running commentary is purgatorial and the views disappointing, though it's certainly true that Amsterdam can look especially enchanting at night when the bridges are illuminated.

Amsterdam's tour operators also offer a wide range of non-nautical excursions, everything from guided cycle rides to a quick zip round the city by bus. A selection is given below, but if you have a specific interest – Dutch art, for example – it's well worth asking at the VVV to see what's on offer.

Tour companies

Holland International Prins Hendrikkade 33 ☎020/625 3035, ⊛www.thatsholland.com. Large tour operator running an extensive range of bus trips from city sightseeing tours (1 daily; 3hr 30min; €26)

to a gallop through Holland on their "Grand Holland Tour" (1 daily except Sat; 8.5hr; €40). The same company also does canal cruises, beginning with the basic one-hour sightseeing trip round the city centre for €8.50 per adult. Boats leave every 15min (9am–6pm) and every 30min (6–10pm) from the jetty facing Centraal Station on Prins Hendrikkade.

Let's Go ☎06/5188 4400, ⊛www .letsgo-amsterdam.com. Tour operator offering various well-organized bike tours around Amsterdam and its environs, including one to Edam and Volendam (see pp.132–134), twice weekly from May to September (4.5hr; €22). Also a "Mystery Walking Tour" around the city centre (May–Sept 2 weekly; 1.5hr; €10). You can book either direct or at the VVV; tours leave from outside the VVV office on Stationsplein.

Mee in Mokum Hartenstraat 18 ☎020/625 1390. Two-hour guided walking tours of the older parts of the city provided by long-time – and older (50+) – Amsterdam residents. Tours once daily on Sat & Sun only; €2.50 per person. Advance reservations required.

Yellow Bike Tours Nieuwezijds Kolk 29, off Nieuwezijds Voorburgwal ☎020/620 6940, ⊛www.yellowbike.nl. This efficient company organizes a lively programme of three-hour guided cycling tours around the city and its environs (April to mid-Oct 1 or 2 daily). Tours cost e17 per person, including the bike. Advance reservations are required.

Costs, money and banks

By west European standards, Amsterdam is fairly expensive when it comes to accommodation, with rooms regularly thirty percent more than in the rest of the country. Food is moderately expensive, but not noticeably so. These costs are partly offset by the low cost of public transport. More precise costs for places to stay and eat are given in the Guide, and you should consult p.143 for general guidelines on accommodation prices. ATMs are routine across the city and are the easiest way to get cash, but currency exchange facilities are widespread too.

If you're prepared to buy your own picnic lunch, stay in hostels, and stick to the least expensive bars and restaurants, you could get by on around **£25/US$40 a day**. Staying in two-star hotels, eating out in medium-range restaurants most nights and drinking

in bars, you'll get through at least **£65/$100 a day** with the main variable being the cost of your room. On **£100/$160 a day** and upwards, you'll be limited only by your energy reserves – though if you're planning to stay in a five-star hotel and to have a big night out, this still won't be enough. As always, if you're travelling alone you'll spend much more on accommodation than you would in a group of two or more: most hotels do have single rooms, but they're fixed at about 75 percent of the price of a double.

Restaurants don't come cheap, but costs remain manageable if you avoid the extras and concentrate on the main courses, for which around £10/$16 will normally suffice – twice that with a drink, starter and dessert. You can, of course, pay a lot more – a top restaurant can be twice as expensive again, and then some.

As for **incidental expenses**, a cup of coffee, a small glass of beer or a wedge of apple cake costs around £1.50/$2.20; today's English newspaper £2/$3; and developing a roll of film an amazing £12/$18. Museum admission prices hover around the £3–4/$4.5–6 mark.

Currency

The **currency** of the Netherlands – like most of the rest of the EU – is the **euro** (€), divided into 100 cents. There are seven euro **notes** – in denominations of €500, €200, €100, €50, €20, €10 and €5, each a different colour and size – and eight different **coins**, €2 and €1, then 50, 20, 10, 5, 2 and 1 cents. Euro coins feature a common EU design on one face, but different country-specific designs on the other. All euro notes and coins can be used in any of the twelve "euro-zone" states. These are the Netherlands, Austria, Belgium, Finland, France, Germany, Greece, Ireland, Italy, Luxembourg, Portugal and Spain. The three remaining EU member states, the UK, Denmark and Sweden, are all currently outside the euro zone.

At the time of writing the rate of exchange is €1.5 to the pound and fractionally under €1 to the dollar. For the most up-to-date rates, check the currency converter website ⓦwww.oanda.com.

Traveller's cheques

The main advantage of buying **traveller's cheques** is that they are a safe way of carrying funds. All well-known brands of traveller's cheque in all major currencies are widely accepted in Amsterdam, with euro and US dollar cheques being the most common. The usual fee for their purchase is one or two percent of face value, though this fee is often waived if you buy the cheques through a bank where you have an account. You'll find it useful to purchase a selection of denominations. When you **cash your cheques**, almost all banks make a percentage charge per transaction on top of a basic minimum charge.

In the event that your cheques are **lost or stolen**, the issuing company will expect you to report it immediately. Make sure you keep the purchase agreement, a record of cheque serial numbers, and the details of the company's emergency contact numbers or the addresses of their local offices, safe and separate from the cheques themselves. Most companies claim to replace lost or stolen cheques within 24 hours.

ATMs, debit and credit cards

Amsterdam has dozens of **ATMs** with a particular concentration in the city centre. Most ATMs give instructions in a variety of languages, and accept a host of **debit cards**, including all those carrying the Cirrus coding. If in doubt, check with your bank to find out whether the card you wish to use will be accepted – and if you need a new (international) PIN. You'll rarely be charged a transaction fee as the banks make their profits from applying different exchange rates. **Credit cards** can be used in ATMs too, but in this case transactions are treated as loans, with interest accruing daily from the date of withdrawal. All major credit cards, including American Express, Visa and Mastercard, are widely accepted in Amsterdam.

Lost and stolen cards

American Express cards ☏020/504 8000; traveller's cheques ☏0800/022 0100.
Diners Club ☏020/654 5511.
Mastercard ☏0800/022 5821.
Visa cards ☏0800/022 3110; traveller's cheques ☏0800/022 5484.

Visa TravelMoney (ⓦwww.visa.com) combines the security of traveller's cheques with the convenience of plastic. It's a disposable debit card, charged up before you leave home with whatever amount you like, separate from your normal banking or credit accounts. You can then access these dedicated travel funds from any ATM that accepts Visa worldwide, with a PIN that you select yourself. Travelex/Interpayment outlets sell the card worldwide (see ⓦwww.travelex.com for locations). When your money runs out, you just throw the card away. Since you can buy up to nine cards to access the same funds – useful for families travelling together – it's recommended that you buy at least one extra card as a back-up in case your first is lost or stolen. The 24-hour Visa customer service line from the Netherlands is ☎0800/022 3110.

Banks and exchange

If you need to change money, Amsterdam's **banks and post offices** usually offer the best deals. Bank opening hours are Monday to Friday 9am to 4pm, with a few also open Thursday until 9pm or on Saturday morning; all are closed on public holidays (see p.34). For post office opening hours, see p.31. Outside these times, you'll need to go to one of the many **bureaux de change** scattered around town. **GWK**, whose main 24-hour branches are at Centraal Station and Schiphol airport, offers competitive rates, as does Thomas Cook, who have branches at Dam 23 (daily 9am–6pm), Damrak 1–5 (daily 8am–8pm) and Leidseplein 31 (daily 9am–6pm). Beware of other agencies though, as some offer great rates but then slap on an extortionate commission, or, conversely, charge no commission but give bad rates. The VVV tourist office also changes money.

Wiring money

Having **money wired** from home using one of the companies listed below is never convenient or cheap, and should only be considered as a last resort. It can actually be slightly cheaper to have your own bank send the money through. For that, you need to nominate a receiving bank in Amsterdam and confirm the arrangement with them before you set the wheels in motion back home – any large branch will do. The sending bank's fees are geared to the amount being transferred and the urgency of the service you require – the fastest transfers, taking two or three days, start at around £25/$40 for the first £300–400/$450–600.

Money-wiring companies

Thomas Cook Canada ☎1-888/823-4732; Ireland ☎01/677 1721; UK ☎01733/318 922; US ☎1-800/287-7362; ⓦwww.us.thomascook.com.
Travelers Express Moneygram Canada ☎1-800/933-3278; US ☎1-800/926-3947; ⓦwww.moneygram.com.
Western Union Australia ☎1800/501 500; Ireland ☎1800/395 395; New Zealand ☎09/270 0050; UK ☎0800/833 833; US and Canada ☎1-800/325-6000; ⓦwww.westernunion.com.

Post, phones and email

As you might expect, the Netherlands in general and Amsterdam in particular has an efficient postal system and a first-rate telephone network, including excellent mobile phone coverage. Telephone booths and mail boxes are liberally distributed across the city – and charges are reasonable.

Post

In Amsterdam, **post offices** are plentiful and mostly open Monday to Friday 9am to 5pm, with the larger ones also open on Saturday mornings from 9am to noon. The main post office (Mon–Fri 9am–6pm, Thurs till 8pm, Sat 10am–1.30pm; ☏020/330 055) is at Singel 250, on the corner with Raadhuisstraat. They have a Poste Restante service; to collect items, you need your passport. Current **postal charges** are €0.50 for a postcard or airmail letter (up to 20g) within the EU; €0.65 airmail to the rest of the world. **Stamps** are sold at a wide range of outlets including many shops and hotels. **Post boxes** are everywhere, but be sure to use the correct slot – the one labelled *overige* is for post going outside the immediate locality.

Phones

Domestic and international **telephone calls** can be made with equal ease from public and private phones. **Phone booths** are common, though the irresistible rise of the mobile means that their numbers will not increase and may well diminish. The vast majority take phone cards or credit cards, but not cash; where this is not the case, they are of the usual European kind, where you deposit the money before you make your call. Most phone booths have English instructions displayed inside. **Phone cards** can be bought at many out-lets, including post offices, tobacconists and VVV offices, and in several specified denominations, beginning at €5. It is worth bearing in mind, however, that phone boxes are provided by different companies and their respective phone cards are not mutually compatible. KPN phones (and cards) are the most common. The cheap-rate period for international calls is between 8pm and 8am during the week and all day at weekends. Numbers pre-fixed ☏0800 are free, while those prefixed ☏0900 are premium-rated; a (Dutch) message before you're connected tells you how much you will be paying for the call. Finally, remember that although most hotel rooms have phones, there is almost always an exorbitant surcharge for their use.

Calling home from abroad with a telephone charge card

One of the most convenient ways of phoning home from abroad is via a **telephone charge card** from your phone company back home. Using a PIN number, you can make calls from most hotels, public and private phones that will be charged to your account – not locally. Since most major charge cards are free to obtain, it's certainly worth getting one at least for emergencies; bear in mind, however, that rates aren't necessarily cheaper than calling from an Amsterdam public phone.

Useful phone numbers

Operator (domestic and international) ☏0800 0410.
Directory enquiries
– domestic ☏0900 8008 (€0.90 per call)
– international ☏0900 8418 (€1.15 per call).

Phoning abroad from Amsterdam
To the UK: ☏0044 + area code minus zero + number.
To the Republic of Ireland: ☏00353 + area code minus zero + number.
To the US or Canada: ☏001 + area code + number.
To Australia: ☏0061 + area code minus zero + number.
To New Zealand: ☏0064 + area code minus zero + number.

Phoning Amsterdam from abroad
From the UK, Ireland and New Zealand: ☏00 + 31 (Netherlands) + 20 (Amsterdam) + number.
From the US and Canada: ☏011 + 31 (Netherlands) + 20 (Amsterdam) + number.
From Australia: ☏0011 + 31 (Netherlands) + 20 (Amsterdam) + number.

In the **US and Canada**, AT&T, MCI, Sprint, Canada Direct and other North American long-distance companies all enable their customers to make credit-card calls while overseas, billed to your home number. Call your company's customer service line for details of the toll-free access code in Amsterdam. In the **UK and Ireland**, British Telecom (☎0800/345 144, ⊛www.chargecard.bt.com) will issue free to all BT customers the BT Charge Card, which can be used in the Netherlands amongst a host of other countries. Alternatively, AT&T (☎0800/890 011, then 888/641-6123 when you hear the AT&T prompt) offers the Global Calling Card.

To call **Australia and New Zealand** from overseas, telephone charge cards such as Telstra Telecard or Optus Calling Card in Australia, and Telecom NZ's Calling Card can be used to make calls abroad, which are charged back to a domestic account or credit card. Apply to Telstra (☎1800/038 000), Optus (☎1300/300 937), or Telecom NZ (☎04/801 9000).

Mobile phones

If you want to use your **mobile phone** in Amsterdam, you'll need to check cellular access and call charges with your phone provider before you set out. Note in particular that you are likely to be charged extra for incoming calls when abroad, as the people calling you will be paying the usual rate. The same sometimes applies to text messages, though in many cases these can now be received easily and at ordinary rates. In Amsterdam, the mobile network covers almost every corner of the city and works on GSM 900/1800. Note that mobiles bought in **North America** need to be **triband** to access the cellular system in Europe.

Email

Amsterdam is well geared up for Internet and email access with a healthy supply of

Internet cafés – see below for a selection. Look out also for the new kid on the Internet block – *internetzuilen* (Internet poles) – fixed pillars in the street with a screen and keyboard, which you access by using a card. The latter are – or at least will be – sold at most large newsagents. Most of the better hotels provide email and Internet access for their guests at free or minimal charge.

One of the best ways to keep in touch while travelling is to sign up for a **free Internet email address** that can be accessed from anywhere, for example YahooMail or Hotmail – accessible through ⊛www.yahoo.com and ⊛www.hotmail.com respectively. Once you've set up an account, you can use these sites to pick up and send mail from any Internet café, or hotel with Internet access. In addition, ⊛www.kropla.com is a useful website giving details of how to plug your laptop in when abroad, as well as listing international phone codes and providing information about electrical systems in different countries.

Recommended Internet cafés

Conscious Dreams Kokopelli Warmoestraat 12 ☎020/421 7000, ⊛www.consciousdreams.nl. A smart shop offering Internet access and even DJs at the weekend. Located in the Red Light District. Daily 11am–10pm; €1 per 30 min.

Dreamlounge Kerkstraat 93 ☎020/626 6907. A small Grachtengordel shop with Internet facility. Mon–Wed 11am–7pm, Thurs–Sat 11am–8pm & Sun noon–5pm; €1 per 30min.

easyInternetcafé ⊛www.easyeverything.com. This international chain has two Internet outlets in Amsterdam – one near Centraal Station at Damrak 33 (daily 7.30am–11.30pm), the other at Reguliersbreestraat 22, near Rembrandtplein (24hr). You can get online for €0.05.

Het Internetcafe Martelaarsgracht 11 ☎020/627 1052, ⊛www.internetcafe.nl. Straightforward Internet café just 100m from Centraal Station. Reasonable rates – €1 per 30min – and open daily (Mon–Thurs & Sun 9am–1pm, Fri & Sat 9am–3pm).

The media

English speakers have a field day in Amsterdam: Dutch TV broadcasts a wide range of British and American programmes, and English-language newspapers are readily available.

The press

There's no difficulty in finding **British newspapers** – they're on sale at almost every newsagent on the day of publication, for around €3.50. Current issues of UK and US magazines are widely available too, as is the *International Herald Tribune*. Centraal Station has several newsagents and you'll always find a good selection of titles here.

Of the **Dutch newspapers**, *NRC Handelsblad* is a right-of-centre paper that has perhaps the best news coverage and a liberal stance on the arts, whilst *De Volkskrant* is a progressive, leftish daily. There's also the popular right-wing *De Telegraaf*, which boasts the largest circulation and has a well-regarded financial section, and *Algemeen Dagblad*, a right-wing broadsheet. Both the middle-of-the-road *Het Parool* ("The Password") and the news magazine *Vrij Nederland* ("Free Netherlands") are the successors of underground Resistance newspapers printed during wartime occupation. The Protestant *Trouw* ("Trust"), another former underground paper, has a centre-left orientation with a religious bent. Bundled in with the weekend edition of the International Herald Tribune is **The Netherlander**, a small but useful business-oriented review of Dutch affairs in English.

TV and radio

Dutch TV isn't up to much, but English-language programmes and films fill up a fair amount of the schedule – and they are always subtitled, never dubbed. Many bars and most hotels are also geared up for (at least a couple of) the big pan-European **cable and satellite** channels – including MTV, CNN and Eurosport – and most cable companies also give access to a veritable raft of foreign television channels, including Britain's BBC1 and BBC2.

As for **Dutch radio**, the one-time stalwart of the squat movement, Radio Honderd, which is only available in and around Amsterdam, at 99.3FM, offers a wide-ranging playlist from world dance to electronica. Jazz Radio, at 99.8FM, speaks for itself. The Dutch Classic FM, at 101.2FM, plays mainstream classical music, with jazz after 10pm. There's next to no English-language programming, but the BBC World Service broadcasts pretty much all day in English on 648kHz (medium wave); between 2am and 7am it also occupies 198kHz (long wave). Scores of radio stations, including all BBC output (www.bbc.co.uk), Voice of America (www.voa.gov), Radio Canada (www.rcinet.ca) and Radio Australia (www.abc.net.au), broadcast online.

Opening hours and public holidays

Although there's recently been some movement towards greater flexibility, opening hours for shops, businesses and tourist attractions – including museums – remain a little restrictive. In addition, travel plans can be disrupted on public holidays, when most things close down, apart from restaurants, bars and hotels, and public transport is reduced to a Sunday timetable.

Opening hours

The Amsterdam weekend fades painlessly into the working week with many smaller **shops and businesses**, even in the centre, staying closed on Monday mornings until noon. Normal **opening hours** are, however, Monday to Friday 8.30/9am to 5.30/6pm and – for shops not businesses – Saturday 8.30/9am to 4/5pm. That said, shops are allowed to open seven days a week from 9am–10pm and an increasing number are doing so; where this isn't the case, many open late on Thursday or Friday evenings. A handful of night shops – *avondwinkels* – stay open round the clock; see p.205 for a list.

Museums, especially those that are state-run, and these are the majority, tend to stick to a pattern – closed on Monday, and open Tuesday to Sunday from 10am to 5pm. The exceptions are the major museums – like the Van Gogh – which open daily from 10am to 5pm or 6pm. Though closed on December 25 and 26 and January 1, the state-run museums mostly adopt Sunday hours on the remaining public holidays, when most shops and banks are closed. Precise details of opening hours are given in the Guide.

Most **restaurants** are open for dinner from about 6 or 7pm, and though many close as early as 9.30pm, a few stay open past 11pm. **Bars**, **cafés** and **coffeeshops** are either open all day from around 10am or don't open until about 5pm; both varieties close at 1am during the week and 2am at weekends. **Nightclubs** generally function from 11pm to 4am during the week, though few open every night, and stay open until 5am on the weekend.

Public holidays

Public holidays (*Nationale feestdagen*) provide the perfect excuse to take to the streets. The most celebrated of them all is **Queen's Day on April 30**, when the Dutch indulge in the equivalent of a national flea market: tradition dictates that each household sells all the junk it has accumulated over the past year on the streets. April 30 is also celebrated in style – and with vim – by the city's gay community (see p.230 for more details).

January 1 New Year's Day
Good Friday (although many shops open)
Easter Sunday
Easter Monday
April 30 Queen's Day
May 5 Liberation Day
Ascension Day
Whit Sunday and Monday
December 25 and 26 Christmas

Trouble and the police

There's little reason why you should ever come into contact with Amsterdam's police force (*politie*), a laid-back bunch in dodgem-sized patrol cars or on bicycles. Few operate on the beat, and in any case Amsterdam is one of the safer cities in Europe: bar-room brawls are highly unusual, muggings uncommon, and street crime less commonplace than in many other capitals.

Petty crime

Almost all the problems tourists encounter in Amsterdam are to do with **petty crime** – pickpocketing and bag-snatching – rather than more serious physical confrontations, so it's as well to be on your guard and know where your possessions are at all times. Thieves often work in pairs and, although **theft** is far from rife, you should be aware of certain ploys, such as: the "helpful" person pointing out "birdshit" (actually shaving cream or similar) on your coat, while someone else relieves you of your money; being invited to read a card or paper on the street to distract your attention; someone in a café moving for your drink with one hand while the other is in your bag as you react; and if you're in a crowd of tourists, watch out for people moving in unusually close.

Sensible **precautions** against petty crime include: carrying bags slung across your neck and not over your shoulder; not carrying anything in pockets that are easy to dip into; and having photocopies of your passport, airline ticket and driving licence, while leaving the originals in your hotel safe. When you're looking for a hotel room, never leave your bags unattended, and similarly if you have a car, don't leave anything in view when you park: vehicle theft is still fairly uncommon, but luggage and valuables do make a tempting target. Again, if you're using a bicycle, make sure it is well locked up – **bike theft** and resale is a big deal here.

If you are robbed, you'll need to go to the **police** to report it, not least because your insurance company will require a police report; remember to make a note of the report number – or, better still, ask for a copy of the statement itself. Don't expect a great deal of concern if your loss is relatively small – and don't be surprised if the process of completing forms and formalities takes ages.

Personal safety

Although it's generally possible to walk around the city without fear of harassment or assault, certain parts of Amsterdam are decidedly shady, and wherever you go at night it's always better to err on the side of caution. In particular, be cautious in and around **Centraal Station**, the **De Pijp** area, south of the Sarphatipark, and in the **Red Light District**, where there's an unpleasant, sometimes threatening undertow amongst the narrow streets between the Oude Kerk and Zeedijk; play safe and avoid these streets if you can or, in the case of Centraal Station, don't wander around looking lost. As a general **precaution**, avoid unlit or empty streets and don't go out brimming with valuables. Using public transport, even late at night, isn't usually a problem, but if in doubt take a taxi.

In the unlikely event that you are **mugged**, or otherwise threatened, never resist, and try to reduce your contact with the robber to a minimum; either just hand over what's wanted, or throw money in one direction and take off in the other. Afterwards go straight to the police, who will be much more sympathetic and helpful on these occasions. Most police officers speak at least some English.

Emergencies

Police, fire service and ambulance
☎112

B

City-centre police stations

HQ Elandsgracht 117 ☎020/5599 111.
De Pijp Pieter Aertszstraat 5.
Jordaan Lijnbaansgracht 219.
Red Light District Warmoesstraat 44.

Drugs

Thousands of visitors come to Amsterdam just to get stoned. It's the one Western city where the purchase of **cannabis** is legal, but perhaps it's worth noting that many Amsterdammers get mightily hacked off with "**drug tourism**".

The Dutch government's attitude to soft drugs is actually much more complex than you might think. The use of cannabis is tolerated but not condoned, with the result being a rather complicated set of **rules and regulations**. The local administration sanctions the sale of cannabis at a few dozen **coffeeshops** (see Chapter Nine for recommendations), but these are not allowed to sell alcohol (or hard drugs) or sell drugs to under-18s, and neither are they allowed to advertise. Furthermore, over-the-counter sales of cannabis are limited to 5g (under one-fifth of an ounce) per purchase, and possession of over 30g (1oz) is illegal. In practice, the 5g and 30g laws are pretty much unenforceable and busts are rare, but note that if the police search you they are technically entitled to confiscate any quantity they find, regardless of whether or not it's less than the legal limit. Outside of the coffeeshops, it's acceptable to smoke in some bars, but many are strongly against it so don't make any automatic assumptions. If in doubt, ask the barperson. "Space cakes" (cakes baked with hashish and sold by the slice), although widely available, count as hard drugs and are illegal. And a word of warning: since all kinds of cannabis are so widely available in coffeeshops, there's no need to buy any on the street – if you do, you're asking for trouble. Dutch drug law is the same throughout the rest of the country, but only in the cities can you anticipate the same relaxed attitude from the police. Needless to say, the one thing you shouldn't attempt to do is take cannabis out of the country – a surprising number of people think (or claim to think) that if it's bought in Amsterdam it can be taken back home legally. Customs officials and drug enforcement officers never believe this story.

As far as **other drugs** go, the Dutch law surrounding magic mushrooms is that you can legally buy and possess any amount so long as they are fresh, but as soon as you tamper with them in any way (dry or process them, boil or cook them) they become illegal. Conscious Dreams, at Kerkstraat 117 (among other shops), has sold mushrooms openly for years, and continues to do so – see p.207. Cocaine, heroin, ecstasy, acid and speed are all as illegal in the Netherlands as they are anywhere else.

Being arrested

If you're **detained** by the police, you don't automatically have the right to a phone call, although in practice they'll probably phone your consulate for you. If your alleged offence is a minor matter, you can be held for up to six hours without questioning; if it is more serious, you can be detained for up to 24 hours.

Travellers with disabilities

Despite its general social progressiveness, the Netherlands is only just getting to grips with the particular requirements of people with mobility problems.

In Amsterdam, the most obvious difficulty is in negotiating the cobbled **streets** and narrow, often broken pavements of the older districts, where the key sights are mostly located. Similarly, provision for people with disabilities on the country's urban **public transport** is only average, although improving – many new buses, for instance, are now wheelchair-accessible. And yet, while it can be difficult simply to get around, practically all **public buildings**, including museums, theatres, cinemas, concert halls and hotels, are obliged to provide access, and do. Places that have been certified wheelchair-accessible now bear an International Accessibility Symbol (IAS). Bear in mind, however, that a lot of the older, narrower **hotels** are not allowed to install lifts, so check first. The national tourist office website ⊛www.visitholland .com has an online search facility within its Services menu, where you can find attractions and accommodation that have a wheelchair available and/or bear an IAS symbol. The tourist board also provides access information and local contact numbers.

If you're planning to use the Dutch train network during your stay and would appreciate assistance on the platform, phone the Bureau Assistentieverlening Gehandicapten (Disabled Assistance Office) on ☎030/235 7822 at least three hours before your train departs, and there will be someone to meet and help you at the station. NS publishes information about train travel for people with disabilities online at ⊛www.ns.nl and in various leaflets, stocked at main stations.

Contacts for travellers with disabilities

UK and Ireland

Access Travel ☎01942/888 844, ⊛www.access-travel.co.uk. Small, personal-service tour operator that can arrange flights, transfers and accommodation for Amsterdam city breaks.

Holiday Care ☎0845/124 9971, Minicom ☎0845/124 9976, ⊛www.holidaycare.org.uk. Provides an information pack for £2.50 which details transport options, accommodation, special services, tour operators and useful contacts for travelling around the Netherlands, Belgium and Luxembourg.

Irish Wheelchair Association ☎01/833 8241, ⊛www.iwa.ie. Useful information about travel abroad.

RADAR (Royal Association for Disability and Rehabilitation) ☎020/7250 3222, Minicom ☎020/7250 4119, ⊛www.radar.org.uk. A good source of advice, with a useful website.

Tripscope ☎0845/758 5641, ⊛www.justmobility .co.uk/tripscope. Registered charity providing free advice on international transport.

US and Canada

Access-Able ⊛www.access-able.com. Online resource for travellers with disabilities.

Directions Unlimited ☎1-800/533-5343 or 914/241-1700. Tour operator.

Mobility International USA ☎541/343-1284, ⊛www.miusa.org. Information and referral services, access guides, tours and exchange programmes.

Society for the Advancement of Travelers with Handicaps (SATH) ☎212/447-7284, ⊛www.sath.org. Non-profit educational organization.

Travel Information Service ☎215/456-9600. Information and referral service.

Twin Peaks Press ☎1-800/637-2256 or 360/694-2462, ⊛disabilitybookshop.virtualave .net. Disability-oriented publisher.

Wheels Up! ☎1-888/389-4335, ⊛www.wheelsup .com. Provides discounted airfare and tour prices and a free monthly newsletter. Comprehensive website.

Australia and New Zealand

ACROD (Australian Council for Rehabilitation of the Disabled) ☎02/6282 4333. Provides lists of travel agencies and tour operators.

Disabled Persons Assembly (NZ) ☎04/801 9100. Resource centre with lists of travel agencies and tour operators.

The Netherlands

Landelijk Bureau Toegankelijkheid National Bureau for Accessibility, Utrecht ☎030/276 9970, ✉sdg@wxs.nl. Part of the Stichting Dienstverleners Gehandicapten (Foundation for Rehabilitation), which promotes accessibility, mobility and technology.
Mobility International Nederland Heidestein 7, 3971 ND Driebergen ☎0343/521795, ✉bijning @worldonline.nl. Largest Dutch information and advice service for people with disabilities.
Stadsmobiel Postbus 2131, 1000 CC Amsterdam ☎ & ✉020/613 4769,

🌐www.stadsmobiel.nl. Provides an accessible shuttle service in and around Amsterdam (including the airport) for members.
Stichting Informatie Gehandicapten (SIG) Zakkedragershof 34–44, Postbus 70, 3500 AB Utrecht ☎030/234 5611. General disability information.
Stichting Recreatie Gehandicapten Postbus 4140, 2003 EC Haarlem ☎023/536 8409, 🌐www.srg-vakanties.nl. Organizes tours around Amsterdam and Europe.

Gay and lesbian travellers

Amsterdam ranks as one of the top gay-friendly holiday destinations in Europe. Attitudes in the city are tolerant, gay bars are plentiful, and support groups and facilities unequalled – see Chapter Twelve.

Contacts for gay and lesbian travellers

UK

🌐**www.gaytravel.co.uk.** Online gay and lesbian travel agent, offering good deals on all types of holiday. Also lists gay- and lesbian-friendly hotels around the world.
Dreamwaves Holidays ☎0870/042 2475, 🌐www.gayholidaysdirect.com. Specializes in exclusively gay package holidays.
Madison Travel ☎01273/202 532, 🌐www.madisontravel.co.uk. Established travel agents specializing in packages to gay- and lesbian-friendly mainstream destinations, and also to gay/lesbian destinations.
Respect Holidays ☎0870/770 0169, 🌐www.respect-holidays.co.uk. Offers exclusively gay packages to popular European resorts and cities.

US and Canada

Damron ☎1-800/462-6654 or 415/255-0404, 🌐www.damron.com. Publisher of the *Men's Travel Guide*, a pocket-sized yearbook full of listings of hotels, bars, clubs and resources for gay men; the *Women's Traveler*, which provides similar listings for lesbians; and *Damron Accommodations*, which provides detailed listings of over 1000 accommodations

for gays and lesbians worldwide. All of these titles are offered at a discount on the website. No specific city guides – everything is incorporated in the yearbooks.
gaytravel.com ☎1-800/GAY-TRAVEL, 🌐www.gaytravel.com. The premier site for trip planning, bookings and general information about international gay and lesbian travel.
International Gay & Lesbian Travel Association ☎1-800/448-8550 or 954/776-2626, 🌐www.iglta.org. Trade group that can provide a list of gay- and lesbian-owned or -friendly travel agents, accommodation and other travel businesses.

Australia and New Zealand

Gay and Lesbian Tourism Australia 🌐www.galta.com.au. Directory and links for gay and lesbian travel worldwide.
Parkside Travel ☎08/8274 1222, ✉parkside@herveyworld.com.au. Gay travel agent associated with local branch of Hervey World Travel; all aspects of gay and lesbian travel worldwide.
Silke's Travel ☎1800/807 860 or 02/8347 2000, 🌐www.silkes.com.au. Long-established gay and lesbian specialist, with the emphasis on women's travel.
Tearaway Travel ☎1800/664 440 or 03/9510 6644, 🌐www.tearaway.com. Gay-specific business dealing with international and domestic travel.

The City

The City

The Old Centre

A msterdam's most vivacious district, the **Old Centre** is an oval-shaped affair whose jingle and jangle of antique streets and narrow canals are confined in the north by the River IJ and to the west and south by the Singel, the first of several canals that once girdled the entire city. This was where Amsterdam began, starting out as a humble fishing village at the marshy mouth of the River Amstel before the local lord gave it some significance by building a castle here in 1204. Sixty years later, the Amstel was dammed – leading to the name Amstelredam – and the village began to flourish as a trading centre, receiving its municipal charter from a new feudal overlord, the Count of Holland, in about 1300. Thereafter, the city developed in stages, each of which was marked by the digging of new canals to either side of the main canal linking the River IJ with Dam square, along today's Damrak. However, time and again, the wooden canalside buildings of medieval Amsterdam went up in smoke, until finally, after a particularly severe fire in 1452, timber was banned in favour of brick and stone – and it's these handsome buildings of the seventeenth and eighteenth centuries which provide the Old Centre with most of its architectural highpoints.

Given the dominance of **Centraal Station** on most transport routes, this is where you'll almost certainly arrive. Immediately outside, on **Stationsplein** – home of the main tourist and transport information offices (see p.22) – you'll be thrust into the city centre's heaving street life of buskers and bicycles, trams and tourists. From here a stroll across the bridge will take you onto **Damrak**, which divided the **Oude Zijde** (Old Side) of the medieval city to the east from the smaller **Nieuwe Zijde** (New Side) to the west. It also led – and leads – to the heart of the Old Centre, **Dam square**, which is overseen by two of the city's most impressive buildings, the **Koninklijk Paleis** (Royal Palace) and the **Nieuwe Kerk** (New Church).

Nowadays, much of the Oude Zijde is taken up by the tentacular **Red Light District**, which stretches across Warmoesstraat and two canals – Oudezijds Voorburgwal and Oudezijds Achterburgwal – before nudging over towards Nieuwmarkt. The prevailing seediness dulls many architectural charms, but

Junkies in the Old Centre

The hang-around **junkies** of the Old Centre are not generally considered dangerous, but they are certainly disconcerting where and whenever they gather in groups – especially when the streets are quiet. It frequently changes, but the edgiest area is just to the east of the Oude Kerk on O.Z. Voorburgwal and O.Z. Achterburgwal with Nieuwmarkt periodically becoming enmeshed too. It almost goes without saying that cutting any kind of drug deal with a street dealer is ill-advised and illegal.

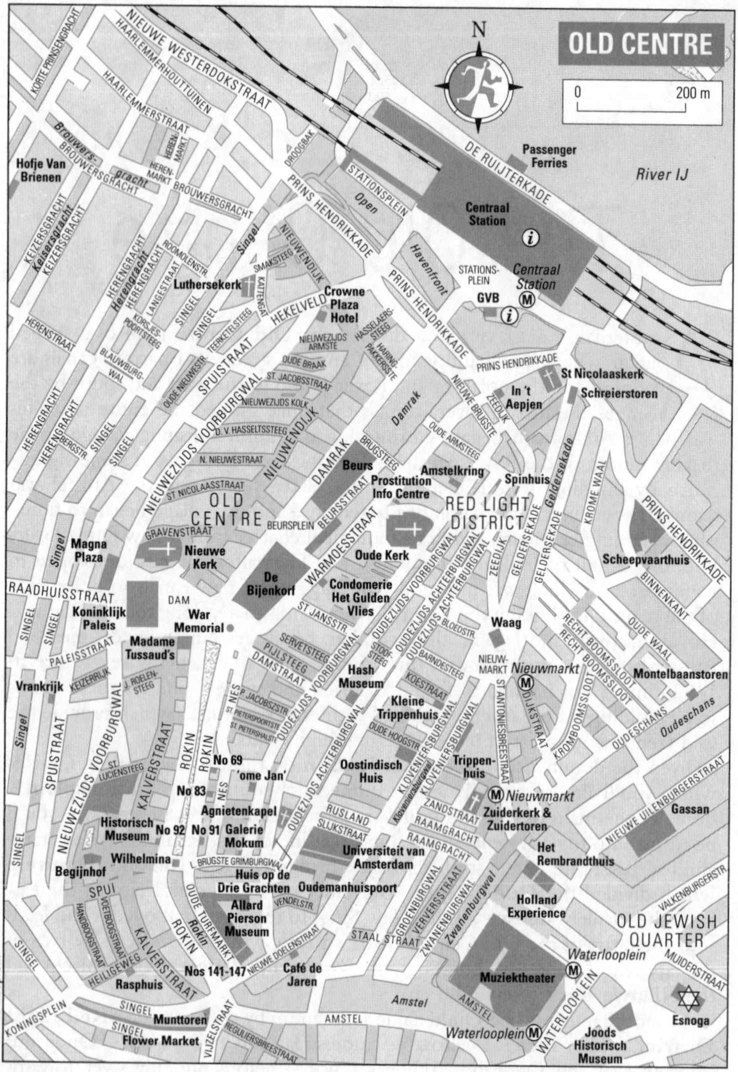

with or without all this industrialized eroticism, be sure to spare time for the delightful **Amstelkring**, a clandestine Catholic church dating from the seventeenth century, and the charming Gothic architecture of the **Oude Kerk**.

Just beyond the reach of the Red Light District is **Nieuwmarkt**, a large and unassuming square that marks the start of **Kloveniersburgwal** which – together with **Groenburgwal** – forms one the most beguiling parts of the Old Centre, with a medley of handsome old houses lining the prettiest of canals. From here, it's a short walk south to the **Muntplein**, a busy square that boasts a floating **flower market** and the distinctive **Munttoren** (Mint Tower).

Muntplein lies at the end of the **Rokin**, a shopping boulevard that runs north to Dam square. Near the Rokin, you'll find a clutch of good museums, but the prime target is the secluded **Begijnhof**, a circle of dignified old houses originally built to house a semi-religious community in the 1340s.

Damrak and the Nieuwe Zijde

Running from Centraal Station to Dam square, the **Damrak** was a canal until 1672, when it was filled in – much to the relief of the locals, who were tired of the stink. The canal had been the medieval city's main nautical artery, with boats sailing up it to discharge their goods right in the centre of town on Dam square. Thereafter, with the docks moved elsewhere, the Damrak became a busy commercial drag, as it remains today, and the Dam became the centre of municipal power.

To the west of the Damrak lies the Old Centre's **Nieuwe Zijde**, whose outer boundary was marked in the 1500s by a defensive wall, hence the name of its principal avenue, **Nieuwezijds Voorburgwal** ("In Front of the Town Wall on the New Side"). The wall disappeared as the city grew, and in the nineteenth century the canal that ran through the middle of the street was earthed in, leaving the unusually wide swathe that you see today. This area was, however, badly mauled by the developers in the 1970s and – give or take a scattering of old canal houses on Nieuwezijds Voorburgwal and maybe the whopping **Lutherse Kerk** – there's no great reason to visit.

Centraal Station and around

With its high gables and cheerful brickwork, the neo-Renaissance **Centraal Station** is an imposing prelude to the city. At the time of its construction in the 1880s, it aroused much controversy because it effectively separated the centre from the River IJ, source of the city's wealth, for the first time in Amsterdam's long history. There was controversy about the choice of architect too. The man chosen, **Petrus J.H. Cuypers**, was a Catholic, and in powerful Protestant circles there were mutterings about the vanity of his designs (he had recently completed the Rijksmuseum – see p.98) and their unsuitability for Amsterdam. In the event, the station was built to Cuypers' design, but it was to be his last major commission; thereafter he spent most of his time building parish churches.

Outside the station, **Stationsplein** is a messy open space, edged by ovals of water, packed with trams and dotted with barrel organs and chip stands, with street performers completing the picture in the summer. Across the water, to the southeast on Prins Hendrikkade, rise the whopping twin towers and dome of **St Nicolaaskerk** (Mon–Sat noon–3pm; free), the city's foremost Catholic Church. Dating back to the 1880s, the cavernous interior holds some pretty dire religious murals, mawkish concoctions only partly relieved by swathes of coloured brickwork. Above the high altar is the crown of the Habsburg Emperor Maximilian, very much a symbol of the city and one you'll see again and again. Amsterdam had close ties with Maximilian: in the late fifteenth century he came here as a pilgrim and stayed on to recover from an illness. The burghers funded many of his military expeditions and, in return, he let the city use his crown in its coat of arms – a practice which, rather surprisingly, survived the seventeenth-century revolt against Spain.

Just along from St Nicolaaskerk, at the top of Geldersekade, is the squat **Schreierstoren** (Weepers' Tower), a rare surviving chunk of the city's medieval wall. Originally, the tower overlooked the River IJ and it was here that women gathered to watch their men folk sail away – hence its name. An old and badly weathered stone plaque inserted in the wall is a reminder of all those sad goodbyes, and another, much more recent, plaque recalls the departure of Henry Hudson from here in 1609. On this particular voyage Hudson stumbled across the "Hudson" river and an island the locals called Manhattan. Hudson founded a colony there and called it New Amsterdam, a colonial possession that was re-named New York after the English seized it in 1664.

If you continue east along Prins Hendrikkade, you soon reach the Scheepvaarthuis (see p.53) and then the Oude Schans canal (see p.52). It's also just a few metres from St Nicolaaskerk to **Zeedijk**, which is the quickest route to the Nieuwmarkt (see p.52). Zeedijk was originally just that – a dike to hold back the sea – and the wooden building at **no. 1** is one of the oldest in the city, built as sailors' lodgings around 1550. It's home to the **In't Aepjen** ("In the Monkeys") bar – as it always has been. As in other such places, sailors were once able to pay their bill by barter if they had whored or gambled away their wages – hardly a rarity. For reasons that remain obscure, trading in pet monkeys was particularly popular here. As for the rest of Zeedijk, it begins promisingly with a huddle of antique buildings, but soon descends into tattiness, with junkies and dealers hanging about in ramshackle doorways, altogether threatening enough to make you hurry on to the open spaces of Nieuwmarkt.

Along Damrak

From Stationsplein, **Damrak**, a wide but unenticing avenue lined with tacky restaurants, bars and bureaux de change, slices south into the heart of the city, first passing an inner harbour crammed with the bobbing canal cruise boats of Amsterdam's considerable tourist industry (see p.27). Just beyond the harbour is the imposing bulk of the **Beurs**, the old Stock Exchange (Tues–Sun 11am–5pm; admission depends on exhibition; ⓦ www.beursvanberlage.nl) – known as the "Beurs van Berlage" – a seminal work designed at the turn of the twentieth century by the leading light of the Dutch Modern movement, Hendrik Petrus Berlage (1856–1934). Berlage re-routed Dutch architecture with this building, forsaking the historicism that had dominated the nineteenth century, and whose prime practitioner had been Cuypers (see p.43). Instead he opted for a style with cleaner, heavier lines, inspired by the Romanesque and the Renaissance, but with a minimum of ornamentation – and in so doing anticipated the Expressionism that swept northern Europe from 1905 to 1925. The Beurs has long since lost its commercial function and nowadays holds a modest exhibition on the history of the exchange, but the building is the main event, from the graceful exposed ironwork and shallow-arched arcades of the main hall through to a fanciful frieze celebrating the stockbroker's trade.

Just up from the Beurs, the enormous **De Bijenkorf** – literally "beehive" – department store extends south along the Damrak. Amsterdam's answer to Harrods, De Bijenkorf posed all sorts of problems for the Germans when they first occupied the city in World War II. It was a Jewish concern, so the Nazis didn't really want their troops shopping here, but it was just too popular to implement a total ban; the bizarre solution was to prohibit German soldiers from shopping on the ground floor, where the store's Jewish employees were concentrated, as they always had been, in the luxury goods section.

The south end of De Bijenkorf abuts Dam square (see opposite).

The Nieuwe Zijde

Running parallel to, and west of, the Damrak, **Nieuwezijds Voorburgwal** kicks off with the **Crowne Plaza Hotel**, at no. 5, formerly the Holiday Inn, built on the site of an old tenement building called **Wyers**. The 1985 clearance of squatters from Wyers ranks among the more infamous of that decade's anti-squatting campaigns, involving a great deal of protest (and some violence) throughout the city. The squatters had occupied the building in an attempt to prevent yet another slice of the city being converted from residential to business use. They were widely supported by the people of Amsterdam, but they could not match the clout of the American hotel company and riot police were sent in; construction of the hotel followed soon after.

From the hotel, it's a short walk along Hekelveld and a right turn down Kattengat to the **Lutherse Kerk**, a whopping seventeenth-century edifice whose copper dome gives this area its nickname, **Koepelkwartier**. It's a grand, self-confident building, seen to best advantage from the Singel canal, but it has been dogged by bad luck: in 1882 the interior was gutted by fire and, although it was repaired, the cost of maintenance proved too high for the congregation, who decamped in 1935. After many years of neglect, the adjacent *Renaissance Hotel* bought the church, turning it into a conference centre. Church domes are a rarity in Amsterdam, but this one was no stylistic peccadillo; until the late eighteenth century, only Dutch Reformed churches were permitted the (much more fashionable) bell towers, so the Lutherans got stuck with a dome.

Doubling back to Nieuwezijds Voorburgwal, you soon reach **Nieuwezijds Kolk**, where the angular, glassy and ultramodern building on the corner is testament to the recent large-scale construction work that has transformed the area. When the underground car park was being dug here, workers discovered archeological remains dating back to the thirteenth century; this turned out to be the castle of the "Lords of Amstel", which, it is thought, had occupied the site when it was open marshland, even before the Amstel was dammed. The series of pedestrianized **alleys** that link Nieuwezijds Voorburgwal to the Damrak to the south of Nieuwezijds Kolk are without much charm. Consequently, it's better to stay on Nieuwezijds Voorburgwal as it heads south, its trees partly concealing a series of impressive canal houses, though these fizzle out as you approach Dam square.

Dam square

Situated at the heart of the city, **Dam square** gave Amsterdam its name: in the thirteenth century the River Amstel was dammed here, and the fishing village that grew around it became known as "Amstelredam". Boats could sail into the square down the Damrak and unload right in the middle of the settlement, which soon prospered by trading herrings for Baltic grain. In the early fifteenth century, the building of Amsterdam's principal church, the Nieuwe Kerk, and thereafter the town hall (now the Royal Palace), formally marked the Dam as Amsterdam's centre, but since World War II it has lost much of its dignity. Today it's open and airy but somehow rather desultory, despite – or perhaps partly because of – the presence of the main municipal **war memorial**, a prominent stone tusk adorned by bleak, suffering figures and decorated with the coats of arms of each of the Netherlands' provinces (plus the ex-colony of Indonesia). The memorial was designed by Jacobus Johannes Pieter Oud (1890–1963), a

De Stijl stalwart who thought the Expressionism of Berlage (see p.44) much too flippant. The Amsterdam branch of **Madame Tussaud's** waxworks is on the Dam too, at no. 20 (daily: mid-July to Aug 9.30am–7.30pm; Sept to mid-July 10am–5.30pm; €17.50, children 5–15 €10, over 60s €15).

The Koninklijk Paleis

Dominating the Dam is the **Koninklijk Paleis**, the Royal Palace (open for guided tours & exhibitions; call for opening hours & admission ☎020/620 4060), though the title is deceptive, given that this vast sandstone structure started out as the city's Stadhuis (town hall), and only had its first royal occupant when Louis Bonaparte moved in during the French occupation (1795–1813). At the time of the building's construction in the mid-seventeenth century, Amsterdam was at the height of its powers. The city was pre-eminent amongst Dutch towns, and had just resisted William of Orange's attempts to bring it to heel; predictably, the council craved a residence that was a declaration of the city's municipal power and opted for a startlingly progressive design by **Jacob van Campen**, who proposed a Dutch rendering of the classical principles revived in Renaissance Italy. Initially, there was opposition to the plan from the council's Calvinist minority, who pointed out that the proposed Stadhuis would dwarf the neighbouring Nieuwe Kerk (see opposite), an entirely inappropriate ordering, so they suggested, of earthly and spiritual values. However, when the Calvinists were promised a new church spire (it was never built) they promptly fell in line and in 1648 work started on what was then the largest town hall in Europe, supported by no less than 13,659 wooden piles driven into the Dam's sandy soil – a number every Dutch schoolchild remembers by adding a "1" and a "9" to the number of days in the year. The poet Constantijn Huygens called the new building "The world's Eighth Wonder / With so much stone raised high and so much timber under". The Stadhuis received its royal designation in 1808, when Napoleon's brother Louis, who had recently been installed as king, commandeered it as his residence. Lonely and isolated, Louis abdicated in 1810 and hightailed it out of the country, leaving behind a large quantity of Empire furniture, most of which is exhibited in the rooms he converted. Possession of the palace subsequently reverted to the city, who sold it to the state in 1935, since when it has been used by royalty on very rare occasions.

The **exterior** of the Stadhuis is very much to the allegorical point: twin tympani depict Amsterdam as a port and trading centre, the one at the front presided over by Neptune and a veritable herd of unicorns. Above these panels are representations of the values the city council espoused – at the front, Prudence, Justice and Peace, to the rear Temperance and Vigilance to either side of a muscular, globe-carrying Atlas. One deliberate precaution, however, was the omission of a central doorway – just in case the mob turned nasty (as they were wont to do) and stormed the place.

The **interior** also proclaims the pride and confidence of the Golden Age; the **Citizen's Hall** contains the enthroned figure of Amsterdam, sumptuously inlaid with brass and marble, looking down on the world laid out at her feet. A good-natured and witty symbolism pervades the building too – cocks fight above the entrance to the Court of Petty Affairs, while Apollo, god of the sun and the arts, brings harmony to the disputes; and a plaque above the door of the Bankruptcy Chamber aptly shows the Fall of Icarus, surrounded by marble carvings depicting hungry rats scurrying around an empty chest and unpaid bills. On a more sober note, death sentences were pronounced at the High Court of Justice at the front of the building, and the condemned were executed in full view on a scaffold outside. Among the **paintings** dotted around the building, most are large-scale historical canvases of little distinction, with the exception of Ferdinand Bol's glossy *Moses the Lawgiver*. The situation could have been very different had Rembrandt, whose career was on the wane, not had his sketches rejected by the city council – a decision which must rank pretty high in any league of major blunders.

Magna Plaza

Behind the Royal Palace, on Nieuwezijds Voorburgwal, you can't miss the old neo-Gothic post office of 1899, now converted into the **Magna Plaza** shopping mall (see p.193). A municipal heavyweight, the post office was never very popular despite its whimsical embellishments, which continued the town's tradition of plonking towers on every major building partly as a matter of civic pride, and partly to contribute to the city's spikey skyline. The architect responsible, a certain C.G. Peters, took a surprising amount of flack for his creation, which was mocked as "postal Gothic".

The Nieuwe Kerk

Vying for importance with the Royal Palace is the adjacent **Nieuwe Kerk** (opening hours & admission vary with exhibitions, but usually daily 10am–6pm; ☎020/638 6909, ⓦwww.nieuwekerk.nl). Despite its name (literally "new church"), it's an early fifteenth-century structure built in a late flourish of the Gothic style, with a forest of pinnacles and high, slender gables. Badly damaged by fire on several occasions and unceremoniously stripped of most of its fittings by the Calvinists, the **interior** is a hangar-like affair of sombre demeanour, whose sturdy compound pillars soar up to support the wooden vaulting of the ceiling. Amongst a scattering of decorative highlights, look out for an extravagant, finely carved mahogany **pulpit** that was fifteen years in the making, a cleverly worked copper **chancel screen** and a flashily Baroque **organ case**. There's also the spectacularly vulgar tomb of Admiral **Michiel de Ruyter** (1607–1676), complete with trumpeting angels, conch-blowing Neptunes and cherubs all in a tizzy. In a long and illustrious naval career Ruyter trounced in succession the Spaniards, the Swedes, the English and the French, and his rise from deck hand to Admiral-in-Chief is the stuff of national legend. His most famous exploit was a raid up the River Thames to Medway in 1667 and the seizure of the Royal Navy's flagship, The Royal Charles; the subsequent Dutch crowing almost drove Charles II to distraction. Ruyter was buried here with full military honours and the church is still used for state occasions: the coronations of queens Wilhelmina, Juliana and, in 1980, Beatrix, were all held here.

After the church, pop into the adjoining *'t Nieuwe Kafé*, which occupies one of the old ecclesiastical lean-tos and where they serve excellent coffee and delicious lunches and snacks.

The Red Light District

The whole area to the east of Damrak, between Warmoesstraat, Nieuwmarkt and Damstraat, is the **Red Light District**, known locally as the "De Walletjes" (Small Walls) on account of the series of low brick walls that contain its canals. The district stretches across the two narrow canals that marked the eastern edge of medieval Amsterdam, Oudezijds Voorburgwal and Oudezijds

Achterburgwal, both of which are now seedy and seamy, though the legalized prostitution here is world renowned and has long been one of the city's most distinctive and popular draws. The two canals, with their narrow connecting passages, are thronged with "**window brothels**" and at busy times the crass, on-street haggling over the price of various sex acts is drowned out by a surprisingly festive atmosphere – entire families grinning more or less amiably at the women in the windows or discussing the specifications (and feasibility) of the sex toys in the shops. Groups of men line the streets hawking the peep shows and "live sex" within – and, unlike in London or New York, there actually is live sex within. There's a nasty undertow to the district though, oddly enough sharper during the daytime, when the pimps hang out in shifty gangs and drug addicts wait anxiously, assessing the chances of scoring their next hit. And don't even think about taking a picture of a "window brothel" unless you're prepared for some major grief from the camera-shy prostitutes. Dodging the dealers, the district also contains two prime attractions, the medieval **Oude Kerk** and the clandestine **Amstelkring** Catholic church.

Warmoesstraat

Soliciting hasn't always been the principal activity on sleazy **Warmoesstraat**. It was once one of the city's most fashionable streets, home to Holland's foremost poet, **Joost van den Vondel** (1587–1679), who ran his hosiery business from no. 110, in between writing and hobnobbing with the Amsterdam elite. Vondel is a kind of Dutch Shakespeare: his *Gijsbrecht van Amstel*, a celebration of Amsterdam during its Golden Age, is one of the classics of Dutch literature, and he wrote regular, if ponderous, official verses, including well over a thousand lines on the inauguration of the new town hall. He had more than his share of hard luck too. His son frittered away the modest family fortune and Vondel lived out his last few years as doorkeeper of the pawn shop on Oudezijds Voorburgwal (see p.51), dying of hypothermia at what was then the remarkable age of 92. Witty to the end, his own suggested epitaph ran:

Here lies Vondel, still and old
Who died – because he was cold.

Vondel's Warmoesstraat house was knocked down decades ago, but the street does have two minor attractions – the **Prostitution Information Centre**, at Enge Kerksteeg 3 (see box on p.49) and the **Condomerie Het Gulden Vlies**, at no. 141, which specializes in every imaginable design and make of condom, in sizes ranging from the small to the remarkable.

Oude Kerk

Just to the east of Warmoesstraat is the city's most appealing church, the **Oude Kerk** (Mon–Sat 11am–5pm, Sun 1–5pm; €4), an attractive Gothic structure with high-pitched gables and finely worked lancet windows. There's been a church on this site since the middle of the thirteenth century, but most of the present building dates from a century later, funded by the pilgrims who came here in their hundreds following a widely publicized miracle. The story goes that, in 1345, a dying man regurgitated the Host he had received here at Communion and when it was thrown on the fire afterwards, it did not burn. The unburnable Host was placed in a chest and installed in a long-lost chapel somewhere off Nieuwezijds Voorburgwal, before finally being transferred to the Oude Kerk a few years later. It disappeared during the Reformation, but to this day thousands of the faithful still come to take part in the annual Stille Omgang, a silent nocturnal procession terminating at the Oude Kerk and held in mid-March. The church is also regularly used for art displays and concerts.

The Protestants cleared the church of almost all of its ecclesiastical tackle during the Reformation, but its largely bare **interior** does hold several interesting features. These include some fruity and folksy misericords, a few faded vault paintings recovered from beneath layers of whitewash in the 1950s and the unadorned memorial tablet of Rembrandt's first wife, Saskia van Uylenburg – it's a couple of metres from the choir organ. Much more diverting, however, are the three beautifully coloured **stained-glass windows** beside the ambulatory in what was once the Chapel of Our Lady. Dating from the 1550s, all three

Commercial sex in Amsterdam

Developed in the 1960s, Amsterdam's liberal approach to social policy has had several unforeseen consequences, the most dramatic being its international reputation as a centre for both drugs (see p.53) and **prostitution**. However, the tackiness of the Red Light District is just the surface sheen on what is a serious attempt to address the reality of sex-for-sale, and to integrate this within a normal, ordered society. In Dutch law, prostituting oneself has long been legal, but the state has always drawn the line at **brothels** and **soliciting in public**. The difficulties this created for the police were legion, so finally, in 1996, a special soliciting zone was established and a couple of years later brothels were legalized in the hope that together these changes would bring a degree of stability to the sex industry. The authorities were particularly keen to get a grip on the use of illegal immigrants as prostitutes and also to alleviate the problem of numbers; the number of "window brothels" is limited, so a significant group of women ply their trade illicitly in bars and hotels. This new legislation is partly the result of a long and determined campaign by the prostitutes' trade union, **De Rode Draad** ("The Red Thread"), which has improved the lot of its members by setting up nascent health insurance and pension schemes.

One of the strongest features of the Dutch approach to commercial sex is its lack of prudery. The **Prostitution Information Centre**, at Enge Kerksteeg 3, in between Warmoesstraat and the Oude Kerk (Tues, Wed, Fri & Sat 11.30am–7.30pm; ☏020/420 7328), is a legally recognized *stichting*, or charitable foundation, set up to provide prostitutes, their clients and general visitors with clear, dispassionate information about prostitution. In addition to selling books and pamphlets, the PIC publishes the *Pleasure Guide* in Dutch and English, which bills itself as "an informative magazine about having a paid love-life". By positioning itself on the commercial interface between the Red Light District and the rest of the city – and devoting itself to aiding communication between the two – the PIC has done much to subvert the old exploitative dominance of underworld pimps.

You can read about the city government's regulations and attitude towards prostitution online at ⓦ www.amsterdam.nl.

△ Condomerie Het Gulden Vlies

depict religious scenes, from left to right the Annunciation, the Adoration of the Shepherds and the Dormition of the Virgin, and each is set above its respective donors. The characters are shown in classical gear with togas and sandals and the buildings in the background are firmly classical too, reflecting both artistic fashion and a belief that Greco-Roman detail was historically accurate. A fourth, contrasting stained-glass window is located on the other side of the ambulatory. A secular piece of 1655, it features the Spanish king Philip IV ceding independence to a representative of the United Provinces (the Netherlands) under the terms of the Treaty of Munster of 1648, which wrapped up the Thirty Years' War. Like the earlier windows, the architectural backdrop is classical, but here it's to emphasize the dignity of the proceedings – and the king and the Dutch emissaries wear contemporary clothes.

The Amstelkring

The front of the Oude Kerk overlooks the northern reaches of **Oudezijds Voorburgwal**, whose handsome facades recall ritzier days when this was one of the wealthiest parts of the city, richly earning its nickname the "Velvet Canal". A few metres north of the church, at Oudezijds Voorburgwal 40, is the clandestine **Amstelkring** (Mon–Sat 10am–5pm, Sun 1–5pm; €6), which was momentarily the city's principal Catholic place of worship and is now one of Amsterdam's most enjoyable museums. In 1578 the city forsook the Catholic Habsburgs and declared for the Protestant rebels in what was known as the *Alteratie* (Alteration). Broadly speaking, the new regime treated its Catholics well – commercial pragmatism has always outweighed religious zeal here – but there was a degree of discrimination; Catholic churches were recycled for Protestant use and their members no longer allowed to practise openly. The result was an eccentric compromise: Catholics were allowed to hold services in any private building providing that the exterior revealed no sign of their activities – hence the development of the city's clandestine churches (*schuilkerken*), amongst which the Amstelkring is the only one to have survived intact.

The Amstelkring, more properly Ons Lieve Heer Op Solder ("Our Dear Lord in the Attic"), occupies the loft of a wealthy merchant's house and is perfectly delightful, with a narrow nave skilfully shoehorned into the available space. Flanked by elegant balconies, the nave has an ornately carved organ at one end and a mock-marble high altar, decorated with Jacob de Wit's mawkish *Baptism of Christ*, at the other. Even the patron of the church, one Jan Hartman, clearly had doubts about de Wit's efforts – the two spares he procured just in case are now displayed behind the altar. The rest of the house has been left untouched, its original furnishings reminiscent of interiors by Vermeer or De Hooch. Amstelkring, meaning "Amstel Circle", is the name of the group of nineteenth-century historians who saved the building from demolition.

Spinhuis

From the Amstelkring cross the canal by the nearest bridge, proceed along Korte Niezel and turn left onto canalside Oudezijds Achterburgwal where, at no. 28, you'll find the **Spinhuis**, once a house of correction for "fallen women", who were put to work here on the looms and spinning wheels. Curiously, workhouses like this used to figure on tourist itineraries: for a small fee the public were allowed to watch the women at work, and at carnival times admission was free and large crowds came to jeer and mock. The justification for this was that shame was supposed to be part of the reforming process, but in fact the municipality unofficially tolerated brothels and the incarcerated women had simply been singled out for exemplary punishment. As the eighteenth-century commentator Bernard de Mandeville observed, "The wary magistrates preserve themselves in the good opinion of the weaker sort of people, who imagine the government is always trying to suppress those [brothels] it really tolerates." The Spinhuis has been turned into offices, but the facade remains pretty much intact, with an inscription by the seventeenth-century Dutch poet Pieter Cornelisz Hooft: "Cry not, for I exact no vengeance for wrong but to force you to be good. My hand is stern but my heart is kind."

From the Spinhuis, it's a brief walk south to the Nieuwmarkt at the northern end of Kloveniersburgwal.

Kloveniersburgwal and around

The outermost of the three eastern canals of fifteenth-century Amsterdam, **Kloveniersburgwal** is a long, dead-straight waterway framed by a string of old and dignified facades. It's altogether one of the most engaging parts of the city, especially at its southern end, where a small pocket of placid waterways and handsome antique canal houses spreads over to neighbouring **Groenburgwal**, a narrow and impossibly pretty waterway. The northern end of Kloveniersburgwal is marked by the cobbled **Nieuwmarkt**, a wide open, sometimes druggy square that is itself within easy walking distance of another pleasant district between two more canals – **Geldersekade** and **Oude Schans**.

Nieuwmarkt and Oude Schans

Nieuwmarkt was long one of the city's most important markets and the place where Gentiles and Jews from the nearby Jewish Quarter – just southeast along St Antoniebreestraat (see p.85) – traded. All that came to a traumatic end during World War II, when the Germans cordoned off the Nieuwmarkt with barbed wire and turned it into a holding pen. After the war, the square's old exuberance never returned and these days the market has all but vanished, though there is a small market for organic food on Saturdays (9am–5pm).

The focus of the square, the sprawling multi-turreted **Waag**, dating from the 1480s, has had a chequered history. Built as one of the city's fortified gates, Sint Antoniespoort, Amsterdam's expansion soon made it obsolete and the ground floor was turned into a municipal weighing-house (*waag*), with the rooms upstairs taken over by the surgeons' guild. It was here that the surgeons held lectures on anatomy and public dissections, the inspiration for Rembrandt's *Anatomy Lesson of Dr Tulp*, displayed in the Mauritshuis Collection in The Hague. Abandoned by the surgeons and the weigh-masters in the nineteenth century, the building served as a furniture store and fire station before falling into disuse, though it has recently been renovated to house a good café-bar and restaurant, *In de Waag* (see p.171).

Strolling along Recht Boomssloot from the northeast corner of Nieuwmarkt, it only takes a couple of minutes to reach the **Montelbaanstoren**, a sturdy tower dating from 1512 that overlooks the **Oude Schans**, a canal dug around the same time to improve the city's shipping facilities. The tower was built to protect the city's eastern flank but its decorative

Drugs in Amsterdam

Amsterdam's liberal policies on commercial sex (see p.49) are similarly extended to **soft drugs**, and the city has an international reputation as a haven for the dope-smoker, though, in fact, this confuses toleration with approval, decriminalization with legality. Many visitors are surprised to find that all drugs, hard and soft, are technically illegal in Amsterdam, the caveat being that since 1976 the possession of small amounts of cannabis (up to 30g/1oz) has been ignored by the police. This pragmatic approach has led to the rise of "smoking" **coffeeshops**, selling bags of dope much in the same way as bars sell glasses of beer.

From its inception, there have been problems with this policy. In part, this is because the Dutch have never legalized the cannabis supply chain – or more specifically that section of it within their national borders – and partly because the thirty-gram rule has proved difficult to enforce. Other complications have arisen because of the difference between Holland's policy and that of its European neighbours. Inevitably, the relative "laxity" of the Dutch has made the country in general and Amsterdam in particular attractive to soft (and arguably hard) **drug dealers**. The Dutch authorities have tried hard to keep organized crime out of the soft drug market, but drug dealing and drug tourism – of which there is an awful lot – irritate many Amsterdammers no end.

In recent years, the French and German governments have put pressure on the Dutch to bring their drug policy into line with the rest of Europe – one concession obliged coffeeshops to choose between selling dope or alcohol, and many chose the latter. Overall however, while the Dutch have found it prudent to keep a rigorous eye on the coffeeshops and emphasize their credentials in the fight against hard drugs, they have stuck to their liberal guns on cannabis. As justification, they cite the lack of evidence to link soft- and hard-drug use and indeed, the country's figures for hard-drug addiction are actually among the lowest in Europe.

Furthermore, by treating drugs as a medical rather than criminal problem, Amsterdam's authorities have been able to pioneer positive responses to **drugs issues**. The city council runs a wide range of rehabilitation programmes and recently decided to overhaul the methadone programme it introduced for heroin addicts in 1979. Here as elsewhere, methadone is now discredited as a means of weaning addicts off heroin and as a result the Dutch began issuing free heroin in tightly controlled quantities to users in 1998, a nationwide trial whose success is still being evaluated.

Nevertheless, for the casual visitor the main blot on the Amsterdam landscape is the groups of **hang-around junkies** who gather in and near the Red Light District, especially amongst the narrow streets and canals immediately to the east of the Oude Kerk (see p.47). The police estimate that there are around a thousand hard-drug users who, as they put it, "cause nuisance", and although the addicts are unlikely to molest strangers, they are a threatening presence. In fairness, however, the police have done their best to clean things up, dramatically improving the situation on the Zeedijk and Nieuwmarkt, which were once notorious for hard drugs, and at the canal bridge on Oude Hoogstraat, formerly nicknamed the "Pillenbrug" – "Pill Bridge".

You can read about the city government's regulations and attitude towards cannabis online at ⓦwww.amsterdam.nl.

spire was added later, when the city felt more secure, by Hendrik de Keyser (1565–1621), the architect who did much to create Amsterdam's prickly skyline.

At the top of Oude Schans, turn left along busy Prins Hendrikkade for the 300-metre amble to the **Scheepvaarthuis** (Shipping Building), an unusual edifice at no. 108 – on the corner of Binnenkant. Completed in 1917, this is one of the flashiest of the buildings designed by the Amsterdam School of architecture, the work of a certain Johann Melchior van der Mey (1878–1949). An almost neurotic edifice, covered with a welter of decoration celebrating the city's marine connections, the entrance is shaped like a prow and surmounted by statues of Poseidon and Amphitrite, his wife. Up above them are female representations of the four points of the compass, whilst slender turrets and Expressionistic carvings playfully decorate the walls.

From here, a five-minute walk takes you back to Nieuwmarkt and the Kloveniersburgwal via Binnenkant.

Along Kloveniersburgwal

Heading south along Kloveniersburgwal from Nieuwmarkt, it's a short hoof to the **Trippenhuis**, at no. 29, a huge overblown mansion complete with Corinthian pilasters and a grand frieze built for the Trip family in 1662. One of the richest families in Amsterdam, the Trips were a powerful force among the **Magnificat**, the clique of families (Six, Trip, Hooft and Pauw) who shared power during the Golden Age. One part of the Trip family dealt with the Baltic trade, another with the manufacture of munitions (in which they had the municipal monopoly), but in addition they also had trade interests in Russia and the Middle East, much like the multinationals of today. In the nineteenth century the Rijksmuseum collection was displayed here, but the house now contains the Dutch Academy of Sciences.

Almost directly opposite, on the west bank of the canal, the **Kleine Trippenhuis**, at no. 26, is, by contrast, one of the narrowest houses in Amsterdam, albeit with a warmly carved facade with a balustrade featuring centaurs and sphinxes. Legend asserts that Mr Trip's coachman was so taken aback by the size of the new family mansion that he exclaimed he would be happy with a home no wider than the Trips' front door – which is exactly what he got; his reaction to his new lodgings is not recorded.

A few metres away, on the corner of Oude Hoogstraat, is the former headquarters of the Dutch East India Company, the **Oostindisch Huis**, a monumental red-brick structure with high-pitched gables and perky dormer windows built in 1605 shortly after the founding of the company. It was from here that the Company organized and regulated its immensely lucrative trading interests in the Far East, importing shiploads of spices, perfumes and exotic woods. This trade underpinned Amsterdam's Golden Age, but predictably the people of what is now Indonesia, the source of most of the raw materials, received little in return. Nevertheless, despite the building's historic significance, the interior is of no interest today, being occupied by university classrooms and offices.

From the Oostindisch Huis, you can either proceed up Oude Hoogstraat to the Hash Museum (see p.55) or keep on Kloveniersburgwal, in which case you'll soon pass **Oudemanhuispoort**, a covered passageway now lined by secondhand bookstalls but formerly part of an almshouse complex for elderly men – hence the unusual name. The passage leads through to Oudezijds Achterburgwal, but stay on the Kloveniersburgwal to take a look at its southern reaches, which are flanked by a comely collection of old canal houses interrupted by the occasional nineteenth-century extravagance. In particular, cross the canal along **Staalstraat** and stop at the second of the two dinky little swing bridges for one of the finest views in the city, down the slender **Groenburgwal** with the Zuiderkerk (see p.85) looming beyond. Nearby also is the *Café de Jaren*, Nieuwe Doelenstraat 20, which offers some of the tastiest meals and snacks in the Old Centre – in bright and knowingly chic surroundings.

The Hash Museum and southern Oudezijds Achterburgwal

From the Oostindisch Huis (see p.54), it's a couple of minutes' walk west to the **Hash Marihuana Hemp Museum**, Oudezijds Achterburgwal 148 (daily 11am–10pm; €5.70), which is still going strong despite intermittent battles with the police. As well as featuring displays on the various types of dope and numerous ways to smoke it, the museum has a live indoor marijuana garden, samples of textiles and paper made with hemp, and pamphlets explaining the medicinal properties of cannabis. There's also a shop selling pipes, books, videos and plenty of souvenirs. Amsterdam's reliance on imported dope ended in the late 1980s when it was discovered that a reddish weed bred in America – "**skunk**" – was able to flourish under artificial lights, and nowadays over half the dope sold in the coffeeshops is grown in the Netherlands. For more information on drugs in Amsterdam see the box on p.53.

The triangular parcel of land at the southern end of **Oudezijds Achterburgwal** is packed with university buildings, mostly modern or nineteenth-century structures built in a vernacular Dutch style. Together they form a pleasant urban ensemble, but the red-shuttered, mullion-windowed early seventeenth-century **Huis op de Drie Grachten** (House on the Three Canals) stands out, sitting prettily on the corner of Oudezijds Achterburgwal and Oudezijds Voorburgwal. Nearby, through an ornate gateway at Oudezijds Voorburgwal 231, is the **Agnietenkapel** (St Agnes Chapel; Mon–Fri 9am–5pm; free, but there's a charge for some exhibitions), originally part of a Catholic convent, but now owned by the university. Upstairs the chapel has a good-looking, first-floor auditorium dating from the fifteenth century; it's used for temporary exhibitions mainly devoted to the university's history. Roughly opposite, just over the footbridge, the large brick and stone-trimmed building at Oudezijds Voorburgwal 302 has long been known as **ome Jan** ("Uncle John's") for its former function as central Amsterdam's pawn shop. The poet Vondel (see p.48) ended his days working here, and a short verse above the fancy stone entranceway, which comes complete with the city's coat of arms, extols the virtues of the pawn shop and the evils of usury.

From ome Jan, it's a couple of hundred metres to the southern end of Oudezijds Voorburgwal, where the **Galerie Mokum** art shop uses the old Jewish nickname for the city; the trams and traffic of Rokin are close by.

Rokin and Spui

Sandwiched between the Singel and the **Rokin**, the southern part of the Old Centre is one of Amsterdam's busiest districts, mostly on account of pedestrianized Kalverstraat, a hectic shopping street. Taken as a whole, it's not a particularly engaging area, but it does have its moments, most enjoyably in the cloistered tranquillity of the **Begijnhof**, at the floating **flower market** near Muntplein and amongst the bars and cafés of the **Spui**. Here also is a brace of moderately diverting museums – the **Amsterdams Historisch Museum** and the archeological **Allard Pierson Museum**.

Along the Rokin to Muntplein

The **Rokin** picks up where the Damrak leaves off, cutting south in a wide sweep that follows the former course of the River Amstel. The Rokin was the business centre of the nineteenth-century city and although it has lost much of its prestige, it is still flanked by an attractive medley of architectural styles incorporating everything from grandiose nineteenth-century mansions to more utilitarian modern stuff. One initial highlight as you stroll south is the handsome Art Nouveau-meets-Art Deco Marine Insurance building at **no. 69**; others are the much earlier canal house at **no. 83** and the attractive stone mansion at **no. 91**. Across the street, at **no. 92**, is the Hajenius cigar shop with its flashy gilt interior, while a prominent equestrian **statue** of Queen Wilhelmina marks the spot where the Rokin hits the canal system. Born in The Hague, **Wilhelmina** (1880–1962) came to the throne in 1890 and abdicated in favour of her daughter, Juliana, 58 years later – a mammoth royal stint by any standard. After her retirement, she wrote *Lonely but not Alone*, which explored her strong religious beliefs, but her popularity was based on her determined resistance to the Germans in World War II, when she was the figurehead of the government-in-exile in London.

Close by, overlooking the canal at Oude Turfmarkt 127, the **Allard Pierson Museum** (Tues–Fri 10am–5pm, Sat & Sun 1–5pm; €4.30) is a good old-fashioned archeological museum in a solid Neoclassical building dating from the 1860s. Spread over two floors – and labelled in English and Dutch – is a wide-ranging albeit fairly small collection of finds retrieved from the Middle East, especially Egypt, Greece and Italy. The particular highlight is the museum's **Greek pottery** with fine examples of both the black- and red-figured wares produced in the sixth and fifth centuries BC. Look out also for the Roman sarcophagi, especially a marble whopper decorated with Dionysian scenes and a very unusual wooden coffin from c.150 AD which is partly carved in the shape of the man held within.

Pushing on down past the museum, **nos. 141–147 Oude Turfmarkt** are classic seventeenth-century canal houses, graced by bottle- and spout-shaped gables. Just beyond, at the end of Rokin, is the **Muntplein**, a dishevelled square where the **Munttoren** of 1480 was originally part of the old city wall. Later, it was adopted as the municipal mint – hence its name – a plain brick structure to which Hendrik de Keyser, in one of his last commissions, added a flashy spire in 1620. A few metres away, the floating **Bloemenmarkt**, or flower market (daily 9am–5pm, though some stalls close on Sun), extends along the southern bank of the Singel. Popular with locals and tourists alike, the market is one of the main suppliers of flowers to central Amsterdam, but its blooms and bulbs now share stall space with souvenir clogs, garden gnomes and Delftware.

From Muntplein, seedy Reguliersbreestraat leads east to the bars and restaurants of Rembrandtplein (see p.74), while the flower market trails along the Singel as far as Koningsplein, at the start of Heiligeweg.

Spui and the Begijnhof

Workaday **Heiligeweg**, or "Holy Way", was once part of a much longer route used by pilgrims heading into Amsterdam. Every other religious reference disappeared centuries ago, but there is one interesting edifice here, the fanciful gateway of the old **Rasphuis** (House of Correction) that now fronts a shopping mall at the foot of Voetboogstraat. The gateway is surmounted by a sculpture of a woman punishing two criminals chained at her sides above the single

The beguinages

One corollary of the urbanization of the Low Countries from the twelfth century onwards was the establishment of **beguinages** (*begijnhoven* in Dutch, *béguinages* in French) in almost every city and town. These were semi-secluded communities, where widows and unmarried women – the **beguines** (*begijns*) – lived together, the better to do pious acts, especially caring for the sick. In **construction**, beguinages follow the same general plan with several streets of whitewashed, brick terraced cottages hidden away behind walls and gates and surrounding a central garden and chapel.

The **origins** of the beguine movement are somewhat obscure, but it would seem that the initial impetus came from a twelfth-century Liège priest, a certain Lambert le Bègue (the Stammerer). The main period of growth came later with the establishment of dozens of new beguinages, like the ones in Ghent and Bruges in Belgium and Breda and Amsterdam in the Netherlands. All were sponsored by the nobility and the later foundations – like the one here in Amsterdam – were established despite the opposition of the Papacy, which had declared against them as a potential source of heresy at the Council of Vienna in 1311.

Beguine communities were different from convents in so far as the inhabitants did not have to take vows and had the right to return to the secular world if they chose. At a time when hundreds of women were forcibly shut away in convents for all sorts of reasons (primarily financial), this element of choice made them an attractive proposition. In the Netherlands. the beguine movement was pretty much polished off by the Reformation – and the Calvinist assertion of the individual's need to have a direct relationship with God without the Church acting as intermediary; the convents closed down too. Almshouses, arguably the predecessors of state subsidized housing, did something to fill the gap.

word Castigatio (punishment). Beneath is a carving by Hendrik de Keyser showing wolves and lions cringing before the whip; the inscription reads "It is a virtue to subdue those before whom all go in dread."

Cut up Voetboogstraat and you soon reach the **Spui,** whose west end opens out into a wide, tram-clanking square flanked by bookshops and popular café-bars. In the middle is a cloying statue of a young boy, known as **'t Lieverdje** ("Little Darling" or "Loveable Scamp"), a gift to the city from a cigarette company in 1960. It was here in the mid-1960s, with the statue seen as a symbol of the addicted consumer, that the playful **Provos** (see p.247) organized some of their most successful *ludiek* (pranks).

A fancy little gateway on the north side of the Spui leads into the **Begijnhof** (daily 10am–5pm; free), where a huddle of immaculately maintained old houses looks onto a central green, their backs to the outside world; if this door is locked, try the main entrance, just a couple of hundred metres north of the Spui on Gedempte Begijnensloot. The Begijnhof was founded in the fourteenth century as a home for the *beguines* – members of a Catholic sisterhood living as nuns, but without vows and with the right of return to the secular world (see box). The original medieval complex comprised a series of humble brick cottages, but these were mostly replaced by the larger, grander houses of today shortly after the Reformation, though the secretive, enclosed design survived. However, a couple of pre-Reformation buildings do remain, including the **Houten Huys**, at no. 34, whose wooden facade dates from 1477, the oldest in Amsterdam and erected before the city forbade the construction of timber houses as an essential precaution against fire. The **Engelse Kerk** (English Reformed Church), which takes up one side of the Begijnhof, is of medieval construction too, but it was taken from the *beguines* and given to Amsterdam's

English community during the Reformation. Plain and unadorned, the church is of interest for its carefully worked pulpit panels, several of which were designed by a youthful **Piet Mondriaan** (1872–1944), the leading De Stijl artist. After they had lost their church, and in keeping with the terms of the Alteratie (see p.242), the *beguines* were allowed to celebrate Mass inconspicuously in the clandestine Catholic **kapel** (chapel; Mon 1–6pm, Tues–Sun 9am–6pm; free), which they established in the house opposite their old church. It's still used today, a homely little place with some terribly sentimental religious paintings, one of which – to the left of the high altar – depicts the miracle of the unburnable Host.

The Amsterdams Historisch Museum

Emerging from the east side of the Begijnhof, turn left onto narrow **Gedempte Begijnensloot** and it's 100m or so to the **Schuttersgalerij** – the Civic Guard Gallery. Here, an assortment of huge group portraits of the Amsterdam militia, ranging from serious-minded paintings of the 1540s through to lighter affairs from the seventeenth century, is displayed for free in a glassed-in passageway. They are interesting paintings, no doubt, and the pick are those by **Nicolaes Pickenoy** (1588–1650), but the finest militia painting by a long chalk – Rembrandt's *The Night Watch* – is exhibited in the Rijksmuseum (see p.102). The Schuttersgalerij is part of the **Amsterdams Historisch Museum** (Amsterdam Historical Museum; Mon–Fri 10am–5pm, Sat & Sun 11am–5pm; €6), which occupies the smartly restored but rambling seventeenth-century buildings of the municipal orphanage. The museum attempts to survey the city's development with a scattering of artefacts and lots of paintings from the thirteenth century onwards. It's a garbled collection, lacking continuity, but at least the labelling is in English and Dutch and there are several worthwhile highlights, beginning with the paintings illustrating the country's former maritime prowess in Room 5, titled "Rulers of the Seas". Room 10, "Social Care & Stern Discipline", examines the harsh paternalism of the city's merchant oligarchy, with paintings depicting the regents of several orphanages, self-contented bourgeoisie in the company of the grateful poor. Nearby, Room 11, "The Art of the Golden Age", is distinguished by three paintings of the surgeons' guild at work – look out for Rembrandt's wonderful *Anatomy Lesson of Dr Jan Deijman* – while the orphanage's own Regentenkamer (Regents' Room; Room C), dating from the seventeenth century, has survived in excellent condition.

The museum is footsteps from **Kalverstraat**, a pedestrianized shopping strip that runs north to Dam square. The street has been a commercial centre since medieval times, when it was used as a calf market. Also close by is **Spuistraat**, liberally sprinkled with bars and restaurants and the possessor of Amsterdam's last remaining **squat**, Vrankrijk (see p.248).

The Grachtengordel

Medieval Amsterdam was enclosed by the **Singel**, part of the city's protective moat, but this is now just the first of five canals that reach right around the city centre, extending anticlockwise from Brouwersgracht to the River Amstel in a "girdle of canals" or **Grachtengordel**. These were dug in the seventeenth century as part of a comprehensive plan to extend the boundaries of a city no longer able to accommodate its burgeoning population. The idea was that the council would buy up the land around the city, dig the canals, and lease plots back to developers. The plan was passed in 1607 and work began six years later, against a backdrop of corruption – Amsterdammers in the know buying up the land they thought the city would soon have to purchase.

Increasing the area of the city from two to seven square kilometres was a monumental task, and the conditions imposed by the council were strict. The three **main waterways** – Herengracht, Keizersgracht and Prinsengracht – were set aside for the residences and businesses of the richer and more influential Amsterdam merchants, while the **radial cross-streets** were reserved for more modest artisans' homes; meanwhile, immigrants, newly arrived to cash in on Amsterdam's booming economy, were assigned, albeit informally, the Jodenhoek (see Chapter Four) and the Jordaan (see Chapter Three). In the Grachtengordel, everyone, even the wealthiest merchant, had to comply with a set of strict and detailed **planning regulations**. In particular, the council prescribed the size of each building plot – the frontage was set at thirty feet, the depth two hundred – and although there was a degree of tinkering, the end result was the loose conformity you can see today: tall, narrow residences, whose individualism is mainly restricted to the stylistic permutations amongst the gables. Even the colour of the front doors was once regulated, with choice restricted to a shade that has since become known as "Amsterdam Green" – still difficult to find outside Holland. It took decades to complete the project, but by the 1690s it was all pretty much finished off – at a time, ironically, when Amsterdam was in economic decline. In essence, therefore,

This chapter covers the full sweep of the Grachtengordel, from Brouwersgracht to the Amstel, but for ease of reference we've considered it as two areas – **Grachtengordel west** and **Grachtengordel south** – divided at roughly the halfway point, Leidsegracht. The Accommodation (see Chapter Eight) and Eating and Drinking (see Chapter Nine) chapters later in the book follow this division too. There's no obvious **walking route** around the Grachtengordel, indeed you may prefer to wander around as the mood takes you, but the description we've given below goes from north to south, taking in all the highlights on the way. On all three of the main canals, **street numbers** begin at Brouwersgracht and increase as you go south.

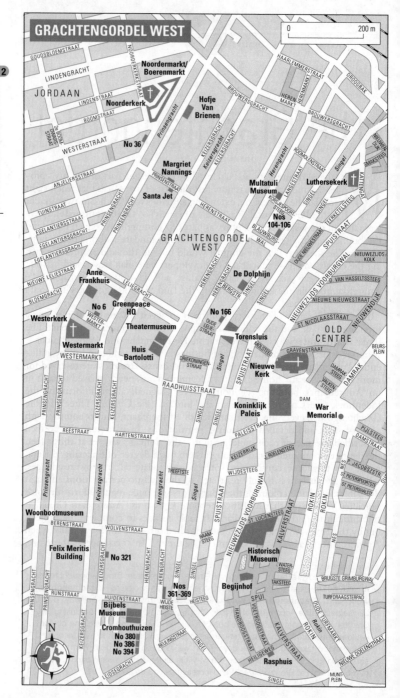

the Grachtengordel is a tribute to the architectural tastes of the city's middle class, an amalgam of personal wealth and aesthetic uniformity – individuality and order – that epitomized Amsterdam's Protestant bourgeoisie in its pomp.

The Grachtengordel is without doubt the most charming part of Amsterdam, its lattice of olive-green waterways and dinky humpback bridges overlooked by street upon street of handsome seventeenth-century canal houses, almost invariably undisturbed by later development. Of the three main canals, **Herengracht** (Gentlemen's Canal) was the first to be dug, followed by the **Keizersgracht**, the Emperor's Canal, named after the Holy Roman Emperor and fifteenth-century patron of the city, Maximilian. Further out still lies the **Prinsengracht**, the Princes' Canal, named in honour of the princes of the House of Orange. It's a subtle cityscape – full of surprises, with a bizarre carving here, an unusual facade stone (used to denote name and occupation) there – and one where the **gables** overlooking the canals gradually evolved. The earliest, dating from the early seventeenth-century, are **crow-stepped gables** but these were largely superseded from the 1650s onwards by **neck gables** and **bell gables**. Some are embellished, many have decorative cornices, and the fanciest, which almost invariably date from the eighteenth century, sport full-scale balustrades. The plainest gables are those of former **warehouses**, where the deep-arched and shuttered windows line up to either side of loft doors, which were once used for loading and unloading goods, winched by pulley from the street down below. Indeed, outside **pulleys** remain a common feature of houses and warehouses alike, and are often still in use as the easiest way of moving furniture into the city's myriad apartments.

The grandest Grachtengordel houses are concentrated along the so-called **De Gouden Bocht** – the Golden Bend – on Herengracht between Leidsestraat and the Amstel. Here, the architectural decorum and arguably the aesthetic vigour of the seventeenth century are left behind for the overblown, French-influenced mansions that became popular with the city's richest merchants in the 1700s. These merchants remodelled the earlier buildings, adding classical features, from tympani and pilasters (though these had been in vogue as early as the 1620s) through to decorative chimney stacks, ornate carvings, balconies and balustrades. Nevertheless, architectural peccadilloes aside, it is perhaps the district's overall atmosphere that appeals rather than any specific sight, with one remarkable exception: the **Anne Frankhuis**, where the young – and now internationally famous – Jewish diarist hid from the Germans in World War II.

Grachtengordel west

Stretching south from the Brouwersgracht to the Leidsegracht, **Grachtengordel west** contains a fine selection of seventeenth-century canal houses. These are at their prettiest along **Herengracht** between Huidenstraat and Leidsegracht, and this is where you'll also find the **Bijbels Museum** (Biblical Museum), home to an odd assortment of models of ancient Jewish temples. However, easily the most popular attraction hereabouts is the **Anne Frankhuis**, on Prinsengracht, which is itself close to the soaring architecture of the **Westerkerk** and the mildly enjoyable **Theatermuseum**.

Brouwersgracht

Running east to west along the northern edge of the three main canals is leafy **Brouwersgracht**, one of the most picturesque waterways in the city. In the seventeenth century, Brouwersgracht lay at the edge of Amsterdam's great harbour. This was where many of the ships returning from the East unloaded their silks and spices, and as one of the major arteries linking the open sea with the city centre, it was lined with storage depots and warehouses. Breweries flourished here too, capitalizing on their ready access to shipments of fresh water. Today the harbour bustle has moved elsewhere, and the **warehouses** have been converted into apartments, their functional architecture dominating the scene. Look down any of the major canals from here and you'll see the gentle interplay of water, brick and stone that gives the city its distinctive draw. Indeed, picking any of the three main canals to head down means missing the other two, unless you're prepared to weave a circuitous route.

South to Leliegracht

Strolling south along **Prinsengracht** from Brouwersgracht, it only takes a minute or two to reach the **Hofje Van Brienen** (daily 6am–6pm & Sat 6am–2pm; free), a brisk, brown-brick courtyard complex at Prinsengracht 85–133. Originally the site of a brewery, the *hofje* was built as an almshouse in 1804 to the order of a certain Aernout van Brienen. A well-to-do merchant, Brienen had locked himself in his own strong room by accident and, in a panic, he vowed to build a *hofje* if he was rescued – he was and he did. The plaque inside the complex doesn't, however, give much of the game away, inscribed demurely with "for the relief and shelter of those in need." Opposite, across the canal, is the **Noorderkerk** (see p.80), a lugubrious pile on the edge of the Jordaan that oversees the **Noordermarkt**, the site of several markets, including a flea market (Mon 9am–1pm & Sat 8am–3pm) and a farmers' produce market (Sat 9am–3pm). Just along the canal from the Noordermarkt, **Prinsengracht 36** has an especially well-proportioned facade, its neck gable, pilasters and pediment dating from the 1650s.

From the Hofje Van Brienen, it's the briefest of walks to the first of the Grachtengordel's cross-streets, **Prinsenstraat/Herenstraat**, where the modest old tradesmen's houses now accommodate flower shops and cafés, greengroceries and more especially clothes shops. It's here you'll find hand-made Latin American items at *Santa Jet*, Prinsenstraat 7 and designer women's clothes at *Margriet Nannings*, Prinsenstraat 8, 15 & 24.

The Multatuli Museum

From Herenstraat, it's a quick gambol to Amsterdam's tiniest museum, the **Multatuli Museum**, just off the Herengracht at Korsjespoortsteeg 20 (Tues 10am–5pm, Sat & Sun noon–5pm; free). This was the birthplace of **Eduard Douwes Dekker**, Holland's most celebrated nineteenth-century writer and a champion of free thinking, who wrote under the pen name Multatuli. Disgusted with the behaviour of his fellow Dutch in their colonies in the East Indies, he returned home to enrage the establishment with his elegantly written satirical novel *Max Havelaar*, now something of a Dutch literary classic. The museum's one room is filled with letters, first editions and a small selection of his furnishings, including the **chaise longue** on which he breathed his last. There's no information in English, but the attendant can tell you everything you might need to know.

The Singel – from Blauwburgwal to Leliegracht

Slipping through to the Singel, turn right along the canal to reach **nos. 104–106**, twin mansions dating to the 1740s and equipped with the largest bell gables in the city – big but not especially pretty. Pushing on, it's a few metres more to the red-brick and stone-trimmed **De Dolphijn** (The Dolphin), at nos. 140–142. This was once home of Captain Banningh Cocq, one of the militiamen depicted in Rembrandt's *The Night Watch* (see p.102), but it takes its name from a late-sixteenth-century Dutch grammar book written by the first owner, one Hendrick Spieghel. Nearby, Singel **no. 166** has the narrowest facade in the city – just 1.8m wide – and it overlooks the **Torensluis**, easily the widest bridge in the Grachtengordel and decorated with a whopping bust of Multatuli (see p.62).

Cut back along Oude Leliestraat and you soon reach **Leliegracht**, one of the tiny radial canals that cut across the Grachtengordel. It's a charming street, an attractive home to a number of bookshops and bars, and it also holds one of the city's finest Art Nouveau buildings, a tall and striking building at the Leliegracht-Keizersgracht junction designed by Gerrit van Arkel in 1905. Originally the headquarters of a life insurance company – hence the two mosaics with angels recommending policies to bemused earthlings – it's now occupied by Greenpeace.

The Anne Frankhuis

In 1957 the Anne Frank Foundation set up the **Anne Frankhuis** (daily: April–Aug 9am–9pm; Sept–March 9am–7pm; closed Yom Kippur; €6.50, 10- to 17-year-olds €3, under-10s free; ⓦ www.annefrank.nl) in the house at Prinsengracht 263 where the young diarist and her family hid from the Germans during World War II. Since the posthumous publication of her diaries, Anne Frank has become extraordinarily famous, in the first instance for recording the iniquities of the Holocaust, and latterly as a symbol of the fight against oppression and, in particular, racism. The house is now one of the most popular tourist attractions in town, but it has managed to preserve a sense of intimacy – and the personal nature of the Franks' sufferings.

The **rooms** the Franks occupied for two years have been left much the same as they were during the war – even down to the movie star pin-ups in Anne's bedroom and the marks on the wall recording the children's heights. Remarkably, despite the number of visitors, there is a real sense of the personal here and only the coldest of hearts could fail to be moved. Apposite video clips on the family in particular and the Holocaust in general give the background. Anne Frank was only one of about 100,000 Dutch Jews who died during World War II, but this, her final home, provides one of the most enduring testaments to its horrors. Her diary has been a source of inspiration to many, including Nelson Mandela.

Westerkerk

Trapped in the achterhuis, Anne Frank liked to listen to the bells of the **Westerkerk** (April–Sept Mon–Sat 10am–4pm; free), just along Prinsengracht, until they were taken away to be melted down for the German war effort. The church still dominates the district, its 85-metre tower (June–Sept Wed–Sat 2–4pm; €3) – without question Amsterdam's finest – soaring graciously above

The story of Anne Frank

The story of **Anne**, her family and friends, is well known. Anne's father, **Otto Frank**, was a well-to-do Jewish businessman who ran a successful spice-trading business and lived in the southern part of the city. He and his family had moved to Amsterdam from Germany to escape Hitler's clutches in December 1933. After the German occupation of the Netherlands, Otto felt – along with many other Jews – that he could avoid trouble by keeping his head down. However, by 1942 it was clear that this would not be possible: Amsterdam's Jews were isolated and conspicuous, being confined to certain parts of the city and forced to wear a yellow star – and roundups were becoming increasingly common too. In desperation, Otto Frank decided – on the advice of two Dutch friends, Mr Koophuis and Mr Kraler – to move the family into the unused back of their warehouse on the Prinsengracht. The Franks went into hiding in July 1942, along with a Jewish business partner and his family, the Van Pels (renamed the Van Daans in the *Diary*). They were separated from the eyes of the outside world by a **bookcase** that doubled as a door. As far as everyone else was concerned, they had fled to Switzerland.

So began the two-year occupation of the **achterhuis**, or back annexe. The two families were joined in November 1942 by a dentist friend, Fritz Pfeffer (the Diary's Albert Dussel). Koophuis and Kraler, who continued working in the front part of the warehouse, regularly brought supplies and news of the outside world. In her diary Anne Frank describes the day-to-day lives of the inhabitants of the annexe: the quarrels, frequent in such a claustrophobic environment; celebrations of birthdays, or of a piece of good news from the Allied Front; and of her own, slightly unreal, growing up (much of which, it's been claimed, was deleted by her father).

Two years later, the atmosphere was optimistic: the Allies were clearly winning the war and liberation seemed within reach. It wasn't to be. One day in the summer of 1944 the Franks were **betrayed** by a Dutch collaborator and the Gestapo arrived and forced Mr Kraler to open up the bookcase. Thereafter, the occupants of the annexe were all arrested and dispatched to Westerbork – the transit camp in the north of the country where all Dutch Jews were processed before being moved to Belsen or Auschwitz. Of the eight from the annexe, only Otto Frank survived; Anne and her sister died of typhus within a short time of each other in Belsen, just one week before the German surrender.

Anne Frank's **diary** was among the few things left behind in the annexe. It was retrieved by one of the people who had helped the Franks and handed to Anne's father on his return from Auschwitz; he later decided to publish it. Since its appearance in 1947, it has been constantly in print, translated into over sixty languages, and has sold millions of copies.

---

its surroundings. On its top perches the crown of Emperor Maximilian, a constantly recurring symbol of Amsterdam (see p.43) and the finishing touch to what was only the second city church to be built expressly for the Protestants. The church was designed by **Hendrick de Keyser** (see box on p.65), and completed in 1631 as part of the general enlargement of the city, but whereas the exterior is all studied elegance, the interior – as required by the Calvinist congregation – is bare and plain.

The church is also the reputed resting place of **Rembrandt**, though the location of his pauper's tomb is not known. Instead, a small memorial in the north aisle commemorates the artist, close to the spot where his son Titus was buried. Rembrandt adored his son – as evidenced by numerous portraits – and the boy's death dealt a final crushing blow to the ageing and embittered artist, who died just over a year later. During renovation of the church in the early 1990s, bones were unearthed that could have been those of Rembrandt – a possibility whose tourist potential excited the church authorities. The obvious way to prove it was through a chemical analysis of the bones' lead content, expected to be unusually high if they were his, as lead was a major ingredient of paint. The bones were duly taken to the University of Groningen for analysis, but the tests proved inconclusive.

Westermarkt

Westermarkt, an open square in the shadow of the Westerkerk, possesses two evocative statues. At the back of the church, beside Keizersgracht, are the three pink granite triangles (one each for the past, present and future) of the **Homo-Monument**. The world's first memorial to persecuted gays and lesbians, commemorating all those who died at the hands of the Nazis, it was designed by Karin Daan and recalls the pink triangles the Germans made homosexuals sew onto their clothes during World War II. The monument has become a focus for the city's gay community and the site of ceremonies and wreath-laying throughout the year, most notably on Queen's Day (April 30), Coming-Out Day (Sept 5) and World AIDS Day (Dec 1). The monument's inscription, by the Dutch writer Jacob Israel de Haan, translates as "Such an infinite desire for friendship". Nearby, on the south side of the church by Prinsengracht, is a small but beautifully crafted **statue of Anne Frank** by the gifted Dutch sculptor Mari Andriessen (1897–1979), who is also the creator of the dockworker statue outside Amsterdam's Portuguese Synagogue (see p.90).

Incidentally, the French philosopher **René Descartes** once lodged at **Westermarkt 6**, a good-looking house with an attractive neck gable and fancy fanlight. Happy that the Dutch were indifferent to his musings, he wrote "Everybody except me is in business and so absorbed by profit-making I could spend my entire life here without being noticed by a soul."

The Theatermuseum and Huis Bartolotti

A few metres from the Westermarkt at Herengracht 168, the **Theatermuseum** (Theatre Museum; Tues–Fri 11am–5pm, Sat & Sun 1–5pm; €3.85) holds a moderately enjoyable collection of theatrical bygones, from props through to stage sets, with a particularly good selection of costumes and posters. The museum, which spreads over into the adjoining buildings, also offers a lively programme of temporary exhibitions and occupies splendid premises. Dating from 1638, **no. 168** has a fetching sandstone facade to a design by **Philip Vingboons** (1607–1678), arguably the most talented architect involved in the creation of the Grachtengordel (see also p.68). The house

---

Hendrick de Keyser

Born in Utrecht, the son of a carpenter, **Hendrick de Keyser** (1565–1621) moved to Amsterdam in 1591. Initially employed as an apprentice sculptor, de Keyser soon ventured out on his own, speedily establishing himself as one of the city's most sought-after sculptor/architects. In 1595 he was appointed the city's official stone mason, becoming city architect too in 1612. His municipal commissions included three churches – the Zuiderkerk (see p.85), the Noorderkerk (see p.80) and the Westerkerk (see p.63) – and the upper storeys of the Munttoren (see p.56). His domestic designs were, however, more playful – or at least ornate – and it was here that he pioneered what is often called **Amsterdam Renaissance style**, in which Italianate decorative details – tympani, octagonal turrets, pilasters, pinnacles and arcading – were imposed on traditional Dutch design. The usual media were red brick and sandstone trimmings – as in the Huis Bartolotti (see p.67).

△ Herengracht

was built for Michael de Pauw, a leading light in the East India Company, and the interior sports an extravagant painted ceiling of the Four Seasons by Jacob de Wit (1696–1754) plus a splendid spiral staircase. Next door, **Huis Bartolotti**, at nos. 170–172, is a tad earlier and a good deal flashier, its pirou-etting facade of red-brick and stone dotted with urns and columns, faces and shells. The house is an excellent illustration of the Dutch Renaissance style, and as such is much more ornate than the typical Amsterdam canal house. The architect was **Hendrick de Keyser** (see box on p.65) and a director of the West India Company, one Willem van den Heuvel, footed the bill. Heuvel inherited a fortune from his Italian uncle and changed his name in his honour to Bartolotti – hence the name of the house.

South to the Woonbootmuseum and the Felix Meritis building

Between Westermarkt and Leidsegracht, the main canals are intercepted by a trio of **cross-streets**, which are themselves divided into shorter streets, mostly named after animals whose pelts were once used in the local tanning industry. There's Reestraat (Deer Street), Hartenstraat (Hart), Berenstraat (Bear) and Wolvenstraat (Wolf), not to mention Huidenstraat (Street of Hides) and Runstraat – a "run" being a bark used in tanning. The tanners are long gone and today the three are eminently appealing **shopping streets**, where you can buy everything from car-pets to handmade chocolates, toothbrushes to beeswax candles.

As for the main canals, the **Woonbootmuseum** (March–Oct Wed–Sun 11am–5pm; Nov–Feb Fri–Sun 11am–5pm; €2.50), opposite Prinsengracht 296, is a Dutch houseboat that doubles as a tourist attraction with a handful of explanatory plaques about life on the water. Some 3000 barges and house-boats are connected to the city's gas and electricity networks. They are regularly inspected and there are strict controls to ensure their numbers don't proliferate. From here, it's one block east along Berenstraat to the **Felix Meritis building**, at Keizersgracht 324. A Neoclassical monolith of 1787, the mansion was built to house the artistic and scientific activities of the epony-mous society, which was the cultural focus of the city's upper crust for near-ly one hundred years. Dutch cultural aspirations did not, however, impress everyone. It's said that when Napoleon visited the city the entire building was redecorated for his reception, only to have him stalk out in disgust, claiming that the place stank of tobacco. Oddly enough, it later became the headquar-ters of the Dutch Communist Party, but they sold it to the council who now lease it to the Felix Meritis Foundation for experimental and avant-garde arts.

Keizersgracht 321 and Hans Van Meegeren

On the other side of the canal, **Keizersgracht 321** is in itself fairly innocuous, but this was once the home of the Dutch art forger **Hans Van Meegeren** (1889–1947). During the German occupation of World War II, Meegeren befriended a German art dealer and sold him – as the agent for Goering – a previously unknown Vermeer. What neither of the Germans realized was that Meegeren had painted it himself. A forger par excellence, Meegeren had devel-oped a sophisticated ageing technique in the early 1930s. He mixed his paints with phenol formaldehyde resin dissolved in benzene and then baked the fin-ished painting in an oven for several hours; the end result fooled everyone, including the curators of the Rijksmuseum, who had bought another "Vermeer" from him in 1941. Indeed, the forgeries may well have never been discovered but for a strange sequence of events. In May 1945 a British captain by the name of Harry Anderson discovered Meegeren's Vermeer in Goering's art collection. Meegeren was promptly arrested as a collaborator and, to get himself out of a pickle, Meegeren soon confessed to this and other forgeries. His reward was a short prison sentence, but he died before he was incarcerated.

Herengracht 361–369 and the Cromhouthuizen

Moving on, double back to cut across Wolvenstraat and turn right for **Herengracht 361–369**, a row of five houses, where you can compare and contrast the main types of **gable**: stepped at no. 361, bell at nos. 365 and 367 and finally neck at no. 369. Across the canal, at Herengracht 364–370, the graceful and commanding **Cromhouthuizen** consist of four matching stone mansions, frilled with tendrils, carved fruit and scrollwork, graced by dinky little bull's-eye windows and capped by elegant neck gables. Built in the 1660s for one of Amsterdam's wealthy merchant families, the Cromhouts, the houses were designed by **Philip Vingboons** (1607–1678), arguably the most inventive of the architects who worked on the Grachtengordel during the city's expansion. As a Catholic, Vingboons was confined to private commissions, inconvenient no doubt, but at a time when Protestants and Catholics were at each other's throats right across Europe, hardly insufferable. Two of the houses have been adapted to hold the Bijbels Museum.

The Bijbels Museum

Despite the grandeur of the facade, the interior of the **Bijbels Museum** (Mon–Sat 10am–5pm, Sun 1–5pm; €5; ⓦ www.bijbelsmuseum.nl) is comparatively plain, though it does boast a handsome spiral staircase and two painted ceilings of classical gods and goddesses by Jacob de Wit. The third floor – where you start a visit – features a model Tabernacle made by a Protestant vicar, one **Leendert Schouten** (1828–1905). Attempts to reconstruct Biblical scenes were something of a cottage industry in the Netherlands in the late nineteenth century, with scores of Dutch antiquarians beavering away, bible in one hand and modelling equipment in the other. Yet Schouten went one step further and made it his lifetime's work – and a popular attraction it was too, with the model attracting scores of visitors to his home. Floor 2 warms to the same theme, with models of the temples of Solomon and Herod, as well as a selection of **bibles**, including the first Dutch-language bible ever printed, dating from 1477, drawn from the museum's collection of over one thousand. A scattering of archeological finds from Palestine and Egypt rounds things off, with more models down below on Floor 1.

Herengracht 380–394 and Leidsegracht

The gracious symmetries of the Cromhouthuizen contrast with the grandiose pretensions of **Herengracht 380**, built in the style of a French château for a tobacco planter in 1889. Ornately dressed, the mansion's main gable is embellished with reclining figures and the bay window by cherubs, mythical characters and an abundance of acanthus leaves; it was the first house in the city to be supplied with electricity. Roughly opposite, across the canal, is the only spot in Amsterdam where the houses come straight out of the water, Venice-like, without the intervention of a pavement.

Close by, **Herengracht 386** is another handsome Philip Vingboons building, whilst **Herengracht 394**, the narrow house with the bell gable at the corner of Leidsegracht, bears a distinctive **facade stone** that refers to the legend of the four Aymon brothers, who are depicted astride their steed. The subject of a popular medieval *chanson*, the legend is all about honour, loyalty and friendship, dynastic quarrels and disputes. Picaresque in form, it doesn't really make much sense, but it revolves around the trials and tribulations of the horse. The clearest part of the tale is the end, where the redoubtable beast repeatedly breaks free from the millstones tied around its neck and refuses to drown. The third time it comes to the surface, the brothers walks away, no longer able to watch the agonies of their animal; assuming he's been abandoned, the horse cries out and promptly drowns.

Herengracht 394 abuts the **Leidsegracht**, a mostly residential canal, lined with chic town houses and a medley of handsome gables. It's a tranquil scene – or at least it would be were it not for the flat-topped tour boats, who use the canal as a short cut, billowing out diesel fumes as they shunt into Prinsengracht. At the west end of Leidsegracht, turn left and keep an eye out for **Prinsengracht 681–693**, where an exquisite set of seven neck gables, one each for the provinces that broke away from the Habsburgs, is one of the most harmonious ensembles in the whole of the Grachtengordel; they were constructed in 1715. From here, it's the briefest of walks to Leidsestraat and Leidseplein (see below).

Grachtengordel south

The southern reaches of the Grachtengordel, **Grachtengordel south**, contain many of the city's proudest and most touted mansions, clustered along **De Gouden Bocht** – the Golden Bend – the curve of Herengracht between Leidsestraat and the River Amstel. It's on this stretch that the merchant elite abandoned the material modesty of their Calvinist forebears, indulging themselves with lavish mansions, whose fancy facades more than hinted at the wealth within. In the late seventeenth and eighteenth centuries, this elite forsook brick for stone and the restrained details of traditional Dutch architecture for an overblown Neoclassicism, their defeat of the Spanish Habsburgs, allied with their commercial success, prompting them to compare themselves with the Greeks and Romans. In the event, it was all an illusion – the bubble burst when Napoleon's army arrived in 1793 – and, although the opulent interiors of two old mansions, the **Museum Willet-Holthuysen** and the **Van Loon Museum**, still give the flavour of those heady days, for the most part all that's left – albeit a substantial legacy – are the wonderful facades.

Grachtengordel south also contains some rather less savoury areas, where ill-considered twentieth-century development has blemished the city – from the seediness of the **Rembrandtplein** to the mediocrity of Vijzelstraat and **Leidseplein**.

Leidseplein

Lying on the edge of the Grachtengordel, **Leidseplein** is the bustling hub of Amsterdam's nightlife, a rather cluttered and disorderly open space that has never had much character. The square once marked the end of the road in from

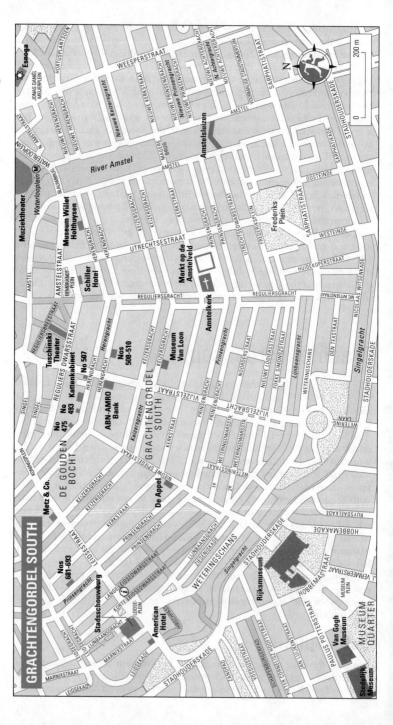

Leiden and, as horse-drawn traffic was banned from the centre long ago, it was here that the Dutch left their horses and carts – a sort of equine car park. Today, it's quite the opposite: continual traffic made up of trams, bikes, cars and pedestrians gives the place a frenetic feel, and the surrounding side streets are jammed with bars, restaurants and clubs in a bright jumble of jutting signs and neon lights. It's not surprising, therefore, that on a good night Leidseplein can be Amsterdam at its carefree, exuberant best.

Leidseplein also contains two buildings of some architectural note. The first is the grandiose **Stadsschouwburg**, a neo-Renaissance edifice dating from 1894 which was so widely criticized for its clumsy vulgarity that the city council of the day temporarily withheld the money for decorating the exterior. Home to the National Ballet and Opera until the Muziektheater (see p.89) was completed on Waterlooplein in 1986, it is now used for theatre, dance and music performances. However, its most popular function is as the place where the Ajax football team (see p.224) gather on the balcony to wave to the crowds whenever they win anything – as they often do.

Close by, just off the square at Leidsekade 97, is the four-star **American Hotel**. One of the city's oddest buildings, it's a monumental and slightly disconcerting rendering of Art Nouveau, with angular turrets, chunky dormer windows and fancy brickwork. Completed in 1902, the present structure takes its name from its demolished predecessor, which was – as the stylistic peccadillo of its architect, one W. Steinigeweg – decorated with statues and murals of North American scenes. Inside the present hotel is the *Café Americain*, once the fashionable haunt of Amsterdam's literati, but now a mainstream location for coffee and lunch. The Art Nouveau decor is well worth a peek – an artful combination of stained glass, shallow arches and geometric patterned brickwork.

Leidsestraat and the Spiegelkwartier

Heading northeast from Leidseplein is **Leidsestraat**, one of Amsterdam's principal shopping streets – a long, slender gauntlet of fashion and shoe shops of little distinction. That said, **Metz & Co**, the department store at the junction with Keizersgracht, does occupy a good-looking stone building of 1891, complete with caryatids and fancy corner dome. At the time of its construction, it was the tallest commercial building in the city – one reason why the owners were able to entice **Gerrit Rietveld** (1888–1964), the leading architectural light of De Stijl, to add a rooftop glass and metal showroom in 1933. The showroom has survived and is now a café offering an attractive view over the city centre; perhaps surprisingly, Rietveld designed just one other building in Amsterdam – the Van Gogh Museum (see p.103).

Two blocks east of Leidseplein is Nieuwe Spiegelstraat, an appealing mixture of bookshops and corner cafés that extends south into Spiegelgracht to form the **Spiegelkwartier**. The district is home to the pricey end of Amsterdam's antiques trade and **De Appel**, a lively centre for contemporary art at Nieuwe Spiegelstraat 10 (Tues–Sun noon–5pm; €2).

The Gouden Bocht

Nieuwe Spiegelstraat meets the elegant sweep of **Herengracht** near the west end of the so-called **De Gouden Bocht** (Golden Bend), where the canal is overlooked by a long sequence of double-fronted mansions, some of the most opulent dwellings in the city. Most of the houses here were extensively remodelled in the late seventeenth and eighteenth centuries. Characteristically, they have double stairways leading to the entrance, underneath which the small door was for the servants, whilst up above the majority are topped off by the ornamental cornices that were fashionable at the time. Classical references are common, both in form – pediments, columns and pilasters – and decoration, from scrolls and vases through to geometric patterns inspired by ancient Greece.

One of the first buildings to look out for on the north side of the canal – just across from (and to the west of) Nieuwe Spiegelstraat – is **Herengracht 475**, an extravagant, if now somewhat gloomy stone mansion decorated with allegorical figures and surmounted by a slender balustrade. Typically, the original building was a much more modest affair, dating to the 1660s, but eighty years later the new owner took matters in hand to create the ornate facade of today. Just along the canal, **no. 493** is similarly grand, though here the building is polished off with an extravagantly carved pediment. Close by, **no. 497** is, by comparison, rather restrained, but the interior has been turned into the peculiar **Kattenkabinet** (Cats' Cabinet; Mon–Fri 9am–2pm, Sat & Sun 1–5pm; €4.50; ⓦ www.kattenkabinet.nl), an enormous collection of art and artefacts relating to cats. They were installed by a Dutch financier, whose own cherished moggy, John Pierpont Morgan, died in 1984; feline fanatics will be delighted. A hop, skip and a jump away, **Herengracht 507** is an especially handsome house, not too grand, its Neoclassical pilasters, pediment, mini-balcony and double-stairway nicely balanced by its slender windows. It was once the home of Jacob Boreel, the one-time major whose attempt to impose a burial tax prompted a riot during which the mob ransacked his house. Opposite, at the corner of Vijzelstraat, is the monumentally inappropriate **Nederlandsche Handelsmaatschappij** building of 1923, a heavyweight structure with Expressionistic flourishes that is now owned by the ABN-AMRO Bank.

On the far side of Vijzelstraat, the facades of **Herengracht 508–510** are well worth a second look too, their neck gables, dating from the 1690s, sporting sea gods straddling dolphins and tritons – half-men, half-fish – trumpeting conch shells to pacify the oceans.

The Museum Willet-Holthuysen

The **Museum Willet-Holthuysen** (Mon–Fri 10am–5pm, Sat & Sun 11am–5pm; €4), beyond Thorbeckeplein (see p.74) and near the Amstel at Herengracht 605, is billed as "a peep behind the curtains into an historic Amsterdam canal house", which just about sums it up. The house itself dates from 1685, but the interior was remodelled by successive members of the coal-trading Holthuysen family until the last of the line, Sandra Willet-Holthuysen, gifted her home and its contents to the city in 1895. Renovated a number of years ago, most of the public rooms, notably the **Blue Room** and the **Dining Room**, have now been returned to their original eighteenth-century Rococo appearance – a flashy and ornate style copied from France, which the Dutch merchants held to be the epitome of refinement and good taste. The chandeliers are mostly gilded, heavy affairs, the plasterwork neat and fancy, and graceful drapes hang to either side of long and slender windows. At the back of the house are the formal **gardens**, a neat pattern of miniature hedges graced by the occasional stone statue. The museum's collection of fine and applied arts belonged to Sandra's husband, Abraham Willet; its forte is glass, silver, majolica and ceramics, including a charming selection of Chinese porcelain exhibited in the Blue Room.

The Amstel and the Magere Brug

Just beyond Willet-Holthuysen, Herengracht comes to an abrupt halt beside the wide and windy **River Amstel**, which was long the main route into the interior, with goods arriving by barge and boat to be traded for the imported materials held in Amsterdam's many warehouses. Turning left here takes you to the Blauwbrug (Blue Bridge) and the Old Jewish Quarter (see p.85), whilst in the opposite direction is the **Magere Brug** (Skinny Bridge), the most famous and arguably the cutest of the city's many swing bridges. Legend has it that the current bridge, which dates back to about 1670, replaced an even older and skinnier version, originally built by two sisters who lived on either side of the river and were fed up with having to walk so far to see each other. From this bridge, it's a few metres further south along the Amstel to the **Amstel sluizen**, the Amstel locks. Every night, the municipal water department closes these locks to begin the process of sluicing out the canals. A huge pumping station on an island out to the east of the city then starts to pump fresh water from the IJsselmeer into the canal system; similar locks on the west side of the city are left open for the surplus to flow into the IJ and, from there, out to sea via the North Sea Canal. The watery content of the canals is thus refreshed every three nights – though, what with three centuries of algae, prams, shopping trolleys and a few hundred rusty bikes, the water is only appealing as long as you're not in it.

To Reguliersgracht and the Museum Van Loon

Doubling back from the Amstel sluizen, turn left along the north side of Prinsengracht and you soon reach the small open space of the **Amstelveld**, an oasis of calm that rarely sees visitors, with the plain seventeenth-century white wooden **Amstelkerk** occupying one of its corners. It's here also that Prinsengracht intersects with **Reguliersgracht**, probably the prettiest of the three surviving radial canals that cut across the Grachtengordel – its dainty humpback bridges and greening waters overlooked by charming seventeenth- and eighteenth-century canal houses.

Proceeding north along Reguliersgracht, turn left along Keizersgracht for the **Museum Van Loon**, at no. 672 (Fri–Mon 11am–5pm; €4.50), which possesses the finest accessible canal house interior in Amsterdam. Built in 1672, the first tenant of the property was the artist Ferdinand Bol, who seems to have been one of the few occupants to have avoided some sort of scandal. The Van Loons, who bought the house in 1884 and stayed until 1945, are a case in point. The last member of the family to live here was Willem van Loon, a banker whose wife, Thora van Loon-Egidius, was *dame du palais* to Queen Wilhelmina. Of German extraction, Thora was proud of her roots and allegedly entertained high-ranking Nazi officials here during the occupation – a charge of collaboration that led to the Van Loons being shunned by polite society. Recently renovated, the **interior** of the house has been returned to its eighteenth-century appearance, a bright and breezy Rococo style of stucco, colourful wallpaper and rich wood panelling. Look out for the ornate copper **balustrade** on the staircase, into which is worked the name "Van Hagen-Trip" (former owners of the house); the Van Loons later filled the spaces between the letters with fresh iron curlicues to prevent their children falling through. The top-floor landing has several pleasant Grisaille **paintings** sporting Roman figures and one of the bedrooms – the "painted room" – is literally decorated with a Romantic painting of Italy, depicting a coastal scene with overgrown classical ruins and diligent peasants – a favourite motif in Amsterdam from around 1750 to 1820. The oddest items are the **fake bedroom doors**: the eighteenth-century owners were so keen to avoid any lack of symmetry that they camouflaged the real bedroom doors and created imitation, decorative doors in the "correct" position instead.

Thorbeckeplein, Rembrandtplein and Reguliersbreestraat

Returning to Reguliersgracht, it's a couple of minutes north to short and slender **Thorbeckeplein**, where a tawdry assortment of bars and restaurants flanks a statue of **Rudolf Thorbecke** (1798–1872), a far-sighted liberal politician and three times Dutch premier whose reforms served to democratize the country in the aftermath of the Europe-wide turmoil of 1848. Thorbeckeplein leads into **Rembrandtplein**, a dishevelled bit of greenery that was formerly Amsterdam's butter market, renamed in 1876. Nowadays, the square claims to be one of the city's nightlife centres, but its crowded restaurants and bars are firmly tourist-targeted. Rembrandt's **statue** stands in the middle, his back wisely turned against the square's worst excesses, which include live (but deadly) outdoor muzak. Of the prodigious number of cafés and bars here, only the café of the *Schiller Hotel* at no. 26 stands out, with an original Art Deco interior somewhat reminiscent of an ocean liner.

The narrow streets edging Rembrandtplein are far from peaceful either. The crumbling alleys to the north contain several of the city's raunchier gay bars, whilst **Reguliersbreestraat** is just supremely tacky. Nevertheless, tucked in among Reguliersbreestraat's slot-machine arcades and sex shops, at nos. 26–28, is the **Tuschinski** (see p.190), the city's most extraordinary cinema, with a marvellously well-preserved Art Deco interior. Opened in 1921 by a Polish Jew, Abram Tuschinski, the cinema boasts Expressionist paintings, coloured marbles and a wonderful carpet, handwoven in Marrakesh to an original design. Tuschinski himself died in Auschwitz in 1942, and there's a plaque in the cinema's foyer in his memory. The network of alleys behind the Tuschinski was once known as **Duivelshoek** (Devil's Corner), and, although it's been tidied up and sanitized, enough backstreet seediness remains to make it a spot to be avoided late at night.

Reguliersbreestraat leads west to Muntplein, for more on which see p.56.

The Jordaan and the Westerdok

L ying to the west of the city centre, the **Jordaan** is a likeable and easily explored area of slender canals and narrow streets flanked by an
agreeable mix of architectural styles, from modest, modern terraces to
handsome seventeenth-century canal houses. Traditionally the home
of Amsterdam's working class, with its boundaries clearly defined by the
Prinsengracht to the east and the Lijnbaansgracht in the west, the Jordaan's
character has in recent years been transformed by a middle-class influx, with
the district now one of the city's most sought-after residential neighbourhoods. Before then, and until the late 1970s, the Jordaan's inhabitants were
primarily stevedores and factory workers, earning a crust amongst the docks,
warehouses, factories and boatyards that extended north beyond
Brouwersgracht, the Jordaan's northern boundary and nowadays one of
Amsterdam's prettiest canals. Specific sights are, however, few and far between
– the best you'll do is probably the **Noorderkerk** – but nonetheless it's still
a pleasant area to wander in.

The pint-sized **Scheepvaartsbuurt** (Shipping Quarter), part of the city's
old industrial belt, edges the Jordaan, falling to either side of
Haarlemmerstraat and its continuation the Haarlemmerdijk, and is now a
mixed shopping and residential quarter. Just beyond lies the **Westerdok**, the
oldest part of the sprawling complex of artificial islands that today sweeps
along the south side of the River IJ, containing many of the city's maritime
facilities. The Westerdok itself was dredged out of the river to provide extra
warehousing and dock space in the seventeenth century. The maritime bustle has pretty much disappeared here, but, after a long period of neglect, the
area is rapidly finding new life as a chichi residential quarter with smart
apartments installed in its warehouses and its clutch of handsome canal
houses revamped and reinvigorated, especially on **Zandhoek**. Finally, the
working-class neighbourhood to the west of the Westerkanaal, which marks
the limit of the Westerdok, is of interest for **Het Schip**, a wonderful example of the Amsterdam School of architecture and perhaps more importantly
an example of social housing at its most optimistic.

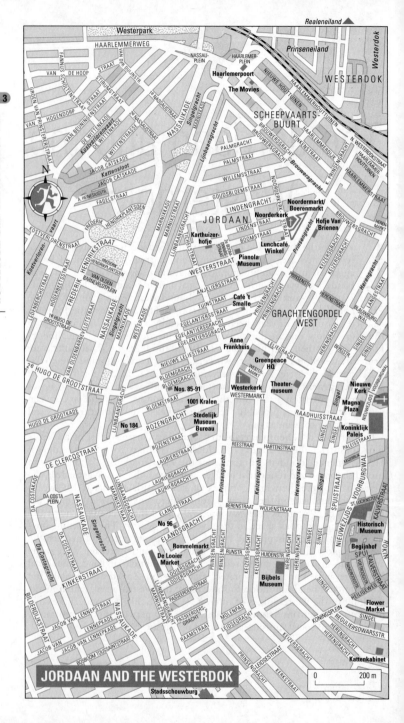

JORDAAN AND THE WESTERDOK

0   200 m

The Jordaan

In all probability the **Jordaan** takes its name from the French word *jardin* ("garden"), since the area's earliest settlers were Protestant Huguenots, who fled here to escape persecution in the sixteenth and seventeenth centuries. Another possibility is that it's a corruption of the Dutch word for Jews, *joden*. Whatever the truth, the Jordaan developed from open country – hence the number of streets and canals named after flowers and plants – into a refugee enclave, a teeming, cosmopolitan quarter beyond the pale of bourgeois respectability. Indeed, when the city fathers planned the expansion of the city in 1610, they made sure the Jordaan was kept outside the city boundaries. Consequently, the Jordaan was not subject to the rigorous planning restrictions of the main *grachten* – Herengracht, Keizersgracht and Prinsengracht – and its lattice of narrow streets followed the lines of the original polder drainage ditches rather than any municipal outline. This gives the district its distinctive, mazy layout, and much of its present appeal.

By the late nineteenth century, the Jordaan had become one of Amsterdam's toughest neighbourhoods, a stronghold of the city's industrial **working class**, mostly crowded together in cramped and unsanitary housing. Unsurprisingly, it was a highly politicized area, where protests against poor conditions were frequent, often coordinated by an influential and well-organized Communist Party. In the postwar period the slums were cleared or renovated, but rocketing property prices in the smarter parts of the city pushed middle-class professionals into the Jordaan from the early 1980s. This process of gentrification was at first much resented, but today the Jordaan is home to many young and affluent "alternative" Amsterdammers, who rub shoulders more or less affably with working-class Jordaaners with long-standing local roots.

Leidsegracht to Elandsgracht

The southern boundary of the Jordaan is generally deemed to be the **Leidsegracht**, though this is open to debate: according to dyed-in-the-wool locals the true Jordaaner is born within earshot of the Westerkerk bells, and you'd be hard-pushed to hear the chimes this far south. The narrow streets and canals just to the north of the Leidsegracht are routinely modern, but **Looiersgracht** (pronounced "lawyers-gracht") does hold, at no. 38, the indoor **Rommelmarket** (daily except Fri 11am–5pm), a large permanent flea market-cum-jumble sale, good for everything from worm-eaten wooden clogs to African masks.

Slightly more upmarket, and a short walk to the north at Elandsgracht 109, is **De Looier antiques market** (daily except Fri 11am–5pm), which is good for picking up Dutch bygones including tiles and ceramics, with a few stalls dealing in particular items or styles such as silver trinkets or delftware. Footballophiles will also want to take a peek at the **sports shop** at

---

The Jordaan's hofjes

One feature of the Jordaan's low-key architectural pleasures is its **hofjes** – almshouses built around a central courtyard and originally occupied by the city's elderly and needy. There were – and are – *hofjes* all over the city (most famously the Begijnhof – see p.57), but there's a concentration here in the Jordaan. Most date back to the seventeenth or eighteenth centuries, but the majority have been rebuilt or at least revamped – and all are still lived in. The Jordaan's most diverting *hofje* is the **Karthuizerhofje**, on Karthuizersstraat (see p.80).

Elandsgracht 96, where **Johan Cruyff** – star of Ajax in the 1970s and one of the greatest players of all time – bought his first pair of football boots.

Elandsgracht to Rozengracht

The streets immediately to the north of Elandsgracht are unremarkable and easily the most agreeable route onwards is along the **Lijnbaansgracht** (Tightrope-walk Canal). This narrow canal threads its way round most of the city centre and here – in between Elandsgracht and Rozenstraat – it's cobbled and leafy, the lapping waters flanked by old brick buildings. On **Rozenstraat** itself, at no. 59, is an annexe of the Stedelijk Museum (see p.106), the **Stedelijk Museum Bureau** (Tues–Sun 11am–5pm; free), which provides space for up-and-coming Amsterdam artists, with exhibitions, installations and occasional lectures and readings.

One block further north, **Rozengracht** lost its canal years ago and is now a busy main road of no particular distinction, though it was here at no. 184 that **Rembrandt** spent the last ten years of his life – a scrolled **plaque** distinguishes his old home. Rembrandt's last years were scarred by the death of his wife Hendrickje in 1663 and his son Titus five years later, but nevertheless it was in this period that he produced some of his finest work, including *The Return of the Prodigal Son*, which is displayed in the Hermitage, Leningrad. Also dated to these years is *The Jewish Bride*, a touchingly warm and heartfelt portrait of a bride and her father completed in 1668 and now in the Rijksmuseum (see p.103). The other place of some interest hereabouts is **1001 Kralen**, a shop at Rozengracht 54, which is packed with every sort of bead imaginable – so much so that it has become something of an Amsterdam institution.

From Rozengracht, it's the shortest of walks to the Westerkerk and the Anne Frankhuis (see p.63).

Rozengracht to Westerstraat

The streets and canals extending north from Rozengracht to Westerstraat form the heart of the Jordaan and hold the district's prettiest moments. Beyond Rozengracht, the first canal is the **Bloemgracht** (Flower Canal), a leafy waterway dotted with houseboats and arched by dinky little bridges, its network of cross-streets sprinkled with cafés, bars and idiosyncratic shops. There's a warm, relaxed community atmosphere here which is really rather beguiling, not to mention a clutch of old and handsome canal houses. Pride of architectural place goes to **nos. 89–91**, a sterling Renaissance building of 1642 complete with mullion windows, crowstep gable, brightly painted shutters and distinctive facade stones, representing a *steeman* (city-dweller), *landman* (farmer) and a *seeman* (sailor). Next door, **nos. 85–87** were built a few decades later – two immaculately maintained canal houses adorned by the bottleneck gables typical of the period.

From Bloemgracht, it's a few metres north to **Egelantiersgracht** (Rose-Hip Canal), where, at no. 12, the **Café 't Smalle** is one of Amsterdam's oldest cafés, opened in 1786 as a *proeflokaal* – a tasting house for the (long gone) gin distillery next door. In the eighteenth century, when quality control was partial to say the least, each batch of *jenever* (Dutch gin) could turn out very differently, so customers insisted on a taster before they splashed out. As a result, each distillery ran a *proeflokaal* offering free samples, and this is a rare survivor. The café's waterside terrace remains an especially pleasant spot to take a tipple (see p.165).

A narrow cross-street – **2e Egelantiersdwarsstraat** and its continuation **2e Tuindwarsstraat** and **2e Anjeliersdwarsstraat** – runs north from Bloemgracht

△ The Jordaan

flanked by many of the Jordaan's more fashionable stores and clothing shops as well as some of its liveliest bars and cafés. At the end is workaday **Westerstraat**, a busy thoroughfare, which is home to the small but fascinating **Pianola Museum** (Sun 11.30am–5.30pm; €3.75), at no. 106, whose collection of pianolas and automatic music-machines dates from the beginning of the twentieth century. Fifteen have been restored to working order. These machines, which work on rolls of perforated paper, were the jukeboxes of their day, and the museum has a vast collection of 14,000 rolls of music, some of which were "recorded" by famous pianists and composers – Gershwin, Debussy, Scott Joplin, Art Tatum and others. The museum runs a regular programme of pianola music concerts, where the rolls are played back on restored machines. Nearby, and also of some interest, is the largest of the Jordaan's hofjes, the **Karthuizerhofje**, Karthuizersstraat 89–171, a substantial courtyard complex established as a widows' hospice in the middle of the seventeenth century, though the present buildings are much later.

The Noorderkerk and the Noordermarkt

At the east end of Westerstraat, overlooking the Prinsengracht, is Hendrik de Keyser's **Noorderkerk** (March–Nov Sat 11am–1pm; free), the architect's last creation and probably his least successful, finished two years after his death in 1623. A bulky, overbearing brick building, it represented a radical departure from the conventional church designs of the time, having a symmetrical Greek cross floor plan, with four equally proportioned arms radiating out from a steepled centre. Uncompromisingly dour, it proclaimed the serious intent of the Calvinists who worshipped here in so far as the pulpit – and therefore the preacher proclaiming the Word of God – was at the centre and not at the front of the church, a symbolic break with the Catholic past. Nevertheless, it's still hard to understand quite how Keyser, who designed such elegant structures as the Westerkerk (see p.63), could have ended up designing this.

The **Noordermarkt**, the somewhat inconclusive square outside the church, holds a **statue** of three figures bound to each other, a poignant tribute to the bloody Jordaanoproer riot of 1934, part of a successful campaign to stop the government cutting unemployment benefit during the Depression. The inscription reads "The strongest chains are those of unity". There is also a **plaque** on the church honouring those Communists and Jews who were rounded up here by the Germans in February 1941. More cheerfully, the square hosts two of Amsterdam's best open-air **markets**. There's an antiques and general household goods market on Monday mornings (9am–1pm) plus a popular Saturday farmers' market, the **Boerenmarkt** (9am–3pm), a lively affair selling organic fruit and vegetables, freshly baked breads and a plethora of oils and spices. Cross an unmarked border though and you'll find yourself in the middle of a Saturday bird market, which operates on an adjacent patch at much the same time, and, if you're at all squeamish, is best avoided – brightly coloured birds squeezed into tiny cages are not for everyone. Incidentally, the *Lunchcafé Winkel*, beside the Noordermarkt at the corner with Westerstraat, sells huge wedges of homemade **apple pie**, which Jordaaners swear is the best in town.

The Lindengracht and Brouwersgracht

Just to the north of the Noorderkerk, the **Lindengracht** ("Canal of Limes") lost its waterway decades ago, but has had a prominent role in local folklore since the day in 1886 when a policeman made an ill-advised attempt to stop an eel-pulling contest. Horrible as it sounds, eel-pulling was a popular pastime hereabouts with tug-o'-war teams holding tight to either end of the poor creature, which was smeared with soap to make the entertainment last a little longer. The crowd unceremoniously bundled the policeman away, but when reinforcements arrived, the whole thing got out of hand and there was a full-scale **riot** – the Paling-Oproer – which lasted for three days and cost 26 lives.

The east end of the Lindengracht intersects with leafy **Brouwersgracht**, which marks the northerly limit of both the Jordaan and the Grachtengordel (see Chapter Two). In the seventeenth century, Brouwersgracht lay at the edge of Amsterdam's great harbour, one of the major arteries linking the open sea with the city centre. Thronged by vessels returning from – or heading off to – every corner of the globe, it was lined with storage depots and warehouses. Breweries flourished here too – hence its name – capitalizing on their ready access to shipments of fresh water. Today, the harbour bustle has moved elsewhere, and the warehouses, with their distinctive spout-neck gables and shuttered windows, formerly used for the delivery and dispatch of goods by pulley from the canal below, have been converted into apartments, some of the most expensive in the city. There are handsome merchants' houses here as well, plus moored houseboats and a string of quaint little swing bridges – altogether one of the most classically picturesque canals in the whole of the city.

The Scheepvaartsbuurt and the Westerdok

Brouwersgracht is also the southern boundary of the **Scheepvaartsbuurt** – the Shipping Quarter – an unassuming neighbourhood which focuses on Haarlemmerstraat and **Haarlemmerdijk**, a long, rather ordinary thoroughfare lined with bars, cafés and food shops. In the eighteenth and nineteenth centuries, this district boomed from its location between the Brouwersgracht and the **Westerdok**, a narrow parcel of land dredged out of the River IJ immediately to the north and equipped with docks, warehouses and shipyards. The construction of these artificial islands took the pressure off Amsterdam's congested maritime facilities and was necessary to sustain the city's economic success. Stretching from the Westerdok to the Oosterdok, Amsterdam's riverside wharves functioned as the heartbeat of the city until the city's shipping facilities began to move away from the centre, a process accelerated by the construction of Centraal Station, slap in the middle of the old quayside in the 1880s. The Westerdok hung on to some of the marine trade until the 1960s, but today – bar the odd small boatyard – industry has to all intents and purposes disappeared and the area is busy re-inventing itself. There is still an air of faded grittiness here, but the old forgotten warehouses – within walking distance of the centre – are rapidly being turned into bijou studios and dozens of plant-filled houseboats are moored alongside the tiny streets.

Haarlemmerdijk and the Haarlemmerpoort

Before World War II the **Haarlemmerstraat** and its westerly extension, the **Haarlemmerdijk**, was a congested thoroughfare, but the trams that once ran here were re-routed and now it's a pleasant if unremarkable pedestrianized strip flanked by shops and cafés. The only architectural high point is the meticulously restored Art Deco interior of **The Movies** cinema (see p.190), near the west end of the street at Haarlemmerdijk 161. Just metres away, the busy Haarlemmerplein traffic junction sports the grandiose Neoclassical **Haarlemmerpoort**, built on the site of a medieval gateway in 1840 for the new king William II's triumphal entry into the city. The euphoria didn't last long. William was a distinguished general, who had been wounded at Waterloo, but as a king he proved too crusty and reactionary to be popular, only accepting mild liberal reforms after extensive rioting in Amsterdam and elsewhere.

At the Haarlemmerpoort, there's a choice of routes: stroll north through the pedestrian tunnel beneath the railway lines for the Westerdok, or push on west for the Westerpark and the striking Expressionism of the Het Schip housing block (see opposite).

The Westerdok

On the far side of the railway line from the Haarlemmerpoort, turn right along Sloterdijkstraat and you soon cross the canal over onto **Galgenstraat** (Gallows Street), once the sight of the municipal gallows, which were clearly visible to passing ships – to discourage potential law-breakers. Galgenstraat bisects the smallest of the Westerdok islands, pint-sized **Prinseneiland**, an indeterminate mix of former warehouses and factories.

Keep going straight along Galgenstraat, over the next canal, and then turn north up Grote Bickersstraat for the bridge over to a second Westerdok island, **Realeneiland**. Here, tiny **Zandhoek** is flanked by a clutch of fine old canal houses dating to the seventeenth century. Several are decorated with distinctive facade stones, including **De Gouden Reael**, whose stone sports a gold coin. Before Napoleon introduced a system of house numbers, these stones were the principal way that visitors could recognize one house from another, and many homeowners went to considerable lengths to make theirs unique. Jacob Real, the Catholic tradesman who owned this particular house, also used the image of a *real* – a Spanish coin – to discreetly advertise his sympathies for the Catholic Habsburgs.

At the top of Zandhoek, cross over the canal and then turn left along Zoutkeetsgracht; another left turn, this time onto Planciusstraat, returns you to the pedestrian tunnel near the Haarlemmerpoort.

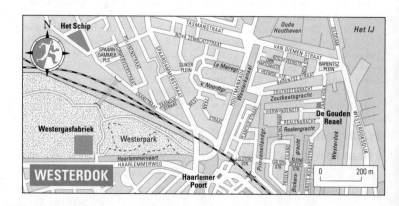

Westerpark and Het Schip

Barely five minutes' walk away to the west of the Haarlemmerpoort is the east entrance to the **Westerpark**, one of the city's smaller and more enticing parks, running alongside a narrow sliver of a canal. At the far end of the park you bump into the old gas factory, the **Westergasfabriek**, a sprawling jumble of neo-Gothic buildings dating from the 1880s. Currently fenced off, it had a brief reincarnation as the city's prime venue for Acid House parties in the early 1990s.

On the north side of the park, about halfway along, a pedestrian tunnel leads under the railway lines to **Zaanstraat**, the southern edge of a working-class neighbourhood that stretches north to the busy Spaarndammer boulevard. Taken as a whole, this part of the city is really rather glum, but hang a left on Zaanstraat and you soon reach Spaarndammerplantsoen, the site of **Het Schip**, a municipal housing block which is a splendid – and pristine – example of the Expressionistic Amsterdam School of architecture. Seven years in the making, from 1913 to 1920, the complex takes its name from its ship-like shape and is graced by all manner of fetching decorative details – from the funnel-like main tower and the intriguing mix-and-match windows through to the sweeping brick facades and balconies. The architect responsible was **Michael de Klerk** (1884–1923), who also designed the two other housing blocks on Spaarndammerplantsoen, though Het Schip is easily the most striking. De Klerk reacted strongly against the influence of Berlage, whose style – exemplified by the Beurs (see p.44) – emphasized clean lines and functionality, opting instead for much more playful motifs. De Klerk also installed a post office in Het Schip and this, with its superb multicoloured tiling, now serves as the **Museum Het Schip** (Wed, Thurs & Sun 2–5pm; €2.50; ⓦ www.hetschip.nl), which explores the history of the Amsterdam School. Politically motivated, De Klerk and his architectural allies were eager to provide high-quality homes for the working class, though their laudable aims were often undermined – or at least diluted - by a tendency to over-elaborate. For details of De Klerk's other major commission in Amsterdam, the De Dageraad housing project, see p.114.

Het Schip is at the terminus of **buses** #22 and 49, which will whisk you back to Centraal Station.

The Old Jewish Quarter and the East

Originally one of the marshiest parts of Amsterdam, prone to regular flooding, the narrow slice of land sandwiched between the curve of the Amstel, Kloveniersburgwal and the Nieuwe Herengracht was the home of Amsterdam's Jews from the sixteenth century up until World War II. By the 1920s, this Old Jewish Quarter, aka the **Jodenhoek** ("Jews' Corner"), was crowded with tenement buildings and smoking factories, but in 1945 it lay derelict – and neither has postwar redevelopment treated it kindly. Its focal point, **Waterlooplein**, has been overwhelmed by a whopping town and concert hall complex, which caused much controversy at the time of its construction, and the once-bustling **Jodenbreestraat** is now bleak and very ordinary, with Mr Visserplein, at its east end, one of the city's busiest traffic junctions. Picking your way round these obstacles is not much fun, but persevere – amongst all the cars and concrete are several moving reminders of the Jewish community that perished in the war. For reasons that remain unclear, the Germans did not destroy all the Jodenhoek's synagogues, and the late seventeenth-century **Esnoga** (Portuguese synagogue) is one of the finest buildings in the city. Close by, four other synagogues have been merged into the fascinating **Joods Historisch Museum** (Jewish Historical Museum), celebrating Jewish culture and custom. As a footnote, Rembrandt spent the best years of his life living in the Jodenhoek and the restored **Het Rembrandthuis** (Rembrandt House) contains a large collection of his etchings.

Immediately to the east of the Old Jewish Quarter lies the **Plantagebuurt**, a trim district spined by the **Plantage Middenlaan**, a wide boulevard that was constructed in the mid-nineteenth century as the first part of the creation of this leafy suburb – one of Amsterdam's first. The avenue borders the city's largest botanical gardens, the **Hortus Botanicus**, and the **zoo** and runs close to the first-rate **Verzetsmuseum** (Dutch Resistance Museum). Just slightly to the north of here are the artificial islands that comprise the **Oosterdok** (East Dock) quarter, dredged out of the River IJ to accommodate warehouses and docks in the seventeenth century. These islands once formed part of a vast maritime complex that spread right along the River IJ. Industrial decline set in during the 1880s, but the area, much like its counterpart the Westerdok (see p.82), is currently being redefined as a residential district, whilst its nautical heyday is recalled by the **Nederlands Scheepvaartmuseum** (Netherlands Maritime Museum).

The Old Jewish Quarter

Throughout the nineteenth century and up to the German occupation, the **Old Jewish Quarter** – the Jodenhoek – was one of the busiest parts of town, its main streets holding scores of open-air stalls selling everything from pickled herrings to pots and pans. Unfortunately, it was also surrounded by canals – and it was these the Germans exploited to create the ghetto that prefigured their policy of starvation and deportation. They restricted movement in and out of the quarter by raising most of the swing bridges (over the Nieuwe Herengracht, the Amstel and the Kloveniersburgwal) and imposing stringent controls on the rest. The Jews, readily identifiable by the yellow Stars of David they were obliged to wear, were not allowed to use public transport or to own a telephone, and were placed under a curfew. Meanwhile, roundups and deportations had begun shortly after the Germans arrived and continued into 1945. At the end of the war, the Jodenhoek lay derelict and, as the need for wood and raw materials intensified in the cold winter that followed, many of the houses were dismantled for fuel, a process of destruction that was completed in the 1970s when the metro was sunk beneath Waterlooplein. By these means, the prewar Jodenhoek disappeared almost without trace, the notable exception being the imposing **Esnoga** (Portuguese Synagogue) and the four connected synagogues of the Ashkenazi Jews, now the **Joods Historisch Museum**. The district's other main sight is the **Het Rembrandthuis**, crammed with the artist's etchings.

St Antoniesbreestraat

Stretching south from Nieuwmarkt, **St Antoniesbreestraat** once linked the city centre with the Jewish quarter, but its huddle of shops and houses was mostly demolished in the 1980s to make way for a main road. The plan was subsequently abandoned, but the modern buildings that now line most of the street hardly fire the soul, even if the modern symmetries – and cubist, coloured panels – of the apartment blocks that spill along part of the street are at least visually arresting. One of the few survivors of all these municipal shenanigans is the **Pintohuis** (Pinto House; Mon & Wed 2–8pm, Fri 2–5pm, Sat 11am–4pm; free), at no. 69, which is now a public library. Easily spotted by its off-white Italianate facade, the mansion is named after Isaac de Pinto, a Jew who fled Portugal to escape the Inquisition and subsequently became a founder of the East India Company (see p.95). Pinto bought this property in 1651 and promptly had it remodelled in grand style, the facade interrupted by six lofty pilasters, which lead the eye up to the blind balustrade. The mansion was the talk of the town, even more so when Pinto had the interior painted in a similar style to the front – pop in to look at the birds and cherubs of the original painted ceiling.

Across the street, through the old archway, the **Zuiderkerk** (Mon 11am–4pm, Tues, Wed & Fri 9am–4pm, Thurs 9am–8pm, free), dating from 1611, was the first Amsterdam church built specifically for the Protestants. It was designed by the prolific architect and sculptor, Hendrick de Keyser (1565–1621), whose distinctive – and very popular – style extrapolated elements of traditional Flemish design, with fanciful detail and frilly towers added wherever possible. The basic design of the Zuiderkerk is firmly Gothic, but the soaring tower is typical of his work, complete with balconies and balustrades, arches and columns. Now deconsecrated, the church has itself been turned into

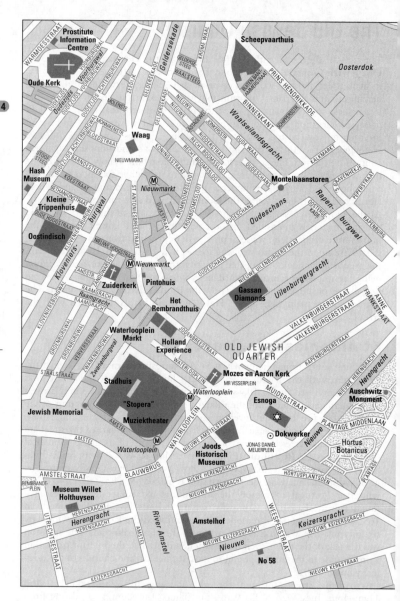

a **municipal information centre** with displays on housing and the environment, plus temporary exhibitions revealing the city council's future plans. The **tower**, which has a separate entrance, can be climbed during the summer (June–Sept Wed–Sat 2–4pm; €3).

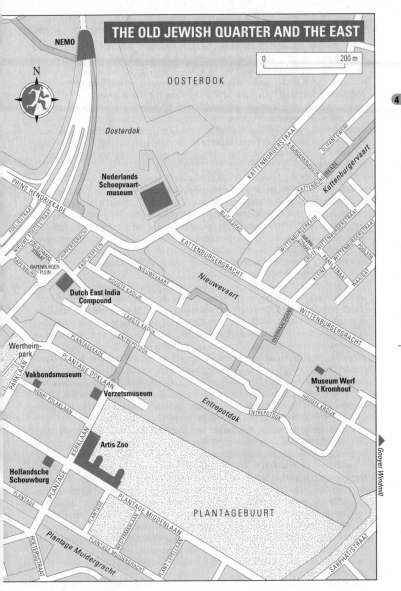

Map labels: NEMO · OOSTERDOK · Oosterdok · Nederlands Scheepvaart-museum · PRINS HENDRIKKADE · FOELIESTRAAT · NIEUWE FOELIESTRAAT · FOELIEDWARS-STRAAT · RAPENBURGERSTRAAT · RAPENBURGER-PLEIN · SCHIPPERSGRACHT · KADIJKSPLEIN · HOOGTE KADIJK · NIEUWEVAART · Nieuwevaart · Dutch East India Compound · LAAGTE KADIJK · ENTREPOTDOK · Wertheim-park · PLANTAGEKADE · PLANTAGE DOKLAAN · PARKLAAN · HENRI POLAKLAAN · Vakbondsmuseum · Verzetsmuseum · Entrepotdok · ENTREPOTDOK · KERKLAAN · Artis Zoo · Hollandsche Schouwburg · PLANTAGE · PLANTAGE MIDDENLAAN · PLANTAGEBUURT · WESTERMANLAAN · PLANTAGE MUIDERGRACHT · PLANTAGE · PLANTAGE MUIDERGRACHT · ROETERSSTRAAT · Plantage Muidergracht · LAAN TEPELLAAN · SARPHATISTRAAT · KATTENBURGERSTRAAT · K. BURGERKRUISSTR · OLIFANTSWERF · KATTENBURGERKADE · Kattenburgervaart · KATTENBURGERKADE · BIJLTJESPAD · KATTENBURGERGRACHT · Nieuwevaart · WITTENBURGERKADE · BAVENSTRAAT · GROTE WITTENBURGERSTRAAT · KLEINE WITTENBURGERSTRAAT · ZANELSTRAAT · POOLSTR · WAAIGAT · OVERHAALSGANG · WITTENBURGERGRACHT · Museum Werf 't Kromhout · HOOGTE KADIJK · Gooyer Windmill

Scale: 0 — 200 m

Jodenbreestraat and Het Rembrandthuis

St Antoniesbreestraat runs into **Jodenbreestraat**, the "Broad Street of the Jews", at one time the main centre of Jewish activity. Badly served by postwar development, this ancient thoroughfare is now short on charm, but in these unlikely surroundings, at no. 6, stands **Het Rembrandthuis** (Rembrandt

From the late sixteenth century onwards, Amsterdam was the refuge of **Jews** escaping persecution throughout the rest of Europe. The **Union of Utrecht**, ratified in 1579, signalled the start of the influx. Drawn up by the largely Protestant northern Dutch provinces in response to the invading Spanish army, the treaty combined the United Provinces (later to become the Netherlands) in a loose federation, whose wheels could only be greased by a degree of religious toleration then unknown elsewhere across the continent. Whatever the Protestants may have wanted, they knew that the Catholic minority (around 35 percent) would only continue to support the rebellion against the Spanish Habsburgs if they were treated well – the Jews benefited by osmosis and consequently immigrated here in their hundreds.

The **toleration** did, however, have its limits: Jewish immigrants were forced to buy citizenship; Christian-Jewish marriages were illegal; and, as with the Catholics, they were only allowed to practise their religion discreetly behind closed doors. A proclamation in 1632 also excluded them from most guilds – effectively withdrawing their right to own and run businesses. This forced them to either excel in those trades not governed by the guilds or introduce new non-guild trades into the city. Nonetheless, by the middle of the eighteenth century the city's Jewish community was active in almost every aspect of the economy, with particular strongholds in bookselling, tobacco, banking and commodity futures.

The first major Jewish influx was of **Sephardic** Jews from Spain and Portugal, where persecution had begun in earnest in 1492 and continued throughout the sixteenth century. In the 1630s the Sephardim were joined in Amsterdam by hundreds of (much poorer) **Ashkenazi** Jews from German-speaking central Europe. The two groups established separate synagogues and, although there was no ghetto as such, the vast majority settled on and around what is now Waterlooplein, then a distinctly unhealthy tract of marshland subject to regular flooding by the River Amstel. Initially known as **Vlooyenburg**, this district was usually referred to as the **Jodenhoek** (pronounced "yo-den-hook"), or "Jews' Corner", though this was not, generally speaking, a pejorative term and neither did the Dutch eschew living here: Rembrandt, for instance, was quite happy to take up residence and frequently painted his Jewish neighbours. Indeed, given the time, the most extraordinary feature of Jewish settlement in Amsterdam was that it occasioned mild curiosity rather than outright hate, as evinced by contemporary prints of Jewish religious customs, where there is neither any hint of stereotype nor discernible demonization.

The restrictions affecting both Jews and Catholics were removed during **Napoleon**'s occupation of the United Provinces, when the country was temporarily renamed the Batavian Republic (1795–1806). Freed from official discrimination, Amsterdam's Jewish community flourished and the Jewish Quarter expanded, nudging northwest towards Nieuwmarkt and east across Nieuwe Herengracht, though this was just the focus of a community whose members lived in every part of the city. In 1882 the dilapidated houses of the Jodenhoek were razed and several minor canals filled in to make way for **Waterlooplein**, which became a largely Jewish marketplace, a bustling affair that sprawled out along St Antoniesbreestraat and Jodenbreestraat.

At the turn of the twentieth century, there were around 60,000 Jews living in Amsterdam, but refugees from Hitler's Germany swelled this figure to around 120,000 in the 1930s. The disaster that befell this community during the German occupation is hard to conceive, but the bald facts speak for themselves: when Amsterdam was liberated, there were only 5000 Jews left and the Jodenhoek was, to all intents and purposes, a ghost town. At present, there are about 25,000 Jews resident in the city, but while Jewish life in Amsterdam has survived, its heyday is gone forever.

House; Mon–Sat 10am–5pm, Sun 1–5pm; €7), whose intricate facade is decorated by pretty wooden shutters and a dinky pediment. Rembrandt bought this house at the height of his fame and popularity, living here for over twenty years and spending a fortune on furnishings – an expense that ultimately contributed to his bankruptcy. An inventory made at the time details the huge collection of paintings, sculptures and art treasures he'd amassed, almost all of which was confiscated after he was declared insolvent and forced to move to a more modest house on Rozengracht in the Jordaan in 1658. The city council bought the Jodenbreestraat house in 1907 and has subsequently revamped the premises on several occasions, most recently in 1999. A string of period rooms now gives a clear impression of Rembrandt's life and times, while the adjoining modern wing displays an extensive collection of Rembrandt's **etchings** as well as several of the original copper plates on which he worked. The biblical illustrations attract the most attention, though the studies of tramps and vagabonds are equally appealing. An accompanying exhibit explains Rembrandt's engraving techniques and there are also regular temporary exhibitions on Rembrandt and his contemporaries; to see his paintings, however, you'll have to go to the Rijksmuseum (see p.98).

Next door, the multimedia **Holland Experience** (daily 10am–6pm; €8, under-16s & over-65s €6.85; ⓦ www.holland-experience.nl) is a kind of sensory-bombardment movie about Holland and Amsterdam, with synchronized smells and a moving floor – not to mention the special 3D glasses. From here, it's a couple of minutes' walk north to **Gassan Diamonds** (frequent guided tours daily 9am–5pm; free), which occupies a large and imposing brick building dating from 1897 on Nieuwe Uilenburgerstraat. Before World War II, many local Jews worked as diamond cutters and polishers, though there's little sign of the industry here today, this factory being the main exception. Tours include a visit to the cutting and polishing areas as well as opportunities to buy diamond jewellery.

Waterlooplein

Jodenbreestraat runs parallel to the **Stadhuis en Muziektheater** (Town Hall and Concert Hall), a sprawling complex whose indeterminate modernity dominates **Waterlooplein**, a rectangular parcel of land that was originally swampy marsh. This was the site of the first Jewish Quarter, but by the late nineteenth century it had become an insanitary slum, home to the poorest of the Ashkenazi Jews. The slums were cleared in the 1880s and thereafter the open spaces of the Waterlooplein hosted the largest and liveliest marketplace in the city, the place where Jews and Gentiles met to trade. In the war, the Germans used the square to round up their victims, but despite these ugly connotations the Waterlooplein was revived in the 1950s as the site of the city's main **flea market** and remains so to this day (Mon–Sat 9am–5pm; for more on markets, see p.207). The market is, however, nowhere as large as it once was, thanks to the town hall and concert hall development. As far as the city council was concerned, the market's reappearance in the 1950s was only a stopgap while they mulled over plans to entirely reinvent the depopulated Jodenhoek. For starters, whole streets were demolished to make way for the motorist – with Mr Visserplein (see p.90), for example, becoming little more than a traffic intersection – and then, warming to their theme in the late 1970s, the council announced the building of a massive new Waterlooplein concert-and-city-hall complex. Opposition was immediate and widespread, but attempts to prevent the building failed, and the Muziektheater opened in 1986, since when it has established a reputation for artistic excellence. One of the story's abiding ironies is that the title of the protest campaign – "**Stopera**" – has passed into common usage to describe the complex.

Inside, amidst all the architectural mediocrity, there are a couple of minor attractions, beginning with the **glass columns** in the public passageway towards the rear of the complex. These give a salutary lesson on the fragility of the Netherlands: two contain water indicating the sea levels in the Dutch towns of Vlissingen and IJmuiden (below knee-level), while another records the levels experienced during the 1953 flood disaster (way above head-height). Downstairs a concrete pile shows what is known as "Normal Amsterdam Level" (NAP), originally calculated in 1684 as the average water level in the river IJ and still the basis for measuring altitude above sea level across Europe. Metres away, in the foyer of the Muziektheater, is a forceful and inventive **memorial** to the district's Jews, in which a bronze violinist bursts through the floor tiles. Outside, at the very tip of Waterlooplein, where the River Amstel meets the Zwanenburgwal canal, there is another memorial – a black stone tribute to the dead of the Jewish resistance; the inscription from Jeremiah translates as:

> If my eyes were a well of tears, I would cry
> day and night for the fallen fighters of my
> beloved people.

Mr Visserplein

Just behind the Muziektheater, on the corner of Mr Visserplein, is the **Mozes en Aaron Kerk**, a rather glum Neoclassical structure built on the site of a clandestine Catholic church in the 1840s. It takes its unusual name from a pair of facade stones bearing effigies of the two prophets that decorated the earlier building. Earlier still, this site was occupied by the house where the philosopher and theologian Spinoza was born in 1632. Of Sephardic descent, Spinoza's pantheistic views soon brought him into conflict with the elders of the Jewish community. At the age of 23, he was excommunicated and forced out of the city, moving into a small village where he survived by grinding lenses. After an attempt on his life, Spinoza moved again, eventually ending up in The Hague, where his free-thinking ways proved more acceptable. He produced his most famous treatise, *Ethics Demonstrated in the Geometrical Order*, in 1674, three years before his death.

Next door to the church, **Mr Visserplein** is a busy junction for traffic speeding towards the IJ tunnel. It takes its name from Mr Visser, President of the Supreme Court of the Netherlands in 1939. He was dismissed the following year when the Germans occupied the country, and became an active member of the Jewish resistance, working for the illegal underground newspaper *Het Parool* ("The Password") and refusing to wear the yellow Star of David. He died in 1942, a few days after publicly – and famously – denouncing all forms of collaboration.

The Esnoga

Unmissable on the corner of Mr Visserplein is the brown and bulky brickwork of the **Esnoga** or **Portugees synagoge** (Portuguese Synagogue; Sun–Fri 10am–4pm; closed Yom Kippur; €3.50), completed in 1675 for the city's Sephardic Jews. One of Amsterdam's most imposing buildings, the central structure, with its grand pilasters and blind balustrade, was built in the broadly Neoclassical style that was then fashionable in Holland. It is surrounded by a courtyard complex of small outhouses, where the city's Sephardim have fraternized for centuries. Barely altered since its construction, the synagogue's lofty interior follows the Sephardic tradition in having the Hechal (the Ark of the Covenant) and *tebah* (from where services are led) at opposite ends. Also traditional is the seating, with two sets of wooden benches (for the men) facing each other across the central aisle – the women have separate galleries up above. A set of superb brass chandeliers holds the candles that remain the only source of artificial light. When it was completed, the synagogue was one of the largest in the world, its congregation almost certainly the richest; today, the Sephardic community has dwindled to just sixty-odd members, most of whom live outside the city centre. In one of the outhouses, a video sheds light on the history of the synagogue and Amsterdam's Sephardim; the mystery is why the Germans left it alone – no one knows for sure, but it seems likely that they intended to turn it into a museum once all the Jews had been polished off.

Jonas Daniel Meijerplein

Next to the synagogue, on the south side of its retaining wall, is **Jonas Daniel Meijerplein**, a scrawny triangle of gravel named after the eponymous lawyer, who in 1796, at the age of just 16, was the first Jew to be admitted to the Amsterdam Bar. It was here in February 1941 that around 400 Jewish men were forcibly loaded up on trucks and taken to their deaths at Mauthausen concentration camp, in reprisal for the killing of a Dutch Nazi during a street fight. The arrests sparked off the **February Strike** (Februaristaking), a general strike in protest against the Germans' treatment of the Jews. It was organized by the outlawed Communist Party and spearheaded by Amsterdam's transport workers and dockers – a rare demonstration of solidarity with the Jews whose fate was usually accepted without visible protest in all of occupied Europe. The strike was quickly suppressed, but is still commemorated by an annual wreath-laying ceremony on February 25, as well as by Mari Andriessen's statue of the **Dokwerker** (Dockworker) here on the square.

Joods Historisch Museum

Across the square, on the far side of the main road, the **Joods Historisch Museum** (Jewish Historical Museum; daily 11am–5pm, closed Yom Kippur; €5) is cleverly shoehorned into four Ashkenazi synagogues dating from the late seventeenth century. For years after the war these buildings lay abandoned, but they were finally refurbished – and connected by walkways – in the 1980s to accommodate a Jewish resource centre and exhibition area. The latter is located in the handsome Grote Synagoge of 1671 and features a fairly small but wide-ranging collection covering most aspects of Dutch Jewish life. Downstairs, in the main body of the synagogue, is a fine collection of religious silverware as well as a handful of paintings and all manner of antique artefacts illustrating religious customs and practices. The gallery above holds a finely judged social history of the city's Jews, tracing their prominent role in a wide variety of industries, both as employers and employees and examining, in brief, the trauma of World War II, complete with several especially moving photographs. For more on Amsterdam during the German occupation, visit the Dutch Resistance Museum (see p.94).

The Plantagebuurt

Developed in the middle of the nineteenth century, the **Plantagebuurt**, with its comfortable streets bordering **Plantage Middenlaan** boulevard, was built as part of a concerted attempt to provide good-quality housing for the city's expanding middle classes. Although it was never as fashionable as the older residential parts of the *grachtengordel*, the new district did contain elegant villas and spacious terraces, making it a first suburban port of call for many aspiring Jews. Nowadays, the Plantagebuurt is still one of the more prosperous parts of the city, in a modest sort of way, and boasts two especially enjoyable attractions – the **Hortus Botanicus** botanical gardens and the **Verzetsmuseum** (Dutch Resistance Museum).

Starting at Centraal Station, **tram** #20 runs along the northern part of Plantage Middenlaan, passing by – or near – all the district's main attractions.

South of Nieuwe Herengracht

With the second phase of the digging of the *grachtengordel*, the three main canals that ringed the city centre were extended beyond the River Amstel up towards the docks along the River IJ – hence "**Nieuwe**" Herengracht, Keizersgracht and Prinsengracht. At first, takers for the new land were few and far between and the city had no option but to offer it to charities at discount prices. One result was the establishment of the whopping **Amstel Hof**, a former *hofje* (alms house) and a stern and especially dreary building, which still stretches out along the Amstel between Nieuwe Herengracht and Nieuwe Keizersgracht. Later, things picked up as many better-off Jews escaped the crowded conditions of the Old Jewish Quarter to live along the new canals, but this community did not survive World War II. One painful reminder of the occupation still stands at **Nieuwe Keizersgracht 58**, a couple of minutes' walk east of – and on the other side of the canal from – the Amstel Hof. From 1940, this house, with its luxurious Neoclassical double doorway and twin caryatids, was the headquarters of the **Judenrat** (Jewish Council), through which the Germans ran the ghetto and organized the deportations. The role of the Judenrat is extremely controversial. Many have argued that they were base collaborators, who hoped to save their own necks by working with the Germans and duping their fellow Jews into thinking that the deportations were indeed – as Nazi propaganda insisted – about the transfer of personnel to new employment in Germany. Just how much the council leaders knew about the gas chambers remains unclear, but after the war the surviving members of the Jewish Council successfully defended themselves against charges of collaboration, claiming that they had been a buffer against the Germans rather than their instruments.

Plantage Middenlaan

From Mr Visserplein, it's a short walk east along Muiderstraat to the lush **Hortus Botanicus** (April–Sept Mon–Fri 9am–5pm, Sat & Sun 11am–5pm, €5; Oct–March Mon–Fri 9am–4pm, Sat & Sun 11am–4pm, €3.40), a pleasant botanical garden at the corner of Plantage Middenlaan and Plantage Parklaan. Founded in 1682, the gardens contain around 6000 plant species (including various carnivorous varieties) on display both outside and in a series of hothouses, including a Three-Climates Glasshouse, where the plants are arranged according to their geographical origins. The garden makes a relaxing break on any tour of central Amsterdam and you can stop off for coffee and

△ Scheepvaarthuis

cakes in the orangery. Across the street, beside the Nieuwe Herengracht canal, is the pocket-sized **Wertheimpark**, where the **Auschwitz monument** is a simple affair with symbolically broken mirrors and an inscription that reads *Nooit meer Auschwitz* ("Auschwitz – Never Again"); it was designed by the Dutch writer Jan Wolkers.

Continue down the right-hand side of Plantage Middenlaan to reach another sad relic of the war, **De Hollandsche Schouwburg**, at no. 24 (daily 11am–4pm except Yom Kippur; free). Formerly a Jewish theatre, the building became the main assembly point for Amsterdam Jews prior to their deportation. Inside, there was no daylight and families were interned in conditions that foreshadowed those of the camps they would soon be taken to. The building has been refurbished to house a small exhibition on the plight of the city's Jews, but the old auditorium out at the back has been left as an empty, roofless shell. A memorial column of basalt on a Star of David base stands where the stage once was, an intensely mournful monument to suffering of unfathomable proportions.

Verzetsmuseum

From De Hollandsche Schouwburg, it's a brief walk northeast along Plantage Kerklaan to both the **Artis Zoo** (see p.219) and, at no. 61, the excellent **Verzetsmuseum** (Dutch Resistance Museum; Tues–Fri 10am–5pm, Mon, Sat & Sun noon–5pm; €4.50; ⓦ www.verzetsmuseum.org). The museum outlines the development of the Dutch Resistance from the German invasion of the Netherlands in May 1940 to the country's liberation in 1945. Thoughtfully presented, the main gangway examines the experience of the majority of the population, dealing honestly with the fine balance between cooperation and collaboration. Side rooms are devoted to different aspects of the resistance, from the brave determination of the Communist Party, who went underground as soon as the Germans arrived, to more ad hoc responses like the so-called **Milk Strike** of 1943, when hundreds of milk producers refused to deliver. Interestingly, the Dutch Resistance proved especially adept at forgery, forcing the Germans to make the identity cards they issued more and more complicated – but without much success. Fascinating old photographs illustrate the (English and Dutch) text along with a host of original artefacts, from examples of illegal newsletters to signed German death warrants. Apart from their treatment of the Jews, which is detailed here, perhaps the most chilling feature of the occupation was the use of indiscriminate reprisals to terrify the population. For the most part it worked, though there were always a minority courageous enough to resist. The museum has dozens of little metal sheets providing biographical sketches of the members of the Resistance – and it's this mixture of the general and the personal that is its real strength.

Vakbondsmuseum

Doubling back along Plantage Kerklaan, take the first right for the **Vakbondsmuseum** (Trade Union Museum; Tues–Fri 11am–5pm, Sun 1–5pm; €3.40), at Henri Polaklaan 9. The museum contains a small exhibition of documents, cuttings and photos relating to the Dutch labour movement, with a section devoted to Henri Polak, the leader of the Diamond Workers' Union and the man responsible for coordinating the successful campaign for the eight-hour working day. However, the building is actually rather more interesting than the exhibition. Built by **Berlage** for the Diamond Workers' Union in 1900, it was designed in a distinctive style that incorporated

Romanesque features – such as the castellated balustrade and the deeply recessed main door – within an Expressionist framework. The striking, brightly coloured interior develops these themes with a beautiful mixture of stained glass windows, stone arches, painted brickwork and patterned tiles. From the outside, the building looks like a fortified mansion, hence its old nickname the Rode Burgt ("Red Stronghold"). This design was not just about Berlage's whims. Acting on behalf of the employers, the police – and sometimes armed scabs – were regularly used to break strikes, and the union believed members could retreat here to hold out in relative safety. On a number of occasions this proved to be the case, leading the idea to be copied elsewhere, especially in Berlin, where it had disastrous consequences for the Left: in the 1930s the National Socialists simply surrounded the trade union strongholds and captured many of the leading activists in one fell swoop.

The Oosterdok

Just to the north of the Plantagebuurt lies the **Oosterdok**, whose network of artificial islands was dredged out of the River IJ to increase Amsterdam's shipping facilities in the seventeenth century. By the 1980s, this mosaic of docks, jetties and islands had become something of a post-industrial eyesore, but since then an ambitious redevelopment programme has turned things around and the area is now reckoned to be one of the most up-and-coming in the city. The obvious sight here is the **Nederlands Scheepvaartmuseum** (Netherlands Maritime Museum).

Entrepotdok

At the northern end of Plantage Kerklaan, just beyond the Dutch Resistance Museum, a **footbridge** leads over to **Entrepotdok**, on the nearest, and most interesting, of the Oosterdok islands. On the far side of the bridge old brick **warehouses** stretch right along the quayside, distinguished by their spout gables, multiple doorways and overhead pulleys. Built by the **Dutch East India Company** in the eighteenth century, they were once part of the largest warehouse complex in continental Europe, a gigantic customs-free zone established for goods in transit. On the ground floor, above the main entrance, each warehouse sports the name of a town or island; goods for onward transportation were stored in the appropriate warehouse until there were enough to fill a boat or barge. The warehouses have been tastefully converted into offices and apartments, a fate that must surely befall the central East India Company **compound**, whose chunky Neoclassical entrance is at the west end of Entrepotdok on Kadijksplein. Founded in 1602, the **Dutch East India Company** was the chief pillar of Amsterdam's wealth for nearly two hundred years. Its high-percentage profits came from importing spices into Europe, and to secure them the company's ships ventured far and wide, establishing trading links with India, Sri Lanka, Indo-China, Malaya, China and Japan, though modern-day Indonesia was always the main event. Predictably, the company had a cosy relationship with the merchants who steered the Dutch government: the company was granted a trading monopoly in all the lands east of the Cape of Good Hope and could rely on the warships of the powerful Dutch navy if they got into difficulty. Neither was their business purely mercantile: the East India Company exercised unlimited military, judicial and political powers in those trading posts it established, the first of which was Batavia in Java in 1619. In the 1750s, the Dutch East India Company went into decline, partly because the British expelled them from most of the best trading stations, but mainly because the company over-borrowed. The Dutch government took it over in 1795.

From Kadijksplein, it's a couple of minutes' walk to the Netherlands Maritime Museum.

The Nederlands Scheepvaartmuseum

The **Nederlands Scheepvaartmuseum** (Netherlands Maritime Museum; Tues–Sun 10am–5pm; mid-June to mid-Sept also Mon 10am–5pm; €7) occupies the old arsenal of the Dutch navy, a vast sandstone structure built in the Oosterdok on Kattenburgerplein. It's underpinned by no less than 18,000 wooden piles driven deep into the river bed at enormous expense in the 1650s. The building's four symmetrical facades are dour and imposing despite the odd stylistic flourish, principally some dinky dormer windows and Neoclassical pediments, and they surround a central, cobbled courtyard. It's the perfect location for a Maritime Museum – or at least it would be if the museum's collection, spread over three floors, was larger; in the event the collection seems a little forlorn, rattling around a building that's just too big.

The ground floor displays a flashy gilded barge built for King William I in 1818 and is used to host temporary exhibitions. The next floor up, devoted to shipping in the seventeenth and eighteenth centuries, is the most diverting. It includes garish ships' figureheads, examples of early atlases and navigational equipment, and finely detailed models of the clippers of the East India Company, then the fastest ships in the world. Contemporary shipbuilders tried hard to make the officers' quarters as domestic as possible – literally a home-from-home – and the fancifully carved, seventeenth-century stern which dominates one of the rooms comes complete with a set of dainty mullion windows. There are oodles of nautical paintings too, some devoted to the achievements of Dutch trading ships, others showing heavy seas and shipwrecks and yet more celebrating the successes of the Dutch Navy. Honed by the long and bloody struggle with Habsburg Spain, the Dutch navy was the most powerful fleet in the world for about thirty years – from the 1650s to the 1680s. Commanded by a series of brilliant admirals – principally Tromp and De Ruyter – the Dutch even inflicted several defeats on the British navy, infuriating Charles II by a spectacular raid up the Thames in 1667. **Willem van de Velde II** (1633–1707) was the most successful of the Dutch marine painters of the period and there's a good sample of his work here – canvases that emphasize the strength and power of the Dutch warship, often depicted in battle. The final floor is devoted to the nineteenth and twentieth centuries and, compared with the one below, fails to excite. There is, however, a whole bunch of minutely precise ships' models, including one of the shipyard on the old Zuider Zee island of Urk. Outside, moored at the museum jetty, is a full-scale replica of an East Indiaman, the *Amsterdam*. It's crewed by actors, and another set of nautical thespians will be needed when the 78-metre *Stad Amsterdam* clipper is completed in the next couple of years.

From the Maritime Museum, there's a choice of routes: if you're heading west the Canal Bus (see p.26) will return you to Centraal Station via the NEMO centre, or you can walk back to the station along Prins Hendrikkade (see p.63) in about fifteen minutes. Alternatively, diligent sightseers can venture further east to the De Gooyer windmill (see opposite).

NEMO

Strolling west from the Maritime Museum along the waterfront Prins Hendrikkade, the foreground is dominated by a massive elevated hood that rears up above the entrance to the IJ tunnel. A good part of this hood is occupied by the large and lavish **NEMO** centre (Tues–Sun 10am–5pm, plus Mon 10am–5pm during school holidays, July & Aug; €10) – just follow the signs for the ground-floor entrance. Recently rebranded, this is a (pre-teenage) kids' attraction par excellence, with all sorts of interactive science and technological exhibits spread over six floors; see p.220 for further details.

Pushing on west along Prins Hendrikkade, it's a brief walk to the **Oude Schans** canal and the Old Centre (see p.52).

Museum Werf 't Kromhout and De Gooyer windmill

Heading east from the Maritime Museum along Kattenburgergracht, you soon reach the bridge that spans the Nieuwe Vaart to reach Hoogte Kadijk, where – by the water's edge at no. 147 – you'll find the **Museum Werf 't Kromhout** (☎020/627 6777 for opening times; €4.50), one of the city's few remaining shipyards. In its heyday, the Oosterdok was littered with shipyards like this one. The first major contraction came at the back end of the nineteenth century when steel and steam replaced timber and few of the existing yards were big enough to make the switch successfully. A number struggled on, including this one, by concentrating on the repair and construction of smaller inshore and canal boats. Even so, 't Kromhout almost went bust in 1969 and was only saved by turning into a combination of operating shipyard and tourist attraction, its display area full of old ship engines and shipyard tools.

Continuing east along Hoogte Kadijk from the Kromhout, it's about 500m to **De Gooyer windmill**, standing tall beside a long and slender canal at Funenkade 5. Amsterdam was once dotted with windmills, used for pumping water and grinding corn, and this is one of the few surviving grain mills; its sails still turn on the first Saturday of the month – wind permitting.

5

The Museum Quarter and Vondelpark

During the nineteenth century, **Amsterdam** burst out of its restraining canals, gobbling up the surrounding countryside. These new outlying neighbourhoods are mostly described in Chapter Six, but Amsterdam's leading **museums**, packed into a relatively small area around the edge of Museumplein, deserve their own chapter. The largest of the museums is the **Rijksmuseum**, which occupies a huge late nineteenth-century edifice overlooking the Singelgracht. Possessing an exceptional collection of **Dutch paintings** from the fifteenth to the seventeenth century, it is perhaps best known for its series of paintings by **Rembrandt**. Close by, the **Van Gogh Museum** boasts the finest assortment of Van Gogh paintings in the world, whilst the **Stedelijk Museum** focuses on modern and contemporary art. The three museums together justifiably form one of Amsterdam's biggest pulls.

Museumplein itself, extending south from Stadhouderskade to Van Baerlestraat, is Amsterdam's largest open space, its wide lawns used for a variety of outdoor activities, from visiting circuses to political demonstrations. There's a **war memorial** here too: the group of slim steel blocks about halfway down the Museumplein commemorates the women of the wartime concentration camps, particularly the thousands who died at Ravensbruck. The text on the right reads: "For those women who defied fascism until the bitter end". At the far end of Museumplein is the **Concertgebouw**, the city's most prestigious classical music concert hall, and it's a short walk along Van Baerlestraat to the sprawling greenery of the **Vondelpark**, Amsterdam's loveliest park.

The Rijksmuseum

At the head of Museumplein, but facing onto the Singelgracht, the **Rijksmuseum** (daily 10am–5pm, €9 – but see box on p.100; ⓦwww.rijksmuseum.nl) is an imposing pile, built in an inventive historic style by Petrus Josephus Hubertus **Cuypers**, also the creator of Centraal Station (see p.43), in the early 1880s. The leading Dutch architect of his day, Cuypers (1827–1921) specialized in neo-Gothic churches, but this commission called for something more ambitious; the result is a permutation of the neo-Renaissance style then popular in

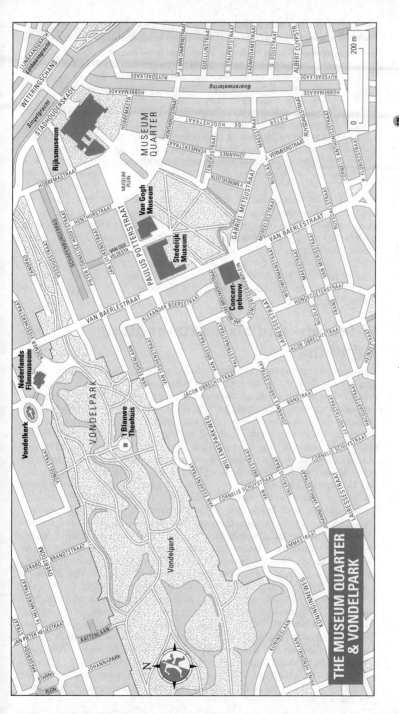

THE MUSEUM QUARTER
& VONDELPARK

Holland, an intricate structure complete with towers and turrets, galleries,
dormer windows and medallions. The museum possesses one of the world's
most comprehensive collections of seventeenth-century **Dutch paintings**,
with twenty or so of **Rembrandt**'s works, plus a healthy sample of canvases by
Steen, Hals, Vermeer and their leading contemporaries. The Rijksmuseum also
owns an extravagant collection of paintings from every other pre-twentieth-
century period of Dutch art and has a vast hoard of applied art and sculpture,
though few if any of these paintings and pieces are likely to appear in the
Philips Wing after December 2003.

Fifteenth- and sixteenth-century paintings

Dating from the fifteenth and sixteenth centuries, the Rijksmuseum's collection of early Flemish – or more properly Netherlandish – paintings, is small but
eclectic. The earliest paintings comprise the highly stylized works of the pre-
Renaissance artists, traditionally known as the "**Flemish Primitives**", whose
preoccupations were exclusively religious. Depicting biblical figures or saints,
these are devotional snapshots, dotted with symbols that provided a readily
understood lexicon for the medieval onlooker. Thus, in the *Madonna
Surrounded by Female Saints*, painted by an unknown artist referred to thereafter
as the **Master of the Virgin Among Virgins**, each of the saints wears a neck-
lace that contains her particular symbol – St Barbara the tower of her impris-
onment; St Catherine the wheel on which she was martyred; the organ of St
Celicia and the wounded heart of St Ursula. However, the most striking paintings in this group are by **Geertgen tot Sint Jans**. His *Holy Kindred*, painted
around 1485, is a skilfully structured portrait of the family of Anna, Mary's
mother, in which the Romanesque nave represents the Old Testament, the
Gothic choir the New. Mary and Joseph are in the foreground and Joseph
holds a lily, emblem of purity, over Mary's head. Behind, on the altar, Abraham
is about to chop off Isaac's head – foreshadowing Jesus's sacrificial death on the
Cross. Geertgen's *Adoration of the Magi* is exquisite too, full of humility and with
an engaging fifteenth-century backdrop of processions, castles and mountains,
while **Jan Mostaert**'s *Tree of Jesse* is crammed with tumbling, dreamlike,
medieval characters. An even clearer picture of the Low Countries in the
Middle Ages appears in *The Seven Works of Charity* by the **Master of Alkmaar**.
Originally hung in St Laurenskerk in the town of Alkmaar (see p.135), each
panel shows the charitable acts expected of those with sufficient piety (and
cash): alms are doled out to the poor with medieval Alkmaar as the backcloth.

Moving on to the sixteenth century, the Rijksmuseum possesses a surprisingly cheeky *Mary Magdalen* by **Jan van Scorel** and a memorable *Carrying of the Cross* by **Quinten Matsys**, long Antwerp's leading painter and a key transitional figure: Matsys was one of the first Netherlandish artists to be influenced by the Italian Renaissance.

The Golden Age

The Rijksmuseum's forte is its collection of paintings from the **Dutch Golden Age**. Included are several wonderful canvases by **Frans Hals**, most notably his expansive *Marriage Portrait of Isaac Massa and Beatrix Laen*. Relaxing beneath a tree, a portly Isaac glows with contentment as his new wife sits beside him in a suitably demure manner. An intimate scene, the painting also carries a detailed iconography: the ivy at Beatrix's feet symbolizes her devotion to her husband, the thistle faithfulness, the vine togetherness and in the fantasy garden behind them the peacock is a classical allusion to Juno, the guardian of marriage. There's also **Dirck van Baburen**'s sensational *Prometheus in Chains* – a work from the Utrecht School, which used the paintings of Caravaggio as its model – and the miniatures of **Hendrick Avercamp**, noted for their folksy and finely detailed skating scenes.

Yet more thoroughly Dutch works are exemplified by the soft, tonal river scenes of the Haarlem artist **Salomon van Ruysdael** and the cool church interiors of **Pieter Saenredam**. In particular, look out for the latter's *Old Town Hall of Amsterdam*, a characteristic work in which the tumbledown predecessor of the current building (now the Royal Palace) witnesses the comings and goings of black-hatted townsmen in the stilted manner of a Lowry. The Rijksmuseum also has in its possession a mixed selection of canvases by some of Rembrandt's better-known pupils, including **Ferdinand Bol**'s *Portrait of Elizabeth Bas*, long thought to be a Rembrandt until the director of the museum proved it otherwise in 1911. Perhaps the most talented of the master's pupils was **Carel Fabritius**, who was killed in 1654 at the age of 32, when Delft's powder magazine exploded. His *Portrait of Abraham Potter*, a restrained, skilful work of soft, delicate hues, contrasts with the same artist's earlier *The Beheading of St John the Baptist*, where the head is served on a platter in piercingly grisly style.

From the latter half of the seventeenth century come **Gerrit Berckheyde**'s crisp depictions of Amsterdam and Haarlem and the carousing peasants of **Jan Steen**. Steen's *Feast of St Nicholas*, with its squabbling children, makes the festival a celebration of disorderly greed, while the drunken waywardness of his *Merry Family* and *The Drunken Couple* verges on the anarchic. Steen knew his bourgeois audience well: his caricatures of the proletariat blend humour with moral condemnation – or at least condescension – a mixture perfectly designed to suit their tastes. Steen was also capable of more subtle works, a famous example being his *Woman at her Toilet*, which is full of associations, referring either to sexual pleasures just had or about to be taken. For example, the woman is shown putting on a stocking in a conspicuous manner, the point being that the Dutch word for stocking, *kous*, is also a slang word for a woman's genitals. By contrast, **Willem van de Velde II**'s preoccupations were nautical, his canvases celebrating either the power of the Dutch navy or the seaworthiness of the merchant marine, as in the churning seas of the superbly executed *Gust of Wind*.

Vermeer is well represented in the museum collection by both *The Love Letter*, which reveals a tension between servant and mistress – the lute on the woman's lap was a well-known sexual symbol – and *The Kitchen Maid*, an exquisitely observed domestic scene, literally right down to the nail – and its shadow – on the background wall. Similarly, in the precise *Young Woman Reading a Letter,* the map behind her hints at the far-flung places her loved one is writing from. **Gerard ter Borch** also depicted innocent scenes, both in subject and title, but his *Woman at a Mirror* glances in a meaningfully anxious manner at her servants, who look on with delicate irony from behind dutiful exteriors; equally, Borch's blandly named *Interior Scene* is set in a brothel. The paintings of **Pieter de Hooch** are less symbolic, more exercises in lighting, but they're as good a visual guide to the everyday life and habits of the seventeenth-century Dutch bourgeoisie as you'll find. So, too, with **Nicholas Maes**, whose caring *Young Woman by the Cradle* is not so much a didactic tableau as an idealization of motherhood.

Rembrandt

Rembrandt's *The Night Watch* of 1642 is the most famous and probably the most valuable of all the artist's pictures. Restored after being slashed in 1975, the painting is of a Militia Company and as such celebrates one of the companies

Rembrandt Harmenszoon van Rijn

Born in Leiden to a family of millers, **Rembrandt Harmenszoon van Rijn** (1606–1669) picked up his first important artistic tips as an apprentice to Pieter Lastman in Amsterdam in the early 1620s. It was here that Rembrandt developed a penchant for mythological and religious subjects, vividly light and rendered with a smooth and glossy finish. After his apprenticeship, in around 1625, Rembrandt went back to Leiden to establish himself as an independent master painter and, this achieved, he returned to Amsterdam some six years later; Rembrandt stayed in Amsterdam for the rest of his life. In the early 1630s Rembrandt concentrated on **portrait painting**, churning out dozens of pictures of the burghers of his day, a profitable business that made him both well-to-do and well known. In 1634 he married **Saskia van Uylenburch** and five years later the couple moved into a smart house on Jodenbreestraat, now the Rembrandthuis museum (see p.87). Things seemed set fair, and certainly Rembrandt's portraits of his wife are tender and loving, but these years were marred by the death of all but one of his children in infancy, the sole survivor being his much loved **Titus** (1641–1668).

In 1642 Rembrandt produced what has become his most celebrated painting, *The Night Watch*, but thereafter his career went into decline, essentially because he forsook portraiture to focus on increasingly sombre and introspective **religious works**. Traditionally, Rembrandt's change of artistic direction has been tied in with the death of Saskia in 1642, but although it is certainly true that Rembrandt was grief-stricken, he was also facing increased competition from a new batch of portrait artists, primarily Ferdinand Bol and Govert Flinck. Whatever the reason, there were few customers for Rembrandt's religious works and he made matters worse by refusing to adjust his spending. The crunch came in 1656, when he was formally declared insolvent, and four years later he was obliged to sell his house and goods, moving to much humbler premises in the Jordaan (see p.78). By this time, he had a new cohabitee, **Hendrickje Stoffels** (a clause in Saskia's will prevented them from ever marrying), and, in the early 1660s, she and Titus took Rembrandt in hand, sorting out his finances and making him their employee. With his money problems solved, a relieved Rembrandt then produced some of his finest paintings, emotionally deep and contemplative works with a rough finish, the paint often daubed almost trowel-like. Hendrickje died in 1663, Titus in 1668, a year before his father.

formed in the sixteenth century to defend the United Provinces against Spain. As the Habsburg threat receded, so the militias became social clubs for the well-heeled, who were eager to commission their own group portraits as signs of their prestige. Rembrandt's *The Night Watch* depicts Amsterdam's **Kloveniersdoelen company**, but the title is actually inaccurate – it got its tag in the eighteenth century when the background darkness was misinterpreted. There were other misconceptions about the painting too, most notably that it was this work that led to the downward shift in Rembrandt's standing with the Amsterdam elite; in fact, there's no evidence that the militia men weren't pleased with the picture, or that Rembrandt's commissions flowed in any more slowly after it was completed.

Though not as subtle as much of the artist's later work, the painting is an adept piece, full of movement and carefully arranged. Paintings of this kind were collections of individual portraits as much as group pictures, and for the artist their difficulty lay in including each single face while simultaneously producing a coherent group scene. Rembrandt opted to show the company preparing to march off, a snapshot of military activity in which banners are unfurled, muskets primed and drums rolled. There are a couple of allegorical figures as well, most prominently a young, spotlit woman who has a bird hanging from her belt, a reference to the Kloveniersdoelen's traditional emblem of a claw. Militia portraits commonly included cameo portraits of the artist involved, but in this case it seems that Rembrandt didn't insert his likeness, though some art historians insist that the pudgy-faced figure peering out from the back between the gesticulating militiamen is indeed the great man himself.

Amongst the other Rembrandts held by the Rijksmuseum is a late *Self-Portrait*, with the artist caught in mid-shrug as the Apostle Paul, a self-aware and defeated old man, and the finely detailed *Portrait of Maria Trip*. There's also his touching depiction of his cowled son, *Titus*, and *The Jewish Bride*, one of his very last pictures, finished in 1667. No one knows who the people are, nor whether they are actually married (the title came later), but the painting is one of Rembrandt's most telling, the paint dashed on freely and the hands touching lovingly, as the art historian and cultural pundit Kenneth Clark wrote, in a "marvellous amalgam of richness, tenderness and trust".

The Van Gogh Museum

Vincent van Gogh (1853–1890) is arguably the most popular, most reproduced and most talked about of all modern artists, so it's not surprising that the **Van Gogh Museum** (daily 10am–6pm; ⓦ www.vangoghmuseum.nl; €7, children 13–17 years €2.50), comprising a fabulous collection of the artist's work, is one of Amsterdam's top attractions. The museum occupies two modern buildings a brief walk west of the Rijksmuseum on the north edge of Museumplein, with the kernel of the collection housed in an angular building designed by a leading light of the De Stijl movement, Gerrit Rietveld, and opened to the public in 1973. Well-conceived and beautifully presented, this part of the museum provides an introduction to the man and his art based on paintings that were mostly inherited from Vincent's art-dealer brother Theo. To the rear of Rietveld's building, and connected by a ground-floor-level escalator, is the ultramodern annexe, an aesthetically controversial structure completed in 1998. The annexe was financed by a Japanese insurance compa-

△ The Rijksmuseum

ny – the same conglomerate who paid $35 million for one of Van Gogh's *Sunflowers* canvases in 1987 – and provides temporary exhibition space. Most of these exhibitions focus on one aspect or another of Van Gogh's art and draw heavily on the permanent collection, which means that the paintings displayed in the older building are regularly rotated. Two paintings you won't see, at least in the foreseeable future, are Van Gogh's *Congregation Leaving the Reformed Church in Nuenen* and *View of the Sea at Scheveningen*, as a robbery recently deprived the museum of both. Even worse was the apparent ease with which the thieves broke in – up a ladder and through a skylight.

The collection

The museum starts on the **ground floor** with a group of works by some of Van Gogh's well-known friends and contemporaries, many of whom influenced his work – Gauguin, Millet, Anton Mauve, Charles Daubigny and others. It then moves on to the works of the man himself, presented for the most part chronologically on the **first floor**. The first paintings go back to the artist's **early years** (1883–1885) in Nuenen, southern Holland, where he was born: dark, sombre works in the main, ranging from an assortment of drab grey and brown still-lifes to the gnarled faces and haunting, flickering light of *The Potato Eaters* – one of Van Gogh's best-known paintings, and the culmination of hundreds of studies of the local peasantry.

Further along, the sobriety of these early works is easily transposed onto the **Parisian** (1886–1888) urban landscape, particularly in the *View of Paris*, where the city's domes and rooftops hover below Montmartre under a glowering, blustery sky. But before long, under the sway of fellow painters and – after the bleak countryside of North Brabant – the sheer colour of the city itself, his approach began to change. This is most noticeable in the views of Montmartre windmills and allotments, a couple of self-portraits, and the pictures from Asnières just outside Paris, where the artist used to travel regularly to paint. In particular, look out for the dazzling movement of *Wheatfield with a Lark* and the disturbing yellows of *Lemons, Pears, Apples, Grapes and an Orange*.

In February 1888 Van Gogh moved to **Arles**, inviting Gauguin to join him a little later. With the change of scenery came a heightened interest in colour, and the predominance of yellow as a recurring motif: it's represented best in such paintings as the *Harvest at La Crau*, and most vividly in the disconcerting juxtapositions of *The Yellow House*. Also from this period comes a striking canvas from the artist's *Sunflowers* series, justly one of his most lauded works, intensely, almost obsessively, rendered in the deepest oranges, golds and ochres he could find. Gauguin told of Van Gogh painting these flowers in a near trance; there were usually sunflowers in jars all over their house.

In 1889 Van Gogh committed himself to the asylum in **St Rémy** after snipping off part of his ear and offering it to a local prostitute. Inside the asylum, his approach to nature became more abstract with trees bent into cruel, sinister shapes and skies coloured purple and yellow, as in the *Garden of St Paul's Hospital*. Van Gogh is at his most expressionistic here, the paint applied thickly, often with a palette knife, especially in the final, tortured paintings done at **Auvers**, where Van Gogh lodged for the last three months of his life. It was at Auvers that he painted the frantic *Ears of Wheat* and *Wheatfield with a Reaper*, in which the fields swirl and writhe under weird, light-green, moving skies. It was a few weeks after completing these last paintings that Van Gogh shot and fatally wounded himself.

The two floors above provide a back-up to the main collection. The **second floor** has a study area with PC access to an excessively detailed computerized account of Van Gogh's life and times, plus a number of sketches and a handful of less familiar paintings. It's here you're likely to find *A Pair of Shoes*, an idiosyncratic painting that used to hang in the house Van Gogh shared with Gauguin in Arles. The **third floor** features more drawings and sketches from the permanent collection as well as notebooks and letters. This floor also affords space to relevant temporary exhibitions illustrating Van Gogh's artistic influences, or his own influence on other artists.

The Stedelijk Museum and Concertgebouw

Amsterdam's number one venue for modern art, the **Stedelijk Museum** (ⓦwww.stedelijk.nl), next door to the Van Gogh Museum, is still at the cutting edge after a hundred years or more. Its permanent collection is wide-ranging and its temporary exhibitions – based both on its own acquisitions and on loaned pieces, and regularly extending to photography and installations – are usually of international standard. It's housed in a grand neo-Renaissance building dating from 1895, but the interior is modern and a new wing was added in the 1950s.

The museum's ground floor has been – and after the refurbishment will probably continue to be – given over to **temporary exhibitions**, often by living European artists. Contemporary Dutch art is a particular favourite, featuring painters such as Jan Dibbets, Rob Scholte and Marlene Dumas. Upstairs, the first floor is expected to stay devoted to the museum's **permanent collection**. Broadly speaking, this starts off with drawings by Picasso, Matisse and their contemporaries, and moves on to paintings by Manet, Monet, Bonnard, Ensor and Cézanne. Mondriaan is well represented too, holding sway among the De Stijl group, from his early, muddy-coloured abstractions to the cool, boldly coloured rectangular blocks for which he's most famous. The museum also has a goodly sample of the work of Kasimir Malevich, his dense attempts at Cubism leading to the dynamism and bold, primary tones of his "Suprematist" paintings – slices, blocks and bolts of colour that shift around as if about to resolve themselves into some complex computer graphic. Other highlights of the Stedelijk's wide collection include several Marc Chagall paintings, and a number of pictures by American Abstract Expressionists Mark Rothko, Ellsworth Kelly and Barnett Newman, plus the odd work by Lichtenstein, Warhol, Jean Dubuffet and Matisse's large cutout, *The Parakeet and the Mermaid*.

Stedelijk Museum renovations

From January 2003 to late 2005 the Stedelijk Museum will be closed for **refurbishment** – and its permanent collection dispersed to other city museums including the Nieuwe Kerk (see p.47).

The Concertgebouw

Across Van Baerlestraat just to the south of the Stedelijk Museum is the **Concertgebouw** (Concert Hall), home of the famed – and much recorded – Royal Concertgebouw Orchestra. When the German composer Brahms visited Amsterdam in the 1870s he was scathing about the locals' lack of culture and, in particular, their lack of an even halfway suitable venue for his music. In the face of such ridicule, a consortium of Amsterdam businessmen got together to fund the construction of a brand-new concert hall and the result was the Concertgebouw, completed in 1888. An attractive structure with a pleasingly grand Neoclassical facade, the Concertgebouw has become renowned among musicians and concertgoers for its marvellous acoustics, though it did have to undergo major repairs when it was discovered that the wooden piles on which it rested were rotting away. The overhaul included the addition of a new, largely glass gallery that contrasts nicely with the red brick and stone of the rest of the building. Although the Concertgebouw attracts the world's best orchestras and musicians, ticket prices can be surprisingly inexpensive – the venue operates an arts-for-all policy – and from September to May there are often free walk-in concerts at lunchtime. For more on Concertgebouw tickets and performances, see p.185.

The Vondelpark and around

Amsterdam is short of green spaces, which makes the leafy expanses of the **Vondelpark**, a short stretch from Museumplein, doubly welcome. This is easily the largest and most popular of the city's parks, its network of footpaths used by a healthy slice of the city's population. The park dates back to 1864, when a group of leading Amsterdammers clubbed together to transform the soggy marshland that lay beyond the Leidsepoort into a landscaped park. The group, who were impressed by the contemporary English fashion for natural (as distinct from formal) landscaping, gave the task of developing the new style of park to the Zocher family, big-time gardeners who set about their task with gusto, completing their work in 1865. Named after the seventeenth-century poet Joost van den **Vondel** (see p.48), the park proved an immediate success and was expanded to its present size (45 hectares) in 1877. It now possesses over 100 species of tree, a wide variety of local and imported plants, and – amongst many incidental features – a **bandstand** and excellent **rose garden**. Neither did the Zochers forget their Dutch roots: the park is latticed with ponds and narrow waterways, home to many sorts of wildfowl. There are other animals too: cows, sheep, hundreds of squirrels, plus, bizarrely enough, a large colony of bright-green parakeets. The Vondelpark has several different children's **play areas** and during the summer regularly hosts free **concerts** and theatrical performances, mostly in its own specially designed open-air theatre.

The Nederlands Filmmuseum and Vondelkerk

Housed in a glum, nineteenth-century building near the northeast corner of the Vondelpark is the **Nederlands Filmmuseum** (Netherlands Film Museum; box office Mon–Fri 9am–10pm, Sat & Sun 1–10pm; ☎020/589

1400, ⓦ www.filmmuseum.nl). It's really more an arthouse cinema (with two screens) than a museum, a showcase for avant-garde films – most of which are shown in their original language, plus subtitles in Dutch (and occasionally English). There are several screenings nightly, plus a matinée on Wednesday afternoons, and the programme often follows a prescribed theme or subject. Look out for news of the free screenings of classic movies on Saturday nights in summer. Metres away, at Vondelstraat 69, the museum's film **library** (Tues–Fri 10am–5pm, Sat 11am–5pm) has a well-catalogued collection of books, magazines and journals, some in English, though they are for reference only and are not loaned out.

Across the street is the lugubrious brown brick hull and whopping spire of the **Vondelkerk**, which has had more than its share of bad luck. Work on the church, which was designed by Cuypers – the architect of Centraal Station and the Rijksmuseum – began in 1872, but the finances ran out the following year and the building was not completed until the 1880s. Twenty years later it was struck by lightning and in the ensuing fire its tower was burnt to a cinder – the present one was added much later. The church always struggled to find a decent-size congregation, but limped on until it was finally deconsecrated in 1979, being turned into offices thereafter.

6

The outer districts

A msterdam is a small city, and the majority of its residential **outer districts** are easily reached from the city centre. The **south** holds most interest, kicking off with the raucous **De Pijp** quarter, home to the Heineken Experience, sited in the company's old brewery, and the 1930s architecture of the **Nieuw Zuid** (New South), which also contains the

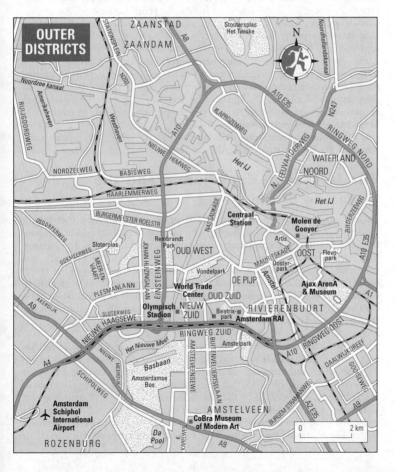

109

enjoyable woodland area of the **Amsterdamse Bos**. As for the other districts, you'll find a good deal less reason to make the effort. Multicultural influences in the **east** give this part of the city some diversity, and this is also the location of the Tropenmuseum, but otherwise it's of little appeal, and the **west** has nothing special at all. Finally, Amsterdam **Noord (north)**, across the IJ, is entirely residential and only relevant if you're cycling through it on the way to open country; the "highlight" of a visit is the short (free) ferry ride there from behind Centraal Station.

De Pijp

Across Boerenwetering, the canal to the east of Museumplein (see p.98), away from the money, lies the busy heart of the Oud Zuid (Old South) – the district known as **De Pijp** ("The Pipe"), Amsterdam's first suburb. New development beyond the Singelgracht began around 1870, but after laying down the street plans, the city council left the actual house-building to private developers. They made the most of the arrangement and constructed long rows of cheaply built and largely featureless five- and six-storey buildings and it is these which still dominate the area today. The district's name comes from the characteristically narrow terraced streets running between long, sombre canyons of brick tenements: the apartments here were said to resemble pipe-drawers, since each had a tiny street frontage but extended deep into the building. De Pijp remains one of the city's more closely knit communities, and is home to a large proportion of new immigrants – Surinamese, Moroccan, Turkish and Asian.

As for public transport, **tram #25**, beginning at Centraal Station, travels the length of De Pijp's main drag, Ferdinand Bolstraat.

The Heineken Experience and the Wetering circuit

On the northern edge of De Pijp, the former Heineken brewery, a whopping modern building beside the Singelgracht canal at Stadhouderskade 78, now holds the **Heineken Experience** (Tues–Sun 10am–6pm; €7.50). The brewery was Heineken's headquarters from 1864 to 1988, when the company was restructured and brewing was moved to a more efficient location out of town. Since then, Heineken has developed the site as a tourist attraction with displays on the history of beer-making in general and Heineken in particular. The old brewing facilities are included on the tour, but for many the main draw is the **free beer**, though the days when you could quaff unlimited quantities are long gone.

Just across the canal from the brewery, the **Wetering circuit** roundabout has two low-key **memorials** to World War II. On the southwestern corner of the roundabout, by the canal, is a sculpture of a wounded man holding a bugle: it was here, on March 12, 1945, that thirty people were shot by the Germans in reprisal for acts of sabotage by the Dutch Resistance – given that the war was all but over, it's hard to imagine a crueller or more futile action. Across the main street, the second memorial commemorates H.M. van Randwijk, a Resistance leader. The restrained wording on the monument translates as:

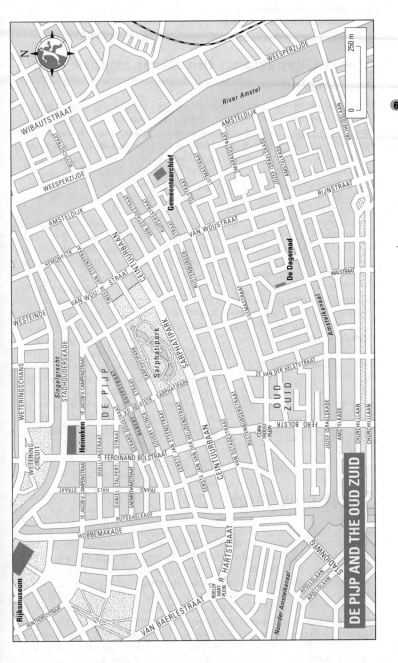

DE PIJP AND THE OUD ZUID

N

250 m

0

River Amstel

WEESPERZIJDE

WIBAUTSTRAAT

RUYSCHSTRAAT

AMSTELDIJK

WEESPERZIJDE

AMSTELDIJK

HEMONY STR

WESTEINDE

WETERINGSCHANS

Singelgracht

STADHOUDERSKADE

WETERING
CIRCUIT

Rijksmuseum

HONTHORSTSTRAAT

Heineken

DE PIJP

1E JACOB V CAMPENSTRAAT

QUELLIJNSTRAAT

HALS-   STRAAT

DANIEL STALPERT-STRAAT

SAENREDAMSTRAAT

FRANS-

RUYSDAELKADE

HOBBEMAKADE

1E JACOB V CAMPENSTRAAT

GERARD DOUSTRAAT

ALBERT   VD HELSSTR

GOVERT FLINCK   STRAAT

FERDINAND BOLSTRAAT

VAN WOU   STRAAT

TWEEDE JAN STEENSTRAAT

GUYPSTRAAT

EERSTE JAN STEENSTRAAT

GOVERT FLINCKSTRAAT

VAN DER HELDENSTRAAT

EERSTE JAN VAN DER HELDENSTRAAT

VAN OSTADESTRAAT

CEINTUURBAAN

RUSTENBURGERSTRAAT

2E VAN DER HELSTSTRAAT

CEINTUURBAAN

Sarphatipark

SARPHATIPARK

Sarphatipark

RUSTENBURGER

UTLMASTRAAT

Gemeentearchief

VAN OSTADESTRAAT

KUIPERSTRAAT

TOLSTRAAT

VAN WOUSTRAAT

De Dageraad

WALSTRAAT

AMSTELDIJK

SMARAGDSTRAAT

UITMASTRAAT

JOZEF ISRAELSKADE

AMSTELKADE

RIJNSTRAAT

Amstelkanaal

OUD
ZUID

FERD BOLSTR

CORN
TROOST
PLEIN

JOZEF ISRAELSKADE

AMSTELKADE

CHURCHILLAAN

CHURCHILLAAN

VRIJHEIDSLAAN

R. HARTSTRAAT

ROELOF
HART
PLEIN

VAN BAERLESTRAAT

Noorder Amstelkanaal

STADIONWEG

APOLLOLAAN

APOLLOLAAN

When to the will of tyrants,
A nation's head is bowed,
It loses more than life and goods –
Its very light goes out.

Albert Cuypstraat, the Sarphatipark and around

Ferdinand Bolstraat, running north–south, is De Pijp's main street, but the long, slim east–west thoroughfare of **Albert Cuypstraat** (pronounced "cowpstraat") is its heart. The daily general **market** held here – which stretches for over a kilometre between Ferdinand Bolstraat and Van Woustraat – is the largest in the city, with a huge array of stalls selling everything from cut-price carrots and raw-herring sandwiches to saucepans and day-glo thongs. Check out, too, the bargain-basement and ethnic shops that flank the market on each side, and the Indian and Surinamese restaurants down the side streets – they're often cheaper than their equivalents in the city centre.

A couple of blocks south of the Albert Cuypstraat market is the leafy **Sarphatipark**, a welcome splash of greenery amongst the surrounding brick and concrete. The park, complete with footpaths and a sinewy lake, was laid out before the construction of De Pijp got underway, and was initially intended as a place for the bourgeoisie to take a picnic.

Heading east from the Sarphatipark, the main **Ceintuurbaan** artery crosses **Van Woustraat** – a long, unremarkable shopping street, though with a number of speciality ethnic food shops – before it reaches the River Amstel. At the river, turn right along Amsteldijk for the short walk south to the **Gemeentearchief** (Municipal Archives; daily 11am–5pm during exhibitions, otherwise Mon–Fri 10am–5pm; ☎020/572 0202; free), on the corner with Tolstraat. Housed in a large and flashy neo-Gothic confection built as the district's town hall in 1895, the archives provide extensive research facilities: all births, marriages and deaths from the early sixteenth century onwards are on record here, and there's also an enormous collection of newspapers, posters, plans and documents. Of more general interest, however, are the temporary exhibitions on the city's past that are held here regularly.

The Nieuw Zuid

Southwest of De Pijp and the Oud Zuid, the **Nieuw Zuid** (New South) encompasses the whole area south of the Noorder Amstel canal to the railway tracks, as well as the old Rivierenbuurt district wedged in between the railway track, the River Amstel and the Amstel canal. By contrast with the Oud Zuid, this was the first properly planned extension to the city since the concentric canals of the seventeenth century. The Dutch architect Hendrik Petrus Berlage (1856–1934) was responsible for the overall plan, but much of the implementation passed to a pair of prominent architects of the Amsterdam School, **Michael de Klerk** (1884–1923) and **Piet Kramer** (1881–1961). By the 1890s, Berlage had broken away from the historicism that had dominated nineteenth-century Dutch architecture, opting instead for a chunky Expressionism, but after his death his two successors departed from Berlage's sobriety altogether, in preference for the playful touches – turrets and bulging windows, sloping roofs and frilly balustrades – that you see in the buildings of the Nieuw Zuid today. Neither was this architectural virtuosity confined to the houses of the well-to-do. In 1901 a reforming Housing Act forced the city council into a concerted effort to clear Amsterdam's slums, a principal result being several quality public housing projects designed by De Klerk and Kramer. There's one extant example in the Westerdok (see p.82) and another here in the Nieuw Zuid, **De Dageraad**, though neither is as fanciful as the duo's phantasmagorical Scheepvaarthuis (see p.53). Cutbacks in the city's subsidy meant that the more imaginative aspects of Berlage's original scheme for the Nieuw Zuid were toned down, but the area's wide boulevards and narrower side streets were completed as conceived. In this, Berlage wanted to reinterpret the most lauded feature of the city's seventeenth-century canals: their combination of monumental grandeur and picturesque scale.

Nowadays the Nieuw Zuid is one of Amsterdam's most sought-after addresses. **Apollolaan**, **Stadionweg** and, a little way to the east, **Churchilllaan** are especially favoured and home to some of the city's most sumptuous properties – huge idiosyncratic mansions set back from the street behind trees and generous gardens. Locals pop to the shops on **Beethovenstraat**, the main drag running south right through the district from the Noorder Amstel canal. Nonetheless, posh residential areas are rarely much fun for the casual visitor and the Nieuw Zuid is no exception. More enticing is the languid greenery of the **Beatrixpark**, and, slightly further out beyond the railway tracks, the sprawling parkland of the **Amsterdamse Bos** – both providing a pleasant interlude from the network of suburban streets.

Apollolaan and around

Apollolaan, a wide residential boulevard just south of the Noorder Amstel canal, is representative of Berlage's intended grand design, but despite its obvious gracefulness, the Nieuw Zuid was far from an instant success with the native Dutch bourgeoisie. Indeed, in the late 1930s the district became something of a Jewish enclave – the family of Anne Frank, for example, lived on Merwedeplein just off Churchilllaan. This embryonic community was swept away during the German occupation, their sufferings retold in Grete Weil's (Dutch-language) novel *Tramhalte Beethovenstraat*. A reminder of those terrible times is to be found at the intersection of Apollolaan and Beethovenstraat, where a **monument** commemorates the reprisal shooting of 29 people here in 1944. Another reminder is the **school** just off Apollolaan on Rubenstraat – itself named after an Amsterdam Resistance fighter who was shot for organizing false identity papers – which was once the headquarters of the Gestapo, and where the Frank family were brought after their capture.

On a different note, Apollolaan is also known for the **Amsterdam Hilton** at no. 138, where John Lennon and Yoko Ono staged their famous week-long "Bed-In" for peace in 1969. Part celebrity farce, part skilful publicity stunt, the couple's anti-war proclamations were certainly heard far and wide, but in Britain the press focused on the supposed evil influence of Yoko on John, which satisfied at least three subtexts – racism, sexism and anti-Americanism.

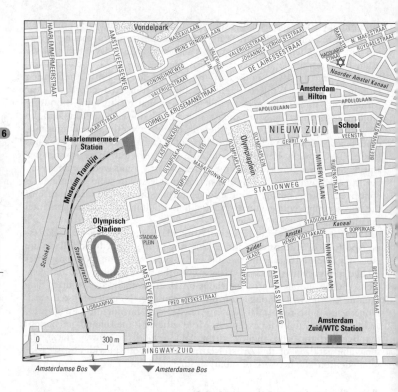

Amsterdamse Bos ▼   ▼ Amsterdamse Bos

Beatrixpark to De Dageraad

From Apollolaan, head south down **Beethovenstraat**, and beyond the Amstel canal, take the first left, Cornelius Dopperkade, for the nearest of several entrances into the **Beatrixpark** (daily dawn to dusk; free). Recently renovated, this appealing park, with its footpaths and walled garden, is latticed by narrow waterways fed by the Amstel canal. It's a pleasant place for a stroll and in summer you can catch free open-air concerts. The park's eastern perimeter is marked by the Boeren Wetering canal, beyond which rises the clumpy **RAI exhibition centre**, a trade and conference complex that was built as part of the city's plan to attract more business trade. It's of little general interest, but if you're at a loose end, you might want to check out one of the centre's many exhibitions. To get there, leave the Beatrixpark at Boerenweteringpad and then follow Wielingenstraat across the canal.

A rather more appealing option is to take a left off Wielingenstraat up Haringvlietstraat, which leads – after about 350m – to the west end of **Churchillaan**. This wide and well-heeled boulevard leads, in its turn, to Waalstraat, which, after crossing the Amstel canal, becomes Pieter Lodewijk Takstraat, a short narrow street that is home to **De Dageraad** ("The Dawn") housing project, completed in 1923 and one of the most successful examples of the Amsterdam School of architecture. Architects De Klerk and Kramer used a

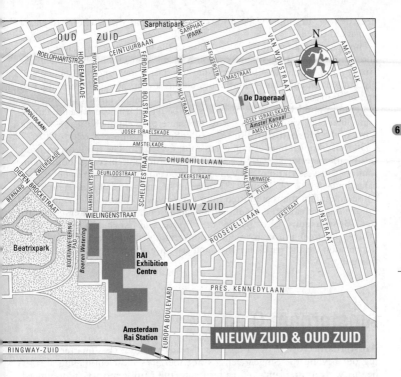

reinforced concrete frame as an underlay to the structure, thus permitting folds, tucks and curves in the brick exterior – a technique known as "apron architecture" (*Schortjesarchitectuur*). The facades are punctuated by strong, angular doors, sloping roofs and turrets, and you'll find a corner tower at the end of every block.

From De Dageraad, you can either walk up to the Albert Cuypstraat market (see p.112), about 800m away to the north, or return to the Churchilllaan to catch tram #12 northwest to the Concertgebouw, and then tram #16 heading west to the Haarlemmermeer Station – for the Amsterdamse Bos.

The Amsterdamse Bos

With eight square kilometres of wooded parkland, the **Amsterdamse Bos** (Amsterdam Forest) is the city's largest open space. Planted during the 1930s, the park was a laudable, large-scale attempt to provide gainful work for the city's unemployed, whose numbers had risen alarmingly following the Wall Street Crash of 1929. Originally a bleak area of flat, marshy fields, it combines a rural feel with that of a well-tended city park – the "forest" tag is something of a misnomer. In the north of the park, the **Bosbaan** is a kilometre-long dead-straight canal, popular for boating and swimming, and there are children's playgrounds and spaces for various sports, including ice skating. There's also a reserve in the south containing bison, buffalo and deer, or you can simply walk or jog your way around a wide choice of clearly marked trails.

The main **entrance** to the Bos is close to the junction of Amstelveenseweg and Van Nijenrodeweg, some 3km south of the west end of the Vondelpark. **Buses** #170, #171 and #172, departing Centraal Station and the Leidseplein, ply Amstelveenseweg and from the nearest bus stop it's about 350m to the east end of Bosbaan, where you can rent a **bike** (March–Oct), much the best way of getting around. Canoes and pedaloes can be rented here too. It's a little more convoluted, but you can also get to this same park entrance on the vintage trams of the **Museumtramlijn** (May–Oct Sun 10.30am–5pm, call ☎020/673 7538 for additional high-season excursions; €3 return). The trams depart from the Haarlemmermeer Station, located beside Amstelveenseweg, about 600m south of the western tip of the Vondelpark. To get to Haarlemmermeer Station, catch buses #170, #171 and #172 or trams #6 and #16 from the centre. The Museumtramlijn trams, imported from as far away as Vienna and Prague, clank south along the eastern edge of the Bos and beyond. The **Bezoekerscentrum het Bosmuseum**, also beside the Bosbaan at Koenenkade 56 (daily 10am–5pm; free), is a visitor information centre that provides maps and basic information on the park's facilities, and has an exhibition on its history and function.

Amsterdam Oost

Amsterdam Oost (East), a rough-and-ready working-class quarter stretching out beyond the Singelgracht, is not the city's most enthralling area. It begins with Amsterdam's old eastern gate, the **Muiderpoort** (pronounced "mao-der-port"), overlooking the canal at the end of Plantage Middenlaan. In the 1770s the gate was revamped in pompous style, a Neoclassical refit complete with a flashy cupola and grandiosely carved pediment. Napoleon staged a triumphal entry into the city through the Muiderpoort in 1811, but his imperial pleasure was tempered by his half-starved troops, who could

barely be restrained from helping themselves in a city of (what was to them) amazing luxury. Despite its general lack of appeal the Oost district does have one obvious attraction – the **Tropenmuseum**, near the Muiderpoort and perched on the corner of another of the city's municipal parks, the **Oosterpark**.

The Tropenmuseum

Across the Singelgracht canal on Mauritskade rises the gabled and turreted **Royal Tropen Instituut** – formerly the Royal Colonial Institute – a sprawling complex which contains the **KIT Tropenmuseum** (Museum of the Tropics; daily 10am–5pm; €6.80, 6- to 17-year-olds €3.40; Ⓦwww .tropenmuseum.nl; tram #9 from Centraal Station), whose entrance is round the side at Linnaeusstraat 2. With its cavernous central hall and three floors of gallery space, the museum has room to focus on all the world's tropical and subtropical zones and impresses with its applied art. Amongst many artefacts, there are Javanese stone friezes, elaborate carved wooden boats from the Pacific, a whole room of masks and, perhaps strangest of all, ritual totem poles cut from giant New Guinea mangroves. The collection is imaginatively presented through a variety of media – slides, videos and sound recordings – and there are creative and engaging displays devoted to such subjects as music-making and puppetry, as well as traditional story-telling. There are also reconstructions, down to sounds and smells, of typical streets in India, China or Africa, plus candid expositions on the problems besetting the developing world, both urban – the ever-expanding slum dwellings of cities like Bombay – and rural, examining such issues as the destruction of the world's tropical rainforests. The permanent collection is enhanced by an ambitious programme of temporary exhibitions.

While you're here, be sure to look in on the **bookshop**, which has a good selection of titles on the developing world, and try the inexpensive **restaurant**, the *Ekeko*, which serves tropical snacks and lunches. Downstairs, the **Tropen Instituut Theater** specializes in Third World cinema, music and dance. Part of the Tropenmuseum is also geared up for children under the age of 12. This section, the **Kindermuseum** (Children's Museum), takes a hands-on approach to the same themes as the main museum but operates restricted opening hours (see p.220).

The Oosterpark and beyond

Behind the Royal Tropen Instituut, the manicured greenery of the **Oosterpark** is a pleasant introduction to the massed housing that extends south and east. A working-class district for the most part, particularly on the far side of Linnaeusstraat, the area also has a high immigrant presence, and the street names – Javastraat, Balistraat, Borneostraat – recall Holland's colonial past. This is one of the city's poorer neighbourhoods, with a sea of ageing terraced houses, though whole streets have been torn down to make way for new and better public housing. One of the few reasons to venture out this way is the **Dapperstraat market** (Mon–Sat 9am–5pm), one block east of Linnaeusstraat. This eastern equivalent to the Albert Cuypstraat market (see p.112) is a diverse affair, where you can pick up a quarter-kilo of Edam at one stall and a fragrant Vietnamese *loempia* at the next.

A second specific attraction, slightly further east, is the recently refurbished **Nederlands Persmuseum** (Dutch Press Museum; Tues–Fri 10am–5pm & Sun noon–5pm; €3.50), housed in the International Institute for Social

History at Zeeburgerkade 10. This tidy museum focuses on the history of the Dutch press since 1618, as revealed in newspapers, leaflets, posters and political cartoons. The collection of the institute itself holds original letters and writings from many of the leading figures of the left including Marx, Lenin and Bakunin. To get there, take tram #7 or #10 (from Leidseplein) to Javaplein, then proceed north along Molukkenstraat over the canal onto Veelaan and keep straight – altogether a 600-metre walk.

Amsterdam West

Of all Amsterdam's outer districts, **Amsterdam West** is probably the least interesting for the visitor, as it's primarily a residential area with only a couple of minor parks as possible attractions. That said, the **Oud West** (Old West), beyond the Singelgracht and north of the Vondelpark, does have a busy Turkish and North African street life, which is seen at its most vigorous at the daily **Katestraat market**, about halfway down **Kinkerstraat** (trams #7 and #17). Beyond, in the **Nieuw West** (New West) districts of Bos en Lommer, De Baarsjes and Overtoomse Veld, the best you'll do is the large but really rather ordinary **Rembrandtpark**.

Amsterdam Noord

Solidly residential, **Amsterdam Noord** (North), on the far side of the River IJ, has flourished since the construction of the IJ tunnel linked it with the city centre in the 1960s. A modern suburban sprawl, the district is short on charm, but the determined can weather the aesthetic gloom to reach the open countryside beyond. The area to head for is the **Waterland**, an expanse of peat meadows, lakes, polders and marshland to the northeast of the built-up area. Until the turn of the twentieth century, this parcel of land was a marshy fen, whose scattered population made a healthy living raising and grazing cattle to be sold in Amsterdam. The Waterland was then made much more tractable by the digging of drainage canals, prompting wealthy Amsterdammers to build their summer residences here. These myriad waterways still pattern the Waterland and are home to a wide range of **waterfowl**, as are the many lakes, the largest of which – abutting the Markermeer, formerly part of the Zuider Zee (see p.131) – is the **Kinselmeer**.

Easily the best way to explore the Waterland is by **bike** and the VVV sells a Waterland leaflet, which outlines a circular, 38-kilometre bike tour. The recommended route begins at the **Adelaarswegveer ferry dock** on the north side of the IJ, from where you follow Meeuwenlaan to the large roundabout at the start of Nieuwendammerdijk. This long thin lane leads east, running parallel to the river, before it meets Schellingwoudedijk and then Durger Dammerdijk at the southern tip of the long dike that stretches up the coast, with the polders and a scattering of tiny villages just inland.

GVB operates two **ferries** across the IJ from behind Centraal Station. Neither ferry (*veer*) takes cars but both carry foot passengers, bicycles and motorbikes for free. Of the two, the **Buiksloterwegveer** (Mon–Sat

6.30am–10.30pm, till 9pm from Buiksloterweg, Sun 11am–6.30pm) – like a huge mobile air-traffic control tower – shuttles back and forth every ten minutes or so, running to the foot of Buiksloterweg. The smaller **Adelaarswegveer** (Mon–Sat 6.20am–11.30pm, Sun 9am–11.30pm) connects with the southern end of Meeuwenlaan, the starting point of the Waterland bike tour; it runs every ten to fifteen minutes.

Day-trips
from the city

Although Amsterdammers may try to persuade you that there's nothing remotely worth seeing outside their own city, the truth is very much the opposite – indeed, you're spoilt for choice. Fast and efficient, the Dutch railway network puts a whole swathe of the Netherlands within easy reach, including all of the **Randstad**, a sprawling conurbation that stretches south and east of Amsterdam and encompasses the country's other big cities, The Hague, Utrecht and Rotterdam. Close to Amsterdam, amidst this urban pile-up, is one delightful medium-sized town – **Haarlem**, whose attractive centre is home to the outstanding Frans Hals Museum. Not only that but Haarlem is also the briefest of train rides from the wide sandy beaches of **Zandvoort**, one of Holland's most popular resorts, and just 13km from the showcase of the country's flower growers, the **Keukenhof gardens**.

To the north of Amsterdam, there's more countryside and less city. The most obvious targets are the old seaports bordering the freshwater **Markermeer**, which forms part of the Ijsselmeer, created when the Afsluitdijk dam cut the former Zuider Zee off from the North Sea in 1932 (see box on p.131). No trains venture out along this coast, but it's an easy bus ride from Amsterdam to the nearest three: the former fishing village of **Marken**, the port of **Volendam** and – best of the lot – the beguiling, one-time shipbuilding centre of **Edam**. Edam is, of course, famous for its cheese, but its open-air **cheese market** is not a patch on that of **Alkmaar**, itself an amiable small town forty minutes by train north from Amsterdam. On the way, most trains pause at **Koog-Zaandijk**, the

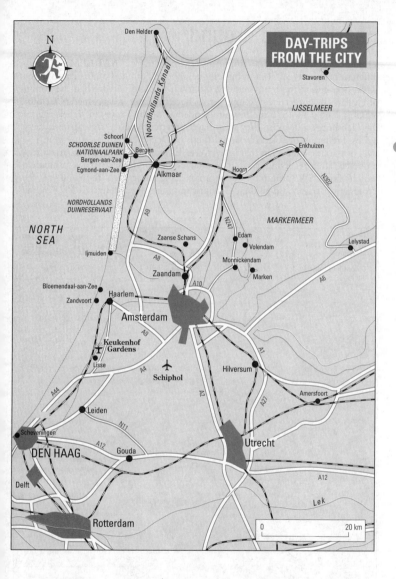

nearest station to the windmills and canals of the recreated Dutch village of
Zaanse Schans, which illustrates rural life as it was in the eighteenth century.
Alkmaar is also within easy striking distance of two pleasant seaside resorts –
Bergen-aan-Zee and **Egmond-aan-Zee** – and the pristine dunes, woods
and beaches of two protected areas, the **Schoorlse Duinen Nationaalpark**
and the **Noordhollands Duinreservaat**.

Public transport to all these destinations from Amsterdam is fast, frequent
and inexpensive.

Haarlem and around

Though only fifteen minutes from Amsterdam by train, **HAARLEM** has a very different pace and feel from its big-city neighbour. Founded on the banks of the River Spaarne in the tenth century, the town first prospered when the counts of Holland decided to levy shipping tolls here, but later it developed as a cloth-making centre. In 1572 the townsfolk sided with the Protestant rebels against the Habsburgs, a decision they must have regretted when a large Spanish army led by Frederick of Toledo besieged them in December of the same year. The siege was a desperate affair that lasted for eight months, but finally the town surrendered after receiving various assurances of good treatment – assurances which Frederick promptly broke, massacring over two thousand of the Protestant garrison and all their Calvinist ministers. Recaptured in 1577 by the

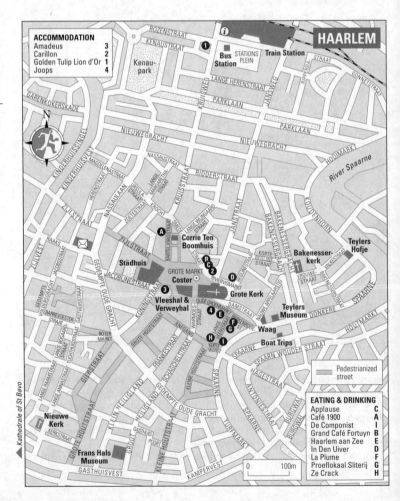

HAARLEM

ACCOMMODATION
Amadeus	3
Carillon	2
Golden Tulip Lion d'Or	1
Joops	4

EATING & DRINKING
Applause	C
Café 1900	A
De Componist	I
Grand Café Fortuyn	B
Haarlem aan Zee	E
In Den Uiver	D
La Plume	F
Proeflokaal Sliterij	G
Ze Crack	H

Pedestrianized street

0   100m

Corrie Ten Boomhuis · Stadhuis · Grote Markt · Coster · Vleeshal & Verweyhal · Grote Kerk · Teylers Museum · Waag · Boat Trips · Bakenesserkerk · Teylers Hofje · Kathedrale of St Bavo · Nieuwe Kerk · Frans Hals Museum

Protestant army of William the Silent, Haarlem went on to enjoy its greatest prosperity in the seventeenth century, becoming a centre for the arts and home to a flourishing school of **painters**. Nowadays, it's an easily absorbed town of around 150,000 people, with a good-looking centre studded with fine old buildings and home to the outstanding **Frans Hals Museum**, located in the almshouse where the artist spent his last, and for some his most brilliant, years.

Well worth an afternoon in itself – maybe even an overnight stay if you're tired of the crowds and grime of Amsterdam – Haarlem is also a short train ride from two coastal resorts: the clumpy modern town of **Zandvoort-aan-Zee**, which is redeemed by its long sandy beach, and **Bloemendaal-aan-Zee**, where the beach is the main event. Both are within easy striking distance of the undeveloped dunes and seashore of the nearby **Nationaalpark de Kennemerduinen**.

The Town

At the heart of Haarlem is the **Grote Markt**, a wide and attractive open space flanked by an appealing ensemble of Gothic and Renaissance architecture, including an intriguing if exceptionally garbled **Stadhuis**, whose turrets and towers, balconies and galleries were put together in piecemeal fashion between the fourteenth and the seventeenth centuries. At the other end of the Grote Markt stands a **statue** of a certain Laurens Coster (1370–1440), who, Haarlemmers insist, is the true inventor of printing. Legend tells of him cutting a letter "A" from the bark of a tree, dropping it into the sand by accident, and, hey presto, he realised how to create the printed word. The statue shows him holding the wooden letter up very earnestly, but most historians agree that it was actually the German Johannes Gutenberg who invented printing, in the early 1440s.

The Grote Kerk

The statue stands in the shadow of the **Grote Kerk** or **Sint Bavokerk** (Mon–Sat 10am–4pm, Sept–March till 3.30pm; €2), a mighty Gothic structure supported by heavy buttresses. The church is surmounted by a good-looking lantern tower directly above the transept crossing, which is actually made of wood, but clad in lead – the original stone version had to be dismantled when, in 1514, it proved too heavy for its supports and was about to crash down. Finally finished in 1538, after 150 years, the church dwarfs the surrounding clutter of higgledy-piggledy streets, and serves as a landmark from almost anywhere in town. Interestingly enough, if you've been to the Rijksmuseum in Amsterdam (see p.98), the Grote Kerk may seem familiar, at least from the outside, since it turns up in several paintings of Haarlem by the seventeenth-century artist Gerrit Berckheyde – only the black-coated burghers are missing.

The **interior** is breathtakingly cavernous, its beauty enhanced by the stark, white power of the vaulting. The present **entrance** (round the back on Oude Groenmarkt) leads into the east end of the church, where the southern ambulatory contains the **tombstone** of the painter Pieter Saenredam and the choir that of Frans Hals. Nearby, next to the south transept, is the **Brewers' Chapel**, where the central pillar bears two black marks – one showing the height of a local giant, the 2.64m-tall Daniel Cajanus, who died in 1749, the other the 0.84m-high dwarf Simon Paap from Zandvoort. Further west still, on the north side of the nave, is the **Dog Whippers' Chapel**, built for the men employed to keep dogs out of the church, and now separated from the nave by an iron grille. At the west end of the church, the mighty Christian Müller **organ** was four years in the making, completed in Amsterdam in 1738. It is

△ Working windmills at Zaanse Schans

said to have been played by Handel and Mozart (the latter on his tour of the country in 1766, at the age of 10) and is one of the biggest in the world, with over five thousand pipes and loads of snazzy Baroque embellishment. Hear it at work at one of the free organ recitals held in the summer (mid-May to mid-Sept Tues 8.15pm, July & Aug also Thurs 3pm; free). Beneath the organ, Jan Baptist Xavery's lovely group of draped marble figures represent Poetry and Music offering thanks to the town, which is depicted as a patroness of the arts – in return for its generous support in the purchase of the organ.

The Vleeshal, Verweyhal and Corrie Ten Boomhuis

Back outside, just beyond the western end of the church, the old meat market, the **Vleeshal**, boasts a flashy Dutch Renaissance facade and its basement is given over to a modest **Archeologisch Museum** (Wed–Sun 1–5pm; free). A couple of doors along, the **Verweyhal** (Tues–Sat 11am–5pm, Sun noon–5pm; €4) features temporary exhibitions of modern art, with special attention given to the local artist Kees Verwey (1900–1995). From the Grote Markt, it's a couple of minutes' walk north to **Corrie Ten Boomhuis**, Barteljorisstraat 19 (Tues–Sat: May–Oct 10am–4pm; Nov–April 11am–3pm; 45min guided tours only; free), where a Dutch family – the Booms – hid fugitives, Resistance fighters and Jews alike, above their watchmaking shop during World War II. The guided tour is instructive and moving in equal measure: the family was betrayed to the Gestapo in 1944 and only one, Corrie Boom, survived.

The Frans Hals Museum

Haarlem's chief attraction, the **Frans Hals Museum** at Groot Heiligland 62 (Tues–Sat 11am–5pm, Sun noon–5pm; €5.40), is a five-minute stroll south from the Grote Markt – take pedestrianized Lange Veerstraat and keep straight as far as Gasthuispoort, where you turn right and then first left. The museum holds a relatively small but eclectic collection of Dutch paintings from the fifteenth century onwards and features a handful of prime works by Hals; the labelling is in English and Dutch. It also occupies an old almshouse complex, a much modified red-brick *hofje* with a central courtyard, where the aged Hals lived out his last destitute years on public funds.

Little is known about **Frans Hals** (c.1580–1666). Born in Antwerp, the son of Flemish refugees who settled in Haarlem in the late 1580s, his extant oeuvre is relatively small – some two hundred paintings and nothing like the number of sketches and studies left behind by Rembrandt. His outstanding gift was as a portraitist, showing a sympathy with his subjects and an ability to capture fleeting expression that some say even Rembrandt lacked. Seemingly quick and careless flashes of colour characterize his work, blended into a coherent whole to create a set of marvellously animated seventeenth-century figures.

The museum begins with the work of other artists: first comes a small group of late fifteenth- and sixteenth-century paintings, the most prominent of which is a triptych from the **School of Hans Memling** and a polished *Adam and Eve* by **Jan van Scorel**. Afterwards, Room 10 features a couple of paintings by the **Haarlem mannerists**, including a work by **Karel van Mander** (1548–1606), leading light of the Haarlem School and mentor of many of the city's most celebrated painters. There's also a curious painting by Haarlem-born **Jan Mostaert** (1475–1555), his *West Indian Scene* depicting a band of naked, poorly armed natives trying to defend themselves against the cannon and sword of their Spanish invaders; the comparison with the Dutch Protestants is obvious. Moving on to Room 11, **Cornelis Cornelisz van Haarlem** (1562–1638)

DAY-TRIPS FROM THE CITY | Haarlem and around

best followed van Mander's guidelines: his *Wedding of Peleus and Thetis* is an appealing rendition of what was then a popular subject, though Cornelisz gives as much attention to the arrangement of his elegant nudes as to the subject. This marriage precipitated civil war amongst the gods and was used by the Dutch as a warning against discord, a call for unity during the long war with Spain. Similarly, and also in Room 11, the same artist's *Massacre of the Innocents* connects the biblical story with the Spanish siege of Haarlem in 1572.

Frans Hals was a pupil of van Mander too, though he seems to have learned little more than the barest rudiments from him. The Hals paintings begin in earnest in Room 21 amongst a set of "Civic Guard" portraits – group portraits of the militia companies initially formed to defend the country from the Spanish, but which later became social clubs for the gentry. Getting a commission to paint one of these portraits was a well-paid privilege – Hals got his first in 1616 – but their composition was a tricky affair and often the end result was dull and flat. With great flair and originality, Hals made the group portrait a unified whole instead of a static collection of individual portraits, his figures carefully arranged, but so cleverly as not to appear contrived. For a time, Hals himself was a member of the Company of St George, and in the *Officers of the Militia Company of St George* he appears in the top left-hand corner – one of his few self-portraits. Hals' later paintings are darker, more contemplative works, closer to Rembrandt in their lighting and increasingly sombre in their outlook. In Room 27, amongst several portraits of different groups of regents, is Hals' *Regents of St Elizabeth Gasthuis*, a serious but benign work of 1641 with a palpable sense of optimism, whereas his twin *Regents* and *Regentesses of the Oudemannenhuis*, currently displayed in Room 21 but often shunted around, is deep with despair. The latter were commissioned when Hals was in his eighties, a poor man despite a successful painting career, hounded for money by the town's tradesmen and by the mothers of his illegitimate children. As a result he was dependent on the charity of people like those depicted here: their cold, self-satisfied faces staring out of the gloom, the women reproachful, the men only marginally more affable. The character just right of centre in the *Regents* painting has been labelled (and indeed looks) drunk, although it is inconceivable that Hals would have depicted him in this condition; it's more likely that he was suffering from some kind of facial paralysis, and his jauntily cocked hat was simply a popular fashion of the time. There are those who claim Hals had lost his touch by the time he painted these pictures, yet their sinister, almost ghostly power as they face each other across the room, suggests quite the opposite. Van Gogh's remark that "Frans Hals had no fewer than 27 blacks" suddenly makes perfect sense.

Look out also for the geometric church interiors of **Pieter Saenredam** in Room 22 and a berserk *Dutch Proverbs* by **Pieter Brueghel the Younger** in Room 24.

Along the River Spaarne

Beyond the Frans Hals Museum, at the end of Groot Heiligland, turn left along the canal and it's a short walk east to the **River Spaarne**, whose gentle curves

---

Excursions from Harlem

Woltheus Cruises, by the river at Spaarne 11 (☎023/535 7723, ⓦwww .woltheus-haarlem.nl), operates several **boat trips** from Haarlem, the most interesting of which is a once- or twice-weekly excursion to Zaanse Schans (July–Sept; 7hr; €14; see p.135).

mark the eastern periphery of the town centre. Turn left again, along riverside Turfmarkt and its continuation Spaarne, to reach the surly stonework of the **Waag** (Weigh House) and then the country's oldest museum, the **Teylers Museum**, located in a grand old building at Spaarne 16 (Tues–Sat 10am–5pm, Sun noon–5pm; €4.50). Founded in 1774 by a wealthy local philanthropist, one Pieter Teyler van der Hulst, the museum should appeal to scientific and artistic tastes alike. It contains everything from fossils, bones and crystals, to weird, H.G. Wells-type technology (including an enormous eighteenth-century electrostatic generator) and sketches and line drawings by Michelangelo, Raphael, Rembrandt and Claude, among others. The drawings are covered to protect them from the light, but don't be afraid to pull back the curtains to take a peek. Look in, too, on the rooms beyond, filled with work by eighteenth- and nineteenth-century Dutch painters, principally Breitner, Israëls, Weissenbruch and, not least, Wijbrand Hendriks, who was once the keeper of the art collection here. Teyler also bestowed his charity on the riverside **Teylers Hofje**, a little way east around the bend of the Spaarne at Koudenhorn 64. With none of the cosy familiarity of the town's other *hofjes*, this is a grandiose affair, a Neoclassical edifice dating from 1787 and featuring solid columns and cupolas. Nearby, the elegant fifteenth-century tower of the **Bakenesserkerk** (no public access), on Vrouwestraat, is a flamboyant, vaguely oriental protrusion on the Haarlem skyline.

Practicalities

With fast and frequent services from Amsterdam, Haarlem's splendid **train station**, a fine example of the Amsterdam School of architecture, is located on the north side of the city centre, about ten minutes' walk from the main square, the Grote Markt. **Cycle rental** is available at the train station for €6 per day. The **bus station** is in front of the train station on Stationsplein and the **VVV** is adjacent (April–Sept Mon–Fri 9am–5.30pm, Sat 9.30am–3.30pm; Oct–March Mon–Fri 9.30am–5.30pm, Sat 10am–2pm; ☎0900/616 1600).

The VVV issues free city maps and brochures and, although there's no strong reason to overnight here, it also has a small supply of **private rooms**, which cost €18.50 per person per night, though note that they are mostly on the outskirts of town. Haarlem also has four central **hotels** (see below) and an HI **hostel**, *Stayokay Haarlem*, near the sports stadium about 3km to the north of the town centre, at Jan Gijzenpad 3 (☎023/537 3793, ℱ023/537 1176; ⓦwww.stayokay.com/haarlem; €17 per bed). Bus #2 runs to the hostel from the station – a ten-minute journey. Finally, **campsites** are dotted along the coast in and around Zandvoort – see p.130.

Haarlem's best **restaurants** and **bars** are conveniently clustered around the Grote Markt and on Oude Groenmarkt, round the back of the Grote Kerk.

Hotels

Amadeus Grote Markt 10 ☎023/532 4530, ℱ023/532 2328, ⓦwww.amadeus-hotel.com. Homely, two-star family hotel with plain but perfectly comfortable en-suite rooms. The front bedrooms have enjoyable views over the main square, their only drawback being the pigeons thrashing around on the window sill. ❷

Carillon Grote Markt 27 ☎023/531 0591, ℱ023/531 4909. Inexpensive place with frugal modern rooms, but friendly atmosphere. Opposite the Grote Kerk. ❶

Golden Tulip Lion d'Or Kruisweg 34 ☎023/532 1750, ℱ023/532 9543. Smart chain hotel housed in a sturdy nineteenth-century building close to the train station. Very comfortable rooms, which offset the dreariness of the setting. ❻

Joops Oude Groenmarkt 20 ☎023/532 2208, ℱ023/532 9549. Large if somewhat spartan rooms immediately behind the Grote Kerk. ❶

Eating and drinking

Café 1900 Barteljorisstraat 10. With an attractive early twentieth-century interior, this has long been a popular café-bar, serving drinks and light meals.

Applause Grote Markt 23a ☎023/531 1425. A chic little bistro serving up Italian food with excellent main courses hovering around €20.

De Componist Korte Veerstraat 1 ☎023/532 8853. Smart Art Nouveau premises and a tasty Dutch menu.

Grand Café Fortuyn Grote Markt 21. A quiet, cosy café-bar with charming 1930s decor, including a tiled entrance and dinky little glass cabinets preserved from its days as a shop.

Haarlem aan Zee Oude Groenmarkt 10 ☎023/531 4884. An eccentric place, where the interior is done out like a Dutch beach, serving a splendid range of seafood, with main dishes averaging around €20–25.

In Den Uiver Riviervismarkt 13. Just off the Grote Markt, this lively and extremely appealing bar has occasional live music.

Proeflokaal Sliterij Lange Veerstraat 7. Intimate and amenable bar – typically Dutch.

Restaurant La Plume Lange Veerstraat 1 ☎023/531 3202. A popular and very affordable restaurant with a range of tasty dishes from pastas through to traditional Dutch.

Ze Crack At the junction of Lange Veerstraat and Kleine Houtstraat. A dim, youthful and smoky bar with good techno and drum and bass.

The bulbfields

The pancake-flat fields extending south from Haarlem towards Leiden are the heart of the Dutch **bulbfields**, whose bulbs and blooms support a billion-dollar industry and some ten thousand growers, as well as attracting tourists in their droves. Bulbs have flourished here since the late sixteenth century, when a certain **Carolus Clusius**, a Dutch botanist and one-time gardener to the Habsburg emperor, brought the first tulip bulb over from Vienna, where it had – in its turn – been brought from modern-day Turkey by an Austrian aristocrat. The tulip flourished in Holland's sandy soil and was so highly prized that it fuelled a massive speculative bubble. At the height of the boom – in the mid-1630s – bulbs were commanding extraordinary prices: the artist Jan van Goyen, for instance, paid 1900 guilders and two paintings for ten rare bulbs, while another set of one hundred bulbs was swapped for a coach and pair of horses. The bubble burst in 1636, thanks to the intervention of the government, and the bulb industry returned to normal, though it left hundreds of investors ruined, much to the satisfaction of the country's Calvinist ministers who had railed against the excesses.

Other types of bulbs were introduced after the tulip and today the **spring flowering sequence** begins in mid-March with crocuses, followed by daffodils and yellow narcissi in late March, and hyacinths and tulips in mid- and late April through to May. Gladioli flower in August. The views from any of the trains heading south from Haarlem can often be sufficient in themselves, the fields divided into stark geometric blocks of pure colour. However, with your own transport you can take in the full beauty of the bulbfields by way of special routes marked by hexagonal signposts – local VVVs sell pamphlets listing the best vantage points – or you can reach the bulb growers' showcase, the **Keukenhof gardens**, easily enough by public transport from Haarlem. Bear in mind also that there are any number of local **flower festivals** and **parades** in mid- to late April – every local VVV has the details.

The Keukenhof gardens

The small town of **LISSE**, halfway between Leiden and Haarlem, is home to the **Keukenhof gardens** (ⓦwww.keukenhof.com; late March to late May daily 8am–7.30pm; €11.50), the largest flower gardens in the world. The Keukenhof was set up in 1949, designed by a group of prominent bulb growers to convert people to the joys of growing flowers from bulbs in their own gardens. Literally the "kitchen garden", its site is the former estate of a fifteenth-century countess, who used to grow herbs and vegetables for her dining table here – hence the name. Some seven million flowers are on show for their full flowering period, complemented, in case of especially harsh winters, by 5000 square metres of glasshouses holding indoor displays. You could easily spend a whole day here, swooning among the sheer abundance of it all, but to get the best of it you need to come early, before the tour buses pack the place. There are several restaurants in the 28 hectares of grounds, and well-marked paths take you all the way through the gardens, which specialize in daffodils, narcissi, hyacinths and tulips.

To get to the Keukenhof by **public transport** from Haarlem, take the train to Leiden (every 20min; 20min) and then catch either the special bus or regular bus #54 (every 30min; 30min) from the adjacent bus station.

The coast

Haarlem is just 5km from the coast at **ZANDVOORT**, a major seaside resort whose agglomeration of modern apartment blocks strings along the seashore behind a wide and sandy beach. As resorts go it's pretty standard – packed in summer, dead and gusty in winter – but the **beach** is excellent and the place also musters a casino and a car-racing circuit. What's more, Zandvoort is one of the few places on the Dutch coast with its own train station (see below): the journey from Amsterdam to Zandvoort only takes thirty minutes, which makes it an easy day-trip – ideal for a spot of sunbathing.

Some 3km north along the coast from Zandvoort are the beachside shacks, dunes and ice-cream stalls of **BLOEMENDAAL-AAN-ZEE**, a pocket-sized resort which possesses several campsites, but should not be confused with workaday Bloemendaal just inland. The resort is also located on the southern edge of the **Nationaalpark de Kennemerduinen**, whose pine woods, lagoons and dunes stretch north as far as the industrial town of **Ijmuiden**, at the mouth of the Nordzeekanaal. Maps of the park are widely available – at petrol stations and local VVVs – and are useful if you intend to negotiate its network of footpaths and cycle trails with everything on offer from an easy kilometre-long ramble to a full-scale 140-kilometre expedition. Bike rental is available in Haarlem and Zandvoort. The park's **visitor centre** is in its southeast corner, just off the **N200** in between Haarlem and Bloemendaal-aan-Zee, and reached from the former on bus #81.

Practicalities

With a half-hourly service from Haarlem, **Zandvoort train station** is only a five-minute walk (if that) from the beach. There are buses from Haarlem too – the **bus station** is in the centre on Louis Davidsstraat. There's no powerful reason to overnight here, but the **VVV** (mid-July to mid-Aug Mon–Thurs 9am–5.15pm, Fri 9am–7pm & Sat 9am–4pm; April to mid-July & mid-Aug to Oct Mon–Fri 9am–5.15pm & Sat 9am–4pm; Nov–March Mon–Fri 9am–12.30pm & 1.30–5pm & Sat 10am–2pm; ☎023/571 7947), a short, signposted walk west of the train station at Schoolplein 1, has a full list of local accommodation. This includes several three- and four-star tower-block **hotels** dotted along the seashore, amongst which the large and slick *NH Zandvoort Hotel*, on the north side of the resort at Burgemeester van Alphenstraat 63 (☎023/576 0760, ⓕ023/571 9094, ⓔnhzandvoort@nh/hotel.nl; ❹), is perhaps the smartest. More modest but perfectly satisfactory options include the *Zuiderbad*, which, with its garish awnings, is on the seashore at Boulevard Paulus Loot 5 (☎023/571 2613, ⓕ023/571 3190, ⓦwww.hotelzuiderbad.nl; ❷). The

VVV also books **private rooms** (❶–❷), but these fill up fast in summer – so ask early in the day or telephone ahead.

Bloemendaal-aan-Zee has two good **campsites**, both among the dunes within comfortable reach of the beach: the sprawling *De Lakens*, at Zeeweg 60 (☎0900/384 6226, ℉025/166 1089, ⓦwww.kennemerduincampings.nl; April–Oct), and *Bloemendaal* at Zeeweg 72 (☎023/573 2178, ℉023/573 2174; April–Sept). **Bus #81** runs from Haarlem train station to Bloemendaal-aan-Zee along the N200; both campsites are just to the north, and within easy walking distance, of this road.

Marken, Volendam and Edam

The turbulent waters of the **Zuider Zee** were once busy with Dutch trading ships plying to and from the Baltic. This Baltic trade was the linchpin of Holland's prosperity in the Golden Age, revolving around the import of huge quantities of grain, the supply of which was municipally controlled to guarantee against famine. The business was immensely profitable and its proceeds built a string of prosperous seaports – including Volendam, Hoorn and Enkhuizen – and nourished market towns like Edam, while the Zuider Zee itself supported numerous fishing villages such as Marken. In the eighteenth century the Baltic trade declined, a process accelerated by the silting up of the Zuider Zee harbours, and the ports were left high and dry economically. Conseqently, with the rapid increase in the Dutch population during the nineteenth century, plans were made to reclaim the Zuider Zee and turn it into farmland. The first part of the scheme was the completion of a dam, the **Afsluitdijk**, across the mouth of the Zuider Zee in 1932, but by the time a second, complementary **barrier** linking Enkhuizen with Lelystad was finished in 1976, the steam had gone out of the project. The old Zuider Zee was never completely drained and most has remained water, with the two dams creating a pair of freshwater lakes – the **Markermeer** and **IJsselmeer**.

These placid, steel-grey lakes are popular with day-tripping Amsterdammers, who come here in their droves to sail boats and visit a string of pretty little towns and villages. These begin on the coast just a few kilometres north of Amsterdam with the picturesque old fishing village of **Marken** and the former seaport of **Volendam**. In the summer it's possible to travel between these two by **boat**, but the trip can also be made – if a little less conveniently – by **bus** via Monnickendam. Buses also link Volendam with **Edam**, a far prettier proposition and much less touristy. You don't necessarily need to make a choice though, since all three places can comfortably be visited in a day.

Marken

Once an island in the Zuider Zee, **Marken** was, until its road connection to the mainland in 1957, pretty much a closed community, supported by a small fishing industry. Despite its proximity to Amsterdam, its biggest problem was the genetic defects caused by close and constant intermarrying, but now it's how to contain the tourists, whose numbers increase yearly. That said, there's no denying the picturesque charms of the island's one and only village – also called **MARKEN** – where the immaculately maintained houses, mostly painted in deep green with white trimmings, cluster on top of artificial mounds

The closing of the Zuider Zee

The towns and villages that string along the east coast of North Holland flourished during Amsterdam's Golden Age, their economies buoyed up by shipbuilding, the Baltic sea trade and the demand for herring. They had access to the open sea via the waters of the **Zuider Zee** (Southern Sea) and, to the north, the connecting **Waddenzee** (Mud Sea). Both seas were comparatively new, created when the North Sea broke through from the coast in the thirteenth century – the original coastline is marked by Texel and the Frisian Islands. However, the Zuider Zee was shallow and tidal, part salt and part freshwater, and accumulations of silt began to strangle its ports from the end of the seventeenth century. Indeed, by the 1750s the Zuider Zee ports were effectively marooned and the only maritime activity was fishing – just enough to keep a cluster of tiny hamlets ticking over, from Volendam and Marken on the sea's western coast, to Stavoren and Urk on the eastern side.

The Zuider Zee may have provided a livelihood for local fishermen, but most of the country was more concerned by the flood danger it posed, as time and again storms and high tides combined to breach the east coast's defences. The first plan to seal off and reclaim the Zuider Zee was proposed in 1667, but the rotating-turret windmills that then provided the most efficient way of drying the land were insufficient for the task and matters were delayed until suitable technology arrived – in the form of the steam-driven pump. In 1891 one **Cornelis Lely** (1854–1929) proposed a retaining dike and his plans were finally put into effect after devastating floods hit the area in 1916. Work began on this dike, the **Afsluitdijk**, in 1920 despite some uncertainty among the engineers, who worried about a possible rise in sea level around the islands of the Waddenzee. In the event, their concerns proved groundless and, on May 28, 1932, the last gap in the dike was closed and the Zuider Zee simply ceased to exist, replaced by the freshwater **IJsselmeer**.

The original plan was to reclaim all the land protected by the Afsluitdijk, and three large-scale land reclamation schemes were completed over the next forty years. In addition, a complementary dike linking Enkhuizen with Lelystad was finished in 1976, thereby creating lake **Markermeer** – a necessary prelude to the draining of another vast stretch of the IJsselmeer. The engineers licked their contractual lips, but they were out of sync with the majority of the population, who were now opposed to any further draining of the lake. Partly as a result, the grand plan was abandoned and, after much governmental huffing and puffing, the Markermeer was left alone.

There were many economic benefits to be had in the closing of the Zuider Zee. The threat of flooding was removed, the country gained great chunks of new and fertile farmland and the roads that were built along the top of the two main retaining dikes brought North Holland within twenty minutes' drive of Friesland. The price was the demise of the old Zuider Zee **fishing fleet**. Without access to the open sea, it was inevitable that most of the fleet would become redundant, though some skippers wisely transferred to the north coast before the Afsluitdijk was completed. Others learnt to fish the freshwater species that soon colonized the Markermeer and IJsselmeer, but in 1970 falling stocks prompted the government to ban trawling. This was a bitter blow for many fishermen and there were several violent demonstrations before they bowed to the inevitable. Today, villages such as Marken and Urk are shadows of their former selves, forced to rely on tourism to survive.

raised to protect them from the sea. There are two main parts to the village, **Havenbuurt**, behind the harbour, and **Kerkbuurt** around the **church** (mid-May to Oct Mon–Sat 10am–5pm; free), an ugly 1904 replacement for its long-standing predecessor. Of the two, Kerkbuurt is the less touristy, its narrow lanes lined by ancient dwellings and a row of old eel-smoking houses, now the **Marker Museum**, Kerkbuurt 44 (April–Sept Mon–Sat 10am–5pm, Sun noon–4pm; Oct Mon–Sat 11am–4pm; €2), devoted to the history of the former island and its fishing industry. Across in the Havenbuurt, one or two of the houses are open to visitors, proclaiming themselves to be "typical" of Marken, and the waterfront is lined by snack bars and souvenir shops, often staffed by locals in traditional costume. It's all a tad prosaic, but now and again you get a hint of how hard life used to be – most of the houses on the waterfront are raised on stilts, allowing the sea to roll under the floors in bad weather, enough to terrify most people half to death.

Practicalities

Marken is accessible direct from Amsterdam on **bus** #111, departing from outside Centraal Station (every 15–30min; 30min). The bus drops passengers beside the car park on the edge of Marken village, from where it's a five-minute walk to the centre. Marken does not have a **VVV** and neither is there anywhere **to stay**. In season a passenger **ferry** links Marken with Volendam (April–Oct daily every 30–45min 11am–5pm; 30min; ☏029/936 3331; €7), but at other times it's a fiddly **bus** trip: take bus #111 back towards Amsterdam, but get off at the **Swaensborch stop** on the edge of Monnickendam village. At Swaensborch, change to bus #110, which runs from Amsterdam to Volendam and Edam.

Volendam

Larger but not nearly as quaint as Marken, the old fishing village of **VOLEN-DAM** has had, by comparison with its neighbour, some rip-roaring cosmopolitan times. In the early years of the twentieth century it became something of an artists' retreat, with both Picasso and Renoir spending time here. The artists are, however, long gone and nowadays Volendam is crammed with day-tripping tourists bobbing in and out of the souvenir stalls that run the length of the main street. Quiet places, never mind pretty ones, are hard to find, but narrow **Meerzijde**, one street back from the harbour, does have its moments in its mazy alleys and mini-canals. One curiosity to look out for is a **plaque** at the corner of Berend Demmerstraat and Josefstraat marking how high the floodwaters of 1916 rose here.

Practicalities

In Volendam bus #110 from Amsterdam and Monnickendam drops passengers on Zeestraat, just along the street from the **VVV**, at no. 37 (April–Sept daily 10am–5pm; Oct–March Mon–Sat 10am–3pm; ☏029/936 3747, ⓦwww .vvv-volendam.nl). From the VVV, it's a couple of minutes' walk to the waterfront. With Amsterdam just a short bus ride away and Edam even nearer (see below), there's absolutely no reason to stay overnight here, but if you do, the long-established *Best Western Spaander* on the waterfront at Haven 15 (☏029/936 3595, ℱ029/936 9615; ❷) is the most attractive option. In the summertime, there is a regular **passenger ferry** to Marken (see p.130).

Edam

Just 3km from Volendam – and further up along the #110 bus route from Amsterdam – you might expect **EDAM** to be jammed with tourists considering the international fame of the rubbery red balls of cheese that carry its name. In fact, Edam usually lacks the crowds and remains a delightful, good-looking and prosperous little town of neat brick houses, swing bridges and slender canals. Founded by farmers in the twelfth century, it experienced a temporary boom in the seventeenth as a shipbuilding centre with river access to the Zuider Zee. Thereafter, it was back to the farm – and the excellent pasture land surrounding the town is still grazed by large herds of cows, though nowadays most Edam cheese is produced elsewhere, even in Germany; "Edam" is the name of a type of cheese and not its place of origin. This does, of course, rather undermine the authenticity of Edam's open-air **cheese market**, held every Wednesday morning in July and August on the Kaasmarkt (10.30am–12.30pm), but it's still a popular attraction and the only time the town heaves with tourists. Edam's cheese market is a good deal more humble than Alkmaar's (see p.136), but it follows the same format, with the cheeses laid out in rows before the buyers sample them. Once a cheese has been purchased, the cheese porters, dressed in the traditional white costumes and straw boaters, spring into action, carrying them off on their gondola-like trays.

The Town

At the heart of Edam is the **Damplein**, a pint-sized main square where an elongated humpbacked bridge has long vaulted the Voorhaven canal, which once used to flood the town with depressing regularity. Also on the square is Edam's eighteenth-century **Stadhuis**, a severe Louis XIV-style structure whose plain symmetries culminate in a squat little tower, and the **Edams Museum** (Tues–Sat 10am–4.30pm, Sun 1.30–4.30pm; €2), housed in an attractive building whose crow-stepped gables date from 1530. Inside, a modest assortment of local bygones is redeemed by the curious floating cellar, supposedly built by a retired sea captain who could not bear the thought of sleeping on dry land. From Damplein, it's a short walk along Grote Kerkstraat to the rambling **Grote Kerk** (April–Oct daily 2–4.30pm; free), on the edge of the fields to the north of the village. This is the largest three-ridged church in Europe, with a huge organ built in 1663 and a vaulted ceiling constructed in wood in an attempt to limit the subsidence caused by the building's massive weight. A handsome, largely Gothic structure, it contains several magnificent **stained-glass windows** dating from 1606 to 1620, mostly heraldic but including historical scenes too. Unfortunately, the church's strong lines are disturbed by the almost comically stubby spire, which was shortened to its present height after a lightning strike started a fire in 1602.

Strolling back from the church, take Matthijs Tinxgracht – one street west of Grote Kerkstraat – along the canal and you'll soon reach the Kaasmarkt, site of both the cheese market and the **Kaaswaag** (Cheese Weighing House), whose decorative panels celebrate – you guessed it – cheese-making and bear the town's coat of arms, a bull on a red field with three stars. From here, it's a couple of hundred metres to the sixteenth-century **Speeltoren**, the elegant tower visible from all over town, and roughly the same distance again – south along Lingerzijde – to the impossibly picturesque **Kwakelbrug** bridge. This leads over to one of Edam's most charming streets, **Schepenmakersdijk**, a cobbled, canalside lane flanked by immaculate gardens and the quaintest of houses.

To explore Edam's every architectural nook and cranny, pop into the VVV, in the Stadhuis (see p.134), and buy their *A Stroll through Edam*.

Practicalities

Leaving Amsterdam every half hour from outside Centraal Station, **bus #110** takes 35 minutes to reach Volendam and 10 minutes more to get to Edam. Edam's **bus station** is on the southwest edge of town, on Singelweg, a five-minute walk from Damplein. There are no signs, but aim for the easily spotted Speeltoren tower: cross the distinctive swing bridge, turn right and follow Lingerzijde as it jinks left and right. From the Speeltoren, it's a few metres east to the Damplein, where the **VVV** (April–Oct Mon–Sat 10am–5pm, plus Sun 1–4.30pm in July & Aug; Nov–March Mon–Sat 10am–3pm; ☎029/931 5125, ⓦwww.vvv-edam.nl) issues town maps and has details of **boat trips** both along the local canals and out into the Markermeer. **Bike rental** is available at Ronald Schot, in the town centre at Grote Kerkstraat 7 (☎029/937 2155); a one-day rental costs about €7.

The VVV also has a selection of **private rooms** (❶–❷), which they will book on your behalf for free. Otherwise, there are three **hotels**, the pick being the charming *De Fortuna*, just round the corner from the Damplein at Spuistraat 3 (☎029/937 1671, Ⓕ029/937 1469, ⓦwww.fortuna-edam.nl; ❹). This three-star hotel, with its immaculate garden flowing down to a canal, has thirty comfortable rooms distributed amongst six cosy little houses. An appealing second choice is the *Damhotel*, which occupies a modernized old inn opposite the VVV (☎029/937 1766, Ⓕ029/937 4031; ❷). The third hotel is the rather more modest, one-star *Harmonie*, in a plain but pleasant canalside house a couple of hundred metres east of the VVV at Voorhaven 92 (☎029/937 1664, Ⓕ029/931 5352; ❶). The nearest **campsite**, *Strandbad*, is east of town near the lakeshore at Zeevangszeedijk 7 (☎029/937 1994; April–Sept) – a twenty-minute walk east along the canal from Damplein.

For **eating**, *De Fortuna* has the best restaurant in town, but eating at the *Damhotel* is barely a hardship – and it's a good deal less expensive; both serve Dutch cuisine.

Zaandam and Zaanse Schans

Every few minutes one of the many trains heading north out of Amsterdam passes through the build-up of settlements collectively known as **Zaanstad**, an untidy sprawl which trails northwest of the city on the far side of the River IJ. Amongst these settlements, two are worth visiting – **Zaandam**, the urban core of Zaanstad, and the museum-village of **Zaanse Schans**, complete with its old wooden cottages and windmills.

Zaandam

From the train it's not an especially enticing prospect, but unassuming **ZAANDAM** is an amiable, largely modern town that merits a brief stop. It was a popular tourist hangout in the nineteenth century, when it was known as "La Chine d'Hollande" for the faintly oriental appearance of its windmills, canals, masts, and row upon row of brightly painted houses. **Claude Monet** spent some time here in the 1870s, and, despite being suspected of spying and under constant police surveillance, immortalized the place in a series of paintings. To see something of Monet's Zaandam, follow the main street, Gedempte Gracht, east from the train station for five minutes, turn right down Damstraat, right again, and left down Krimp and you'll be rewarded with a pretty harbour, spiked with masts and fringed by wooden houses. On Krimp itself, at no. 23, is the town's main claim to fame, the **Czaar Petershuisje** (April–Oct Tues–Sun 1–5pm, Nov–March Sat & Sun only 1–5pm; €2), where the Russian

Tsar Peter the Great stayed when he came to study shipbuilding here. In those heady days, Zaandam was an important shipbuilding centre, and the Tsar made four visits, the first in 1697 when he arrived incognito and stayed in the simple home of one Gerrit Kist, who had formerly been employed by the Tsar. A tottering wooden structure enclosed within a brick shelter, the house is little more than two tiny rooms, decorated with a handful of portraits of a benign-looking emperor and the graffiti of tourists going back to the mid-nineteenth century. Among the few things to see is the cupboard bed in which Peter is supposed to have slept, together with the calling cards and pennants of various visiting Russian delegations; around the outside of the house is an exhibition on the shipbuilding industry in Zaandam. Napoleon is said to have remarked on visiting the house, "Nothing is too small for great men."

Zaanse Schans

Most visitors to Zaanstad are, however, on their way to the recreated Dutch village of **Zaanse Schans**. The village is made up of around thirty cottages, windmills and workshops assembled from all over the region, in an energetic and endearing attempt to reproduce a Dutch village as it would have looked in the eighteenth and early nineteenth century. Spread over a network of narrow canals beside the River Zaan, it's a pretty spot and deservedly popular, with the particular highlight being the seven working **windmills**, giant industrial affairs used – amongst other things – to cut wood, grind mustard seeds and produce oil. This is the closest place to Amsterdam to see working windmills and there's a scattering of other attractions too, notably a **Bakkerij** (bakery), **Kaasboerderij** (cheese-making workshop) and a **Klompenmakerij** (clog-making workshop). Opening times vary, but almost every structure is open daily, except sometimes on Mondays, from April to October, and at the weekend only from November to March. Precise times are available from the visitor centre – the **Bezoekerscentrum**, on the east side of the village beside the car park (daily 8.30am–5pm; ☎075/616 8218, ⓦ www.zaanseschans.nl). It's actually possible to walk round Zaanse Schans at any time and in the evening or early morning you may well have the place pretty much to yourself. Finally, there are also enjoyable hour-long **boat trips** on the River Zaan from the jetty near the De Huisman mustard windmill (April–Oct daily 11am–4pm, every hour; €6).

It's about 800m to Zaanse Schans from the **nearest train station**, Koog-Zaandijk, two stops up the line from Zaandam.

Alkmaar and around

Forty minutes from Amsterdam by train – and thirty from Koog-Zaandijk (see above) – the little town of **ALKMAAR** was founded in the tenth century in the middle of a marsh. It takes its name from the auk, a diving bird which once hung around here in numbers, as in *alkeen meer*, or auk lake. Just like Haarlem, the town was besieged by Frederick of Toledo, but heavy rain flooded its surroundings and forced the Spaniards to withdraw in 1573, an early Dutch success in their long war of independence. Alkmaar's agreeable, partially canalized centre is still surrounded by its medieval moat, part of which has been incorporated into the Noordhollandskanaal, itself part of a longer network of waterways running north from Amsterdam to the Waddenzee.

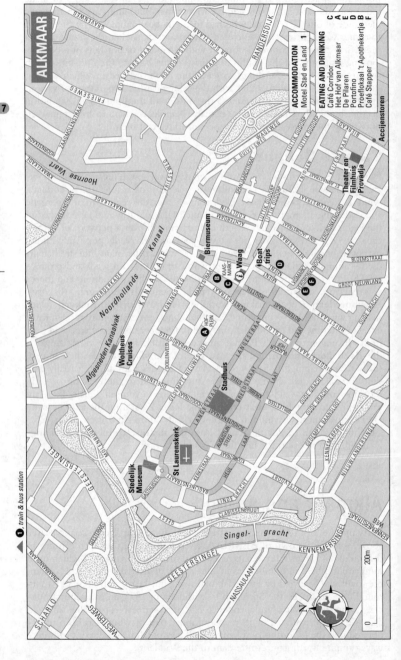

ALKMAAR

▲ ◗ train & bus station

ACCOMMODATION
Motel Stad en Land   1

EATING AND DRINKING
Café Corridor   C
Het Hof van Alkmaar   A
De Pilaren   E
Portofino   D
Proeflokaal 't Apothekertje B
Café Stapper   F

Biermuseum
KAAS-MARKT
Waag
Boat trips
Theater en Filmhuis Provadja
Accijenstoren

Wolthuis Cruises
Afgesneden Kanaalvak
Stadhuis
St Laurenskerk
Stedelijk Museum

Singel- gracht

N

0   200m

Alkmaar has a cluster of impressive medieval buildings, but is best known for its much-touted **kaasmarkt** – **cheese market** (mid-April to mid-Sept Fri 10am–noon), an ancient affair that these days ranks as one of the most extravagant tourist spectacles in Holland. Cheese has been sold on the main square here since the 1300s, and although it's no longer a serious commercial concern, the market remains popular and continues to draw the crowds. If you want a good view be sure to get there early, as by opening time the crowds are already thick on the ground. The ceremony starts with the buyers sniffing, crumbling, and finally tasting each cheese, followed by intensive bartering. Once a deal has been concluded, the cheeses – golden discs of Gouda mainly, laid out in rows and piles on the square – are borne away on ornamental carriers by groups of four porters (*kaasdragers*) for weighing. The porters wear white trousers and shirt plus a black hat whose coloured bands – green, blue, red or yellow – represent the four companies that comprise the cheese porters' guild. Payment for the cheeses, tradition has it, takes place in the cafés around the square.

The Town

Even if you've only come for the cheese market, it's well worth seeing something of the rest of the town before you leave. On the main square, the **Waag** (Weighing House) was originally a chapel dedicated to the Holy Ghost – hence the imposing tower – but was converted and given its delightful east gable shortly after the town's famous victory against the Spanish. The gable is an ostentatious Dutch Renaissance affair bedecked with allegorical figures and decorated with the town's militant coat of arms. Nowadays, the Waag holds the **VVV** (see p.138) and the **Kaasmuseum** (Cheese Museum; April–Oct Mon–Thurs & Sat 10am–4pm, Fri 9am–4pm; €2.50), with displays on the history of cheese, cheese-making equipment and suchlike. Just off the north side of the square, the **Biermuseum de Boom**, housed in the old De Boom brewery at Houttil 1 (April–Oct Tues–Fri 10am–4pm, Sat & Sun 1.30–4pm; Nov–March Tues–Sun 1–4pm; €2.50), has displays tracing the brewing process from the malting to the bottling stage, aided by authentic props from this and other breweries. There's lots of technical equipment, enlivened by mannequins and empty bottles from once innumerable Dutch brewers – though few, curiously, from De Boom itself. It's an engaging museum, lovingly put together by enthusiasts, and there's a shop upstairs where you can buy a huge range of beers and associated merchandise, as well as a downstairs bar serving some eighty varieties of Dutch beer.

Heading south from the Waag along Mient, it's a few metres to the jetty from where boat trips (see below) leave for a quick zip round the town's central canals – an enjoyable way to spend 45 minutes. At the south end of Mient, the

Boat trips

Boat trips around Alkmaar leave from the jetty on Mient (April–Oct daily, hourly 11am–5pm, plus additional departures during the cheese market; 25min; €4). There are also longer trips to Zaanse Schans (mid-May to late Oct 2–3 weekly; 6hr; €10 one-way, €15 return) and even to Amsterdam (mid-June to mid-Sept weekly; 9hr; €13 one-way, €21 return); ask at the VVV for further details or contact the operators, **Woltheus Cruises**, at the Kanaalkade jetty, on the north side of the centre (℡072/511 4840; ⊛www.woltheuscruises.nl).

open-air **Vismarkt** (Fish Market) marks the start of the **Verdronkenoord** canal, whose attractive medley of facades and gables leads down to the spindly **Accijenstoren** (Excise Tower), part harbour master's office, part fortification built during the long struggle with Spain in 1622. Turn left at the tower along Bierkade and you'll soon reach **Luttik Oudorp**, another attractive corner of the old centre, a slender canal jammed with antique barges that leads back to the Waag.

One block south of the Waag, pedestrianized **Langestraat** is Alkmaar's main and mundane shopping street, whose only notable building is the **Stadhuis**, a florid affair, half of which (the Langestraat side and tower) dates from the early sixteenth century. At the west end of Langestraat lurks **St Laurenskerk** (June to mid-Sept Tues–Sat noon–5pm; free), a Gothic church of the late fifteenth century whose pride and joy is its huge **organ**, commissioned at the suggestion of the diplomat and political bigwig Constantijn Huygens in 1645. The case was designed by Jacob van Campen, the architect who was later to design Amsterdam's town hall (see p.46), and decorated with paintings by Caesar van Everdingen (1617–1678) illustrating the triumph of David. The artist's seamless brushstrokes and willingness to kowtow to the tastes of the burgeoning middle class were to make him a wealthy man. In the apse is the tomb of Count Floris V, penultimate in the line of medieval counts of North Holland, who did much to establish the independence of the towns hereabouts and was murdered for his trouble by jealous nobles in 1296.

Across from the church, in the newly enlarged cultural centre, the **Stedelijk Museum** (Municipal Museum; Tues–Fri 10am–5pm, Sat & Sun 1–5pm; €3.40) displays pictures and plans of the siege of 1573, along with an assortment of seventeenth-century paintings. Amongst the latter is a striking *Holy Family* by Gerard van Honthorst (1590–1656), a Mannerist who specialized in glossy portraits of high officials. There's also work by Pieter Saenredam and Maerten van Heemskerck (1498–1574), a transitional figure who was tutored in the Dutch Mannerist style before a visit to Italy in 1532 changed the direction of his work. Greatly impressed by the Italians, Heemskerck returned home to paint in the style of Michelangelo, populating his large canvases with muscular men-of-action and buxom women.

Practicalities

From Alkmaar's **train** and **bus station**, it's about ten minutes' walk to the centre of town: keep straight outside the station along Spoorstraat, take the first right down Snaarmanslaan and then left at busy Geesterweg, which leads over the old city moat to St Laurenskerk. From the church, it's another five minutes' walk east along Langestraat to the **VVV**, housed in the Waag on Waagplein (Mon–Fri 10am–5.30pm, Thurs till 9pm April–Oct, Sat 9.30am–5pm; ☎072/511 4284). Alkmaar only takes an hour or two to explore, but if you decide to stay the VVV has plenty of **private rooms** for €32 per double per night, including breakfast, though most places are on the outskirts of town and en-suite rooms are rare. Failing that, Alkmaar has one recommendable central **hotel**, the *Motel Stad en Land*, a plain and simple, trim and modern two-star establishment opposite the bus station, beside a busy road at Stationsweg 92 (☎072/512 3911, ℱ072/511 8440; ❷).

For **food**, Alkmaar is well served by *Het Hof van Alkmaar*, which occupies delightful old premises just off Nieuwesloot at Hof van Sonoy 1 (☎072/512 1222). During the day this restaurant offers inexpensive sandwiches, snacks and pancakes, and at night they serve up tasty Dutch cuisine – it's the best place in town. As a substitute, you might try *Portofino*, an old-fashioned Italian place close to the Waag at Mient 5; pizzas here start at €6. Alkmaar has two main groups of **bars**, one on Waagplein, the other around the Vismarkt, at the end of the Verdronkenoord canal. Among the former, the pick is *Proeflokaal 't Apothekertje*, an old-style bar, open until 2am, with an antique-cluttered interior and a laid-back atmosphere. Metres away, *Café Corridor* is younger and plays loud music late into the night. On Verdronkenoord, *De Pilaren* is another noisy place, though catering to a rather cooler crowd, some of whom take refuge in the *Café Stapper* next door, if the music gets too much.

Bergen and the Schoorlse Duinen Nationaalpark

Bus #160 leaves Alkmaar train station every fifteen minutes or so – hourly on Sunday – for the ten-minute ride to **BERGEN**, a cheerful village whose main square, the **Plein**, is an amiable affair flanked by good-looking, vaguely rustic buildings. Bus #160 stops on the Plein and from here it's a short walk to the **Museum Kranenburgh**, a fine-arts museum housed in a handsome Neoclassical villa at Hoflaan 26 (Tues–Sun 1–5pm; €4.50). Bergen has been something of a retreat for artists since the late nineteenth century and the museum features the work of the Expressionist Bergen School, which was founded here in 1915. Greatly influenced by the Post-Impressionists, especially Cézanne, none of the group is original enough to stand out, but taken as a whole it's a delightful collection and one that is supported by an imaginative programme of temporary exhibitions. These often focus on the two contemporaneous Dutch schools that were to have much more artistic impact – De Ploeg and De Stijl (see p.261). In addition, and warming to this artistic past, the local council organizes all sorts of cultural events in Bergen, including open-air sculpture displays and concerts, whilst the village also boasts a scattering of chichi art-for-sale galleries.

From Bergen's Plein, local bus #410 (Mon–Sat 6 daily) makes the thirty-minute trip northwest to the hamlet of **SCHOORL**, travelling along the eastern border of the **Schoorlse Duinen Nationaalpark**, whose wooded dunes stretch 5km west to the sea – one of the widest undeveloped portions of the whole Dutch coastline. The park is criss-crossed by cycling and walking trails and for all but the briefest of visits you should pick up a map from Bergen **VVV**, at Plein 1, before you set out (Mon–Fri 10am–5.30pm & Sat 10am–1pm; ☎072/581 3100).

The coast: Bergen-aan-Zee and Egmond-aan-Zee

Heading west from Bergen, **bus #262** (daily, every 30min) takes ten minutes to travel the 5km to the coast at **BERGEN-AAN-ZEE**, a pleasant, pocket-sized resort where the main event is the long sandy beach with its thick border of grassy dunes. To either side is pristine coastline: the Schoorlse Duinen Nationaalpark (see above) stretches out to the north, while the woods and dunes of the **Noordhollands Duinreservaat**, with their abundance of footpaths and cycle trails, extend south. If you fancy a night here, the *Hotel Nassau-Bergen*, at Van der Wijckplein 4 (☎072/589 7541, ℱ072/589 7044, 🌐www.hotel-nassau.nl; ❹), has every convenience – from an outdoor swimming pool to tennis courts – and is situated just 50m from the beach. The **VVV** is just along the street at no. 8 (☎072/581 2400).

Another coastal option, just 11km from Bergen-aan-Zee, is the slightly larger resort of **EGMOND-AAN-ZEE**, in the middle of the dunes of the Noordhollands Duinreservaat and in the shadow of a whopping lighthouse. To get there, take **bus #165** from Alkmaar train station (daily every 30min; 30min). Egmond has a **VVV** too – at Voorstraat 82a (☏072/506 1362).

Listings

Listings

Accommodation

Accommodation in Amsterdam can be extremely difficult to find, and is often a major expense: even hostels are pricey for what you get, and the hotels are among the most expensive in Europe. The city's compactness means that you'll almost inevitably end up somewhere central, but if you arrive without a reservation you'll still need to search hard to find somewhere decent. At peak times of the year – July and August, Easter and Christmas – you'd be advised to book well ahead; hotel rooms and even hostel beds can be swallowed up remarkably quickly. Most of the places we've listed – even the larger hostels – will accept bookings from abroad by fax or email (in fact a lot of hostels will not accept phone bookings during peak season), although the cheaper ones may require some guarantee of payment (such as a credit card number). You can also reserve rooms in advance by contacting the **Netherlands Reservations Centre** (℡0031/299 689 144; ℱ0031/299 689 154, ⓦwww.hotelres.nl) or ⓦwww.bookings.nl, both of which allow you to view availability and prices before making a booking. Once you've arrived, the city's VVVs (tourist offices) will make hotel reservations on your behalf either in advance or on the same day for a €3 fee, but note that during peak periods and weekends they get extremely busy with long and exhausting queues. They also sell a booklet on hotels in Amsterdam for €3.50. For VVV locations and opening times, see p.22.

Where to stay

To help you choose a place to stay, we've **divided our listings by area**, using the same headings as in the guide chapters – "The Old Centre", "The Grachtengordel", etc. All the hostels, hotels and B&Bs we describe are marked

Accommodation prices

The hotels and guesthouses detailed throughout this chapter have been graded according to the price categories listed below. Prices given are for the least expensive double room during the high season, including breakfast. Single rooms, where available, usually cost between sixty and eighty percent of a double. For hostel accommodation we've used the code if they have double rooms, otherwise we've specified the actual price per person for dorm beds. Note that in the low season prices can drop by as much as two categories and that many of the larger hotels have rooms at various prices.

❶ below €65	❹ €95–120	❼ €180–230
❷ €65–80	❺ €120–150	❽ €230–300
❸ €80–95	❻ €150–180	❾ €300 and above

on the **colour maps** at the end of the book.

If you choose to stay in the **Old Centre**, you'll never have to search for nightlife. Cheap hotels abound in the Red Light District, as you might expect – and this is the first place to start looking if money is tight, although women travellers may find it intimidating. However, there's also a good selection of quiet, reasonably priced places in more agreeable locations on and near the canals, close to restaurants and shopping areas.

The **western section** of the **Grachtengordel** canal ring is only a few minutes' walk from the bustle of Dam square, but it has a number of quiet canalside hotels; the Anne Frank House and several of the city's smaller museums are here too. The least expensive places are mostly strung along Raadhuisstraat, one of the city's most traffic-choked streets.

The **Grachtengordel's southern section** is an appealing area to stay, whether you're looking for bustling nightlife or peace and quiet. There are plenty of hotels for all budgets close to the bars and restaurants of Leidseplein and Rembrandtplein, plus a number of very pleasant, occasionally stylish options along the surrounding canals.

Staying in the **Jordaan** puts you in among the locals and well away from the hustle and bustle of the tourist centres. There's no shortage of bars and restaurants in this up-and-coming area either – and some of the most beautiful of the city's canals are here too – but you'll be at least fifteen minutes' walk from the bright lights. Beware that Marnixstraat and Rozengracht are busy traffic streets.

Very few tourists venture out to the **Old Jewish Quarter**: the streets and canals off the main traffic arteries of Weesperstraat and Plantage Middenlaan are purely residential, with very few bars or restaurants. Consequently, although you're pretty much guaranteed a quiet night's sleep here, you'll be a tram ride away from any of the main sights.

The main reason for staying out of the centre in the **Museum Quarter** is to be close to the city's three leading museums – although the nightlife around Leidseplein is also within easy striking distance. There are no canals in the area, and Overtoom and 1e Constantijn Huygensstraat constantly rumble with traffic, but there are plenty of quiet and comfortable hotels in the smaller side streets, as well as two of the city's best hostels on the edge of the leafy expanse of the Vondelpark.

There's not too much reason to venture out into the city's far-flung suburbs, but the **outer districts** do possess two noteworthy hotels (see p.154).

For specifically **gay** or gay-friendly hotels, see Chapter Twelve.

Many of Amsterdam's buildings have narrow, very steep **staircases**, and many do not have lifts; indeed in the older houses, the insertion of lifts is actually illegal. If this is a consideration for you, check before you book.

Note that all directions given are from Centraal Station (abbreviated as "CS").

Campsites

There are several **campsites** in and around Amsterdam, most of them readily accessible by car or public transport. The four listed below are recommended by the VVV, which divides them into two self-explanatory classifications, "youth" and "family campsites". The latter are the more suitable for touring caravans and mobile homes. For information on city campsites throughout the Netherlands check out ⓦ www.stadscampings.nl.

Youth campsites

Vliegenbos Meeuwenlaan 138 ⓣ 020/636 8855, ⓕ 020/632 2723, ⓦ www.vliegenbos.com. Bus #32, #36 or nightbus #73 from CS; drivers take Exit S116 off the A10. A relaxed and friendly site, just a ten-minute bus ride into Amsterdam North from CS. Facilities include a general shop, bar and restaurant. Rates are €7.25 per night per person with hot showers included. There are also huts with bunk beds and basic cooking facilities, for €45.30 per night for four people; phone ahead to check availability. Under-16s need to be accompanied by an adult; no pets. Open all year.
Zeeburg Zuiderzeeweg 20 ⓣ 020/694 4430, ⓕ 020/694 6238, ⓦ www.campingzeeburg.nl. Bus #22 to Kramatweg from CS, or tram #14 from Dam square; drivers take Exit S114 off the A10. Slightly better equipped than the *Vliegenbos*, but more difficult to get to. Rates are €2–4 per person, plus €3.50 for a tent, €2.50 for a motorbike and €4 for a car. Hot showers are an extra 80 cents. Cabins sleeping two and six people are €16.25 per person per night, including bed linen. The shop sells freshly baked bread, and the bar sometimes has live music. Open all year.

Family campsites

Amsterdamse Bos Kleine Noorddijk 1, Aalsmeer ⓣ 020/641 6868, ⓕ 020/640 2378, ⓔ camping@dab.amsterdam.nl. Yellow NZH bus #171 from CS; by car take Exit 6 off the A9 towards Aalsmeer. Facilities include a bar, shop and restaurant, but this campsite is a long way out, on the southern reaches of the lush and well-kept Amsterdam Bos (forest). Rates are €4.45 per person per night (children under 3 are free), hot showers included, plus €2.35 for a car, €5.60 for a camper van and €3.30 for a caravan. Huts sleeping up to four cost €38.60 a night, which includes a gas stove. Open April to mid-Oct.
Gaasper Camping Loosdrechtdreef 7 ⓣ 020/696 7326, ⓕ 020/696 9369. Metro Gaasperplas, or Exit S113 off A9. Campsite just the other side of the Bijlmermeer housing complex in Amsterdam Zuidoost (Southeast), and easily reached from Centraal Station by metro. Very close to the open-air Gaasperplas park, which has facilities for all sorts of outdoor activities. Rates are €4 (€1.75 for under-12s), plus €5.25 per tent, €3.50 for a car, €5.75 for a caravan. Open mid-March to December.

Apartments and houseboats

For groups or families especially, short-term **apartment** rentals can work out cheaper than staying in a hotel, with the further advantages of privacy and the convenience (or at least economy) of self-catering. Apartments sleeping four or five can often be found for the same price as a double room in a hotel. **Houseboats** tend to be significantly more luxurious and expensive. Both are often organized through local hotels.

Acacia Lindengracht 251, 1015 KH Amsterdam ⓣ 020/622 1460, ⓕ 020/638 0748, ⓔ acacia.nl@wxs.nl. Studios and apartments.
Amsterdam House Amstel 176a, 1017 AE Amsterdam ⓣ 020/626 2577, ⓕ 020/626 2987, ⓔ amshouse@euronet.nl. Apartments and houseboats.

Café*ine* Korte Lijnbaanssteeg 1 ⓦ www .amsterdamapartment.com. Apartments for rent above an Italian-style coffee bar.
Gasthuismolen Apartments Gasthuismolensteeg 10, 1016 AN Amsterdam ⓣ 020/626 6043, ⓕ 020/638 3479, ⓔ info@hotel-hoksbergen.nl. Apartments.

Hostels

If you're on a tight budget, the cheapest central option is to take a dormitory bed in a **hostel**, and there are plenty to choose from: Hostelling International places, unofficial private hostels, even Christian hostels. Most hostels will either provide (relatively) clean bed linen or charge a few euros for it; your own sleeping bag might be a better option. Many hostels also lock guests out for a short period each day to clean the place; and some set a nightly curfew, though these are usually late enough not to cause too much of a problem. Many hostels don't accept reservations from June to August.

The cheapest **dorms** you'll find are the Christian hostels, around €15.50 per person per night; although the average elsewhere is closer to €20. Much more and you might as well be in a hotel room. A few otherwise friendly, good-value places have a policy of **charging more at the weekends** than during the week – a price hike of as much as €5 that can come as an unpleasant surprise. Note that you can pay the same for a bed in a sixteen-person dorm as you'd pay to be in a four-person dorm elsewhere: any place that won't allow you to see the dorm before you pay is worth avoiding. If you want a little extra privacy, many hostels also offer triples, doubles and singles for much less than you'd pay in a regular hotel, though the quality and size of rooms can leave a lot to be desired.

The Old Centre

Anna Spuistraat 6 ☎020/620 1155. Small hostel, with two large seventeen-bed dorms on the ground floor at €18 per bunk. Decorated Bedouin-style, though rooms are rather impersonal; shower rooms are curtained off to the side at reception. OK for short stays. No bookings; 2min from CS.

Bob's Youth Hostel Nieuwzijds Voorburgwal 92 ☎020/623 0063, ℱ020/675 6446. An old favourite with backpackers and a grungy crowd, *Bob's* is lively and smoky. Small dorms at €17 per person, including breakfast in the coffeeshop on the ground floor (which also does cheap dinners). They also let four apartments (€70 for two people, €80 for three). However, they kick everyone out at 10am to clean, which is not so good if you want a lie in; 10min from CS.

Bulldog Low-Budget Hotel Oudezijds Voorburgwal 220 ☎020/620 3822, ℱ020/627 1612, ⊛www.bulldog.nl. Part of the Bulldog coffeeshop chain, and recently renovated into "a five-star hotel for backpackers". Bar and DVD lounge downstairs complete with leather couches and soft lighting. Dorms with TV and shower start at €26, including breakfast, linen and wake-up service. Also double rooms, as well as fully equipped luxury apartments available from €130. Tram #4, #9, #16 or #24 to Dam, then a 3min walk. ❸

Durty Nelly's Warmoesstraat 115–117 ☎020/638 0125, ℮nellys@xs4all.nl. Good-quality partitioned dorms above a packed Irish pub, with a cooked breakfast, sheets and lockers included (€22 per person, €25 weekends). Street-side dorms are better lit and airier; 5min from CS.

Flying Pig Downtown Nieuwendijk 100 ☎020/420 6822, ℱ020/624 9516, ⊛www .flyingpig.nl. Clean, large and well run by ex-travellers familiar with the needs of backpackers. Free use of kitchen facilities, no curfew, and there's a late-night coffeeshop next door. Hostel bar open all night. Justifiably popular, and a very good deal, with dorm beds for €19–25 depending on the size of the dorm; queensize bunks sleeping two also available. €10 deposit for sheets and keys. During the peak season you'll need to book well in advance. See also the *Flying Pig Palace*, p.148; 5min from CS.

Kabul Warmoesstraat 38–42 ☎020/623 7158, ℱ020/620 0869. Large and bustling with basic rooms sleeping between one and sixteen people. €21 in peak season, including use of all facilities. Not always as clean as it might be, but there's no lockout or curfew and you can book in advance. Groups welcome; 3min from CS.

Last Waterhole Oudezijds Armsteeg 12 ☎020/624 4814, ℱ020/427 4985, ⊛www .lastwaterhole.nl. Long-established friendly

Amsterdam dosshouse, this graffitied hostel is well due for a refit – the shower rooms leave a lot to be desired. Large twelve-person dorms, with sheets and towels included; €16 per person during the week (watch out for the weekend price hike). No breakfast. The dorm price includes storage space, but no lock, so make sure you bring your own. Live blues and rock bands every night; beer served in chilled glasses; 3min from CS.

Meeting Point Warmoesstraat 14 ⊤ 020/627 7499, ⨍ 020/330 4774, ⓔ info @hostel-meetingpoint.nl. Warm and cosy central hostel with space in twelve- to eighteen-bed dorms going for €16 per person during the week. Cash only. Four-person dorms also available from €92. Breakfast of bread, jam and eggs €2.50. Checkout 10am. Private bar and pool table for guests; 2min from CS.

The Shelter City Barndesteeg 21 ⊤ 020/625 3230, ⨍ 020/623 2282, ⓦ www.shelter.nl. A non-evangelical Christian youth hostel smack in the middle of the Red Light District. At €15.50 these are some of the best-value beds in Amsterdam, with bed linen, shower and sizeable breakfast included. Dorms are single-sex, lockers require a €5 deposit and there's a midnight curfew (1am at weekends). You might be handed a booklet on Jesus when you check in, but you'll get a quiet night's sleep and the sheets are clean. Metro Nieuwmarkt.

Stay Okay Stadsdoelen Kloveniersburgwal 97 ⊤ 020/624 6832, ⨍ 020/639 1035, ⓦ www.stayokay/stadsdoelen. The closest to Centraal Station of the two official hostels, with clean, semi-private dorms at €17.50 for members, who get priority in high season; non-members pay €20.65. Price includes linen, breakfast and locker, plus use of communal kitchen. Guests get a range of discounts on activities in the city too, and you can also book Eurolines bus tickets here, with card holders receiving a ten percent discount. The bar overlooks the canal and serves good-value if basic food, and there's a 2am curfew (though the door opens for three 15min intervals between 2am and 7am). Metro Nieuwmarkt, or tram #4, #9, #16, #20, #24 or #25 to Muntplein. The other HI hostel is the *Stay Okay Vondelpark*, which is better equipped for large groups (see p.148).

Grachtengordel south

Euphemia Fokke Simonszstraat 1–9 ⊤ & ⨍ 020/622 9045, ⓦ www.euphemiahotel.com. Situated a shortish walk from Leidseplein and the major museums, with a likeable laid-back atmosphere and big, basic rooms with TVs. Doubles, and three- and four-bed rooms (for a steep €50 per person), drop to half price during the low season. Breakfast not included. Minimum two-night stay at weekends, booking advised. Tram #16, #24 or #25 to Weteringcircuit. ⑤

Hans Brinker Kerkstraat 136 ⊤ 020/622 0687, ⨍ 020/638 2060. Well-established and rau-cously popular Amsterdam cheapie, which has over 500 beds. Dorm beds go for around €21 including breakfast. Singles and doubles also available. The facilities are good: free Internet after 10pm, disco every night, and dorms are basic and clean; near to the buzz of Leidseplein too. A hostel to head for if you're out for a good time (and not too bothered about getting a deep night's sleep), though be prepared to change dorms several times during your stay. Walk-in policy only. Tram #1, #2 or #5 to Prinsengracht. ①

International Budget Hotel Leidsegracht 76 ⊤ 020/624 2784, ⨍ 020/626 1839, ⓔ info @internationalbudgethotel.com. An excellent budget option on a peaceful little canal in the heart of the city, with the same owners as the *Euphemia* (see above). Small, simple rooms sleeping up to four (from €30 per person), with singles and doubles available. Young, friendly staff. Tram #1, #2 or #5 to Prinsengracht. ②

The Jordaan and the Westerdok

The Shelter Jordan Bloemstraat 179 ⊤ 020/624 4717, ⨍ 020/627 6137, ⓦ www.shelter.nl. The second of Amsterdam's two Christian youth hostels (the other is *Shelter City*, see above). Great value at €15.50 per bed, with breakfast and bed linen included. Dorms are single-sex, lockers require a €5 deposit and there's a 2am curfew. Friendly and helpful staff, plus a decent café. Sited in a particularly beautiful part of the Jordaan, close to the Lijnbaansgracht canal. Tram #13, #14 or #17 to Marnixstraat.

The Museum Quarter and Vondelpark

Flying Pig Palace Vossiusstraat 46 ⓣ020/400 4187, ⓕ020/470 5159, ⓦwww.flyingpig.nl. The better of the two *Flying Pig* hotels, facing the Vondelpark and close to the city's most important museums. Immaculately clean and well maintained by a staff of travellers, who understand their backpacking guests. Free use of kitchen facilities, no curfew and good tourist information. Ten-bed dorms start at €18 per person and there are a few two-person queensize bunks at €27, as well as double rooms. Great value. Tram #1, #2 or #5 to Leidseplein, then walk. ❶–❷

Stay Okay Vondelpark Zandpad 5 ⓣ020/589 8996, ⓕ020/589 8955, ⓦwww.stayokay /vondelpark. Well located and, for facilities, the better of the city's two HI hostels, with a bar, restaurant, TV lounge, free Internet access and bicycle shed, plus various discount facilities for tours and museums. HI members have priority in high season and pay €2.50 less than non-members. Member rates are €21 per person in the dorms, including use of all facilities, shower, sheets and breakfast. Singles, doubles and rooms sleeping up to six are available. Secure lockers; lift; no curfew. To be sure of a place in high season you'll need to book at least two months ahead. Tram #1, #2 or #5 to Leidseplein, then walk. ❷

Hotels and B&Bs

Aside from a couple of ultra-cheap places, most of Amsterdam's **hotels** start at around €60 for a double, and although some form of breakfast – "Dutch" (bread and jam) or "English" (eggs) – is normally included in the price at all but the cheapest and the most expensive hotels, some places give the barest value for your money. Given this state of affairs, it's advisable to ask to see the room first before you slap down any money, and if you don't like it refuse it. A number of hotels in Amsterdam have large three- or four-bed family rooms available from €150. Rooms ambitiously dubbed "penthouses" are popular with large groups and are usually located on the top floor as far away from other guests as possible. Most hotel prices include tax, but some of the more expensive places charge five percent on top of quoted prices.

There are relatively few **bed-and-breakfasts** in Amsterdam, although they are on the increase and we've listed some of the best. Holiday Link, Postbus 70-155, 9704 AD Groningen (ⓣ050/313 3535, ⓕ050/313 3177 ⓦwww .holidaylink.com), can send you a book for €15 that lists reputable B&Bs throughout the country.

The Old Centre

AMS City Centre Nieuwezijds Voorburgwal 50 ⓣ020/422 0011, ⓕ020/420 0357, ⓦwww.ams.nl. A three-star hotel which is sparklingly clean, but nevertheless rather soulless. En-suite rooms with TV and tea- and coffee-making facilities. 10min from CS. ❻

Amsterdam House (Eureka) 's-Gravelandseveer 3 ⓣ020/624 6607, ⓕ020/624 1346, ⓦwww.amsterdamhouse.com. Considering it's just across the Amstel from Rembrandtplein, this delightful hotel is located in a surprisingly quiet part of town. Rooms are small but clean and pleasant, the staff are friendly, and you're perfectly

positioned for the nightlife. Tram #4, #9, #16, #24 or #25 to Muntplein. ❷

Botel Amstel Moored at Oosterdokskade 2 ⓣ020/626 4247, ⓕ020/639 1952. Despite the seeming romance of a floating hotel, the rooms are all identically poky and connected by claustrophobic corridors. Something a bit different certainly, but, in-house movies or not, staying here is like spending your holiday on a cross-Channel ferry. Breakfast extra. Minimum three-night stay at weekends; 2min from CS. ❸

The Crown Oudezijds Voorburgwal 21 ⓣ020/626 9664, ⓕ020/420 6473, ⓦwww.hotelthecrown.com. Friendly hotel overlooking a canal. Rooms with large twin beds from €45 per person, without breakfast. Triples, quads and six-person rooms also available, some with a view. Two-night minimum stay at weekends. Very safe, despite the location. Late bar until 3am; 3min from CS. ❸

Delta Damrak 42 ☏ 020/620 2626, ℱ 020/620 3513, ⓦ www.delta-hotel.com. If you really want to stay on Damrak, try this place first – uninspired, plain and characterless, but comfortable enough, it's one of the better options on a generally unappealing street; 10min from CS. ❺

France Oudezijds Kolk 11 ☏ 020/535 3777, ℱ 020/535 3788, ℮ info@francehotel.nl. Spartan hotel on a tiny, very beautiful and little-used canal in the heart of the Old Centre. Small, comfortable rooms, if a little characterless. Payment on arrival; 2min from CS. ❻

De Gerstekorrel Damstraat 22–24 ☏ 020/624 1367, ℱ 020/623 2640, ℮ gersteko@euronet.nl. Small, simple hotel, steps away from the Dam, with large, brightly decorated and well-lit rooms. Pleasant staff and good buffet breakfast €9.50, but on a noisy street, so ask for a back room. One of the cheaper options within this price range. No ground-floor rooms. Tram #4, #9, #16, #24 or #25 to Dam square. ❺

The Globe Oudezijds Voorburgwal 3 ☏ 020/421 7424, ℱ 020/421 7423, ℮ manager@the-globe.demon.nl. A popular hotel and sports-screen bar, which is a favourite with those on all-day drinking binges. In addition to rooms they have dorm beds from €19, a little more on the weekend. €20 key deposit. Breakfast is an extra €4.20; 5min from CS. ❸

Grand Oudezijds Voorburgwal 197 ☏ 020/555 3111, ℱ 020/555 3222, ⓦ www.thegrand.nl. Originally a Royal Inn dating from 1578, and after that the Amsterdam Town Hall, this fine Classical building is a handsome affair and one of the city's architectural high points. The rooms are large and well-appointed and decorated in crisp, modern style. All facilities including an inside pool. Tram #4, #9, #16, #24 or #25 to Dam square. ❾

Grand Hotel Krasnapolsky Dam 9 ☏ 020/554 9111, ℱ 020/622 8607, ⓦ www.nh-hotels.com. A huge and strikingly good-looking, mid-nine-teenth-century building, this luxurious hotel occupies an entire side of Dam square. If you can't afford the rack-rate (€265 or more for a double), scrape together

enough for lunch in the charming Winter Garden, a spectacular atrium in the heart of the hotel. Tram #4, #9, #16, #24 or #25 to Dam square. ❽

Hotel de l'Europe Nieuwe Doelenstraat 2–8 ☏ 020/531 1777, ℱ 020/531 1778, ⓦ www .leurope.nl. Very central hotel which retains a wonderful *fin-de-siècle* charm, with large, well-furnished rooms and a very attractive riverside terrace. Liveried staff and a red carpet on the pavement outside complete the picture. €320 without breakfast and tax. Tram #4, #9, #16, #24 or #25 to Muntplein. ❾

Nes Kloveniersburgwal 137–139 ☏ 020/624 4773, ℱ 020/620 9842, ⓦ www.hotelnes.nl. Extremely pleasant and quiet, with a lift; well-positioned away from noise but close to shops and nightlife. Helpful staff. Prices vary, depending on the view. Tram #4, #9, #16, #24 or #25 to Muntplein. ❻

Rho Nes 5 ☏ 020/620 7371, ℱ 020/620 7826, ⓦ www.rhohotel.com. A very comfortable hotel in a quiet alley off Dam square. Boasts an extraordinary high-ceilinged lounge, originally built as a theatre in 1908. The place looks a bit run-down from the outside, but it's still a fine city-centre option, with helpful and welcoming staff. Towards the top end of its price bracket. Tram #4, #9, #16, #24 or #25 to Dam square. ❻

Rokin Rokin 73 ☏ 020/626 7456, ℱ 020/625 6453, ⓦ www.rokinhotel.com. Three-star family hotel which has recently undergone major expansion. Doubles from €75, including breakfast. Private car park. New building has a lift. Tram #4, #9, #16, #24 or #25 to Dam or Spui. ❷

Tourist Inn Spuistraat 52 ☏ 020/421 5841, ℱ 020/427 0900, ⓦ www.tourist-inn.nl. Popular budget hotel, with clean and comfortable rooms and friendly staff. Six-person dorms with TV (€25), doubles without shower from €80. Triples and quads also available. Higher weekend rates. Lift access; 5min from CS. ❸

Travel Beursstraat 23 ☏ 020/626 6532, ℱ 020/627 1250, ℮ travelhotel@hotmail.com. Small, simple hotel on a dingy street. Inside it's very clean and comfortable, with a quiet 24-hour bar and no curfew. Light years away from the backpacker places nearby and 10min from CS. ❹

Utopia Nieuwezijds Voorburgwal 132 ☏ 020/626 1295, ℱ 020/622 7060, ⓦ www.hotelutopia.nl.

Self-proclaimed "smokers' hotel" above a coffeeshop with tiny, musty rooms over the street, reached by a near-vertical staircase. Basic, and generally welcoming, though we've had complaints about unhelpful staff during peak season. 10min from CS. **❶**
Victoria Damrak 1–5 ⊕ 020/623 4255, ⑨ 020/625 2997, ⓔ vicres@parkplazahotels.nl. The *Victoria* is one of the landmarks of the city – a tall, elegant building, wonderfully decorated throughout – and one of the classiest hotels, with every possible amenity. Opposite CS. **❾**
Vijaya Oudezijds Voorburgwal 44 ⊕ 020/626 9406, ⑨ 020/620 5277, ⓦ www.hotelvijaya.com. Stately old canal house in the heart of the Red Light District, with plain rooms and accommodating management, who also own an Indian restaurant of the same name. Clean, but no lift; 10min from CS. **❸**
Winston Warmoesstraat 123 ⊕ 020/623 1380, ⑨ 020/639 2308, ⓦ www.winston.nl. Popular but noisy hotel designed for an arty crowd. Rooms (sleeping from one to six) are light and airy, some en-suite, some with a communal balcony, and many are specially commissioned "art" rooms, including the Durex Room, Heineken Room and Schiffmacher Room (the management plans to refurbish all the rooms in this way over the next few years). Lift and full disabled access. 10min from CS. **❸**

Grachtengordel west

Ambassade Herengracht 341 ⊕ 020/555 0222, ⑨ 020/555 0277, ⓦ www.ambassade-hotel.nl. Elegant canalside hotel made up of ten seventeenth-century houses, with elegant furnished lounges, a well-stocked library and comfortable en-suite rooms. Breakfast is an extra €14, but well worth it. Tram #1, #2 or #5 to Spui. **❼**
Aspen Raadhuisstraat 31 ⊕ 020/626 6714, ⑨ 020/620 0866, ⓦ www.hotelaspen.nl. One of a number of inexpensive hotels situated in the Art Nouveau crescent of the Utrecht Building. Family-run with basic but tidy rooms, which are checked every day. Tram #13, #14 or #17 to Westermarkt. **❷**
Blakes Keizersgracht 384 ⊕ 020/530 2010, ⑨ 020/530 2030, ⓔ hotel@blakes.nl. The latest Anouchka Hempel hotel (there are already two in London), housed in a seventeenth-century building, centred on a beautiful courtyard and terrace. Both the decor and

the restaurant menu combine Oriental and European styles. Each of the 26 rooms is opulently decorated, featuring exposed beams and natural fabrics. Luxury suites overlook the Keizersgracht canal. Hip without being pretentious. Doubles from €370. Tram #1, #2 or #5 to Keizersgracht. **❾**
Brian Singel 69 ⊕ 020/624 4661, ⑨ 020/625 3958, ⓔ hotelbrian@hotmail.com. A cheap and friendly hotel in a good spot; €54 for a very basic but clean double, including breakfast and free tea and coffee throughout the day. Less positively, its compact rooms and narrow stairways means it suffers from "slamming door syndrome" late at night; not the best place if you're looking for somewhere peaceful; 10min from CS. **❶**
Canal House Keizersgracht 148 ⊕ 020/622 5182, ⑨ 020/624 1317, ⓦ www.canalhouse.nl. Magnificently restored seventeenth-century building, centrally located on one of the principal canals. Comfortable rooms, but generally brusque staff. Tram #13, #14 or #17 to Westermarkt. **❺**
Clemens Raadhuisstraat 39 ⊕ 020/624 6089, ⑨ 020/626 9658, ⓦ www.clemenshotels.nl. Friendly, well-run budget hotel, close to the Anne Frank House and museums. One of the better options along this busy main road. Individually decorated doubles without shower from €70, with shower €110. Breakfast extra. All rooms offer free Internet connection, and you can rent laptops for €8. Prices stay the same throughout the year, with seasonal offers. Tram #13, #14 or #17 to Westermarkt. Recommended. **❷–❹**
Estherea Singel 303–309 ⊕ 020/624 5146, ⑨ 020/623 9001, ⓔ estherea@xs4all.nl. Chic, standard hotel converted from a row of canal houses; though they lack the personal touch, the rooms are all of a high quality. Tram #1, #2 or #5 to Spui. **❽**
Galerij Raadhuisstraat 43 ⊕ 020/624 8851, ⑨ 020/420 7725. One of the Raadhuisstraat budget options. Basic rooms (ask for a quieter one at the back) with clean sheets but well-worn blankets. Doubles for €70, but prices go up a little on the weekend. Tram #13, #14 or #17 to Westermarkt. **❷**
Hegra Herengracht 269 ⊕ 020/623 7877, ⑨ 020/623 8159. Welcoming atmosphere and relatively inexpensive for the location, on a beautiful stretch of the canal. Rooms are

small but comfortable; a few have a private bath instead of a shower. Tram #1, #2 or #5 to Spui. ②–③

Hoksbergen Singel 301 ⓣ020/626 6043, ⓕ020/638 3479, ⓔhotelhoksbergen@wxs.nl. Friendly, standard-issue hotel, with a light and open breakfast room overlooking the canal. Basic en-suite rooms, all with telephone and TV. Self-catering apartments also available. Tram #1, #2 or #5 to Spui. ③–④

't Hotel Leliegracht 18 ⓣ020/422 2741, ⓕ020/626 7873, ⓔth.broekema@hetnet.nl. Extremely pleasant hotel located along a quiet canal. Owned by the proprietor of an antique shop, who believes in making people feel at home. Eight spacious rooms, large beds, TV, fridge and either bath or shower. No groups. Minimum three-night stay at the weekend. Tram #13 or #17 to Westermarkt. ⑤

Keizersgracht Keizersgracht 15 ⓣ020/625 1364, ⓕ020/620 7347. Terrific location on a major canal close to the station with a good mixture of clean, though somewhat jaded, singles and doubles, plus rooms sleeping up to four people. Breakfast not included; 5min from CS. ③

Pax Raadhuisstraat 37 ⓣ020/624 9735. Straightforward city-centre cheapie, owned by two brothers, Philip and Peter. A mixture of fair-sized rooms sleeping one to four persons, but plans are afoot to refurbish the rooms in the minimalist white style of the large double on the top floor. In the meantime, as with most of the hotels along here, ask for a room at the back. Cash only. Tram #13, #14 or #17 to Westermarkt. ②

Pulitzer Prinsengracht 315 ⓣ020/523 5235, ⓕ020/627 6753, ⓦwww.starwood.com. An entire row of seventeenth-century canal houses creatively converted into a five-star chain hotel. Very popular with visiting businessfolk, but although the public areas are tastefully decorated and the breakfasts very good, the modern rooms lack character and some – considering the price – are very disappointing. From €300 for a double. Tram #13, #14 or #17 to Westermarkt. ⑨

Toren Keizersgracht 164 ⓣ020/622 6033, ⓕ020/626 9705, ⓔhotel.toren@tip.nl. Fine example of an imaginatively revamped seventeenth-century canal house, once the home of a Dutch prime minister and now popular with American visitors. Opulently designed en-suite doubles with a touch of

class from €130. Some deluxe rooms have a Jacuzzi. Friendly and efficient staff. Tram #13, #14 or #17 to Westermarkt. Something of a snip. ⑤

Wiechmann Prinsengracht 328–332 ⓣ020/626 3321, ⓕ020/626 8962, ⓦwww.hotelweichmann .nl. Canal-house restoration, family-run for fifty years, with dark wooden beams and restrained style throughout. Large, bright rooms with TV and shower, kept in perfect condition. Close to the Anne Frank House. Prices stay the same throughout the year. Tram #13, #14 or #17 to Westermarkt. ⑤

Grachtengordel south

De Admiraal Herengracht 563 ⓣ020/626 2150, ⓕ020/623 4621. Friendly hotel close to the nightlife, with wonderful canal views. Breakfast an extra €5. Reception sometimes closes during the day. Tram #4, #9 or #14 to Rembrandtplein. ②

Agora Singel 462 ⓣ020/627 2200, ⓕ020/627 2202, ⓔagora@worldonline.nl. Nicely located, small and amiable hotel right near the flower market; doubles cost upwards of €110, three- and four-bed rooms proportionately less. You'll pay more for a canal view. Same rates throughout the year. Tram #1, #2 or #5 to Koningsplein. ④

American Leidsekade 97 ⓣ020/556 3000, ⓕ020/556 3001, ⓔamerican@6C.com. Landmark Art Deco hotel dating from 1902 (and in pristine, renovated condition), right on Leidseplein and the water. Large, double-glazed, modern doubles from around €330. If you can't afford to stay, don't leave Amsterdam without soaking up some of the atmosphere at the popular and superbly decorated *Café Américain* overlooking the square. Tram #1, #2 or #5 to Leidseplein. ⑨

Armada Keizersgracht 713–715 ⓣ020/623 2980, ⓕ020/623 5829, ⓔhotelarmada @chello.nl. Large if slightly tatty rooms close by the Amstel. Triples and quads also available. Tram #4 to Keizersgracht. ③

Dikker & Thijs Fenice Prinsengracht 444 ⓣ020/620 1212, ⓕ020/625 8986, ⓦwww.dtfh.nl. Small and stylish hotel on a beautiful canal close to all the shops. Rooms vary in decor but all include a minibar, telephone and TV – those on the top floor give a good view of the city; there is a lift too, but it's small and old-fashioned. Tram #1, #2 or #5 to Prinsengracht. ⑦–⑧

Het Leidseplein Korte Leidsedwarsstraat 79 ☏ 020/627 2505, ℱ 020/623 0065, ⊛ www .leidsepleinhotel.nl. Scruffy, low-maintenance hotel handily placed for frenetic Leidseplein, but on a noisy and tacky street. Steep and narrow staircase. Rooms basic but spacious with TV and minibar. Tram #1, #2 or #5 to Leidseplein. ❸

De Leydsche Hof Leidsegracht 14 ☏ 020/623 2148. Stately, privately run canal house on one of the smaller and quieter waterways. It looks a bit run-down from the outside, but the rooms are comfortably sized and each has an en-suite shower. Tram #1, #2 or #5 to Keizersgracht. Closed October 1 to April 1. ❶

Maas Leidsekade 91 ☏ 020/623 3868, ℱ 020/622 2613, ⊛ www.hemhotels.nl. Modern hotel on a quiet stretch of water; clean, nicely decorated and well-equipped, en-suite rooms – ask for one with a waterbed! Rooms from €95, marginally more for a canal view. Tram #1, #2 or #5 to Leidseplein. ❹

Marcel van Woerkom Leidsestraat 87 ☏ & ℱ 020/622 9834, ⊛ www.marcelamsterdam.com. Well-known, popular B&B run by an English-speaking graphic designer and artist, who attracts like-minded people to this stylish restored house. Four en-suite doubles available for two, three or four people sharing. Relaxing and peaceful amidst the buzz of the city, with regulars returning year after year, so you'll need to ring well in advance in high season. Breakfast not included, but there are tea- and coffee-making facilities. ❹

De Munck Achtergracht 3 ☏ 020/623 6283, ℱ 020/620 6647, ⊛ www.hoteldemunck.com. Fine, family-run hotel in a quiet spot steps from the Amstel, with clean, light and well-maintained rooms. The Sixties-style breakfast room sports a Wurlitzer jukebox with a good collection of 1960s hits. Booking recommended. Tram #4 to Frederiksplein. ❹

Op de Gracht Prinsengracht 826 ☏ 020/626 1937, ℱ 202/489 1916, ℮ opdegracht@hetnet.nl. B&B in a good-looking canal house on one of the main canals; run by the very pleasant Jolanda Schipper. Two rooms tastefully decorated, both with en-suite bathroom. Minimum stay two nights. Tram #4 from CS to Prinsengracht. ❸–❹

Prinsenhof Prinsengracht 810 ☏ 020/623 1772, ℱ 020/638 3368, ⊛ www.hotelprinsenhof.com.

Tastefully decorated, this is one of the city's top budget options with doubles at €60 without shower. Booking essential. Tram #4 to Prinsengracht. ❶–❷

Quentin Leidsekade 89 ☏ 020/626 2187, ℱ 202/622 0121. Very friendly small hotel, often a stopover for artists performing at the Melkweg (see p.182). Welcoming to all, and especially well-regarded among gay and lesbian visitors, but families with children might feel out of place. Tram #1, #2 or #5 to Leidseplein. ❸

Schiller Karena Rembrandtplein 26–36 ☏ 020/554 0700, ℱ 020/624 0098, ℮ nhschiller@nh-hotels.nl. Once something of a hangout for Amsterdam's intellectuals, the Schiller still has one of the city's better-known and more atmospheric bars on its ground floor. Named after the renowned painter and architect, whose works are liberally sprinkled throughout the hotel. Fetching Art Deco furnishings in all the public areas. The drawback is its location – on tacky Rembrandtplein. Tram #4, #9 or #14 to Rembrandtplein. ❼

Seven Bridges Reguliersgracht 31 ☏ 020/623 1329. Perhaps the city's most charming hotel – and certainly one of its better-value ones. Takes its name from its canalside location, which affords a view of no less than seven dinky little bridges. Beautifully decorated, its spotless rooms are regularly revamped. Small and popular, so often booked solid. Breakfast is served in your room and prices vary depending on the view. Recommended. Tram #4 or #9 to Prinsengracht. ❹–❻

The Jordaan and the Westerdok

Acacia Lindengracht 251 ☏ 020/622 1460, ℱ 020/638 0748, ℮ acacia.nl@wxs.nl. Well-kept hotel, along a quiet canal. Situated right on a corner, so some of the rooms have panoramic views of the water and streets below. They also let self-catering apartments. Doubles from €80 as well as three-, four- and five-bed rooms available. A fifteen-minute walk from CS. ❸

De Bloeiende Ramenas Haarlemmerdijk 61 ☏ 020/624 6030, ℱ 020/420 2261, ℮ myhotel@ibn.net. Welcoming and friendly hotel with large, basic rooms at sensible prices, though those at the front can be a bit noisy. Located to the northwest of the centre, away from the nightlife, but with good access to the city's markets; 15min from CS. ❶

Calendula Goldbloom's Goudsbloemstraat 132 ☎020/428 3055, ⓕ020/776 0075, ⓦwww.calendulas.com. Comfortable and well-furnished B&B, off an unassuming street, close to the Noordermarkt. Has a couple of spacious double rooms, each with TV, and a shared bathroom. Bus #18 to Willemstraat. ❹

Johanna's Van Hogendorpplein 62 ☎020/684 8596, ⓕ020/413 3056, ⓔjohannas@planet.nl. A privately run B&B, very friendly and helpful to newcomers. It's a little difficult to get to, situated out near the Westergasfabriek, but is excellent value. Two double rooms only, so be sure to call before you set out. Tram #10 from Leidseplein to Van Limburg Stirumplein. ❸

La Bohème Marnixstraat 415 ☎020/624 2828, ⓕ020/627 2897, ⓔhotel@bohemeA200.nl. One of the best of the many, many hotels spreading up the Marnixstraat from Leidseplein, this small establishment with super-friendly staff has en-suite doubles for €110. Tram #1, #2 or #5 to Leidseplein. ❹

Mark's B&B Van Beuningenstraat 80a ☎020/776 0056, ⓕ020/682 7372, ⓦwww.geocities.com/CollegePark/Plaza/3686. Comfortable and stylishly decorated B&B, with two doubles, which can be booked as one apartment. No breakfast but use of fridge provided along with tea and coffee facilities. Rooms are non-smoking. There's a pleasant garden terrace too. Tram #10 to de Wittenkade, or a five-minute taxi ride from CS. Minimum booking two nights; price band depends on length of stay. ❷–❸

Van Onna Bloemgracht 102 ☎020/626 5801, ⓦwww.netcentrum.com/onna/. A quiet, well-maintained, family-run place on a tranquil canal, still retaining some of its original fixtures dating back over three hundred years. Simple setup, no TV, no smoking and cash payment only. Rooms sleeping up to four people for €40 per person, including all services. Booking advised. Tram #13, #14 or #17 to Westermarkt. ❸

The Old Jewish Quarter and the East

Adolesce Nieuwe Keizersgracht 26 ☎020/626 3959, ⓕ020/627 4249, ⓔadolesce@xs4all.nl. Large, popular and welcoming hotel, with

neat if unspectacular rooms and a large dining room and bar. Tram #9 or #14 to Waterlooplein. ❸

Amstel Inter-Continental Professor Tulpplein 1 ☎020/622 6060, ⓕ020/622 5808, ⓦwww.interconti.com. The absolute top-of-the-range – one of the best and most luxurious hotels in the country. Favoured by visiting celebrities and renovated a few years ago in sumptuous style to the tune of €50 million. If you have the money, splash out on a night of ultimate style and class; cheapest doubles from €395. If you're in a regal mood, check out the Royal Suite from €2890 per night. Metro Weesperplein. ❾

Fantasia Nieuwe Keizersgracht 16 ☎020/623 8259, ⓕ020/622 3913, ⓦwww.fantasia-hotel.com. Nicely situated family-run hotel on a broad, quiet canal just off the Amstel; the rooms are well maintained, connected by quaint, narrow corridors, and there are also some very attractive attic rooms for €75. Triples and quads also available. Tram #9 or #14 to Waterlooplein. ❷

De Hortus Plantage Parklaan 8 ☎020/625 9996, ⓕ020/625 3958, ⓦwww.hotelhortus.com. Smoker-friendly hotel close to the Hortus Botanicus. Rooms vary in size, from two- to twelve-person, and maintenance is kept to a minimum, but they're clean, and the common room, equipped with pool table and coffee machine, has a good atmosphere. Note that you need to confirm your booking two days prior, though, otherwise you'll lose the room. All rooms €25 per person. Tram #9 to Artis Zoo. ❶

Hotel Arena 's-Gravesandestraat 51 ☎020/850 2410, ⓕ020/850 2415, ⓦwww.hotelarena.nl. A little way east of the centre, in a renovated old convent on the edge of the Oosterpark, this place has recently been revamped, transforming a popular hostel into a hip three-star hotel complete with split-level rooms and minimalist decor. Despite the odd pretentious flourish, it manages to retain a relaxed vibe attracting both businessfolk and travellers alike. Lively bar, intimate restaurant, and late-night club (Fri & Sat) located within the former chapel. Doubles start from €125. Metro Weesperplein, then walk, or tram #6 from Leidseplein to Korte 's-Gravensandestraat. ❺

Kitty Plantage Middenlaan 40 ☎020/622 6819. Located above a butcher's and run by a pensioner, this quiet, large old house is a little out from the centre, but in an interesting neighbourhood close to the Zoo. Decent-sized rooms from €60 a double. Tram #9 or #14 to Plantage Badlaan. **❶–❷**

Rembrandt **Plantage Middenlaan 17 ☎020/627 2714, ℱ020/638 0293, ℮info@rembrandt.nl.** Elegant hotel with a dining room dating from the sixteenth century, though the building itself is nowhere near as old. Rooms are decorated in crisp modern style, with wood interiors and are en suite. Tram #9 to Artis Zoo. Minimum two-night stay in high season. **❷–❸**

The Museum Quarter and Vondelpark

Acro **Jan Luyckenstraat 44 ☎020/662 5538, ℱ020/675 0811, ℗www.acro-hotel.nl.** Excellent, modern hotel with stylish rooms, a plush bar and self-service restaurant (breakfast only). Well worth the money; reserve at least two months in advance. Tram #2 or #5 to Van Baerlestraat. **❸**

AMS Atlas **Van Eeghenstraat 64 ☎020/676 6336, ℱ020/671 7633, ℗www.ams.nl.** Situated near the Vondelpark and occupying an attractive Art Nouveau building, the Atlas is a personable modern hotel with every convenience and comfort, plus an à la carte restaurant. Small, tranquil and very welcoming. Discounts often available. One of the fourteen hotels in the AMS Hotel Group whose establishments range from two- to four-star. Tram #2 to Jacob Obrechtstraat. **❺**

AMS Hotel Holland **P.C. Hooftstraat 162 ☎020/676 4253, ℱ020/676 5956, ℗www.ams.nl.** Comfortable, quiet and welcoming hotel at the end of the street near the Vondelpark. Tram #2 or #5 to Hobbemastraat **❹**

AMS Museum **P.C. Hooftstraat 2 ☎020/662 1402, ℱ020/673 3918, ℗www.ams.nl.** Large, standard-issue but very well-maintained hotel, next door to the Rijksmuseum. Tram #2 or #5 to Hobbemastraat. **❻**

AMS Toro **Koningslaan 64 ☎020/673 7223, ℱ020/675 0031, ℗www.ams.nl.** Lovely hotel in two very comfortably furnished early twentieth-century town houses on a peaceful residential street by the southern reaches of the Vondelpark. Has its own garden and terrace overlooking a lake in the park. Tram #2 to Emmastraat. **❼**

Bema **Concertgebouwplein 19b ☎020/679 1396, ℱ020/662 3688, ℮postbus@hotel_bema.demon.nl.** Large, clean

rooms within a huge house under the canny eye of the friendly English-speaking manager-owner. The rooms aren't modern (the beds can be a bit uncomfortable), but they're full of funky character. Handy for concerts and museums. Triples and quads available too. Tram #5 to Museumplein. **❷**

Fita **Jan Luyckenstraat 37 ☎020/679 0976, ℱ020/664 3969, ℗www.fita.nl.** Mid-sized, friendly family-run hotel in a quiet spot between the Vondelpark and the museums. Comfortable en-suite doubles (extra bed €23). All rooms non-smoking. Tram #2 or #5 to Van Baerlestraat. **❹**

Jan Luycken **Jan Luyckenstraat 58 ☎020/573 0730, ℱ020/676 3841, ℗www.janluyken.nl.** Part of the Bildererg hotel group, this elegant hotel is located in an imposing nineteenth-century town house. Stylish and comfortable in equal measure. Tram #2 or #5 to Van Baerlestraat. **❼**

Karen McCusker **Zeilstraat ☎020/679 2753 (mornings), ℗www.bedandbreakfastamsterdam .net.** Small B&B run by an Englishwoman who moved to Amsterdam in 1979. Cosy and clean, Laura Ashley-style double rooms in her home, close to the Vondelpark, cost around €60 (€80 for the room with a roof terrace). Ring first, because the owner isn't always resident and you'll also need to reserve well in advance. Tram #2 to Amstelveenseweg. **❶–❷**

Parkzicht **Roemer Visscherstraat 33 ☎020/618 1954, ℱ020/618 0897.** Quiet unassuming little hotel on a pretty backstreet near the Vondelpark and museums, with an appealingly lived-in look – clean and characterful. Closed between Dec and March. Tram #1 to 1e Constantijn Huygensstraat. **❷**

Piet Hein **Vossiusstraat 53 ☎020/662 7205, ℱ020/662 1526, ℗www.hotelpiethein.nl.** Calm, low-key and stylish, tucked away on a quiet street running past the Vondelpark, midway between Leidseplein and the Concertgebouw. Bar with leather couches open till 1am. Lift access. At the lower end of its price bracket. Tram #2 or #5 to Hobbemastraat. Recommended. **❺**

Prinsen **Vondelstraat 38 ☎020/616 2323, ℱ020/616 6112, ℗www.prinsenhotel.demon.nl.** Family-style hotel on the edge of the Vondelpark; quiet and with a large, secluded back garden. Marginally higher rates at the weekend. Tram #1 to 1e Constantijn Huygensstraat. **❺**

Verdi Wanningstraat 9 ☎020/676 0073,
☏020/673 9070. Small and simple hotel with
basic but comfortable rooms near the
Concertgebouw. Basic doubles from €75,
with some en suites for €125. Tram #5 to
Museumplein. ❷

Zandbergen Willemsparkweg 205 ☎020/676
9321, ☏020/676 1860, ⊛www.hotel-zandbergen
.com. Light, airy, family-run hotel on a busy
street near the Vondelpark; the rooms are
clean and spacious. Tram #2 to Jacob
Obrechtstraat. ❺

The outer districts

Hilton Apollolaan 138 ☎020/710 6000,
☏020/710 6080, ⊛www.amsterdam.hilton.com.
Way outside the centre in the distinctly
upmarket Nieuw Zuid, with everything
you'd expect, including a Yacht Club,
health club and a fine Italian restaurant.
Doubles hover around the €240 mark, but
it's only really worth considering if you can
afford to soak up a bit of 1960s nostalgia
in its (admittedly stunning) Lennon and Ono
suite, where the couple held their famous
1969 "Bed-In" for peace; one night here
will set you back €875. Tram #5 or #24 to
Apollolaan. ❽

Van Ostade Van Ostadestraat 123 ☎020/679
3452, ☏020/671 5213,
✉info@.bicyclehotel.com. Friendly, youthful
place not far from the Albert Cuyp market
in the Pijp, it bills itself as a "bicycle hotel",
renting bikes (€5 per day) and giving advice
on routes and suchlike. Basic but clean
rooms, with or without shower. Good
breakfast. Garage parking for cars (€15),
though you'll need to book in advance.
Tram #25 to Ceintuurbaan. ❷–❹

Eating and drinking

A msterdam is a great city to go **drinking** in, fuelled by Holland's proximity to two of the premier beer-drinking nations in Europe – Belgium, where monks more or less invented modern beer, and Germany, famous for its beer consumption – and the city's selection of bars is one of its real pleasures. As for **eating**, this may not be Europe's culinary capital, but there's a good supply of **ethnic restaurants**, especially Indonesian, Chinese and Thai, and the prices (by big-city standards) are hard to beat. Amsterdam's tradition of **eetcafés** and **bars** serving adventurous food for a good price in a relaxed and unpretentious setting is a huge plus too. This said, however, it's worth bearing in mind that Dutch service is not known for its speed, and isn't always the most friendly.

Dutch **mealtimes** are a little idiosyncratic. Breakfast tends to be later than you might expect, and other meals tend to be eaten earlier. If you choose to eat breakfast out of your hotel, you'll find few cafés open before 8 or 8.30am. The standard Dutch lunch hour is from noon to 1pm, and most restaurants are at their busiest between 7 and 8pm, (and may stop serving altogether by 10pm).

For such a small city, Amsterdam is filled with places to eat and drink, and you should have no trouble finding somewhere convenient and enjoyable to suit your budget. On Friday and Saturday nights it's advisable to start early (between 6 and 7pm) or make a **reservation**, if you want to find a place at your favourite choice. While the Red Light District area has more than its fair share of tacky, low-quality establishments, there are plenty of good restaurants scattered all over the city, and in much of the centre you can find a bar on almost every corner.

With Amsterdam's singular approach to the sale and consumption of marijuana, you might choose to enjoy a joint after your meal rather than a beer: we've included in this chapter a selection of **"coffeeshops"** where you can buy and smoke grass. If you want to avoid dope smoke, there are plenty of places throughout the city where you can sit in the afternoon with a cup of coffee and a sandwich; they have taken to calling themselves **tearooms** instead. Non-smokers should beware that wherever you go it's almost impossible to avoid cigarette smoke.

What to eat

Dutch **restaurant food** tends to be higher in protein content than imagination: steak, chicken and fish, along with filling soups and stews, are staple fare. Many places offer *dagschotels* (dish of the day, generally available for as long as the restaurant is open), a meat and two vegetable combination for which you'll pay around €8 bottom line, for what tend to be enormous portions. The fish is generally high-quality but not especially cheap (€10 and up, on average).

Dutch cheese

Holland's **cheeses** have an unjustified reputation abroad for being bland and rubbery, possibly because they only export the nastier products and keep the best for themselves. In fact, Dutch cheese can be delicious, although there isn't the variety you get in, say, France or Britain. Most are based on the same soft, creamy *Goudas*, and differences in taste come with the varying stages of maturity – young, mature or old (*jong*, *belegen* or *oud*). *Jong* cheese has a mild flavour, *belegen* is much tastier, while *oud* can be pungent and strong, with a flaky texture not unlike Italian Parmesan. Generally, the older they get, the saltier they are. Among the other cheeses you'll find are the best-known round, red *Edam*, made principally for export and (quite sensibly) not eaten much by the Dutch; *Leidse*, which is simply *Gouda* with cumin seeds; *Maasdammer* and *Leerdammer*, strong, creamy and full of holes; and Dutch-made *Emmentals* and *Gruyères*. The best way to eat cheese here is the way the Dutch do it, in thin slices cut with a special cheese knife (*kaasschaaf*) rather than large hunks. See p.203 for recommended cheese shops. Street markets are a good place to shop too; try the organic farmers' produce market on Saturday at the Noordermarkt, p.208.

Many places advertise "tourist menus" costing an average of €9 which are usually extremely dull.

A wide selection of **vegetarian** restaurants offer full-course set meals for around €9, or hearty dishes for €8 or less. Bear in mind that they often close early. Another cheap stand-by is **Italian** food: pizzas and pasta dishes start at a fairly uniform €5–6 in all but the ritziest places. **Chinese** and **Thai** restaurants are also common, as are (increasingly) **Spanish** ones, all of which serve well-priced, filling food. But Amsterdam's real speciality is its **Indonesian** restaurants, a consequence of the country's imperial adventures and well worth checking out. You can eat à la carte – nasi goreng and bami goreng (rice or noodles with meat) are ubiquitous dishes, and chicken or beef in peanut sauce (*sateh*) is available everywhere too. Alternatively, order a *rijsttafel*: boiled rice and/or noodles served with a number of spicy side dishes and hot sambal sauce on the side. Eaten with the spoon in the right hand, fork in the left, and with dry white or rosé wine or beer, this doesn't come cheap, but it's delicious and is normally more than enough for two.

In **bars** you can expect to find sandwiches and rolls (*boterhammen* and *broodjes*) – often open, and varying from a simple slice of cheese to something so embellished it's a complete meal – as well as more substantial fare. Dutch classics include **broodje halfom**, a roll with a combination of thinly sliced salted beef and liver eaten with mustard, and broodje warm vlees, thinly sliced warm pork served with sateh sauce. In the winter, **erwtensoep** (aka snert) is available in most bars. At around €5 a serving, this thick pea soup with smoked sausage, accompanied by a portion of smoked bacon on pumpernickel, makes a great-value lunch. Or there's **uitsmijter**: one, two or three fried eggs on buttered bread, topped with a choice of ham, cheese or roast beef – at around €7, it's another good budget lunch.

What to drink

The beverage drunk most often in Amsterdam's bars is **beer**. The three leading brands of Dutch beer – Amstel, Grolsch and Heineken – are worldwide bestsellers, but are available here in considerably more potent formats than the insipid varieties shunted out for export. Beer is usually served in small measures, around half a pint (ask for *een pils*), much of which will be a frothing head. Different beers come in different glasses – Oranjeboom, for instance, is served in a *vaasje*; white beer (*witbier*), which is light, cloudy and served with lemon, has its own tumbler; and most of the speciality Belgian beers have individual stemmed glasses.

Jenever, Dutch gin, is not unlike English gin but a bit weaker and a little oilier; it's made from molasses and flavoured with juniper berries. Served in small glasses it is traditionally drunk straight, often knocked back in one gulp with much hearty back-slapping. There are a number of varieties: oud (old) is smooth and mellow, jong (young) packs more of a punch – though neither is terribly alcoholic. Ask for a *borreltje* (straight jenever), a *bitterje* (with angostura bitters) or, if you've a sweeter tooth, try a *bessenjenever* – blackcurrant-flavoured gin; for a glass of beer with a jenever chaser, ask for a *kopstoot*.

Other drinks you'll see include numerous Dutch **liqueurs**, notably advocaat (eggnog), and the sweet blue *curaçao*; and an assortment of lurid-coloured **fruit brandies**, which are best left for experimentation at the end of an evening. There's also the Dutch-produced brandy, *Vieux*, which tastes as if it's made from prunes but is in fact grape-based.

Dutch **coffee** is black and strong, and comes in disappointingly small cups. It is often served with *koffiemelk* (evaporated milk); ordinary milk is offered only occasionally. If you want white coffee (café au lait), ask for a *koffie verkeerd*. Most bars also serve cappuccino, although bear in mind that many stop serving coffee altogether around 11pm.

Tea generally comes with lemon, if anything; if you want milk you have to ask for it. **Hot chocolate** is also popular, served hot or cold: for a real treat drink it hot with a layer of fresh whipped cream on top.

Breakfast, fast food and snacks

In all but the very cheapest hostels and the most expensive hotels, **breakfast** (*ontbijt*) will be included in the price of the room. Though usually nothing fancy, it's always very filling: rolls, cheese, ham, hard-boiled eggs, jam and honey or peanut butter are the principal ingredients. If you're not eating in your hotel, many bars and cafés serve breakfast, and those that don't invariably offer rolls and sandwiches.

For the rest of the day, eating cheaply and well, particularly on your feet, is no real problem, although those on the tightest of budgets may find themselves dependent on the dubious delights of **Dutch fast food**. This has its own peculiarities. Chips – *frites* – are the most common standby (*Vlaamse* or "Flemish" are the best), either sprinkled with salt or smothered with huge gobs of mayonnaise (sometimes known as *fritesaus*); some alternative toppings are curry, goulash, peanut or tomato sauce. Chips are often complemented with *kroketten* – spiced meat (usually either veal or beef) in hash covered with breadcrumbs and deep-fried – or *fricandel*, a frankfurter-like sausage, made from offal. All these are available over the counter at evil-smelling fast-food places (FEBO is the most common chain), or from heated glass compartments outside. As an alternative there are also a number of **Indonesian take-aways**, serving *sateh* and noodle dishes in an "open-kitchen" atmosphere.

Tastier, and good both as a snack and a full lunch, are the **fish specialities** sold from street kiosks: salted raw herrings, smoked eel, mackerel in a roll, mussels, and various kinds of deep-fried fish; tip your head back and dangle the fish into your mouth, Dutch-style. Other, though far less common, street foods include **pancakes** (*pannekoeken*), sweet or spicy (more widely available at sit-down restaurants), **waffles** (*stroopwafels*) doused with maple syrup, and, in November and December, *oliebollen*, deep-fried dough balls with raisins and

Food delivery

Having food delivered to your door is still far from the norm in Amsterdam, and so something of a rarity. As well as the places listed below, there are many pizza lines, which deliver pizza for free in response to a telephone call. However, the quality of these varies dramatically, and you shouldn't expect anything better than basic. Pizzas usually start at around €6.50. All food delivery lines open in the late afternoon, and most close down by 10pm.

Koh-I-Noor ☎020/623 3133, ⊛www.koh-i-noor-reastaurant.nl. Delivers good-quality, reasonably priced Indian food (see p.173).

Kong Ming Rijnstraat 67 ☎020/644 5377. Delicious Chinese, Thai and Cantonese dishes, in 45 minutes.

Mousaka Express ☎020/675 7000. Just what you'd expect, with a long delivery menu of Greek speciality dishes; mousaka starts at €7.50 (vegetarian from €6), taramasalata for €3 and a mixed grill for two for €25.

Porto Ercole ☎020/624 7654. A wide range of all kinds of Italian food for delivery, from cold and hot antipasti through twenty styles of pizza, fresh homemade pasta and lasagne, to fillet steak and a fine tiramisu. Drop by Vijzelstraat 97 (Grachtengordel south) to pick up a menu.

Soup en Zo ☎020/623 2962. Freshly made soups every day, ranging from peanut to chickpeas and spinach, all wholesome, filling and tasty. Takeaway (at Nieuwe Spiegelstraat 54 and Jodenbreestraat 94) and delivery service.

Taco Mundo ☎0900/123 8226. Substantial portions of Mexican fast food.

Terang Boelan ☎020/620 9974. Will deliver a *rijsttafel* and other Indonesian specialities to your door for around €10.

Top Thai ☎020/683 1297, ⊛www.dinnersite.nl/amsterdam/topthai. The well-known restaurant does deliveries too. They take at least sixty minutes, but are well worth the wait (see p.172).

Two in One ☎020/612 8488. Excellent, reasonably priced Indian and Surinamese food for delivery, at around €7.50 per person.

candied peel, traditionally eaten on New Year's Eve. Dutch **cakes and biscuits** are always good and filling, best eaten in a *banketbakkerij* with a small serving area; or buy a bag and eat them on the go. Apart from the ubiquitous *appelgebak* – a wedge of apple tart flavoured with cinnamon – other things to try include *spekulaas*, a cinnamon biscuit with a gingerbread texture, and *amandelkoek*, cakes with a biscuity outside and melt-in-the-mouth almond paste inside.

Kroketten and frites outlets

FEBO Leidsestraat and Reguliersbreestraat (Grachtengordel south), Damrak (Old Centre) and other locations. The most obvious place to get a *kroket*, but not a bad choice. Ask for it on a roll with some mustard.

Holtkamp Vijzelgracht 15 (Grachtengordel south). More of a pastry shop, but they do sell homemade, fresh-fried *kroketten*, including a shrimp version. Closed Sun.

Kwekkeboom Reguliersbreestraat 36 (Grachtengordel south). Bakery selling pastries, pies, rolls and *kroketten*. There are a couple of small tables out the back.

Van Dobben Korte Reguliersdwarsstraat 5 (Grachtengordel south). For most people this is *the* place to come for a *kroket*. Open till 1am during the week, 2am on Fri & Sat, Sun till 9pm.

Vlaamse Friethuis Voetboogstraat 33 (Old Centre). The best chips in town; take-away only. Daily noon–6pm.

△ One of the city's many cafés

Bars and cafés

There are, in essence, two kinds of Amsterdam bar. The traditional, old-style bar is the **brown café** – a *bruin café* or *bruine kroeg*; these are cosy places so called because of the dingy colour of their walls, stained by years of tobacco smoke. As a backlash, slick, self-consciously modern **designer bars** have sprung up, many of them known as "grand cafés", which tend to be as un-brown as possible and geared towards a largely young crowd. We've included details of the more established ones, although these places come and go – something like seventy percent are said to close down within a year of opening.

Bars, of either kind, **open** daily at around 10am or 5pm; those that open in the morning do not close at lunchtime, and both stay open until around 1am during the week, 2am at weekends (sometimes until 3am).

Another type of drinking spot – though there are very few of them left – is the **tasting houses** (*proeflokalen*), originally the sampling rooms of small private distillers, now tiny, stand-up places that sell only spirits and close around 8pm.

A growing trend in Amsterdam is **Irish pubs**: at the last count there were ten in and around the city centre, all featuring Guinness and other stouts on tap, Gaelic music of varying quality, and English football live via satellite most weekends. The clue to their success seems to lie much more in the football than the fiddlers – all have rapidly become "locals" for the relatively large numbers of British and Irish living and working in Amsterdam, and although at quiet times the clientele might include a smattering of Amsterdammers, most of the (generally male) drinkers in these places are expats rather than locals.

Many bars – often designated **eetcafés** – offer a complete food menu, and most will make you a sandwich or a bowl of soup; at the very least you can snack on hard-boiled eggs from the counter. Some of the best bars specializing in food are listed in the "Restaurants" section, pp.170–179.

For listings of **gay bars** see Chapter Twelve.

Prices are fairly standard everywhere, and the only time you'll pay through the nose is when there's music, or if you're foolish (or desperate) enough to step into the obvious tourist traps around Leidseplein and along Damrak. Reckon on paying roughly €1.70 for a standard-measure small beer, €2.20 for a glass of wine and €2.40 for a shot of *jenever*.

The Old Centre

Belgique Gravenstraat 2. Tiny and very appealing bar behind the Nieuwe Kerk that specializes in brews from Belgium.

Bern Nieuwmarkt 9. Casual and inexpensive brown café patronized by a predominantly arty clientele. Run by a native of Switzerland, its speciality is, not surprisingly, excellent and alcoholic cheese fondue.

Blincker St Barberenstraat 7. Squeezed between the top end of Nes and Oudezijds Voorburgwal, this hi-tech theatre bar, all exposed steel and hanging plants, is more comfortable than it looks.

De Brakke Grond Nes 43. Modern, high-ceilinged bar and *eetcafé* often full of people discussing the performances they've just seen at the adjacent theatre.

De Buurvrouw St Pieterspoortsteeg 29. Dark, noisy bar with a wildly eclectic crowd; a great alternative place to head for in the centre.

Cul de Sac Oudezijds Achterburgwal 99. Down a long alley in what used to be a seventeenth-century spice warehouse, this is a handy retreat from the Red Light District. Small, quiet and friendly.

Dante Spuistraat 320. Is it a bar? Is it an art gallery? It's both and there are just as many people sitting drinking as there are perusing what's on the walls.

Dantzig Zwanenburgwal 15. Easy-going grand café, right on the water behind Waterlooplein, with comfortable chairs, friendly service and a low-key, chic atmosphere. Food served at lunchtime and in the evenings.

De Drie Fleschjes Gravenstraat 16. Tasting house for spirits and liqueurs, which once would have been made on the premises. No beer, and no seats either; its clients tend to be well heeled or well soused (often both). Closes 8pm.

Droesem Nes 41. On a thin, theatre-packed alley behind the Dam, this is a highly recommended wine bar. Wine comes in carafes filled from the barrel, along with a high-quality choice of cheeses and other titbits to help it on its way.

Durty Nelly's Warmoesstraat 115. Irish pub in the heart of the Red Light action. With a clean and well-run hostel above, this is one of the better expat Brit/Irish meeting places, packed for the weekend football shown live by satellite.

De Engelbewaarder Kloveniersburgwal 59. Once the meeting place of Amsterdam's bookish types, this is still known as a literary café. It's relaxed and informal, with live jazz on Sunday afternoons.

De Engelse Reet Begijnensteeg 4. More like someone's front room than a bar – indeed, all drinks mysteriously appear from a back room. Photographs on the wall record generations of sociable drinking.

Gaeper Staalstraat 4. Convivial brown café packed during the school year with students from the university across the canal. Good food and seating outside for people-watching.

't Gasthuis Grimburgwal 7. Another brown café popular with students. Both this place and *Gaeper* are run by brothers, so it's in more or less the same style.

Gollem Raamsteeg 4. Small, noisy bar with a huge array of different beers. A genial barman dispenses lists to help you choose.

Hard Rock Café Oudezijds Voorburgwal 246. Not the overblown burger joint found worldwide, but a small, crowded (smoking) bar showing 1970s-style videos to similarly styled customers. Patronized mainly by those in Amsterdam for the weed.

Harry's American Bar Spuistraat 285. One of a number of smooth and classy hangouts at the Spui end of Spuistraat – brown bar meets jazz café. Great selection of cocktails too.

Het Doktertje Roozenboomsteeg 4. Tiny, dark, brown café with stained glass to keep you from the world outside. Liqueurs fill the wall behind the tiny bar. A place to be enchanted.

Het Paleis Paleisstraat 16. Bar that's a favourite with students from the adjoining university buildings. Refurbished in a trendy style, they also have an adjoining Italian-style café.

Hoppe Spui 18. One of Amsterdam's longest-established and best-known bars, and one of its most likeable, frequented by the city's businessfolk on their wayward way home. Summer is especially good, when the throngs spill out onto the street.

De Jaren Nieuwe Doelenstraat 20. One of the grandest of the grand cafés, overlooking the Amstel next to the university, with three floors, two terraces and a cool, light feel. A great place to nurse the Sunday paper – unusually you'll find English ones here. Reasonably priced food too, and a great salad bar. From 10am.

De Koningshut Spuistraat 269. In the early evening, at least, it's standing room only in this small, spit-and-sawdust bar, popular with office folk on their way home or to dinner.

Latei Zeedijk 174. A lovely shop and café in one, selling bric-a-brac and serving good espresso and lunches, with a different menu every week.

Lokaal 't Loosje Nieuwmarkt 32. Quiet old-style brown café that's been here for two hundred years and looks it. Wonderful for late breakfasts and pensive afternoons.

Luxembourg Spui 22. The prime watering-hole of Amsterdam's advertising and media brigade. If you can get past the crowds, it's actually an elegant bar with a good (though pricey) selection of snacks. Overlooks the Singel at the back.

Mappa Nes 59. Theatre bar popular with a young crowd. Elegantly brown with mirrors, a pink marble bar and meals for around €10.

Mercurius Prins Hendrikkade 20. Cool, spacious bar and restaurant attached to a conference centre hosting live TV shows and Sunday-night jazz singers.

't Nieuwe Kafé Adjoining the Nieuwe Kerk, facing Gravenstraat. Smart bistro-style café popular with shoppers, serving good, reasonably priced lunches. Great pancakes too.

Ot en Sien Buiksloterweg 27. Brown café in a row of seventeeth-century *dijkhuisjes*, serving Dutch beers and filled with locals. A good stopoff when taking a cycling trip along the Noord-Hollandskanaal.

De Pilserij Gravenstraat 10. Roomy bar behind

the Nieuwe Kerk that has a comfortable back room and plays good jazz. Above all, though, it's the authentic nineteenth-century surroundings that appeal – little has changed, even down to the cash register.
Scheltema Nieuwezijds Voorburgwal 242. Journalists' bar, now only frequented by more senior newshounds and their occasionally famous interviewees, since all the newspaper headquarters along here have since moved to the suburbs. Faded early twentieth-century feel, with a reading table and meals.
Schuim Spuistraat 189. Popular and spacious alternative grand café with retro furniture, attracting an unpretentious crowd.
Tapvreugd Oude Hoogstraat 11. Far and away the most amicable of the loud, crowded music bars on this and surrounding streets.
Vrankrijk Spuistraat 216 ⊛ www.vrankrijk.org. The best and most central of Amsterdam's few remaining squat bars, threatened periodically with closure. Cheap drinks, hardcore noise, and almost as many dogs-on-strings as people. Buzz to enter. From 10pm.
Wilhelmina Dok Noordwal 1. A good place to get some fresh air on the waterfront and enjoy a good lunch or dinner; at its best on late summer evenings. Take the ferry to Adelaarsweg behind CS and walk to the orange building.
Wynand Fockink Pijlsteeg 31. Hidden just behind Dam square. One of the older *proeflokalen*. Frequented by local street musicians.

Grachtengordel west

Aas van Bokalen Keizersgracht 335. Unpretentious local bar with good food. Great collection of Motown tapes. Very small, so go either early or late.
De Admiraal Herengracht 319. Large and uniquely comfortable *proeflokaal*, with a vast range of liqueurs and spirits to explore.
't Arendsnest Herengracht 90. Dutch beers specialist selling eight varieties on draught. Selected with true dedication by the owner, who delights in filling you in on the relative properties of each. Open from 4pm.
Belhamel Brouwersgracht 60. Kitschy bar/restaurant with an Art Nouveau-style interior and excellent, though costly, French food. The main attraction in summer is one of the most picturesque views in Amsterdam.

De Doffer Runstraat 12. Small, affable bar with food and a billiards table.
Hegeraad Noordermarkt 34. Lovingly maintained, old-fashioned brown café with a fiercely loyal clientele. The back room, furnished with red plush and paintings, is the perfect place to relax with a hot chocolate.
De Klepel Prinsenstraat 22. Quiet bar where people come to play chess. English newspapers, plus soup and a daily dish for €5–9.
Het Molenpad Prinsengracht 653. This is one of the most appealing brown cafés in the city – a long, dark, dusty bar that also serves remarkably good food. Fills up with a young, professional crowd after 6pm. Recommended.
De Prins Prinsengracht 124. Boisterous professionals' bar, with a wide range of drinks and a well-priced menu. A great place to drink in a nice part of town. Food served from 10am to 10pm.
Sjaalman Prinsengracht 178. Small bar with a pool table and Thai food. Good in the summer when the church tower is lit up.
't Smackzeyl Brouwersgracht 101. Uninhibited drinking hole on the fringes of the Jordaan (corner of Prinsengracht). One of the few brown cafés to have Guinness on tap; also an inexpensive menu of light dishes.
Spanjer & van Twist Leliegracht 60. A gentle place, which comes into its own on summer afternoons, with chairs lining the most peaceful stretch of water in the city centre.
Twee Prinsen Prinsenstraat 27. Cornerside people-watching bar that's a useful starting place for touring the area. Its heated terrace makes it possible to sit outside even in winter.
De Twee Zwaantjes Prinsengracht 114. Tiny Jordaan bar whose live accordion music and raucous singing you'll either love or hate. Fun, in an oompah-pah sort of way.
Van Puffelen Prinsengracht 377. A café and restaurant adjacent to each other. The café is an appealing place to drink, with a huge choice of international beers and a reading room; the restaurant (daily 6–11pm) serves French food, which, though not cheap, is usually well worth it.

Grachtengordel south

Café Americain *American Hotel*, **Leidseplein 28.** The terrace bar here was the gathering place for Amsterdam media people for years, and it's worth coming at least once, if only for the decor: Art Nouveau frills coordinated down to the doorknobs. A place to be seen, with prices not surprisingly above average.

Bamboo Lange Leidsedwarsstraat 66. Legend has it Chet Baker used to live upstairs and jam on stage to pay his rent. These days the *Bamboo* is an unpretentious, friendly bar playing Seventies and Eighties music. Open from 9pm.

Black & White Leidseplein 18. No-nonsense bar, whose "rolling stone" emblem at the front is a good indicator of the loud rock music within. A large good-time crowd on Saturday night.

Bolle Jan Korte Reguliersdwarsstraat 7. Unrestricted and forthright Dutch café with folksingers and music.

The Brasil Music Bar Lange Leidsedwarsstraat 70. Brazilian music and football bar. Free entry, but you need to buy a drink.

De Duivel Reguliersdwarsstraat 87. Tucked away on a street of bars and coffeeshops, this is the only hip-hop café in Amsterdam, with continuous beats and a clientele to match. Opposite the hip-hop coffeeshop *Free I*.

Het Hok Lange Leidsedwarsstraat 134. Games bar, where you can play backgammon, chess or draughts, or just drink against a backdrop of clicking counters. Pleasingly unpretentious after the plastic restaurants of the rest of the street, though women may find the overwhelmingly male atmosphere off-putting.

Het Land van Walem Keizersgracht 449. A chic bar-café – cool, light, and vehemently un-brown. The clientele is stylish, and the food is a kind of hybrid French-Dutch; there's also a wide selection of newspapers and magazines, including some in English. Breakfast in the garden during the summer is a highlight. Usually packed.

Huyschkaemer Utrechtsestraat 137. Attractive, small, local bar-restaurant on a street renowned for its eateries, which is a favourite watering-hole of arty students. At weekends the restaurant space is turned into a dance floor.

Klein Wiener Wad Utrechtsestraat 135. Small, self-consciously modern café; trendy and unavoidably intimate.

De Koe Marnixstraat 381. A fine, popular café amongst many in this area. Being slightly further out from the Leidseplein, it's one of the less busy options when the others are jammed full.

De Kroon Rembrandtplein 15. Calling itself a media café because of its location next to the Amsterdam Salto Telvision Studio, this first-floor place is decorated in Victorian style. Attracts a smarter-than-average crowd, and serves a reasonable menu including tournedos steak and tilapia fillet.

L & B Korte Leidsedwarsstraat 82. A cosy bar, rather misplaced among the touristy restaurants and clubs of this part of town. Has a selection of two hundred different whiskies and bourbons from around the world. Open until 3am.

Lux Marnixstraat 403. The most trendy option among this stretch of cafés, drawing a young alternative crowd. Loud music. Open late.

Morlang Keizersgracht 451. Bar/restaurant of the new wave, yuppie variety (much like the *Walem* next door), serving good food for around €10. Occasional live music.

Mulligan's Amstel 100. By far the best Irish pub in the city, with an authentic atmosphere, superb Gaelic music and good service.

Mulliners Wijnlokaal Lijnsbaansgracht 267. Upmarket wine bar (around €3 a glass, €10 a bottle), serving food as well. Good atmosphere.

Oosterling Utrechtsestraat 140. Stone-floored local bar-cum-off-licence that's been in the same family since the middle of the last century. Very quiet – home to some serious drinkers.

Reynders Leidseplein 6. The last real option if you want to sit out on the Leidseplein. A remnant of days long gone, with aproned waiters and an elegant interior.

Schiller Rembrandtplein 26. Art Deco bar of the hotel upstairs (see p.152), authentic in both feel and decor, and offering a genteel escape from the tackiness of much of Rembrandtplein.

Terzijde Kerkstraat 59. Within a stone's throw of Leidsestraat, this is a peaceful but sometimes crowded bar used by locals and students, surprisingly showing Dutch international football matches on a big screen.

Vive la Vie Amstelstraat 7. Small, campy bar, patronized mostly, but not exclusively, by women and transvestites.

The Wave Kerkstraat 23. Amsterdam's only central karaoke bar. Open late.

De Wetering Weteringstraat 37. Tucked away out of sight off the Spiegelgracht, this is a wonderfully atmospheric local brown café, complete with wood beams, sleeping cat and, during the winter, an open fire.

De Zotte Proeflokaal Raamstraat 29. Belgian hangout on the edge of the Jordaan. Food, liqueurs and hundreds of different types of beer.

The Jordaan and the Westerdok

Chris Bloemstraat 42. Very proud of itself for being the Jordaan's (and Amsterdam's) oldest bar, dating from 1624. Comfortable, homely atmosphere.

Duende Lindengracht 62. Wonderful little tapas bar with good, cheap tapas (from €2) to help your drink go down. Also includes a small venue in the back for live dance and music performances, including regular flamenco.

Du Lac Haarlemmerstraat 118. Very appealing Art Deco grand café, with plenty of foliage.

Gambit Bloemgracht 20. Chess bar, with boards laid out all day until midnight.

De Kat in de Wijngaert Lindengracht 160. Hefty *bessenjenevers* and an enticing name, "Cat in the Vineyard".

Nol Westerstraat 109. Probably the epitome of the jolly Jordaan singing bar, a luridly lit dive, popular with Jordaan gangsters and ordinary Amsterdammers alike. Opens and closes late, especially at weekends, when the back-slapping joviality and drunken singalongs keep you here until closing time.

De Reiger Nieuwe Leliestraat 34. The Jordaan's main meeting place, an old-style café filled with modish Amsterdammers. Affordable good food.

Saarein Elandsstraat 119. Notorious for years for its stringent women-only policy, *Saarein* has recently opened its doors to men. Though some of the former glory of this café is gone, it's still a warm, relaxing place to take it easy, with a cheerful atmosphere. Also a useful starting point for contacts and information. Closed Mon.

Café SAS Marnixstraat 79. An artists' bar and café backing onto a canal, open all day, with couches, armchairs and all kinds of cosiness, enhanced after dark by candlelight.

't Smalle Egelantiersgracht 12. Candle-lit and comfortable, with a barge out front for relaxed summer afternoons. One of the highlights of the city (see p.78).

De Tuin 2e Tuindwarsstraat 13. The Jordaan has some marvellously unpretentious bars, and this is one of the best: agreeably unkempt and always filled with locals.

The Old Jewish Quarter and the East

De Druif Rapenburgerplein 83. Possibly the city's first bar, and one of its most beguiling, yet hardly anyone knows about it. Its popularity with the locals lends it a village pub feel.

East of Eden Linnaeusstraat 11. A wonderfully relaxed little place right near the Tropenmuseum. Appealing combination of high-ceilinged splendour and gently waving palm trees, with James Dean thrown in on top. Well worth a sunny afternoon.

Entredok Entrepotdok 64. Perhaps the best of a growing number of bars in this up-and-coming area. The clientele hails from the surrounding hi-tech offices, though increasingly from the residential blocks in between, too.

De Groene Olifant Sarphatistraat 126. Metres from the Muiderpoort, this is a characterful old wood-panelled brown café, with floor-to-ceiling windows and an excellent, varied menu.

't IJ In the De Gooyer windmill, Funenkade 7. The beers (Natte, Zatte and Struis), brewed on the premises, are extremely strong. A fun place to drink yourself silly. Wed–Sun 3–8pm.

Kanisinmeiland Levantkade 127. One of the first cafés in the former docks area with a prime waterfront spot. A relaxing terrace, with good sandwiches, away from it all. There's a choice of three soups in the evening and they bake their own apple pie. Take the small ferry from CS.

De Nieuwe Vaart Oostenburgergracht 187. Traditional Dutch café with slots for amateur singers. Once a month, the talent is broadcast on A1 MokumTV, the local Amsterdam TV station.

Tisfris St Antoniesbreestraat 142. Colourful, split-level café and bar near the Rembrandt House, and minutes from Waterlooplein. Youthful and popular.

De Wereldbol Pireusplein 59. A cheap eatery in amongst the pricier restaurants of KNSM island. Serves good salads and the menu changes weekly. Gorgeous views of the antique barges and houseboats. Inexpensive. Closed Mon & Tues.

't Blauwe Theehuis Vondelpark 5 ⊛www.blauwetheehuis.nl. Beautiful tea-room/café housed in a circular building from the De Stijl period. A good place for breakfast and for open-air dancing with DJs on Fri & Sat nights; jazz on Thursday. Daily 9am till late.

Cobra Museumplein. A modern café set up during the renovation of the square, with paintings from the twentieth-century CoBrA movement. The terrace has become the new hotspot for Amsterdam's professional couples and their kids. The club sandwiches are pricey but good; the coffee could be better.

Ebeling Overtoom 52. Alternative, but not overly raucous, bar within a few minutes of Leidseplein, housed in an old bank – with the toilets in the vaults.

Keyser Van Baerlestraat 96 ☎020/671 1441. In operation since 1905, and right next door to the Concertgebouw, this café/restaurant exudes *fin-de-siècle* charm, with ferns, gliding bow-tied waiters, and a dark, carved-wood interior. Prices are slightly above average, especially for the food, but it's a wonderful place nonetheless. You'll need to make bookings for the restaurant, and dress accordingly. Closed Sun.

Vertigo Vondelpark 3. Attached to the Film Museum, this is a pleasant spot to while away a sunny afternoon (or take refuge from the rain), with a spacious interior and a large terrace overlooking the park.

De Vondeltuin Vondelpark 7 ☎020/664 5091. Peaceful terrace on the Amstelveen side of the Vondelpark serving tapas, fresh salads and pancakes, next to the in-line skate rental. A picnic or barbecue in the park including skate rental can be arranged for €19. April–Oct daily 11am–1am; Nov–March Sat & Sun noon–5pm.

Welling J.W. Brouwersstraat 32. Supposedly the traditional haunt of the gloomy Amsterdam intellectual, *Welling* is usually packed solid with performers and visitors from the Concertgebouw next door.

Wildschut Roelof Hartplein 1. Large and congenial bar famous for its Art Deco trimmings. Not far from the Concertgebouw, with the Amsterdam School architecture all around.

De Pijp

Duvel 1e van der Helststraat 59. An *eetcafé* on a pedestrianized street adjacent to Albert Cuypstraat. Handy if you've come to shop in the market.

De Engel Albert Cuypstraat 182.Excellent if you're longing for some space while shopping in the crowded market. This is a beautifully restored café with a mezzanine floor and angels painted on the wall. Sunday-morning brunch concerts by local music students.

Kingfisher Ferdinand Bolstraat 24. A cool Amsterdam café, good for a beer or an after-dinner coffee.

Café Krull Sarphatipark 2. On the corner of 1e van der Helststraat, a few metres from the Albert Cuyp, this is an atmospheric place on a lively corner. The actual *krull* (curve) is the nearby men's urinoir designed in a curve. Drinks, snacks and jazz all day long from 11am.

Coffeeshops

Art, architecture and canals aside, a large proportion of visitors to Amsterdam have come for one thing: the **drugs**. Amsterdam remains just about the only city in the world where you can stand in a public place and announce in a loud, clear voice that you intend to buy and smoke a large, well-packed joint, and then do just that in front of the watching police. In theory, purchases of up to 5g of cannabis, and possession of up to 30g (the legal limit), are tolerated; in practice, most coffeeshops around the city offer discounted bulk purchases of 50g with impunity (though bear in mind that if the police do search you they're entitled to confiscate any amount they find). No one will ever call the police on you in Amsterdam for discreet, personal dope-smoking, but if in doubt about whether smoking is OK in a given situation, ask somebody – the worst you'll get will be a "no".

The first thing you should know about Amsterdam's **coffeeshops** is that locals use them too. The second thing you should know is that the only ones locals use are outside the Red Light District. Practically all the coffeeshops you'll run into in the centre are worth avoiding, either for their decor, their deals or their clientele. Plasticky, neon-lit dives abound, pumping out mainstream varieties of house, rock or reggae at ear-splitting level; the dope on offer is usually limited and of poor quality. A short time exploring the city will turn up plenty of more congenial, high-quality outlets for buying and enjoying cannabis, light years away from the tack of the city centre.

When you first walk into a coffeeshop, it isn't immediately apparent how to buy the stuff – it's illegal to advertise cannabis in any way, which includes calling attention to the fact that it's available at all. What you have to do is ask to see the **menu**, which is normally kept behind the counter. This will list all the different hashes and grasses on offer, along with (if it's a reputable place) exactly how many grammes you get for your money. Most of the stuff is sold either per gramme, or in bags worth €5 or €10 (the more powerful it is, the less you get). The in-house dealer will be able to help you out with queries.

The **hash** you may come across originates in various countries and is pretty self-explanatory, apart from *Pollem*, which is compressed resin and stronger than normal. **Marijuana** is a different story, and the old days of imported Colombian, Thai and sensimelia are fading away; taking their place are limitless, potent varieties of Nederwiet, Dutch-grown under UV lights. Skunk, Haze and Northern Lights are all popular types of Dutch weed, and should be treated with caution – a single spliff of Skunk can lay you low (or high) for hours. You would be equally well advised to take care with **space-cakes**, which are widely available: you can never be sure exactly what's in them; they tend to have a delayed reaction (up to two hours before you notice anything strange); and once they kick in, they can bring on an extremely intense, bewildering high – 10–12 hours is common. Some large coffeeshops, such as the *Bulldog*, refuse to sell them, and advise you against buying elsewhere. You may also come across cannabis seeds for growing your own. While Amsterdammers are permitted to grow five small marijuana plants for "domestic consumption", the import of cannabis seeds is illegal in any country – don't even think about trying to take some home.

Most coffeeshops open around 10am or 11am and close around midnight.

The Old Centre

The Bulldog Oudezijds Voorburgwal 90, 132 & 218; Singel 12. The biggest and most famous of the coffeeshop chains; see p.168 for details.

Dampkring Handboogstraat 29. Colourful coffeeshop with loud music and laid-back atmosphere, known for its good-quality hash.

Extase Oude Hoogstraat 2. Part of a chain run by the initiator of the Hash Museum. Considerably less chichi than the better-known coffeeshops.

Grasshopper Oudebrugsteeg 16; Nieuwezijds Voorburgwal 57. One of the city's more welcoming coffeeshops, though at times overwhelmed by tourists.

Homegrown Fantasy Nieuwezijds Voorburgwal 87a. Attached to the Dutch Passion seed company, this sells the widest selection of marijuana in Amsterdam, most of it local.

Josephine Baker Oude Hoogstraat 27. Once known as the *Café de Dood* – "Café of the Dead" – after the studiously wasted youth who patronize it – this is the loudest and most squalid hangout in the area.

Kadinsky Rosmarijnsteeg 9 and Zoutsteeg 9. Strictly accurate deals weighed out to a background of jazz dance. Chocolate chip cookies to die for.

Rusland Rusland 16. One of the first Amsterdam coffeeshops, a cramped but vibrant place that's a favourite with both dope fans and tea addicts (it has 43 different kinds). A cut above the rest.

Smoking Bull Lange Niezel 13. A relaxed place amongst the rumble of the Red Light District, with a good choice of music.

De Tweede Kamer Heisteeg 6. A friendly coffeeshop, in a tiny alley off Spui, with experienced staff and an enormous variety.

Grachtengordel west

Grey Area Oude Leliestraat 2. High-class coffeeshop with menu (and prices) to match.

La Tertulia Prinsengracht 312. Tiny corner coffeeshop, complete with indoor rockery and tinkling fountain. Much better outside, though, as it's on a particularly beautiful stretch of the canal.

Siberië Brouwersgracht 11. Set up by the former staff of *Rusland* and notable for the way it's avoided the overcommercialization of the larger chains. Very relaxed, very friendly, and worth a visit whether you want to smoke or not.

Grachtengordel south

Borderline Amstelstraat 37. Opposite the *iT* disco, with gently bouncing house beats. Open until 2.30am Fri & Sat.

The Bulldog Leidseplein 15; Korte Leidsedwarsstraat 49. The biggest and most famous of the coffeeshop chains, and a long way from its pokey Red Light District dive origins. The main Leidseplein branch (the Palace), housed in a former police station, has a large cocktail bar, coffeeshop, juice bar and souvenir shop, all with separate entrances. It's big and brash, not at all the place for a quiet smoke, though the dope they sell (packaged up in neat little brand-labelled bags) is reliably good.

Free I Reguliersdwarsstraat 70. Tiny place that looks and feels like an African mud hut, except for the hip-hop beats. Grass specialists.

Global Chillage Kerkstraat 51. Celebrated slice of Amsterdam dope culture, always comfortably filled with tie-dyed stone-

heads propped up against the walls, so chilled they're horizontal.

Mellow Yellow Vijzelgracht 33. Sparse but bright coffeeshop with a small but good-quality dope list. A little out of the way, but makes up for it in friendliness.

The Otherside Reguliersdwarsstraat 6. Gay coffeeshop (in Dutch, "the other side" is a euphemism for gay). Crowded and fun, this is a place for anyone to mix.

Stix Utrechtsestraat 21. The quietest branch of an Amsterdam institution in dope-smoking. You can get it all here: a coffee, a newspaper and a smoke.

The Jordaan and the Westerdok

Barney's Breakfast Bar Haarlemmerstraat 102. Not exactly a coffeeshop, but not exactly a café either, *Barney's* is simply the most civilized place in town to enjoy a big joint with a fine breakfast.

Free City Marnixstraat 233. Crowded coffeeshop done up in *Mad Max* style and favoured by local "professional" smokers.

Paradox 1e Bloemdwarsstraat 2. If you're fed up with the usual coffeeshop food offerings of burgers, cheeseburgers or double cheeseburgers, *Paradox* satisfies the munchies with outstanding natural food, including spectacular fresh fruit concoctions. Closes 8pm.

Pink Floyd Haarlemmerstraat 44. Cool corner shop. Daily 9am–8pm.

The Real Thing 2e Laurierdwarsstraat 58. Down to earth, sober but friendly coffeeshop. Serving coffee with apple pie for €1.80 only. Open from 5pm.

De Pijp

Greenhouse Tolstraat 4; Waterlooplein 345; O.Z. Voorburgwal 191. Consistently sweeps the boards at the annual Cannabis Cup, with medals for its dope as well as "Best Coffeeshop". Tolstraat is a way down to the south (tram #4), but worth the trek: if you're only buying once, buy here.

Yo-Yo 2e Jan van der Heijdenstraat 79. About as local as it's possible to get. Down in the Pijp, to the east of the Sarphatipark, a small, airy little place to seek out smoking solitude.

EATING AND DRINKING | Coffeeshops

Tearooms

Amsterdam's **tearooms** roughly correspond to the usual concept of a café – places that are generally open all day, might serve alcohol but definitely aren't bars, don't allow dope-smoking, but serve good coffee, sandwiches, light snacks and cakes. Along with *eetcafés* tearooms make good places to stop off for lunch, or to spend a quiet time reading or writing without distractions. They're open daily 10am–6pm.

The Old Centre

Arnots Singel 441. Just around the corner from Heiligeweg, a basement café serving some of the best coffee in town along with wholemeal sandwiches and freshly squeezed apples. A great summertime spot with people spilling out onto the pavement. Closed Sun.

Cafe*ine* Korte Lijnbaanssteeg 1. An Italian-style coffee bar where you can have a quick espresso standing at the counter. They also have apartments for rent (see p.145). Open from 8am.

Café Esprit Spui 10a. Swish modern café, with wonderful sandwiches, rolls and superb salads.

Juicebar Tasty & Healthy Korte Lijnbaanssteeg 8. It looks like a snackbar but all they serve is fresh juice; good for a quick energy recharge.

Puccini Staalstraat 21. Lovely cake and chocolate shop-cum-café, with wonderful handmade pastries and good coffee. Close to Waterlooplein.

Villa Zeezicht Torensteeg 3. Small and central, this all-wood café serves excellent rolls and sandwiches, plus some of the best apple cake in the city, fresh-baked every ten minutes or so.

Grachtengordel west

Baton Espresso Corner Herengracht 82. Convivial tearoom with a huge array of sandwiches. In a central location, handy for cheap lunches, good muffins and croissants.

Buffet van Odette & Yvette Herengracht 309. Just walking past will get your tastebuds going; a serious treat for breakfast or lunch.

Dialoog Prinsengracht 261a. A few doors down from the Anne Frank House, one long room filled with paintings, restrained classical music, and downstairs, a gallery of Latin American art. Good choice of sandwiches and salads too.

Greenwood's Singel 103. Small, English-style teashop in the basement of a canal house. Pies and sandwiches, pots of tea – and a decent breakfast.

Lunchcafé Winkel Noordermarkt 43. A popular café on the corner with Westerstraat; something of a rendezvous on Saturday and Monday mornings, when the market's in full flow. Some of the most delicious apple cake in the city.

Pompadour Patisserie Huidenstraat 12. A great patisserie specializing in handmade chocolates.

Grachtengordel south

Backstage Utrechtsedwarsstraat 67. Run by former cabaret stars the Christmas Twins (Greg and Gary), this offbeat place also sells knitwear and African jewellery.

Bagels & Beans Keizersgracht 504. The latest bagel eatery, *B&B* makes some of the most creative and delicious snacks, attracting a young clientele: their version of strawberries and cream cheese is a big favourite in the summer. The "Beans" part of the name refers to the coffee you can have to accompany your bagel. Also a branch in De Pijp (see p.170).

Gary's Muffins Prinsengracht 454; Reguliersdwarsstraat 53. The first New York bagels in town, with big, American-style cups of coffee (and half-price refills) and tasty fresh-baked muffins. Reguliersdwarsstraat branch open until 3am.

Metz Keizersgracht 455. Pleasantly appointed café on the top floor of the Metz department store, offering panoramic views over the city centre. Routine department store food, though.

Café Panini Vijzelgracht 3. Tearoom-cum-restaurant with good sandwiches, plus pasta dishes in the evening.

Studio 2 Singel 504. Pleasantly situated tearoom with a delicious selection of rolls, sandwiches and English breakfast.

The Jordaan and the Westerdok

Arnold Cornelis Elandsgracht 78.
Confectioner with a snug tearoom.
J.G. Beune Haarlemmerdijk 156. Age-old
chocolatier with a tearoom attached.
The Coffee Company Haarlemmerdijk 62.
Relaxed place for reading newspapers;
whole and ground beans for sale as well.
Gary's Muffins Marnixstraat 121. Branch of
the New York bagel-and-muffin teashop,
with the biggest cups of coffee around.
Sunday newspaper heaven.
Jordino Haarlemmerdijk 25. Small tearoom
with an enormous variety of chocolates,
pastries and ice cream all year long.

Newdeli Haarlemmerstraat/Herenmarkt. A
bright, light place with lovely Italian rolls
and pastas. Also quality spring water.
Schranserijen 2e Anjeliersdwarsstraat 6.
Small place with very tasty hot chocolate.

De Pijp

Bagels & Beans Ferdinand Bolstraat 70. The
southern branch of this popular bagel joint,
just opposite the Albert Cuyp – see p.169
for more details.
Granny 1e van der Helststraat 45. Just off the
Albert Cuyp market, with terrific *appelgebak* and *koffie verkeerd*.

Restaurants

Dutch cuisine is firmly rooted in the meat, potato and cabbage school of
cooking – but as a recompense, the country's colonial adventures have ensured
there's a wide range of non-Dutch restaurants.

In the reviews of restaurants and *eetcafés* that follow, we've indicated the
average **cost** for a main course without drinks within each listing, but as a
broad guide, very few places charge more than €20 for a main dish; in fact you
can often get a sizeable, quality meal at many *eetcafés* and smaller restaurants for
€9 or less. Bars and cafés are also worth checking out: many serve food, and at
lunchtime it's possible to fill up cheaply with a bowl of soup or a French bread
sandwich (see p.161).

The majority of *eetcafés* are **open** all day; most restaurants open at 5 or 6pm.
The Dutch eat out early – very rarely later than 9pm – and restaurants normally close their doors at 10 or 11pm, though you'll still be served if you're
already installed. Times can vary a little according to season or how busy things
are that night. Vegetarian restaurants tend to close even earlier than this. Unless
indicated otherwise, all the places we've listed are open seven days a week, from
5 or 6pm until 10 or 11pm. At anywhere we've described as Moderate or
Expensive, it's sensible to call ahead and reserve a table. Larger restaurants will
probably take major credit cards, but *eetcafés* and smaller restaurants almost certainly won't. All restaurant and café bills include 17.5 percent sales tax as well
as a fifteen percent service charge. **Tipping** on top of this is completely
optional, though usually expected – if service merits it, the custom is generally
to hand some change directly to your server rather than adding it to the bill.

The Old Centre

Chinese

Hoi Tin Zeedijk 122 ☎020/625 6451. One of
the best places in Amsterdam's rather
dodgy Chinatown, this is a constantly busy
place with an enormous menu (in English
too) including some vegetarian dishes.
Worth a try. Daily noon–midnight. Moderate.

Dutch

Het Karbeel Warmoesstraat 58 ☎020/627
4995. Cheese is what it is about here,
serving anything from a simple
Amsterdammertje – a brown roll with
mature cheese – to a fondue. Daily
9.30am–midnight. Inexpensive.
De Silveren Spiegel Kattengat 4 ☎020/624
6589. There's been a restaurant in this location since 1614, and "The Silver Mirror" is

> **Budget:** Under €9
> **Inexpensive:** €9–13.50
> **Moderate:** €13.50–18
> **Expensive:** Over €18
> Prices are the average cost per person for a main course without drinks.

one of the best in the city, with a delicately balanced menu of Dutch cuisine. The proprietor lives on the coast and brings in the fish himself. Spectacular food, with a cellar of 350 wines to complement it. Four-course dinner for two at a table set with silver is a cool €100, though you can get away with a main course for €28. Closed Sun. Expensive.

Van Beeren Koningsstraat 54 ☏ 020/622 2329. Huge portions of the simplest Dutch fare – cabbage, mashed potato and steaming stew. Daily 5.30–9.30pm. Budget.

Fish

Kopke Adega Koggestraat 1 ☏ 020/622 4587. Mediterranean-style fish restaurant, which also has a bar serving tapas from 4pm. Moderate.

Werkendam St Nicolaasstraat 43 ☏ 020/428 7744. Stylish, affordable restaurant in one of the alleys running from Nieuwezijds Voorburgwal to Nieuwendijk, largely frequented by local professionals. Efficient and friendly staff. Expensive.

French and Belgian

De Compagnon Guldenhandsteeg 17 ☏ 020/620 4225. This restaurant tends to be fully booked well in advance, but you might get in for lunch. With its split-level wooden floors it has an Old Amsterdam atmosphere, traditional food and a wine menu with a choice of 400 bottles. Expensive.

Hemelse Modder Oude Waal 9 ☏ 020/624 3203. Tasty meat, fish and vegetarian food in French–Italian style at reasonable prices in an informal atmosphere. Highly popular (especially among the gay community). Closed Mon. Moderate.

Het Begijntje Begijnensteeg 8 ☏ 020/624 0528. A good, simple French kitchen, close to the most enchanting *hofje* in Amsterdam. Closed Sun. Expensive.

In de Waag Nieuwmarkt ☏ 020/422 7772. Comfortable and stylish Belgian café-

restaurant with uniformed staff. Daily 10am–midnight. Moderate.

Luden Spuistraat 304 ☏ 020/622 8979. Excellent French restaurant that does fine value *prix fixe* menus, for which you can expect to pay €18–20, as well as a more moderately priced à la carte menu and brasserie. Moderate.

Tolhuis Buiksloterweg 7 ☏ 020/636 0270. Just opposite the back of Centraal Station on the other side of the IJ, this is a heartwarming place for a late breakfast, lunch or dinner. Closed Sunday. Moderate.

Fusion

Palmers Zeedijk 4 ☏ 020/427 0551. French fusion restaurant (set up, according to the menu, by an ex-aviator who crashed over Greenland and married an Eskimo) with such dishes as grilled salmon in coriander and soy sauce. Inexpensive.

Supperclub Jonge Roelensteeg 21 ☏ 020/344 6400. Five-course dinner served at 8pm in a cool, white, loungy environment. Afterwards you can dance downstairs in the club.

Indonesian

Kantjil en de Tijger Spuistraat 291 ☏ 020/620 0994. High-quality food averaging around €30 per person, served in a stylish wood-panelled grand café. Moderate–Expensive.

Sie Joe Gravenstraat 24 ☏ 020/624 1830. Small café-restaurant which is great value for money. The menu is far from extensive, but comprises well-prepared, simple dishes such as *gado gado*, *sateh*, *rendang* and soups. Mon–Sat 11am–7pm, Thurs till 8pm. Budget.

Italian

Tonio Nieuwezijds Voorburgwal 346. A small family-run Italian café serving good cheap Italian staples. All served with salad. Daily 9am–7pm. Budget.

Vasso Roozenboomsteeg 12 ☏ 020/626 0158. Genuine, creative restaurant on the corner of Het Spui, housed in three curvy sixteenth-century buildings. Polite and attentive service. Moderate.

Japanese

Kobe House Nieuwezijds Voorburgwal 77 ☏ 020/622 6458. Ultra-cool Japanese interior and a little overpriced, but serving good sushi and tepanyaki. Moderate.

Stereo Sushi Jonge Roelensteeg 4 ☏020/777 3010. Funky sushi restaurant whose accessories include tip-up chairs to make space for a dance floor and small TV screens in the toilets showing cult movies and Manga films. DJ until 3am on Fridays and Saturdays, otherwise till 1am. Daily from 7pm. Inexpensive.

Pancakes

Pannekoekhuis Upstairs Grimburgwal 2 ☏020/626 5603. Minuscule place in a tumbledown house opposite the university buildings, with sweet and savoury pancakes at low prices. Student discount. Wed–Fri noon–7pm, Sat & Sun noon–6pm. Budget.

Spanish

Centra Lange Niezel 29 ☏020/622 3050. Cantina with a wonderful selection of Spanish food, masterfully cooked, genially served and in the running for Amsterdam's best. Daily 1–11pm. Inexpensive.

Thai

Bird Zeedijk 77 ☏020/420 6289. A packed canteen-like restaurant with good views of the hustle and bustle in the street. Quality food for a good price and Thai versions of all your favourite European pop songs. Budget.

De Klaes Compaen Raamgracht 9 ☏020/623 8708. Good Thai food at affordable prices. Daily 5–9.45pm. Moderate.

Lana Thai Warmoesstraat 10 ☏020/624 2179. Among the best Thai restaurants in town, with seating overlooking the water of Damrak. Quality food, chic surroundings but high prices. Closed Tues. Expensive.

Tom Yam Staalstraat 22 ☏020/622 9533. High-quality Thai restaurant in the middle of town. The branches at Prinsengracht 42 and Utrechtsestraat 55 do takeaway. Moderate–Expensive.

Top Thai Nieuwebrugsteeg 26 ☏020/320 8920; Herenstraat 22; 2e Const. Huygenstraat 64. A popular set of restaurants boasting some of the best Thai food in Amsterdam, with spicy, authentic dishes at a good price, and a friendly atmosphere. For a complete burn-out try one of their chilli salads. Inexpensive.

Vegetarian

Green Planet Spuistraat 122 ☏020/625 8280. Cute mezzanine café with lots of tofu dishes and a varied international menu from wraps to couscous and ravioli. Next to the university language centre. Inexpensive.

Grachtengordel west

Dutch

De Voordeur Herenstraat 14 ☏020/624 2229. Affordable restaurant servinf modern Dutch cuisine. Closed around Christmas and New Year. Inexpensive.

't Zwaantje Berenstraat 12 ☏020/623 2373. Old-fashioned Dutch restaurant with a nice atmosphere and well-cooked, reasonably priced food. Well known for its liver and onions. Moderate.

French and Belgian

Bar5 Prinsenstraat 10 ☏020/428 2455. Spectacularly designed café open for lunch with brilliant club sandwiches and a good atmosphere for dinner. Moderate.

Bordewijk Noordermarkt 7 ☏020/624 3899. A chic restaurant serving stylish French cuisine – a favourite of Johannes van Dam, Amsterdam's most famous food critic. Moderate–Expensive.

Chez Georges Herenstraat 3 ☏020/626 3332. A highly rated, upmarket Belgian eatery, where the emphasis is on meat; dishes €22 and up. Closed Wed & Sun. Expensive.

> **Budget:** Under €9
> **Inexpensive:** €9–13.50
> **Moderate:** €13.50–18
> **Expensive:** Over €18
> Prices are the average cost per person for a main course without drinks.

Christophe Leliegracht 46 ☏020/625 0807. Classic Michelin-starred restaurant on a quiet and beautiful canal, drawing inspiration from the olive-oil-and-basil flavours of southern France and the chef's early years in North Africa. His aubergine terrine with cumin has been dubbed the best vegetarian dish in the world. Try for a table well in advance. Closed Sun. Expensive.

Damsteeg Reestraat 28 ☎020/627 8794.
Superb French-inspired cuisine with more
than the occasional Dutch gastronomic
flourish. In a charmingly renovated old
canal house. Expensive.

Intermezzo Herenstraat 28 ☎020/626 0167.
Good French–Dutch cooking at above-
average prices, but worth every penny.
Closed Sun. Moderate.

Lieve Herengracht 88 ☎020/624 9635. Belgian
restaurant with a pleasant atmosphere,
although reports of the food (from €18
upwards) are mixed. Expensive.

D'Theeboom Singel 210 ☎020/623 8420.
Classic, ungimmicky French cuisine –
around €30 for two courses.
Moderate–Expensive.

Fusion

Blakes Keizersgracht 384 ☎020/530 2010.
Restaurant in the newly opened *Blakes*
hotel. Japanese-style decorated interior,
with some Dutch extras, while the food is a
fusion of Japanese, Thai and European
styles – and somewhat overpriced.
Expensive.

Greek, Balkan and Turkish

Turquoise Wolvenstraat 22 ☎020/624 2026.
Good Turkish restaurant with a beautiful
long bar, giving it a café-like atmosphere.
Inexpensive.

De Twee Grieken Prinsenstraat 20 ☎020/625
5317. Refined Greek cuisine in a romantic
atmosphere. Moderate–Expensive.

Indian

Koh-I-Noor Westermarkt 29 ☎020/623 3133.
One of the city's better Indian restaurants
and deservedly popular. Takeaway too.
Inexpensive.

Purna Hartenstraat 29 ☎020/623 6772. The
speciality here is spicy tandoori. Closed
Tues. Inexpensive.

Italian

Prego Herenstraat 25 ☎020/638 0148. Small
restaurant serving exceptionally high-quality
Mediterranean cuisine from €30 or so for
two courses. Polite and friendly staff.
Expensive.

Indonesian

Cilubang Runstraat 10 ☎020/626 9755. Small

restaurant, with a friendly atmosphere,
serving well-presented, spicy dishes.
Moderate.

Pancakes

The Pancake Bakery Prinsengracht 191
☎020/625 1333. Open all day, this place in a
beautiful old house on the canal has a
large selection of (filled) pancakes from €5,
many big enough to count as a meal. Daily
noon–9.30pm. Budget.

Surinamese and Caribbean

Amigo Rozengracht 5 ☎020/623 1140. Basic,
but good-value-for-money Surinamese
restaurant close to the Westerkerk. Daily
except Wed 2–10pm. Budget.

Rum Runners Prinsengracht 277 ☎020/627
4079. Caribbean-style bar/restaurant situated in the old Westerkerk hall. Expensive
cocktails, but well-priced if not always dev-
astatingly tasty food. Moderate.

Thai

Top Thai Herenstraat 22 ☎020/623 4463. See
"The Old Centre" p.172. Inexpensive.

Vegetarian and organic

Bolhoed Prinsengracht 60 ☎020/626 1803.
Something of an Amsterdam institution.
Familiar vegan and vegetarian options from
the daily changing menu, with organic beer
to wash it down. More expensive than you
might imagine. Daily noon–10pm.
Moderate.

Grachtengordel south

African

Axum Utrechtsedwarsstraat 85 ☎020/622 8389.
Small Ethiopian *eetcafé*, open from 5pm,
with a choice of fifteen authentic dishes.
Budget.

Pygmalion Nieuwe Spiegelstraat 5a ☎020/420
7022. Good spot for both lunch and dinner,
popular among locals. South African dishes
include crocodile steaks, and there's a
good selection of sandwiches and
authentic Afrikaner desserts. Moderate.

The Americas

Castell Lijnbaansgracht 252 ☎020/622 8606.
Cosy restaurant with an old brown hearth

and homely atmosphere, serving barbe-
cued food. The cocktails certainly hit the
mark. Fri & Sat until 1.30am. Moderate.
Iguazu Prinsengracht 703 ☎020/420 3910. For
carnivores only: a superb Argentinian–
Brazilian restaurant, with perhaps the best
fillet steak in town. Daily noon–midnight.
Moderate.
Mister Coco's Thorbeckeplein 8 ☎020/627
2423. Bustling, determinedly youthful
American restaurant that lives up to its
own slogan of "lousy food and warm
beer". Cheap, though (try the all-you-can-
eat spare ribs), and very lively.
Inexpensive.
Los Pilones Kerkstraat 63. Cheerful Mexican
bar and restaurant serving authentic food,
popular with local expats. The Mexican
owner collects tequilas and is more than
happy to serve them to you. Moderate.

> **Budget**: Under €9
> **Inexpensive**: €9–13.50
> **Moderate**: €13.50–18
> **Expensive**: Over €18
> Prices are the average cost per
> person for a main course without
> drinks.

Dutch

De Blonde Hollander Leidsekruisstraat 28
☎020/623 3014. Dutch food in generous
quantities – something of a boon in an otherwise touristy, unappealing part of town.
Expect to share a table. Inexpensive.
Piet de Leeuw Noorderstraat 11 ☎020/623 7181.
Amsterdam's best steakhouse, dating from
the 1940s. Excellent steaks, and mouthwa-
tering desserts. Mon–Fri noon–11pm, Sat &
Sun 5–11pm. Inexpensive.

Fish

Brasserie de Kelderhof Lange
Leidsedwarsstraat 53 ☎020/622 0682.
Extension of the well-known Prinsengracht
restaurant, serving delicious fish dishes in a
modern and light Mediterranean setting.
Daily noon–10.30pm. Moderate.
Le Pêcheur Reguliersdwarsstraat 32 ☎020/624
3121. Beautiful restaurant with a well-balanced menu (the four-course set menu is
good value at around €35). Lovely garden
terrace in the summer. Open for lunch.
Closed Sun. Moderate.

De Oesterbar Leidseplein 10 ☎020/626 3463.
Veteran restaurant overlooking the
Leidseplein action, popular with a largely
older clientele. Worth it if everywhere else
is full, particularly, of course, if you're an
oyster fan. Daily noon–midnight. Moderate.

French and Belgian

Bonjour Keizersgracht 770 ☎020/626 6040.
Classy French cuisine in a romantic setting;
particularly good charcoal-grilled dishes.
Set menus from €22. Closed Mon & Tues.
Moderate.
Kitch Utrechtsestraat 42 ☎020/625 9251. Well-
designed restaurant with a water tap at
your table, Eighties music and suitably hip
waitresses. Expensive.
Le Zinc ... et les Dames Prinsengracht 999
☎020/622 9044. Wonderfully atmospheric little
place serving good-quality, simple fare for an
average of €22; there's a particularly good
wine list. Closed Mon & Sun. Expensive.
Quartier Latin Utrechtsestraat 49 ☎020/622
7419. Small, cosy place, good for a quiet,
romantic dinner. Undemanding food and
service. Closed Mon. Moderate.
Van de Kaart Prinsengracht 512 ☎020/625
9232. A new creative force is in town with an
excellent and surprising menu including lob-
ster carpaccio, home cured bacon and
pumpkin-stuffed ravioli. The selection of
wines complements superbly the tastes created in the kitchen. Moderate–Expensive.

Fusion

Inez IPSC Amstel 2 ☎020/639 2899. Glitzy
first-floor restaurant overlooking the flower
market, Munt and Amstel and frequented
by arty professionals. Daily noon–3pm &
7–11.30pm. Expensive.

Greek, Balkan and Turkish

Aphrodite Lange Leidsedwarsstraat 91
☎020/622 7382. Refined Greek cooking in a
street where you certainly wouldn't expect
it. Fair prices too. Daily 5pm–midnight.
Inexpensive.

Indian

Shiva Reguliersdwarsstraat 72 ☎020/624 8713.
The city's most outstanding Indian restaurant in terms of quality and price, with a
wide selection of dishes, all expertly prepared. Vegetarians well catered for. Highly
recommended. Inexpensive.

Indonesian

Bojo Lange Leidsedwarsstraat 51 ☏ 020/622 7434. Also round the corner at Leidsekruisstraat 12. One of the best-value Indonesian places in town. Recommended for its young, lively atmosphere and late opening hours, but the food is very much a hit-and-miss affair, and you'll have to wait a long time both for a table and service. Mon–Wed 4pm–2am, Thurs & Sun noon–2am, Fri & Sat noon–4am. Budget.

Puri Mas Lange Leidsedwarsstraat 37 ☏ 020/627 7627. Exceptionally good value for money, on a street better known for rip-offs. Friendly and informed service preludes spectacular *rijsttafels*, both meat and vegetarian. Recommended. Moderate.

Sahid Jaya Reguliersdwarsstraat 26 ☏ 020/626 3727. Excellent restaurant where you can eat outside surrounded by a beautiful flower garden. Helpful and friendly staff. Moderate.

Tempo Doeloe Utrechtsestraat 75 ☏ 020/625 6718. Reliable, quality place close to Rembrandtplein. As with all Indonesian restaurants, be guided by the waiter when choosing – some of the dishes are very hot indeed. Moderate.

Tujuh Maret Utrechtsestraat 73 ☏ 020/427 9865. Impressive Indonesian food, notable for its rich combinations without compromising on authentic taste. Tues–Sun noon–10pm. Moderate.

Italian

D'Antica Reguliersdwarsstraat 80 ☏ 020/623 3862. An authentic Italian kitchen where the food is true and the stories too. No pizza. Closed Sun & Mon. Expensive.

Ponte Arcari Herengracht 534 ☏ 020/625 0853. Small corner restaurant with a terrace squeezed in by the canal and a view of seven bridges, serving a small choice of traditional, fresh food. Lunch and dinner Tues–Fri. Moderate.

Rimini Lange Leidsedwarsstraat 75 ☏ 020/622 7014. Surprisingly cheap pizza and pasta, most of it well-prepared. Daily 3–11.30pm. Budget.

Japanese

Japan-Inn Leidsekruisstraat 4 ☏ 020/675 9892. Warm and welcoming restaurant in the middle of the Leidseplein buzz. Kitchen open till midnight. Inexpensive.

Tomo Reguliersdwarsstraat 131 ☏ 020/528 5208. Quality, hip Japanese grill and sushi place, popular with young professional people. Moderate–Expensive.

Yoichi Weteringschans 128 ☏ 020/622 6829. High-class Japanese cuisine in an improbable dark-brown, old Dutch atmosphere. Closed Wed. Expensive.

Zushi Amstel 20 ☏ 020/330 6882. High-tech sushi bar, serving colour-coded dishes on a conveyor belt running along the bar. Daily noon–midnight. Inexpensive.

Pancakes

Le Soleil Nieuwe Spiegelstraat 56 ☏ 020/622 7147. Pretty little restaurant (once visited by the Queen) which makes some great pancakes – try one with ginger and raisins. Open until 6pm. Budget.

Spanish

Pata Negra Utrechtsestraat 124 ☏ 020/422 6250. Big smoked hams hanging from the ceiling and an innkeeper who wants to know what you're drinking and how fast. Lovely tapas. Daily 2–11.30pm.

Thai

Dynasty Reguliersdwarsstraat 30 ☏ 020/626 8400. Festive choice of Indochinese food, with Vietnamese and Thai options; not for the shoestring traveller. The subdued atmosphere suits the prices (average €35). Closed Tues. Expensive.

Thai Corner Restaurant Kerkstraat 66 ☏ 020/627 8239. Cosy, family-run little Thai place, with a welcoming atmosphere. Daily 5pm–midnight. Inexpensive–Moderate.

Vegetarian and organic

Deshima Weteringschans 65 ☏ 020/625 7513. A little difficult to spot (it's in the basement), this is actually a macrobiotic food store, with a small restaurant attached. Mon–Fri noon–2pm. Inexpensive.

Golden Temple Utrechtsestraat 126 ☏ 020/626 8560. Laid-back place with a little more soul than the average Amsterdam veggie joint. Well-prepared, lacto-vegetarian food and pleasant, attentive service. No alcohol and non-smoking throughout. Inexpensive.

De Vrolijke Abrikoos Weteringschans 76 ☏ 020/624 4672. All ingredients, produce and processes are organic or environmentally friendly in this restaurant that serves fish and meat as well as vegetarian dishes. Closed Tues. Inexpensive–Moderate.

The Jordaan and the Westerdok

Dutch

Claes Claesz Egelantiersstraat 24 ☎020/625 5306. Exceptionally friendly Jordaan restaurant that attracts a good mixed crowd and serves excellent Dutch food. Live music from Thursday to Saturday, and Sunday's "theatre-dinner" sees various Dutch theatrical/musical acts between the courses. Often has (pricey) special menus to celebrate occasions like Easter or the Queen's Birthday. Closed Mon. Moderate.

De Eenhoorn 2e Egelantiersdwarsstraat 6 ☎020/623 8352. A less attractive alternative to *De Eettuin* (see below) but just down the road and serving a similar menu so handy if it's full. Inexpensive.

De Eettuin 2e Tuindwarsstraat 10 ☎020/623 7706. Hefty portions of Dutch food, with salad from a serve-yourself bar. Non-meat eaters can content themselves with the large, if dull, vegetarian plate, or the delicious fish casserole. Inexpensive.

Koevoet Lindenstraat 17 ☎020/624 0846. The "Cow's-Foot" – or, alternatively, the "Crowbar" – is a traditional Jordaan *eetcafé* serving a creative menu with some excellent sauces. Closed Sun & Mon. Moderate.

Fish

Albatros Westerstraat 264 ☎020/627 9932. Family-run restaurant serving some mouth-wateringly imaginative fish dishes. A place to splash out and linger over a meal. Closed Wed. Expensive.

French and Belgian

Café Amsterdam Watertorenplein 6 ☎020/682 2666. An old factory with parts of the turbines still in the huge dining room; popular with families. There's a lovely terrace outside too. However, although the menu looks promising the actual experience is a bit bland. Moderate.

De Gouden Reael Zandhoek 14 ☎020/623 3883. Fine French food (€20 and up) in a unique setting up in the western harbour. The bar, as described in the novel of the same name by Jan Mens, has a long history of association with the dockworkers. Mon–Fri noon–10pm, Sat 5–10pm. Expensive.

Jurriaans Egelantiersgracht 72 ☎020/622 7887. Friendly French-Belgian restaurant serving steaks and grilled fare to a mixed clientele. Also has a bar with seven draught beers on tap. Inexpensive.

Fusion

Banana Rama Westerstraat 91 ☎020/638 1039. Small, intimate Filipino restaurant with a choice of tastes and nice cocktails. Moderate.

Summum Binnendommersstraat 13 ☎020/770 0407. Not just another fusion menu, this time mixing North African and Asiatic spices with French/Italian flavours, the cooks try every combination they feel like making. Closed Mon. Moderate.

De Tropen Palmgracht 39 ☎020/421 5528. A small French fusion restaurant, with a menu to match, but the food is perfectly flavoured, using ingredients from all over the world. An open kitchen, so you can view the action. Closed Mon & Tues. Budget–Inexpensive.

> **Budget**: Under €9
> **Inexpensive**: €9–13.50
> **Moderate**: €13.50–18
> **Expensive**: Over €18
> Prices are the average cost per person for a main course without drinks.

Indian

Himalaya Haarlemmerstraat 11 ☎020/622 3776. Cosy and welcoming atmosphere, with a good selection to choose from. Inexpensive.

Italian

Capri Lindengracht 61 ☎020/624 4940. Good café-restaurant with much of the joyful atmosphere of the neighbouring market on Saturday. Inexpensive.

Cinema Paradiso Westerstraat 186 ☎020/623 7344. A romantic combination of an old Amsterdam moviehouse and a modern interior, serving pizza, antipasti, risotto and a pasta of the day. Popular but no reservations. Inexpensive–Moderate.

Da Noi Haarlemmerdijk 128 ☏020/620 1409. A friendly open-kitchen restaurant where two chefs prepare three- or five-course dinners, from an à la carte menu. A place to settle down for the evening and enjoy Italian food beyond pasta and pizza. Expensive.

Hostaria 2e Egelantiersdwarsstraat 9 ☏020/626 0028. A traditional Italian restaurant serving lovely food, expertly prepared. Tues–Sun 7–10.30pm. Moderate.

Toscanini Caffe Lindengracht 75 ☏020/623 2813. Authentic food prepared in front of your eyes; very popular, so book ahead. Expensive.

Yam Yam F. Hendrikstraat 90 ☏020/681 5097. Top pizzeria and trattoria in a simple 1950 retro-style dining room. Classic pizzas with fresh rucola or truffle sauce attract all the hip young parents from the neighbourhood. Closed Mon. Moderate.

Spanish

Casa Tobio Lindengracht 31 ☏020/624 8987. Small Jordaan restaurant that doles out vast servings of Spanish food; cut costs and risk annoying the management by sharing a paella for two among three. There have been reports of surliness, though. Closed Wed. Inexpensive.

Surinamese and Caribbean

Harlem Haarlemmerstraat 77 ☏020/330 1498. Soulfood for breakfast, lunch and dinner. DJ on Sundays.

Thai

Rakang Thai Elandsgracht 29 ☏020/620 9551. Richly decorated restaurant with friendly service. The food is fresh and delicious and not too highly spiced. Next door the takeaway is of similarly good quality. Expensive.

Vegetarian and organic

Burger's Patio 2e Tuindwarsstraat 12 ☏020/623 6854. Despite the name (the site used to be occupied by a butcher's), there isn't a burger in sight in this young and convivial vegetarian Italian restaurant where you compose your own main course from several given options. Inexpensive.

De Vliegende Schotel Nieuwe Leliestraat 162 ☏020/625 2041. Perhaps the best of the city's cheap and wholesome vegetarian restaurants, the "Flying Saucer" serves delicious food in large portions. Lots of space, a peaceful ambience and a good notice board. Budget.

The Old Jewish Quarter and the East

African and Middle Eastern

Kilimanjaro Rapenburgerplein 6 ☏020/622 3485. Bright African restaurant in a bedraggled part of town, serving such delicacies as Tanzanian antelope, Moroccan *tajine* and Ethiopian pancakes. Small, simple and super-friendly. Closed Mon. Moderate.

King Salomon Waterlooplein 239 ☏020/625 5860. Approved by the Rabbi of Amsterdam, this restaurant has a fairly average kosher menu. Moderate.

Fish

éénvistwéévis Schippersgracht 6 ☏020/623 2894. An uncomplicated fish restaurant serving an interesting selection of sealife. Closed Mon. Inexpensive.

French and Belgian

Koffiehuis van de Volksbond Kadijksplein 4 ☏020/622 1209. Formerly a Communist Party café and apparently the place where the local dockworkers used to receive their wages, this is now an Oosterdok neighbourhood restaurant. Budget–Inexpensive.

Indonesian

Anda Nugraha Waterlooplein 339 ☏020/626 6064. Lively restaurant serving moderately spicy Indonesian food. Well-prepared dishes using fresh ingredients, but the selection is small. There's a very pleasant terrace in the summer. Inexpensive.

Italian

Rosario Peperstraat 10 ☏020/627 0280. Very attractive restaurant slightly out of the way in a relatively unexplored corner of Amsterdam. Good Italian food. Closed Sun & Mon. Expensive.

The Museum Quarter and Vondelpark

African

Lalibela 1e Helmersstraat 249 ☏020/683 8332.

Another excellent Ethiopian restaurant, with a well-balanced menu and attentive service. Tram #1 or #6 to Jan Pieter Heyenstraat. Inexpensive.

Dutch

Loetje Joh. Vermeerstraat 52 ☏ 020/662 8173. One of the two best steakhouses in town (the other one being *Piet de Leeuw*). Kitchen open 11am–10pm, closed on Sun. Sat no lunch. Inexpensive.

French and Belgian

Brasserie Joffers Willemsparkweg 163 ☏ 020/673 0360. Small café-like brasserie with a terrace at the front, serving delicious soups and poultry dishes. Mon–Fri 8am–10pm, Sat 8am–6pm, Sun 9am–6pm. Moderate.

Gent aan de Schinkel Theophile de Bockstraat 1 ☏ 020/388 2851. Lovely corner restaurant on a busy shipping canal. Belgian and fusion cuisine and a huge range of bottled Belgian beers to enjoy on their perfect summer terrace. Just outside the other entrance to the Vondelpark, across the cyclist bridge. Moderate.

Le Garage Ruysdaelstraat 54 ☏ 020/679 7176. This elegant restaurant is popular with a media crowd and their hangers-on, since it's run by a well-known Dutch TV cook. An eclectic French and Italian menu; call to reserve a week ahead, dress to impress and bring at least €35 or so per person. Daily 6–11pm, Mon–Fri also noon–2pm. Expensive.

Vossius Hobbemastraat 2 ☏ 020/577 4100. Haute cuisine (set menus or à la carte) served in modern surroundings at steep prices. But this is the home of Robert Kranenborg, one of the best chefs in town, so you won't be disappointed. Expensive.

Greek

Dionysos Overtoom 176 ☏ 020/689 4441. Good Greek restaurant a little to the south of Leidseplein, with the distinct added advantage of serving until 1am. Phone ahead if you're going to turn up after midnight. Daily 5pm–1am. Inexpensive.

Indian

Dosa Overtoom 146 ☏ 020/616 4838. Halfway along the Vondelpark, a cheap restaurant

on the corner serving Southern- as well as the more usual Northern-style cuisine. Budget.

Indonesian

Orient Van Baerlestraat 21 ☏ 020/673 4958. Excellently prepared dishes, with a wide range to choose from; vegetarians are very well taken care of, and the service is generally good. Expect to pay around €25 for a *rijsttafel*. Moderate–Expensive.

Sama Sebo P.C. Hooftstraat 27 ☏ 020/662 8146. Amsterdam's best-known Indonesian restaurant, especially for its *rijsttafel* – although the prices may initially put you off, it's easy to eat quite reasonably by choosing à la carte dishes, and the food is usually great. Closed Sun. Inexpensive–Moderate.

> **Budget:** Under €9
> **Inexpensive:** €9–13.50
> **Moderate:** €13.50–18
> **Expensive:** Over €18
> Prices are the average cost per person for a main course without drinks.

Thai

Top Thai 2e Const. Huygenstraat 64 ☏ 020/683 1297. See "The Old Centre", p.172.

Vegetarian and organic

De Groene Gewoonte 2e Helmersstraat 3 ☏ 020/689 8952. Delicious organic and vegan food, accompanied by organic wines, served at tables made from recycled wood. Moderate.

De Pijp

The Americas

Il Cantinero Marie Heinekenplein 4 ☏ 020/670 6921. A reasonable place for tapas with a choice of good-value Argentinian, Mexican, Caribbean and Surinamese dishes. Worth a visit for its live salsa bands. Moderate.

Dutch

Hap Hmm 1e Van Der Helststraat 33 ☏ 020/618 1884. Dutch meals like *stampots*, beans with bacon and onion, chicken and cauli-flower, and fish on Fridays from €5. Budget–Inexpensive.

Italian

L'Angoletto Hemonystraat 2. Everyone's favourite Italian, always packed out – as you'll see from the condensation on the two big windows; the long wooden tables and benches create a very sociable atmosphere. Not everything they serve is on the menu so keep an eye on the glass show-case in front of the kitchen for any spe-cials. No bookings, so just turn up and hope for the best. Closed Sat. Inexpensive. **Mambo Pasta** 1e van der Helststraat 66. Lovely small café with only three tables; antipasti, rolls, lasagne and pizzas made with Italian love. Mon–Sat 9am–8pm. Inexpensive

Japanese

Hotel Okura Ferdinand Bolstraat 333 ☏020/678 7111. The two restaurants in this five-star hotel – the sushi restaurant *Yamazato*, and the grill-plate restaurant *Teppan-Yaki Sazanka* – serve the finest Japanese cui-sine in the city. Reckon on at least €45 per person. Both are also open for lunch noon–2.30pm. Expensive.

Middle Eastern

Artist 2e Jan Steenstraat 1 ☏020/671 4264. A small Lebanese restaurant just off Albert Cuypstraat. Inexpensive. **Eufraat** 1e van der Helststraat 72 ☏020/672 0579. Basic *eetcafé* in the midst of the cos-mopolitan Pijp district, serving Syrian food which just about translates to the very un-Syrian setting. Daily 11am–midnight. Inexpensive.

Spanish

La Pipa Gerard Doustraat 50 ☏020/679 2318. A great favourite with the Spanish community

in Amsterdam, with good food, sometimes accompanied by spontaneous flamenco performances. Inexpensive **Mas Tapas** Saenredamstraat 37 ☏020/664 0066. Moorish-style restaurant with mosaic tiles everywhere, serving tapas and an interesting variety of main dishes. Inexpensive–Moderate.

Surinamese

Warung Marlon 1e van der Helststraat 55 ☏020/671 1526. Surinamese takeaway and popular hangout for lunch, rapidly gaining a loyal clientele. Lively atmosphere. Daily except Tues 11am–8pm. Budget. **Warung Swietie** 1e Sweelinckstraat 1 ☏020/671 5833. Cheap and cheerful Surinamese–Javanese *eetcafé*. Daily except Wed 11am–9pm. Budget.

Thai

Cambodja City Albert Cuypstraat 58–60 ☏020/671 4930. Thai and Vietnamese restaurant serving delicious meat fondues, soups and prawn dishes, and run by a friendly, but no-nonsense, lady who pro-vides good service. Inexpensive–Moderate.

Turkish

Saray Gerard Doustraat 33 ☏020/671 9216. Excellent Turkish eatery down in the Pijp neighbourhood. Popular with students. Moderate.

Vegetarian and organic

De Waaghals Frans Halsstraat 29 ☏020/679 9609. Well-prepared organic dishes in this cooperative-run restaurant near the Albert Cuyp. Tues–Sun 5–9.30pm. Inexpensive. **De Witte Uyl** Frans Halsstraat 26 ☏020/670 0458. Good restaurant serving free-range poultry and meat and organic vegetables when available. Closed Sun & Mon. Moderate.

Entertainment and nightlife

A
lthough Amsterdam is not generally considered one of the world's major cultural centres, the quality and quantity of music, dance and film on offer here are high – largely thanks to the government's long-term subsidy to the arts. With its uniquely youthful population, the city is at the cutting edge in many ways, though its strengths lie in the graphic arts and new media rather than the performing arts. In fact, there can be a marked lack of daring in Dutch performance, which may have something to do with the stable and homogeneous nature of Dutch society, and its high standard of living. If you spend any time in Amsterdam you're bound to come across plenty of fringe and mainstream events, many of them spontaneous and entertaining, though lacking perhaps the inventiveness or perspective of New York and London. That said, though, Amsterdam buzzes with places offering a wide range of affordable entertainment and you'll never find yourself at a loss for something to do.

Information and tickets

For information about **what's on**, a good place to start is the **Amsterdam Uitburo**, or **AUB**, the cultural office of the city council, which is housed in a corner of the Stadsschouwburg theatre on Leidseplein (daily 10am–6pm, Thurs until 9pm; ℗0900/0191). You can get advice here on anything remotely cultural, as well as tickets and copies of what listings magazines there are. Critical English-language listings of clubs, live music gigs and film screenings are hard to find, and your best bet, until some enterprising publisher fills the obvious gap, is to keep an eye out for posters, billboards and notices advertising upcoming events in the city. The **Luckystrike shop** in the Leidsestraat is also worth a visit: upstairs there's an information counter offering current music, club and party news.

Of the **listings magazines**, there's a choice of the AUB's own monthly *Uitkrant*, which is comprehensive and free, but in Dutch; or you could settle for the VVV's bland and uncontroversial English-language *What's On In Amsterdam*. The newspaper *Het Parool*'s Wednesday entertainment supplement, *Uit en Thuis*, is one of the most up-to-date reference sources. Take a look, too, at the AUB's *Uitlijst* notice boards, which include a weekly update on pop music events. Any cinema can provide the long, thin, fold-out *Week Agenda*, which gives details of all films showing in the city that week (Thursday to Wednesday). Bars and restaurants often stock similar fortnightly or monthly listings leaflets. *SHARK*, a printed pamphlet listing Amsterdam's clubs, bars and cafés, each with a personal review, and including a gay supplement, is available at the Athenaeum News Centre at Spui and a few other cafés and bookshops around town.

Tickets for most performances can be bought at the Uitburo (for a €2 fee) and VVV offices, or reserved by phone through the **AUB Uitlijn** (☎0900/0191 at €0.40 per min) for a one-percent booking fee. You can also buy tickets for any live music event in the country at the GWK bureau de change offices at the Leidseplein and larger train stations, and the post office at Singel 250, again for around a one-percent fee. Obviously the cheapest way to obtain tickets is to turn up at the venue itself. Some major performance venues – the Carré, Muziektheater, Stadsschouwburg and others – sell tickets for each other's productions at no extra cost through the Kassadienst plan. If you're under 26, the AUB is the place to go for a **Cultureel Jongeren Passport** (**CJP**), which costs €11 and gets you reductions on entry to theatres, concerts and *filmhuizen*. Generally the only people eligible for **discounts** at cultural events are students, over-65s (though most places will only take Dutch ID) and CJP card-holders.

Rock, folk and world music

As far as **live music** goes, Amsterdam is a regular tour stop for many major artists, and something of a testing ground for current rock bands. Until recently, **Dutch rock and pop** was almost uniformly dire, but mercifully times have changed, and Dutch groups nowadays can lay claim to both quality and originality. Look out for the celebrated Zuco 103 and other members of the dance/hip-hop scene, or try to catch rock bands such as Bløf, Spinvis and Junky XL. Anouk is a popular draw whenever she plays. Bear in mind, too, that Amsterdam is often on the tour circuit of up-and-coming British bands – keep an eye on the listings.

With the construction of the brand-new 50,000-seat Amsterdam ArenA out in the southeastern suburbs of the city, Amsterdam has finally gained the **stadium** rock venue it has craved for years. However, the Amsterdam ArenA is taking some time to catch on, and, aside from the Bon Jovi brand of superstar, most major stadium acts still choose to play at Rotterdam's Ahoy sports hall. The Heineken Music Hall, a simple but acoustically impressive black box, close to the ArenA, hosts smaller acts, while the three dedicated **music venues** in Amsterdam city centre – the Paradiso, the Melkweg and the Arena (not to be confused with the ArenA) – are all much smaller, and supply a constantly changing seven-days-a-week programme of music to suit all tastes (and budgets). Alongside the main venues, the city's clubs, bars and multimedia centres sporadically host performances by live bands. As far as **prices** go, for big names you'll pay anything between €20 and €30 a ticket; ordinary gigs cost €7.50–12.50, although some places charge a membership (*lidmaatschap*) fee on top.

The Dutch **folk music** tradition in Amsterdam is virtually extinct, although interest has been revived of late by the new duo, Acda and de Munnik. There are still one or two touring folk singers who perform traditional *smartlappen* ("torchsongs") at the Carré Theatre, and at a few sympathetic venues such as *De Nieuwe Vaart* and *Bolle Jan* (see p.164). But the best place to catch these traditional songs – a brash and sentimental adaptation of French chansons – is still in the cafés of the Jordaan, such as *Nol* and the *Twee Zwaantjes*, where they sprang from (see p.165).

More accessible is **world music**, for which there are several good venues including the Tropenmuseum theatre, the Melkweg (with a World Roots festival in June) and Akhnaton.

Aside from summer Sundays in the Vondelpark, Amsterdam doesn't have many **outdoor music festivals**; the biggest events are the Drum Rhythm and Racism Beat It festivals, usually held in May and August respectively (see p.230), which are multi-venue extravaganzas attracting world-class acts, and for classical music, the Grachtenfestival in the last week of August (see p.231). Of the festivals outside the city, the most famous is the Pink Pop Festival in June, down in the south at the Draf en Renbaan in Landgraaf, near Maastricht. Others include the spring Dance Valley Festival in Spaarnwoude, halfway between Amsterdam and Haarlem; the May Goffert Pop in Nijmegen; Lowlands held at Biddinghuizen; and the June Park Pop, in The Hague. Dates are variable, so check with the VVV before making plans.

Major venues

Amsterdam ArenA ArenA Boulevard (Outer Districts) ☎020/311 1333, ⊛www .amsterdamarena.nl. The home soccer stadium for Ajax also hosts live music events featuring world-class artists. Metro or train to Bijlmer station.

Arena 's-Gravensandestraat 51 (Old Jewish Quarter and the East) ☎020/694 7444, ⊛www .hotelarena.nl. Part of the major reorganization of what used to be the *Sleep-In* hostel, the Arena is a multimedia centre featuring live music and cultural events, and has a bar, coffeeshop and restaurant. It's also still one of the city's better hostels. Awkwardly located out to the east of the centre (trams #6 and #10), its intimate hall tends to feature underground bands from around the world and clubnights. Start time around 9.30pm.

Heineken Music Hall ArenA Boulevard (Outer Districts) ☎0900-musichall, ⊛www.heineken-music-hall.nl. A high-tech music venue attracting international bands ranging from Sisters of Mercy to Massive Attack. The bar has an efficient system using plastic tokens. Metro or train to Bijlmer station.

Melkweg ("Milky Way") Lijnbaansgracht 234a (Grachtengordel south) ☎020/531 8181, ⊛www.melkweg.nl. Probably Amsterdam's most famous entertainment venue, and these days one of the city's prime arts centres, with a young, hip clientele. A former dairy (hence the name) just round the corner from Leidseplein, it underwent a four-year renovation programme between 1995 and 1999, and now has two separate halls for live music, putting on a broad range of bands covering everything from reggae to rock, all of which lean towards the "alternative". Late on Friday and Saturday nights,

excellent offbeat disco sessions go on well into the small hours, sometimes featuring the best DJs in town. As well as the gigs, there's also a fine monthly film programme, a theatre, gallery, and bar and restaurant (Marnixstraat entrance). Wed–Sun 2–9pm (dinner from 5.30pm). Concerts start between 9pm and 11pm.

Paradiso Weteringschans 6–8 (Grachtengordel south) ☎020/626 4521, ⊛www.paradiso.nl. A converted church near the Leidseplein, with bags of atmosphere, featuring bands ranging from the up-and-coming to the Rolling Stones. It has been known to host classical concerts, as well as debates and multimedia events (often in conjunction with the nearby Balie centre). Bands usually get started around 9pm.

Smaller venues

Akhnaton Nieuwezijds Kolk 25 (Old Centre) ☎020/624 3396, ⊛www.akhnaton.nl. A "Centre for World Culture", specializing in African and Latin American music and dance parties. On a good night, the place heaves with people.

AMP KNSM-laan 13 (Old Jewish Quarter and the East) ☎020/418 1111, ⊛www.ampstudios.nl. Way out in the eastern harbour district, this rehearsal space and recording studio features live bands, a jazz and a percussion festival. Bus #28 or #39 from CS.

De Buurvrouw Pieterspoortsteeg 29 (Old Centre) ☎020/625 9654. Eclectic alternative bar featuring loud local bands.

Cruise Inn Zeeburgerdijk 271 (Old Jewish Quarter and the East) ☎020/692 7188. Off the beaten track, but with great music from the 1950s and 1960s. Saturday is R&B night.

De Heeren van Aemstel Thorbeckeplein 5 (Grachtengordel south) ☎ 020/620 2173, ⓦ www.deheerenvanaemstel.nl. Warm atmospheric café with swinging soul and funk gigs almost every day.

Korsakoff Lijnbaansgracht 161 (Grachtengordel west) ☎ 020/625 7854. Late-night performances by some of the better-known local grunge bands, in a lively setting with cheap drinks and a post-punk clientele. Free admission.

Last Waterhole Oudezijds Armsteeg 12 (Old Centre) ☎ 020/624 4814, ⓦ www.lastwaterhole.nl. In the depths of the Red Light District, this is the favoured spot for Amsterdam's biker set, who join the crowd from the hostel upstairs for the regular jam sessions.

Maloe Melo Lijnbaansgracht 163 (Grachtengordel west) ☎ 020/420 4592, ⓦ www.maloemelo.nl. Next door to the *Korsakoff*, a dark, low-ceilinged bar, with a small back room featuring lively local bluesy acts.

Meander Café Voetboogstraat 5 (Old Centre) ☎ 020/625 8430, ⓦ www.cafemeander.nl. Daily live music of the soul, funk and blues variety.

Mulligans Amstel 100 (Grachtengordel south) ☎ 020/622 1330. Irish bar that is head and shoulders above the rest for atmosphere and authenticity, with Gaelic musicians and storytellers most nights for free.

OCCII Amstelveenseweg 134 (Museum Quarter and Vondelpark) ☎ 020/671 7778, ⓦ www.occii.org. Cosy former squat bar at the far end of the Vondelpark, with live alternative music.

Tropen Instituut Theater Linnaeusstraat 2 (Old Jewish Quarter and the East) ☎ 020/568 8500, ⓦ www.kit.nl.theater. Part of the Tropical Institute, this formal theatre specializes in the drama, dance, film and music of the developing world. A great place for ethnic music and to pick up on acts that you wouldn't normally get to see.

Winston International Warmoesstraat 123 (Old Centre) ☎ 020/623 1380, ⓦ www.winston.nl. Adventurous small venue, that does a good line in camp entertainment, with bingo Vegas nights and the like. Hip-hop, rock and jazz bands Wed–Sat.

Jazz and Latin

For **jazz** fans, Amsterdam can be a treat. Since the 1940s and 1950s, when American jazz musicians began moving to Europe to escape discrimination back home, the city has had a soft spot for jazz. Paris stole much of the limelight, but Chet Baker lived and died in Amsterdam, and he and any number of legendary jazzbos could once be found jamming into the small hours at the *Casablanca* on Zeedijk. Although Zeedijk has changed a lot since then, there's still an excellent range of jazz venues for such a small city, varying from tiny bars staging everything from Dixieland to avant-garde, to the *Bimhuis* – the city's major jazz venue – which plays host to both international names and homegrown talent. Saxophonists Hans Dulfer, Willem Breuker and Theo Loevendie, and percussionist Martin van Duynhoven, are among the **Dutch musicians** you might come across – and they're well worth catching if you get the chance.

It's worth remembering, too, that the Netherlands has one of the best jazz festivals in the world, the **North Sea Jazz Festival**, held in the Congresgebouw in The Hague during July – information from PO Box 87840, 2508 DE The Hague (☎ 015/215 7756, ⓕ 015/215 8393, ⓦ www.northseajazz.nl). Comprising three days and nights of continuous jazz on twelve stages, the festival regularly involves over 700 musicians, among them world-class performers from Oscar Peterson to James Brown, Chuck Berry to Guru's Jazzmatazz. Tickets cost from about €45 a day, with supplements for the big names. Special late-night trains are laid on to bring revellers back to Amsterdam after the gigs – hotel rooms in The Hague are booked up months in advance. **October** is also a good time to catch jazz, with extra concerts and small festivals held all over the country.

The Dutch connection with **Surinam** – a former colony tucked in between Venezuela and Brazil – means that there is a sizeable **Latin American** community in the city, and plenty of authentic salsa and other Latin sounds to be discovered.

Venues

Akhnaton Nieuwezijds Kolk 25 (Old Centre) ☎020/624 3396, ⓦwww.akhnaton.nl. A crowded, lively venue that often puts on Latin music.

Café Alto Korte Leidsedwarsstraat 115 (Grachtengordel south) ☎020/626 3249. It's worth hunting out this legendary little jazz bar just off Leidseplein for the quality modern jazz every night from 10pm until 3am (and often much later). It's big on atmosphere, though slightly cramped, but entry is free, and you don't have to buy a (pricey) beer to hang out and watch the band.

Bimhuis Oude Schans 73–77 (Old Centre) ☎020/623 1361, ⓦwww.bimhuis.nl. The city's premier jazz venue for almost 28 years, with an excellent auditorium and ultramodern bar. Concerts Thurs–Sat, free sessions Mon–Wed. There's also free live music in the bar on Sun at 4pm. Concert tickets are for sale on the day only.

Bourbon Street Leidsekruisstraat 6 (Grachtengordel south) ☎020/623 3440, ⓦwww.bourbonstreet.nl. Friendly bar with a relaxed atmosphere and quality blues and jazz nightly until 3am.

Casablanca Zeedijk 26 (Old Centre) ☎020/625 5685, ⓦwww.casablanca-amsterdam.nl. A shadow of its former self, though still hosting live jazz every night and Sunday afternoon.

De Engelbewaarder Kloveniersburgwal 59 (Old Centre) ☎020/625 3772. Excellent live jazz sessions Sunday afternoon and evening.

't Geveltje Bloemgracht 170 (Jordaan and the Westerdok) ☎020/623 9983, ⓦwww.jazzcafe -gevel.demon.nl. A jazz café offering workshops through the week with a professional jam session on Fridays. Open until 3am. Closed Sat and Sun.

IJsbreker Weesperzijde 23 (Old Jewish Quarter and the East) ☎020/693 9093, ⓦwww .ijsbreker.nl. Principally a venue for contemporary music (see p.186), but with occasional avant-garde and free-jazz evenings.

Le Maxim Leidsekruisstraat 35 (Grachtengordel south) ☎020/624 1920. Intimate piano bar that's been going since the Sixties, with live music nightly.

Pompoen Spuistraat 2 (Old Centre) ☎020/521 3000, ⓦwww.pompoen.nl. Live jazz from Monday to Saturday at 9pm. Sunday café chantant – jazz vocalists and a three-course meal.

Classical, opera and contemporary music

There's no shortage of **classical music** concerts in Amsterdam, with two major orchestras based in the city, plus regular visits by other Dutch orchestras. The **Royal Concertgebouw Orchestra** remains one of the most dynamic in the world, and occupies one of the finest concert halls to boot. The other resident orchestra is the **Netherlands Philharmonic**, based at the Beurs van Berlage concert hall, which has a wide symphonic repertoire and also performs with the Netherlands Opera at the Muziektheater. Among visiting orchestras, the Rotterdam Philharmonic and the Utrecht Symphony have world-class reputations, as does the Radio Philharmonic Orchestra, based in Hilversum outside Amsterdam.

As far as **smaller classical ensembles** go, Dutch musicians pioneered the use of **period instruments** in the 1970s, and Ton Koopman's Amsterdam Baroque Orchestra and Frans Brüggen's Orchestra of the 18th Century are two internationally renowned exponents. Koopman's Amsterdam Baroque Choir and the Amsterdam Bach Soloists are also pre-eminent. As well as the main concert halls, a number of Amsterdam's churches (and former churches) host regular performances of classical and chamber music – both types of venue are

ENTERTAINMENT AND NIGHTLIFE | Classical, opera and contemporary music listed here, see below. Others, including the huge Nieuwe Kerk on Dam square, the Westerkerk, the Noorderkerk, the Mozes en Aaronkerk on Waterlooplein, and the tiny Amstelkerk on Kerkstraat, as well as numerous small churches out in the residential south and west, occasionally put on one-off concerts, often at very reasonable prices.

The most prestigious venue for **opera** is the Muziektheater (otherwise known as the Stopera) on Waterlooplein, which is home to the Netherlands Opera company – going from strength to strength under the guidance of Pierre Audi – as well as the National Ballet. Visiting companies sometimes perform here, but more often at the Stadsschouwburg and the Carré Theatre.

As far as **contemporary music** goes, the IJsbreker centre on the Amstel is a leading showcase for musicians from all over the world. Local talent is headed by the Asko and Schoenberg ensembles, as well as the Nieuw Ensemble and the Volharding Orchestra. Look out also for Willem Breuker and Maarten Altena, two popular musicians who successfully combine improvised jazz with composed new music.

The most prestigious multi-venue Dutch festival by far is the annual **Holland Festival** every June (info ☏020/530 7111), which attracts the best domestic mainstream and fringe performers in all areas of the arts, as well as an exciting international line-up. Otherwise, one of the more interesting music-oriented events is the **piano recital** held towards the end of August on a floating stage outside the *Pulitzer Hotel* on the Prinsengracht – with the whole area floodlit and filled with small boats, and every available spot on the banks and bridges taken up, this can be a wonderfully atmospheric evening. Also around this time – and from two ends of the musical spectrum – Utrecht plays host to the internationally renowned **Early Music Festival**, and Amsterdam holds the **International Gaudeamus Music Week**, a forum for debate and premier performance of cutting-edge contemporary music.

All the major venues listed below, as well as some of the churches, have wheelchair access, though you should call ahead if you need assistance.

Venues

Beurs van Berlage Damrak 213 (Old Centre) ☏020/627 0466, ☜www.beursvanberlage.nl. The splendid interior of the former stock exchange (see p.44) has been put to use as a venue for theatre and music. The resident Netherlands Philharmonic and Netherlands Chamber Orchestra perform in the huge but comfortable Yakult Zaal and the AGA Zaal, the latter a very strange, glassed-in room-within-a-room.

Carré Theatre Amstel 115–125 (Grachtengordel south) ☏020/622 5225, ☜www.theatercree.nl. A splendid hundred-year-old structure (originally built for a circus) which represents the ultimate venue for Dutch folk artists, and hosts all kinds of top international acts: anything from Russian folk dance to *La Cage aux Folles*, with reputable touring orchestras and opera companies squeezed in between.

Concertgebouw Concertgebouwplein 2–6 (Museum Quarter and Vondelpark) ☏020/671 8345, ☜www.concertgebouw.nl. After a facelift and the replacement of its crumbling foundations in the early 1990s, the Concertgebouw is now looking – and sounding – better than ever. The acoustics of the Grote Zaal (Large Hall) are unparalleled, and a concert here is a wonderful experience. The smaller Kleine Zaal regularly hosts chamber concerts, often by the resident Borodin Quartet. Though both halls boast a star-studded international programme, prices are on the whole very reasonable, €30–40, and €13 for the sponsored Sunday morning events. Free Wednesday lunchtime concerts are held from Sept to May (doors open 12.15pm, arrive early), and in July and August there's a heavily subsidized series of summer concerts. Look out also for occasional swing/jazz nights.

Engelse Kerk Begijnhof 48 (Old Centre) ☏020/624 9665. The church with the biggest programme – three to four performances a week, lunchtime, afternoon and evening, with an emphasis on period instruments.

IJsbreker Weesperzijde 23 (Old Jewish Quarter and the East) ☎020/693 9093, ⓦwww.ijsbreker.nl. Out of the town centre by the Amstel, with a delightful terrace on the water. Has a large, varied programme of international modern, chamber and experimental music, as well as featuring obscure, avant-garde local performers. Concerts are occasionally held in the Planetarium of the Artis Zoo.

Marionette Theatre Nieuwe Jonkerstraat 8 (Old Centre) ☎020/620 8027, ⓦwww.marionettetheater.nl. Continues an old European tradition with its performances of operas by Mozart and Offenbach. Although they're touring Holland and the rest of Europe for most of the year, the wooden marionettes return to Amsterdam around May, October and Christmas. Call for details of performances, and to find out about their opera dinners.

Muziektheater Waterlooplein (Old Jewish Quarter and the East) ☎020/625 5455, ⓦwww.muziektheater.nl. Part of the €150 million complex that includes the city hall. The theatre's resident company,

Netherlands Opera, offers the fullest, and most reasonably priced, programme of opera in Amsterdam. Tickets go very quickly. Look out for free lunchtime concerts Sept–May.

Oude Kerk Oudekerksplein 23 (Old Centre) ☎020/625 8284. Hosts organ and carillon recitals, as well as occasional choral events. In summer, in conjunction with the Amstelkring Museum, the church organizes a series of "walking" concert evenings, consisting of three separate concerts at different venues, with time for coffee and a stroll between each.

Stadsschouwburg Leidseplein 26 (Grachtengordel south) ☎020/624 2311, ⓦwww.stadsschouwburgamsterdam.nl. These days somewhat overshadowed by the Muziektheater, but still staging significant opera, theatre and dance, as well as hosting visiting English-language theatre companies.

Waalse Kerk Oudezijds Achterburgwal 157 (Old Centre); information from the Old Music Society on ☎020/236 2236. Weekend afternoon and evening concerts of early music and chamber music.

Theatre and cabaret

Surprisingly for a city that functions so much in English, there is next to no **English-language drama** to be seen in Amsterdam. A tiny handful of part-time companies put on two or three English productions during the summer; there are also performances by touring groups at the theatres listed below and at other venues dotted around town.

English-language **comedy** and **cabaret**, on the other hand, has become a big thing in Amsterdam, spearheaded by the resident and extremely successful Boom Chicago comedy company. During the summer in particular, a number of small venues host mini-seasons of English-language stand-up comedy and cabaret, with touring British performers, and material that's generally targeted at visitors to the city.

Most of Amsterdam's larger theatre companies concentrate either on foreign works in translation or Dutch-language theatre, neither of which is likely to be terribly interesting for the non-Dutch speaker. However, there are plenty of **avant-garde** theatre groups in the city, much of whose work relies on visual rather than verbal impact, as well as one or two companies devoted to **mime** (including the famous Griftheater). Look out also for performances at the Amsterdam Marionette Theatre (see above). The Amsterdamse Bos Theatre (ⓦwww.bostheater.nl) might also be worth checking out, performing summertime, open-air Shakespeare plays (in Dutch). It's an atmospheric evening, with audiences picnicking before the show.

The main event to watch out for, apart from the mainstream Holland Festival (see p.231), is the summer-long **Over Het IJ Festival** (info ☎020/636 1083), a showcase for all kinds of theatre and performance arts at big, often outdoor locations in Amsterdam North (thus "over the IJ"). With a great many interesting fringe companies taking part, including the celebrated Dogtroep, productions are often surprising and exciting. In June there is also the **International Theatre School Festival** (info ☎020/626 1241), when the four theatres on Nes, a tiny alley running from Dam square parallel to Rokin, host productions by local and international theatre schools.

Major venues

De Balie Kleine Gartmanplantsoen 10 (Grachtengordel south) ☎020/623 2904, ⓦwww.balie.nl. A multimedia centre for culture and the arts, located off the Leidseplein, which often plays host to drama, debates, international symposia and the like, sometimes in conjunction with the Paradiso next door.

Boom Chicago Korte Leidsedwarsstraat 12 (Grachtengordel south) ☎020/423 0101, ⓦwww.boomchicago.nl. Something of a phenomenon in Amsterdam in recent years, this rapid-fire improv comedy troupe performs nightly to crowds of both tourists and locals, and has received rave reviews from *Rough Guide* readers, the Dutch press and *Time* magazine alike. With inexpensive food, the cheapest beer in town (in pitchers, no less!), and a Smoke Boat Cruise following the show at 10.30pm, the comedy need not be funny – but it is.

Carré Theatre See p.185. A chunky old building on the eastern bank of the Amstel that, aside from its folk associations, hosts all kinds of top international acts, with the emphasis on hit musicals.

Comedy Café Max Euweplein 29 (Grachtengordel south) ☎020/638 3971, ⓦwww.comedycafe.nl. Small cabaret theatre with a bar that sometimes hosts English-language acts.

Kleine Komedie Amstel 56 (Grachtengordel south) ☎020/624 0534, ⓦwww.kleinekomedie.nl. One of Amsterdam's oldest theatres, established in 1786, with occasional English-language shows, and performances by the odd pop megastar.

Melkweg See p.182. At the centre of the city's cultural scene, this is often the first-choice venue for foreign touring companies.
Stadsschouwburg See p.186. Often hosts productions on tour from London or New York.

Avant-garde and mime

Bellevue Leidsekade 90 (Grachtengordel south) ☎020/624 7248, ⓦwww.theaterbellevue.nl.
De Brakke Grond Nes 45 (Old Centre) ☎020/626 6866, ⓦwww.brakkegrond.nl. Mainly Flemish productions. See also ⓦwww.nestheaters.nl.
CompagnieTheater Kloveniersburgwal 50 (Old Centre) ☎020/520 5320, ⓦwww .theatercompagnie.nl.
Cosmic Theater Nes 75 (Old Centre) ☎020/622 8858, ⓦwww.cosmictheater.nl. Cross-cultural productions.
Dasarts Haarlemmerweg 8–10 (Jordaan and the Westerdok) ☎020/586 9636, ⓦwww.dasarts.nl. Not a venue as such but a global clubhouse for theatremakers, a think-tank and postgraduate institute, with international workshops and performances.
De Engelenbak Nes 71 (Old Centre) ☎020/624 0394, ⓦwww.engelenbak.nl.
Felix Meritis Keizersgracht 324 (Grachtengordel south) ☎020/623 1311.
Frascati Nes 63 (Old Centre) ☎020/626 6866. ⓦwww.nestheaters.nl.
De Nieuw Amsterdam Grote Bickerstraat 2 (Jordaan and the Westerdok) ☎020/627 8672, ⓦwww.denieuwamsterdam.nl. Multicultural focus on non-Western productions.
Nieuwe de la Mar Marnixstraat 404 (Grachtengordel south) ☎020/623 3462, ⓦwww.nieuwedelamar.nl.

Dance

Of the major **dance companies** based in Amsterdam, the largest and most prestigious is the Muziektheater's National Ballet, under Wayne Eagling. Also working regularly in Amsterdam are the noted Dutch choreographers Toer van

Schayk and Rudi van Dantzig, while for **folk dance** fans the excellent Folkloristisch Danstheater is based in the city. However, a constant feature of dance in Holland is the prevalence of non-Dutch choreographers and dancers, and the work of William Forsyth, Lloyd Newson, Saburo Teshigawara and others is regularly on show.

Of the other major Dutch dance companies, which can be seen on tour in Amsterdam – or in nearby Rotterdam and The Hague – the most innovative is The Hague's Netherlands Dance Theatre, with a repertoire of ballet and modern dance featuring inspired choreography by Jiri Kylian and Hans van Manen. The oldest company in the country, the Scapino Ballet (based in Rotterdam), has spruced up its image and is gathering a new generation of admirers.

On a smaller scale, Amsterdam is particularly receptive to the latest trends in **modern dance**, and has many experimental dance groups, often incorporating other media into their productions; small productions staged by dance students also abound. Look out for performances by the Dans Werkplaats Amsterdam and the extraordinary Cloud Chamber company, as well as the mime specialists Griftheater, and Shusaku Takeuchi's vast, open-air water-based extravaganzas. Modern dance and movement theatre companies from outside Amsterdam that often perform in the city include the Rotterdamse Dansgroep, who mainly focus on New York modern dance; Introdans, similar in style to the Netherlands Dance Theatre; and Djazzex, fine exponents of jazz dance.

Dance festivals are a little thin on the ground: **Julidans**, which is held in the Stadsschouwburg every July, is the leading event in the city. Two festivals in The Hague to watch for are the **Holland Dance Festival** (info ☎ 070/361 6142), which takes place every two years (October 2003 and 2005) and attracts many leading international companies; and **CaDance** (info ☎ 070/363 7540), which premieres contemporary dance works. The Hague is just 45 minutes away from Amsterdam by regular trains from Centraal Station.

Venues

Cosmic Theater See p.187. A modern dance and theatre company featuring young professionals with a multicultural background.
Dans Werkplaats Amsterdam Arie Biemondstraat 107 (Jordaan and the Westerdok) ☎ 020/689 1789, ⊛ www.euronet.nl/~dwa/. A dance studio staging occasional productions at its own studio, Het Veem and other locations in the city.
Folkloristisch Danstheater Kloveniersburgwal 87 (Old Centre) ☎ 020/623 9112. Original folk dance from around the world, with international choreographers brought in to work with the dancers.

Het Veem Van Diemenstraat 410 (Jordaan and the Westerdok) ☎ 020/626 0112, ⊛ www .hetveemtheater.nl. Old warehouse converted into dance studios and a theatre.
Melkweg See p.182. Upstairs in this pop and world music venue, there is a little theatre with modern and funky productions.
Muziektheater See p.186. Home of the National Ballet, but with a third of its dance schedule given over to international companies.
Stadsschouwburg See p.186. Host to the Julidans dance festival in July as well as staging regular productions.

Film

Most of Amsterdam's commercial **cinemas** are huge, multiplex picture palaces showing a selection of general releases. There's also a scattering of film houses (*filmhuizen*) showing **revival and art films** and occasional retrospectives; and Amsterdam's multimedia centres often organize film and video programmes too. Two Amsterdam cinemas worth a visit no matter what's showing are the extravagantly Art Deco Tuschinski and the atmospheric The Movies (see p.190).

Pick up a copy of the **Week Agenda** from any cinema for details of all films showing in the city, or check Ⓦ www.filmladder.nl. For details of gay and lesbian film programmes, see p.214. Weekly programmes change on Thursdays.

All foreign movies playing in Amsterdam (almost no Dutch movies turn up, anyway) are shown in their **original language** and subtitled in Dutch – which is fine for British or American fare, but a little difficult if you fancy Tarkovsky or Pasolini. If you're interested in seeing a non-English-language movie, check with the venue whether it's been **subtitled** in English (*Engels Ondertiteld*) before you go. Films are almost never dubbed into Dutch: if they are, *Nederlands Gesproken* will be printed in the listings. Most major cinemas have four showings a day: two in the afternoon, two in the evening; some also have midnight shows on Fridays and Saturdays.

Tickets can cost around €7 for an evening show Friday to Sunday, though it's not hard to find a ticket for €5 during the week. Prices at the *filmhuizen* are slightly lower, and can drop to as little as €4 for a 10am Sunday showing. Aside from occasional film festivals held by the likes of Amnesty International, Amsterdam's only regular event is the fascinating **International Documentary Film Festival** in November/December (info ℡020/620 1826, Ⓦ www.idfa.nl), where 200 documentaries from all over the world are shown in ten days. The festival has established itself as the biggest international documentary festival in the world. Simultaneously, there's the **Shadowfestival**, held at the Melkweg and showcasing alternative documentaries. Whereas the Dutch Film Festival, held each September in Utrecht, features only home-grown productions, January's **Rotterdam Film Festival** (info ℡010/411 8080, Ⓦ www.filmfestivalrotterdam.com) is truly international, with screenings of well over a hundred art movies from all parts of the world, as well as the usual accompanying lectures and seminars.

Filmhuizen and arthouse cinemas

De Balie Off Leidseplein (Grachtengordel south) ℡020/553 5100, Ⓦ www.balie.nl. Cultural centre for theatre, politics, film and new media, showing movies on Friday and Saturday nights, often with English subtitles.

Cavia Van Hallstraat 52 (Jordaan and the Westerdok) ℡020/681 1419, Ⓦ www .filmhuiscavia.nl. Incongruously sited above a martial arts centre, this is one of the best of the small *filmhuizen*, with an eclectic and non-commercial programme of international movies. Tram #10.

Cinecenter Lijnbaansgracht 236 (Grachtengordel south) ℡020/623 6615, Ⓦ www.cinecenter.nl. Opposite the Melkweg, this shows independent and quality commercial films, the majority originating from non-English-speaking countries, shown with an interval.

Filmmuseum Vondelpark 3 (Museum Quarter and Vondelpark) ℡020/589 1400, Ⓦ www .filmmuseum.nl. Subsidized by the government since the 1940s, the Filmmuseum holds literally tens of thousands of prints. Dutch films show regularly, along with all kinds of movies from all corners of the world. Silent movies often have live piano accompaniment, and on summer weekend evenings there are free open-air screenings on the terrace. Also many cheap matinees. Most movies have English subtitles.

Kriterion Roeterstraat 170 (Old Jewish Quarter and the East) ℡020/623 1708, Ⓦ www .kriterion.nl. Stylish duplex cinema close to Weesperplein metro. Shows arthouse and quality commercial films, with late-night cult favourites. Friendly bar attached. Tram #6, #7, #10.

Melkweg See p.182. As well as music, art and dance, the Melkweg manages to maintain a consistently good monthly film and video programme, ranging from mainstream fodder through to obscure imports. Tram #1, #2 or #5 to Leidseplein.

The Movies Haarlemmerdijk 161 (Jordaan and the Westerdok) ☎020/624 5790, ⓦwww
.themovies.nl. A beautiful Art Deco cinema, and a charming setting for independent films. Worth visiting for the bar and restaurant alone, fully restored to their original sumptuousness. Late shows at the weekend. Tram #3.

Rialto Ceintuurbaan 338 (De Pijp) ☎020/675 3994, ⓦwww.rialtofilm.nl. The only fully authentic arthouse cinema in Amsterdam, showing an enormously varied programme of European and World movies, supplemented by themed series and classics. Refurbished in 1999, the cinema now boasts a large café open to the public, and, thanks to the set-up of volunteer staff, the place has a friendly and welcoming atmosphere. On Saturday afternoons there's a talk entitled "Documentaire Salon", in which documentary film-makers discuss their work (tickets €7). Tram #3, #24 or #25 from the centre.

Smart Cinema 1e Const. Huygensstraat 10 (Outer Districts) ☎020/427 5951. The best non-mainstream movies and a free videoshow on Wednesday and Sunday at 5pm. There's also a trendy international restaurant with DJs, and occasional exhibitions. Tram #1, #3, #6 or #12 to Overtoom.

Tropen Instituut Theater See p.183. Attached to the Tropenmuseum, this theatre concentrates mostly on music and dance, but puts on ad hoc film shows and themed film festivals from around the world. Tram #6, #9 and #10.

Tuschinski Theater Reguliersbreestraat 26 no phone, ⓦwww.filmladder.nl. Fabulous Art Deco theatre famous for its handwoven carpet and painted wallpaper, this film house shows the more arty offerings from the mainstream list.

De Uitkijk Prinsengracht 452 (Grachtengordel south) ☎020/623 7460 ⓦwww.uitkijk.nl. The oldest cinema in the city (pronounced "out-kike"), in a converted canal house with no bar, no ice cream and no popcorn – but low prices. Shows popular movies for months on end.

Clubs and discos

Clubbing in Amsterdam is not the exclusive, style-conscious business it is in many other capitals. There is no one really extravagant night spot, especially since the closure of the *Roxy* in 1999, and most Amsterdam clubs – even the hip ones – aren't very expensive or difficult to get into. As for the music itself, as in so many other things, Amsterdam is not at the cutting edge of experimentation: hip-hop has its devotees, as do modern and retro funk, jazz and underground trance and lounge, but unless you go looking for something special, a random dip into a club will probably turn up mellow, undemanding **house** beats.

That said, though, the craze for pumped-up, 200bpm+ **"gabber"** (pronounced the Dutch way, with a throaty "kh" at the beginning), laid on at vast arenas for thousands of shaven-headed speed-freaks, has now slowed down to techno in clubs at the rim of the city such as *Hemkade* and *The Powerzone*, or is confined to the Dance Valley Festival in August (see p.231). If you can find a techno event (check for flyers at Midtown Records, Nieuwendijk 104 ☎020/638 4252), expect to pay a hefty €25 or more for entry, although it'll go on until dawn and flyers for after-hours parties will circulate during the night. Unlike many other places around Europe, there are now practically no **illegal raves** or parties in and around Amsterdam, and the last squat venues in the harbour areas have finally made way for apartment buildings; the old days of acid warehouse parties are well and truly over.

Most clubs have very reasonable **entry prices**, hovering between €7.50 and €10 at weekends and then dropping to €5 during the week, sometimes going as low as €2.50, especially in the gay scene. A singular feature of Amsterdam clubbing, however, is that you tip the bouncer: if you want to get back into the same place next week, €1 or €2 in the palm of his hand will do very nicely. Drinks prices are just slightly more expensive than in cafés at around €3–4 but not excessively hiked up and, as in the rest of the city, toilets cost money (20c or 50c). **Dress codes** are minimal or nonexistent, except where we've noted in the listings below. As far as **drugs** go, smoking joints is generally fine – though if you can't see or smell the stuff, ask the barman if it's OK. Should you need reminding, ecstasy, acid and speed are all completely illegal, and you can expect less than favourable treatment from the bouncers (and the law) if you're spotted with anything.

Although all the places listed below **open** at either 10pm or 11pm, there's not much point turning up anywhere before midnight; unless stated otherwise, everywhere stays open until 5am on Friday and Saturday nights, 4am on other nights.

For **news** and flyers about clubs, upcoming parties and raves, drop in to Clubwear House, at Herengracht 265, or the Hair Police and Conscious Dreams, next door to each other at Kerkstraat 115 and 117.

Finally, there are a couple of clubs **outside Amsterdam** that you might see advertised around town. *Stalker*, in Haarlem (☏023/531 4652), is a small place with a dedicated following and a consistently adventurous music policy, while the equally popular *Hemkade* in Koog aan de Zaan (☏075/628 5829, ☻www.hemkade.nl), attracts British and European DJs to its weekend parties.

For gay and lesbian clubs see Chapter Twelve.

Venues

020 Nieuwezijds Voorburgwal 165 (Old Centre). A groovy, funky place with no attitude, where every night is arranged by a different organizer. Wednesday is lounge, Thursday salsa, Friday deep house, Saturday commercial house and Sunday jazz, sometimes with live acts.

Arena See p.182. Part of a large hostel-cum-multimedia centre, with popular dance parties on Fri and Sat.

Backdoor Amstelstraat 32a (Grachtengordel south) ☏020/620 2333, ☻www.backdoor.nl. Relaxed club that's oriented towards soul, funk and lounge. Saturday night is a mixed gay/straight extravaganza night.

't Blauwe Theehuis Open-air dancing in the Vondelpark with DJs on Friday and Saturday nights.

Dansen bij Jansen Handboogstraat 11 (Old Centre) ☏020/620 1779, ☻www .dansenbijjansen.nl. Founded by – and for – students, and very popular. Open nightly; €2.50, but officially you need student ID to get in.

Du Lac Haarlemmerstraat 118 (Jordaan and the Westerdok) ☏020/624 4265. Rather trendy bar with R&B and soul DJs from Thurs till Sun.

Escape Rembrandtplein 11 (Grachtengordel south) ☏020/622 3542, ☻www.escape.nl. What once used to be a tacky disco is now home to Amsterdam's hottest Saturday night, "Chemistry", every so often featuring Holland's top DJ, Dimitri. A vast place, with room for 2000 people (although you may still have to queue). Closed Sun.

Korsakoff See p.183. Small, dark grunge club, featuring live bands as well as alternative rock and noise nights. Free.

Loveboat De Ruiterkade, steiger 4, behind Centraal Station (Old Centre). Famous DJ partyship giving monthly dresscoded parties.

Mazzo Rozengracht 114 (Grachtengordel west) ☏020/626 7500, ☻www.mazzo.nl. One of the city's hippest and most laid-back clubs, with a choice of music to appeal to all tastes. Perhaps the easiest-going bouncers in town. Open nightly.

Melkweg See p.182. After the bands have finished, this multimedia centre plays host to some of the most enjoyable theme nights around, everything from African dance parties to experimental jazz-trance.

The Ministry Reguliersdwarsstraat 12 (Old Centre) ☏020/623 3981. A new club trying to catch a wide brand of party people and featuring quality DJs. Speed garage, house and R&B. Monday-night jam session with the local jazz talent. Open late.

Nieuwezijds Lounge Nieuwezijds Voorburgwal 169 (Old Centre) ☎ 020/622 7510. An average lounge club where everybody pretends to work for MTV. Mon–Thurs & Sun till 3am, Fri & Sat till 4am.

More Rozengracht 133 (Grachtengordel west) ☎ 020/344 6402, ⊛ www.expectmore.nl. Trying to be the coolest club in town, but not hitting the mark. Girls-only night once a month called "Habiba".

Odeon Singel 460 (Grachtengordel south) ☎ 020/624 9711, ⊛ www.odeontheater.nl. This converted seventeenth-century building is one of the oldest venues in the city. Its stylishly elegant interior is divided into four floors ranging from the top floor's student vibe to African beats in the basement. Open nightly.

Panama Oostelijke Handelskade 4 (Old Jewish Quarter and the East) ☎ 020/311 8686, ⊛ www.panama.nl. The newest club in town, host to a wide variety of live gigs and themed club nights. There is a theatre and a restaurant too. Funky.

Paradiso Weteringschans 6–8 (Grachtengordel south) ☎ 020/623 7348, ⊛ www.paradiso.nl. One of the principal venues in the city, which on Fridays turns into the unmissable VIP (Vrijdag In Paradiso) Club, from midnight onwards. Also hosts one-off events – check listings.

The Powerzone Danielgoedkoopstraat 1–3 (Outer Districts) ☎ 020/681 8866, ⊛ www .thepowerzone.nl. Weekend partyzone, with good trance and techno DJs. Metro Spaklerweg.

Sinners in Heaven Wagenstraat 3 (Grachtengordel south) ☎ 020/620 1375, ⊛ www .sinners.nl. Rembrandtplein club churning out lots of R&B and house, with a dressed-up clientele consuming long drinks.

Café Sol Rembrandtsplein 18 (Grachtengordel south) ☎ 020/330 3279. ⊛ www.djcafesol.nl. DJ café where the emphasis is on loud music rather then anything else.

Winston Kingdom Warmoestraat 129 (Old Centre) ☎ 020/623 1380, ⊛ www.winston.nl. Small venue adjacent to the *Winston Hotel*, with club nights and performances. See p.150.

Shops and markets

Variety is the essence of Amsterdam **shopping**. Whereas in other capitals you can spend days trudging around in search of something interesting, here you'll find every kind of store packed into a relatively small area that's nearly always pleasant to wander around. Throw in a handful of great **street markets**, and Amsterdam's shopping possibilities look even better. There are, of course, the obligatory generic malls and pedestrianized shopping streets, where you can find exactly the same stuff you'd see at home (only more expensive), but where Amsterdam scores is in some excellent, unusual **speciality shops** – designer clocks, rubber stamps, Indonesian arts, condoms, to name just a few.

Shopping in Amsterdam can be divided roughly by **area**, with similar shops often huddled together in neighbouring streets. While exploring, bear in mind that the major canals are mostly given over to homes and offices, and it's along the small radial streets that connect them that many of the most interesting and individual shops are scattered. Broadly, the **Nieuwendijk/Kalverstraat** strip running through Dam square in the Old Centre is home to high-street fashion and mainstream department stores – Saturday afternoon here can be a hellish experience. **Magna Plaza**, just behind the Royal Palace, is a marvellous, striped castle of a building that used to be the main post office, but has now been transformed into a covered mall on five floors, all pricey espressos and teenagers on the escalators. **Koningsplein** and **Leidsestraat** used to be home to the most exclusive shops; these days many of them have fled south, though there's still a surprisingly good selection of affordable designer shoe and clothes stores. The **Jordaan**, to the west, is where many local artists ply their wares: you can find individual items of genuine interest here, as well as more specialized and adventurous clothes shops and some affordable antiques. Less affordable antiques – the cream of Amsterdam's renowned trade – can be found in the Spiegelkwartier, centred on **Nieuwe Spiegelstraat**, while to the south, **P.C. Hooftstraat**, **Van Baerlestraat** and, further south still, **Beethovenstraat** play host to designer clothiers, upmarket ceramics stores, confectioners and delicatessens.

The consumer revolution is noticeably absent from Amsterdam's cobbled alleys, and the majority of shops you'll come across are individual small businesses rather than chains: in Amsterdam it's the shopworker, not the consumer, who reigns supreme, as evidenced by both the limited **opening hours** of most shops and the relatively high prices. The majority of shops take Monday morning off, not opening up until noon or 1pm and closing again at 6pm. On Tuesday, Wednesday and Friday, hours are the standard 9am to 6pm, although the larger shops in the centre have shifted towards a 7pm closing time. Thursday is late-opening night (*koopavond*), with most places staying open from 9am until 9pm. Saturday hours are normally 8.30 or 9am to 5 or 5.30pm, and all except the larger shops on the main streets are closed on Sunday. A few "night shops" are open between roughly 4pm and 1am; see the box on p.205.

Most small and medium-sized shops – and even some of the larger ones – won't accept **payment by credit card**: don't take it for granted in anywhere but the biggest or most expensive places. Shops that do will accept the usual range of major cards, but never traveller's cheques.

Antiques

By necessity, this is only a sample of what's on offer – you'll find many more **antiques** shops in every corner of Amsterdam.

Affaire D'Eau Haarlemmerdijk 150 (Jordaan and the Westerdok) ☎020/422 0411. Antique bathtubs, taps, sinks and toilets.

Blitz Nieuwe Spiegelstraat 37a (Grachtengordel south) ☎020/623 2663. Chinese ceramics.

Couzijn Simon Prinsengracht 578 (Grachtengordel south) ☎020/624 7691. Antique toys and dolls.

Dick Meijer Keizersgracht 539 (Grachtengordel south) ☎020/624 9288. Egyptian, Roman and pre-Columbian antiquities.

Eduard Kramer Nieuwe Spiegelstraat 64 (Grachtengordel south) ☎020/638 8740. Specialists in fifteenth- to twentieth-century Dutch tiles, with a marvellous selection.

Elisabeth Hendriks Nieuwe Spiegelstraat 61 (Grachtengordel south) ☎020/623 0085. Snuff bottles.

Gallery de Munt In the Munttoren, Muntplein 12 (Old Centre) ☎020/623 2271. The best outlet for gifts of antique delftware, pottery, hand-painted tiles and the like.

Harrie van Gennip Govert Flinckstraat 402 (De Pijp) ☎020/679 3025. A huge collection of old and antique stoves from all parts of Europe, lovingly restored and all in working order.

Jan Beekhuizen Nieuwe Spiegelstraat 49 (Grachtengordel south) ☎020/626 3912. European pewter from the fifteenth century onwards.

Jan Best Keizersgracht 357 (Grachtengordel west) ☎020/623 2736. Famed antique lamp shop, with some wonderfully kitsch examples.

Thom & Lenny Nelis Keizersgracht 541 (Grachtengordel south) ☎020/623 1546. Medical antiques and spectacles.

Tóth Ikonen Nieuwe Spiegelstraat 68 (Grachtengordel south) ☎020/420 7359. Antique Russian icons.

Van Dreven & Toebosch Nieuwe Spiegelstraat 33 (Grachtengordel south) ☎020/625 2732. Antique clocks, barometers and music boxes.

Van Hier tot Tokio Prinsengracht 262 (Grachtengordel west) ☎020/428 2682. Japanese furniture, crafts, kimonos etc. A split-level store with a good variety of quality items.

De Vredespijp 1e Van der Helststraat 5–11 (De Pijp) ☎020/676 4855. Art Deco furniture and decorative pieces.

Art supplies, postcards and posters

Art Unlimited Keizersgracht 510 (Grachtengordel south) ☎020/624 8419. Enormous card and poster shop, with excellent stock. All kinds of images: good for communiqués home that don't involve windmills.

Cortina Reestraat 22 (Grachtengordel west). Note blocks, diaries and address books in every possible design.

De Lach 1e Bloemdwarsstraat 14 (Jordaan and the Westerdok) ☎020/626 6625. Fairy-tale movie poster shop.

Paper Moon Singel 419 (Grachtengordel west) ☎020/626 1669. Well-stocked card shop.

Quadra Herengracht 383 (Grachtengordel west) ☎020/626 9472. Original advertising posters from 1900 onwards.

Van Beek Stadhouderskade 63 (De Pijp) ☎020/662 1670. Long-established outlet for art materials. Graphic arts supplies are sold at the Weteringschans 201 branch.

Van Ginkel Bilderdijkstraat 99 (Oud West) ☎020/618 9827. Supplier of art materials, with an emphasis on print-making.

Vlieger Amstel 52 (Grachtengordel south) ☎020/623 5834. Every kind of paper downstairs, every kind of paint upstairs.

Bikes

Bikes can be **rented** from Centraal Station (and other train stations), or from a number of private outlets all over town – see "Directory", p.233. When **buying** a bike, don't be tempted by anything you're offered on the street or in a bar – more often than not you'll end up with a stolen bike. Try instead the shops listed below, which rent, sell and repair bikes of all qualities. If you find that no one in the shop speaks English, check out the glossary of basic bike terms on p.273.

Bike City Bloemgracht 70 (Jordaan and the Westerdok) ☎020/626 3721. The best of the sale-and-rental shops for service and quality – try here first.

Fietsenmakerij Damstraat Damstraat 20 (Old Centre) ☎020/625 5092. Bike repair and rental.

Freewheel Akoleienstraat 7 (Jordaan and the Westerdok) ☎020/627 7252. Women-run bike repairs and sales. Tues–Fri 9am–6pm, Sat 9am–5pm.

Ligfietswinkel Waterspiegelplein 10H (Amsterdam West) ☎020/686 9396, ⊚www.ligfietswinkel.nl. Bike shop which also arranges cycling tours to the green areas just outside Amsterdam on the first Sunday of every month. Wed, Fri & Sat 10am–6pm.

Lohman De Clercqstraat 70 (Oud West) ☎020/618 3906. New and used racing bikes.

MacBike Centraal Station West, Waterlooplein ☎020/620 0985; **MacBike Too** Marnixstraat 220 ☎020/626 6964; and at Leidseplein ☎020/528 7688; ⊚www.macbike.nl. Well-respected rental-and-sales firm, which organizes city tours as well.

't Mannetje Frans Halsstraat 28 (De Pijp) ☎020/679 2139, ⊚www.manbike.nl. This shop makes bicycles to personalized designs, whether you want to get your kids on board too or indulge in some extreme sports. They have dealers in London, Berlin and Brussels as well. Closed Sun & Mon.

Kronan Tesselschadestraat 1E (Museum Quarter and Vondelpark) ☎020/627 0005, ⊚www.kronan.nl. More of a craze than a cycling revolution. Kronan builds good-looking, if heavy and rather slow bikes featuring a very small main cogwheel.

Soulcycle Nieuwe Herengracht 33 (Old Jewish Quarter and the East) ☎020/771 5484. BMX bikes and accompaning streetwear.

Ton Kroonenberg Van Woustraat 59 (De Pijp) ☎020/671 6466. Repairs and sales; helpful and courteous service.

Zijwind Fietsen Ferdinand Bolstraat 168 (De Pijp) ☎020/673 7026. A bicycle repair shop run by women; they also have a few secondhand bikes for sale. Tues–Fri 9am–6pm, Sat 10am–5pm.

Books and magazines

Virtually all Amsterdam bookshops stock at least a small selection of **English-language books**, though prices are always inflated (sometimes dramatically). In the city centre it's possible to pick up most English **newspapers** the day they come out, and English-language **magazines** are widely available too, from newsstands and bookshops. The **secondhand** and **antiquarian** booksellers listed below are only the most accessible; for a comprehensive list, pick up the *Antiquarian & Secondhand Bookshops of Amsterdam* leaflet at any of them. For gay and lesbian bookstores see Chapter Twelve.

General bookstores

American Book Center Kalverstraat 185 (Old Centre) ☎020/625 5537. Vast stock, all in English, with lots of imported US magazines and books. Students get ten percent discount.

Athenaeum Spui 14 (Old Centre) ☎020/623 3933. Excellent all-round bookshop with an adventurous stock – though it's basically a Dutch store. Also the best source of international newspapers and magazines.

The English Bookshop Lauriergracht 71 (Jordaan and the Westerdok) ☎020/626 4230. A small but quirky collection of titles, many of which you won't find elsewhere.

Martyrium Van Baerlestraat 170 (Oud Zuid) ☎020/673 2092. Mostly remaindered stock, but none the worse for that – English-language paperbacks and hardbacks galore.

Scheltema Holkema Vermeulen Koningsplein 20 (Grachtengordel south) ☎020/523 1411. Amsterdam's biggest and best bookshop. Six floors of absolutely everything (mostly in Dutch). Open late and on Sundays.

De Slegte Kalverstraat 48 (Old Centre) ☎020/622 5933. The Amsterdam branch of a nationwide chain specializing in new and used books at a discount.

Waterstone's Kalverstraat 152 (Old Centre) ☎020/638 3821. Amsterdam branch of the UK high-street chain, with four floors of books and magazines. A predictable selection, but prices are sometimes cheaper here than elsewhere.

Zwart op Wit Utrechtsestraat 149 (Grachtengordel south) ☎020/622 8174. Small but well-stocked store. Open on Sunday afternoons and until 7pm during the week.

Secondhand and antiquarian

Barry's Book Exchange Kloveniersburgwal 58 (Old Centre) ☎020/626 6266. Rambling old shop with a crusty proprietor. Huge, dark and dusty.

Boekenmarkt Spui (Old Centre). Open-air book market every Friday – see p.208.

Book Traffic Leliegracht 50 (Grachtengordel west) ☎020/620 4690. An excellent and well-organized selection, run by an American.

Brinkman Singel 319 (Grachtengordel west) ☎020/623 8353. A stalwart of the Amsterdam book trade, Brinkman has occupied the same premises for forty years.

Egidius Haarlemmerstraat 87 (Jordaan and the Westerdok) ☎020/624 3255; Nieuwezijdsvoorburgwal 334 (Old Centre) ☎020/624 3929. A good selection of literature, art and poetry, plus a gallery selling lithographs.

Fenix Frans Halsstraat 88 (De Pijp) ☎020/673 9459. Irish literature, and a good range of books on Celtic history and culture, as well as general prehistory.

De Kloof Kloveniersburgwal 44 (Old Centre) ☎020/622 3828, ☜www.dekloof.nl. Enormous higgledy-piggledy used bookshop on four floors. Great for a rummage. All in English and mostly science and philosophy. Open Thurs, Fri & Sat.

A. Kok Oude Hoogstraat 14 (Old Centre) ☎020/623 1191. Antiquarian stock, especially strong on prints and maps.

Magic Galaxies Oude Schans 140 (Old Centre) ☎020/627 6261. Run by a couple whose spare time is spent collecting science fiction, fantasy and other esoteric books, many of which are in English. Run from home, so call first.

Oudemanhuispoort Book Market See p.208.

Timboektoe & Wonderbook Verversstraat 4 (Old Centre) ☎020/6200 568. English paperbacks, travel literature and books on technical innovation.

Vrouwen In Druk Westermarkt 5 (Grachtengordel west) ☎020/624 5003. Secondhand books, all by women authors.

Art and architecture

Architectura & Natura Leliegracht 22 (Grachtengordel west) ☎020/623 6186. Books on architecture and interior design.

Art Book Van Baerlestraat 126 (Museum Quarter and Vondelpark) ☎020/644 0925. The city's best source of high-gloss art books. Check out also the shops of the main museums, particularly the Stedelijk.

Boekie Woekie Berenstraat 16 (Grachtengordel west) ☎020/639 0507. Books by and on Dutch artists and graphic designers.

Lankamp & Brinkman Spiegelgracht 19 (Grachtengordel south) ☎020/623 4656. Art and applied arts, antiques and collectables, plus a good general stock.

Mendo Berenstraat 11 (Grachtengordel west) ☎020/612 1216, ☜www.mendo.nl. Magazines and books on photography and graphic design.

Nijhoff en Lee Staalstraat 13a (Old Centre) ☎020/620 3980. Art and design titles, specializing in books on the art of printing, typography and lithography.

Comics and graphic novels

CIA (Comic Import Amsterdam) Zeedijk 31a (Old Centre) ☎020/620 5078. What it says.

Lambiek Kerkstraat 78 (Grachtengordel south) ☎020/626 7543, ☜www.lambiek.nl. The city's largest and oldest comic bookshop and gallery, with an international stock. Their website features the biggest comiclopedia in the world. Due to rebuilding of their premises they are temporarily relocating from June 2003; check their website for the latest news.

Stripwinkel Kapitein Rob 2e Egelantiersdwarsstraat 7 (Jordaan and the Westerdok) ☏020/622 3869. Cartoon books old and new.
Vandal Com-x Rozengracht 31 (Jordaan and the Westerdok) ☏020/420 2144. US comic imports, as well as related toys, games and masks.

Computer

Boek N Serve Ferdinand Bolstraat 151 (De Pijp) ☏020/664 3446. Good range of computer literature and travel guides. You can get coffee and surf the Internet too.
Computer Collectief Amstel 312 (Grachtengordel south) ☏020/638 9003. Vast collection of books, software and magazines, and an eminently knowledgeable staff.

Cookery

Kookboekhandel Runstraat 26 (Grachtengordel west) ☏020/622 4768. Cookery books in a variety of languages, mostly English; also some out-of-print surprises. The owner is a well-known Dutch cookery journalist, who can get decidedly grumpy if you don't show a little knowledge.
Lankamp en Brinkman Spiegelgracht 19 (Grachtengordel south) ☏020/623 4656. The general stock here focuses on art, but the shop is also known for its good selection of wine books.

Language

Athenaeum See p.195. Excellent all-round bookshop with a first-rate selection of dictionaries and phrase books.
Intertaal Van Baerlestraat 76 (Museum Quarter and Vondelpark) ☏020/671 5353. Teach-yourself books and dictionaries in every language you can think of.
Scheltema Holkema Vermeulen See p.196. Amsterdam's biggest and best bookshop has an excellent range of language books and all sorts of stuff on the Dutch and their habits.

Politics and society

El Hizjra Singel 300a (Grachtengordel west) ☏020/420 0568. Books on the Middle East and the Arab world.
Fort van Sjakoo Jodenbreestraat 24 (Jewish Quarter and the East) ☏020/625 8979. Anarchist bookshop stocking a wide selection of radical political publications.

Pantheon St Antoniesbreestraat 132 (Old Centre) ☏020/622 9488. General bookshop with a strong political and Middle East section.
Pegasus Singel 367 (Grachtengordel west) ☏020/623 1138. The best politics collection in the city.
Tropenmuseum Bookstore Linnaeusstraat 2 (Amsterdam Oost) ☏020/568 8295. Books on Third World politics and culture, many in English.

Religion and occult

Au Bout du Monde Singel 313 (Grachtengordel west) ☏020/625 1397. Astrology, philosophy, psychology and mysticism, with classical music playing while you browse.
International Evangelist Bookshop Raadhuisstraat 14 (Grachtengordel west) ☏020/620 1859. Bibles and Christian books.
Kirchner Leliegracht 32 (Grachtengordel west) ☏020/624 4449. A bible in almost every language and some good scholarly works.
Kirchner Antiquariaat Prinsengracht 260 (Grachtengordel west) ☏020/615 9377. Secondhand literature on a broad range of religious subjects.

Theatre and film

Cine-Qua-Non Staalstraat 14 (Old Centre) ☏020/625 5588. Mostly English titles on film and cinema history.
International Theatre and Film Books Leidseplein 26a (Grachtengordel south) ☏020/622 6489. Books and magazines on all aspects of the stage and screen.

Travel

A la Carte Utrechtsestraat 110 (Grachtengordel south) ☏020/625 0679. Large and friendly travel bookshop.
Evenaar Singel 348 (Grachtengordel west) ☏020/624 6289. Concentrates more on travel literature than guidebooks.
Jacob van Wijngaarden Overtoom 97 (Museum Quarter and Vondelpark) ☏020/612 1901. The city's best travel bookshop, with knowledgeable staff and a huge selection of books and maps. Also inflatable and illuminated globes.
Pied-à-Terre Singel 393 (Grachtengordel west) ☏020/627 4455. Hiking maps for Holland and beyond, most in English.
Stadsboekwinkel Amsteldijk 112 (De Pijp) ☏020/572 0299. The shop for all books on

Amsterdam: architecture, transport, history, urban planning, geography, etc.

Women's

Vrouwen in Druk Westermarkt 5 (Grachtengordel west) ⊕020/624 5003. "Women in Print" stocks secondhand books by female authors, with a large English selec-

tion. Mon–Fri 11am–6pm, Sat 11am–5pm.

Xantippe Unlimited Prinsengracht 290 (Grachtengordel west) ⊕020/623 5854. Amsterdam's foremost women's bookshop, with a wide selection of new feminist titles in English. Mon 1–7pm, Tues–Fri 10am–7pm, Sat 10am–6pm, Sun 10am–5pm.

Clothes and accessories

When it comes to **clothes**, Amsterdam is in many ways an ideal place to shop: prices aren't too high and the city is sufficiently compact to save lots of shoe leather. On the other hand, don't expect the huge choice of, say, London or New York. The city's **department stores** (see p.201) tend to be conservative, and the Dutch disapproval of ostentation means that the big international designers stay out of the limelight. What you will find are good-value, if somewhat dull, mainstream styles along Kalverstraat and Nieuwendijk, with better stuff along Rokin and Leidsestraat, and the really fancy goods down in the south of the city on P.C. Hooftstraat, Van Baerlestraat and Beethovenstraat. More interestingly, there's a fair array of one-off youth-oriented and secondhand clothing shops dotted around the Jordaan, on Oude and Nieuwe Hoogstraat, and along the narrow streets that connect the major canals west of the city centre. For **secondhand clothes** the Waterlooplein flea market (see p.208) is a marvellous hunting ground. For children's clothes, see "Kids' Amsterdam", p.221. What follows is a brief rundown of some of the more exciting outlets.

New and designer clothes

Agnès B Rokin 126 (Old Centre) ⊕020/627 1465. Shop of the French designer.

America Today In Magna Plaza mall (Old Centre) ⊕020/638 8447; also at Sarphatistraat 48 (Amsterdam Oost). Hugely popular outlet for classic US brands, imported direct and sold cheap.

Analik Hartenstraat 36 (Grachtengordel west) ⊕020/422 0561, ⊛www.analik.nl. Experimental but always stylish clothes for women. Bold mixes of fabrics and colours and styles.

Antonia Gasthuismolensteeg 18 and 6a (Grachtengordel west) ⊕020/627 2433. A gathering of adventurous Dutch designers who started under one roof, and have now split into male and female sites. Good for shoes and bags too.

Cora Kemperman Leidsestraat 72 (Grachtengordel south) ⊕020/625 1284. Well-made, elegantly relaxed designer clothes for women that won't break the bank.

Diversi 1e Leliedwarsstraat 6 (Jordaan and the Westerdok) ⊕020/625 0773. Small but inspired collection of reasonably priced,

mainly French clothes for women.

Edgar Vos P.C. Hooftstraat 136 (Museum Quarter and Vondelpark) ⊕020/671 2748 & Beethovenstraat 57 (Nieuw Zuid). Amsterdam shop of the Dutch *haute couture* designer: power styles for women and a good casual range too.

G & G Prinsengracht 514 (Grachtengordel south) ⊕020/622 6339. Men's clothing in larger sizes.

Hemp Works Nieuwendijk 13 (Old Centre) ⊕020/421 1762. Not all hemp is like sackcloth – check out the silky hemp shirts and jeans.

Local Service Keizersgracht 400 (Grachtengordel west) ⊕020/626 6840. Men's and women's fashions. Ultra-trendy and expensive.

Margriet Nannings Prinsenstraat 8, 15 & 24 (Grachtengordel west) ⊕020/620 7672. Designer clothes for men and women, casual and chic. Wonderful handbags and jewellery too.

Marianne van der Wilt Geldersekade 43d (Old Centre) ⊕020/620 0264. Top designs in leather.

Mateloos Bilderdijkstraat 62 (Oud West) ☎020/683 2384, & Kinkerstraat 77. Clothes for women in larger sizes.

De Mof Haarlemmerdijk 109 (Jordaan and the Westerdok) ☎020/623 1798. Basically an industrial clothier, selling heavy-duty shirts, baggy overalls and the like for rock-bottom prices.

Raymond Linhard Van Baerlestraat 50 (Museum Quarter and Vondelpark) ☎020/679 0755. Cheerful, well-priced separates.

Reflections P.C. Hooftstraat 66 (Museum Quarter and Vondelpark) ☎020/664 0040. The absolute crème de la crème of designer clothing for men and women, with price tags to match.

Robin & Rik Runstraat 30 (Grachtengordel west) ☎020/627 8924. Handmade leather clothes and accessories for men and women.

Robin's Bodywear Nieuwe Hoogstraat 20 (Old Centre) ☎020/620 1552. Affordable lingerie store with a wide stock.

Sissy Boy Leidsestraat 15 (Grachtengordel south) ☎020/623 8949; also at Van Baerlestraat 12 (Museum Quarter and Vondelpark) & Kalverstraat 210 (Old Centre). Simply designed but pricey clothes for men and women.

Solid Haarlemmerdijk 20 (Jordaan and the Westerdok) ☎020/627 4114. Interesting and very fashionable womenswear.

Street and clubwear

Clubwear House Spuistraat 242 (Old Centre) ☎020/622 8766. The place for everything to do with clubbing in Amsterdam, from flyers to fabulous clothes. DJs play in-store on Saturdays.

Cream Leidsestraat 56 (Grachtengordel south) ☎020/420 3094. Frivolous clubwear, jeans and jumpers.

Cyberdog Spuistraat 250 (Old Centre) ☎020/330 6385. Conveniently close to Clubwear House, this shop is a tad more cutting-edge in its creations.

Kosiuko Huidenstraat 8 (Grachtengordel west) ☎020/320 0223. Outlet store with colourful T-shirts and funky jeans.

Ksisk Kerkstraat 115 (Grachtengordel south). Punky store.

Punch St Antoniesbreestraat 73 (Old Centre) ☎020/626 6673. Doc Martens and Lonsdale.

Rodolfo's Magna Plaza mall (Old Centre) ☎020/623 1214; also at Sarphatistraat 59 (Amsterdam Oost). Huge collection of in-line skates and skateboards and the latest fashion to go with them.

Secondhand clothes

Daffodil Jacob Obrechtstraat 41 (Museum Quarter and Vondelpark) ☎020/679 5634. Designer labels only in this posh secondhand shop down by the Vondelpark.

The End Nieuwe Hoogstraat 26 (Old Centre) ☎020/625 3162. Unspectacular but inexpensive streetwear.

Jojo Huidenstraat 23 ☎020/623 3476; also at Runstraat 9 (both Grachtengordel west). Decent secondhand clothes from all eras. Particularly good for trench coats and 1950s jackets.

Kelere Kelder Prinsengracht 285 (Grachtengordel west). Goldmine for used alternative clothing. Fri–Sun 1–6pm.

Lady Day Hartenstraat 9 (Grachtengordel west) ☎020/623 5820. Good-quality secondhand fashion at reasonable prices.

Laura Dols Wolvenstraat 7 (Grachtengordel west) ☎020/624 9066. Vintage clothing and lots of hats.

Second Best Wolvenstraat 18 (Grachtengordel west) ☎020/422 0274. Classy cast-offs.

Zipper Huidenstraat 7 (Grachtengordel west) ☎020/623 7302; also at Nieuwe Hoogstraat 10 (Old Centre). Used clothes selected for style and quality – strong on jeans and flairs. Prices are high, but it's very popular, and everything is in good condition.

Shoes and accessories

Big Shoe Leliegracht 12 (Grachtengordel west) ☎020/622 6645. All designs and styles for larger-sized female feet.

Body Sox Leidsestraat 35 (Grachtengordel south) ☎020/627 6553. Socks, tights and stockings in every conceivable colour and design.

Bonnier Haarlemmerstraat 58 (Jordaan and the Westerdok) ☎020/626 4991. Very reasonably priced bag and umbrella shop.

Dr Adam's Oude Doelenstraat 5 (Old Centre) ☎020/622 3734; also at Leidsestraat 25 (Grachtengordel south) and P.C. Hooftstraat 90 (Museum Quarter and Vondelpark). One of the city's broadest selections of shoes.

The English Hatter Heiligeweg 40 (Old Centre) ☎020/623 4781. Ties, hats and various other accessories, alongside classic menswear from shirts to cricket sweaters.

Fred de la Bretonière St Luciesteeg 9 ☎020/623 4152; also at Utrechtsetstraat 77 (both Grachtengordel south). Designer famous for his high-quality handbags and shoes, sold at reasonable prices.

△ Old-style grocery store

De Grote Tas Oude Hoogstraat 6 (Old Centre) ☏020/623 0110. Family-run store now in the third generation, selling a wide selection of serious bags, briefcases and suitcases.
Hoeden M/V Herengracht 422 (Grachtengordel west) ☏020/626 3038. Designer hats galore, from felt Borsalinos to straw Panamas. Gloves and umbrellas too; intimidating prices, though.

Jan Jansen Rokin 42 (Old Centre) ☏020/625 1350. Famous Dutch designer selling hand-made shoes with frivolous designs.
Warmer Leidsestraat 41 (Grachtengordel south) ☏020/427 8011. A step ahead in designer shoes and boots. Bags too.
Zwartjes Utrechtsestraat 123 (Grachtengordel south) ☏020/623 3701. Classical and modern shoes, all leather.

Department stores and malls

Amsterdam's **department stores**, like many of the city's shops are pretty conservative. More exciting is **Magna Plaza**, in the old post office building at Nieuwezijds Voorburgwal 182, behind Dam square, which is not a department store but a covered mall sheltering all kinds of outlets, from stationery to underwear. Alternatively, try the **Kalvertoren**, another covered mall on Kalverstraat, close to the Munt, with a range of general high-street outlets. The glass lift in the centre takes you up to the *HEMA* restaurant, a wonderful belvedere and a good place for coffee and simple lunches.

De Bijenkorf Dam 1 (Old Centre) ☏020/621 8080. Dominating the northern corner of Dam square, this is the city's top shop, a huge bustling place (the name means bee-hive) that has an indisputably wide range. Departments to head for include household goods, cosmetics and kidswear; there's also a good choice of newspapers and magazines.
HEMA Nieuwendijk 174 (Old Centre) ☏020/623 4176; also in the Kalvertoren and branches out of the centre. A kind of Dutch Woolworth's, but of a better quality: good for stocking up on toiletries and other essentials, and occasional designer delights – it's owned by De Bijenkorf, and you can sometimes find the same items at knockdown prices. Surprises include wine and salami in the back of the shop, and sometimes a bakery and cheese counter. Their Fotoservice is convenient and gives same-day delivery.
Maison de Bonneterie Rokin 140 (Old Centre) ☏020/626 2162. Apart from the building, which rises through balustraded balconies to a high central dome, nothing special: very conservative and, on the whole, extremely expensive. Small lunch café as well. By appointment to Her Majesty.

Metz & Co. Keizersgracht 455 (Grachtengordel south) ☏020/624 8810. Upmarket department store with the accent on Liberty prints (it used to be owned by Liberty's of London), stylish ceramics and designer furniture of the kind that's exhibited in modern art museums: just the place to pick up a Rietveld chair. If your funds won't stretch quite that far, settle for a cup of coffee in the top-floor Rietveld restaurant, which gives great views over the city.
Peek & Cloppenberg Dam 20 (Old Centre) ☏020/623 2837. Less a department store than a multistorey clothes shop with some painfully middle-of-the-road styles. Nonetheless, an Amsterdam institution.
Vroom & Dreesmann Kalverstraat 203 (entrance also from Rokin; Old Centre) ☏020/622 0171. The main Amsterdam branch of a middle-ground nationwide chain, just near Muntplein. It's pretty unadventurous, but take comfort from the fact that the restaurant is quite outstanding (for a department store), and they bake fresh bread on the premises as well. Check out also the listening stands in the CD section on the top floor – the best place for a free Mozart recital with a canal view.

Food and drink

Amsterdam's talent for small specialist outlets extends to food as much as anything else. While the city's supermarkets may not impress, there's a whole host of **speciality food stores** where you can buy anything from local fish to imported Heinz beans. We've also listed a selection of **wine and spirits shops**, chosen for their location, specialities or simply because they're good value.

Supermarkets

Supermarkets are rather thin on the ground in the city centre, and most are throwbacks to the 1970s; going supermarket shopping in Amsterdam will probably be the only occasion when you'll long for the impersonal efficiency of back home. Aisles are narrow, trolleys are battered (you need a euro coin to de-chain them), there are too many people and not enough choice. If you're buying fruit or vegetables, you'll need to weigh and price them yourself (unless a price is given per item, *per stuk*) – put them on the scale, press the little picture, then press *BON* to get a sticky barcode. If you're buying beer, juice or water in **bottles** (glass or plastic), a deposit of €0.10–0.45 will be added on at the checkout; you get it back when you return the empties – to a different store if you like. Unless you have a bag for all your stuff, you'll have to pay about €0.35 for an own-brand one. Most supermarkets conform to regular shop hours (see p.193).

Albert Heijn Koningsplein 4 (Grachtengordel south) ☎020/624 5721. Amsterdam's main branch of a nationwide chain but still small, crowded and expensive. There are other central branches at Nieuwezijds Voorburgwal/Dam, Nieuwmarkt and Joodenbreestraat, but prices are lower in those further out of the centre: Haarlemmerdijk 1 (Jordaan and the Westerdok), Overtoom 454 (Museum Quarter and Vondelpark), Vijzelstraat 117 (Grachtengordel south) and Westerstraat 79 (Jordaan and the Westerdok). Variable opening hours, currently Mon–Sat 10am–10pm, Sun noon–6pm.

Dirk van den Broek Heinekenplein 25 (De Pijp) ☎020/611 0812. Beats Albert Heijn hands down in everything except image. Cheaper across the board; bigger too. Trams #16, #24 or #25. Mon–Sat roughly 9am–9pm. More branches dotted around

the suburbs.

HEMA See p.201. Known amongst locals for its affordable wines of likeable quality, birthday cakes and smoked sausages, they also sell nice cookies, cheese, bread and sometimes sliced meat.

De Natuurwinkel Weteringschans 133 (Grachtengordel) ☎020/638 4083. Main branch of a chain selling only organic food (thus a little more expensive). Much better tasting fruit and vegetables than anywhere else; also grains, pulses and Bon Bon Jeanette chocolates. Superb bread. Smaller branches around town. Mon–Sat 7am–8pm, Thurs till 9pm, Sun 11am–6pm.

Beer, wine and spirits

The **legal age** at which you can be sold beer is 16; for wines and spirits you need to be 18. The Dutch word for an off-licence (liquor store) is *slijterij*.

De Bierkoning Paleisstraat 125 (Old Centre) ☎020/625 2336. The "Beer King" is aptly named: 850 different beers, with matching glasses to drink them from.

Chabrol Haarlemmerstraat 7 (Jordaan and the Westerdok) ☎020/622 2781. All kinds of alcohol from all parts of the world. A fine selection of wines, and the staff are extremely knowledgeable.

Chateau P.C. Hooft Honthorststraat 1 (Museum Quarter and Vondelpark) ☎020/673 0102. Extensive but expensive: fifty malt whiskies, forty champagnes, and Armagnac from 1886.

Drinkland Spuistraat 116 (Old Centre) ☎020/638 6573. Largest off-licence in the centre of the city.

Elzinga Wijnen Frederiksplein 1, corner of Utrechtsestraat (Grachtengordel south) ☎020/623 7270. High-quality wines from around the world.

Gall & Gall Nieuw Zijds Voorburgwal 226 (Old Centre) ☎020/421 8370. Most central branch of the largest off-licence chain in Amsterdam. Other outlets at Van Baerlestraat 85, 1e van der Helststraat 82, Rozengracht 72 and Utrechtsestraat 67.

Vintner Otterman Keizersgracht 300 (Grachtengordel west) ☏020/625 5088. Small, exclusive selection of French wines to weep for.

Bread, pastries and sweets

Along with the outlets selling cholesterol- and sugar-packed goodies, we've listed some places where you can buy healthier baked goods. Note that a *warme bakkerij* sells bread and rolls baked on the premises; a *banketbakkerij* sells pastries and cream cakes.

J.G. Beune Haarlemmerdijk 156 (Jordaan and the Westerdok) ☏020/624 8356. Handmade cakes and chocolates in an old-style interior.

Bon Bon Jeanette Centraal Station (Old Centre) ☏020/421 5194. Organic, handmade, additive-free, preservative-free, low-sugar chocolates – surprisingly delicious.

Gary's Muffins Prinsengracht 454 (Grachtengordel south) ☏020/420 1452. The best, most authentic New York bagels (and muffins) in town. Branches at Marnixstraat 121 (Jordaan and the Westerdok) and at Reguliersdwarsstraat 53 (Grachtengordel south), the latter open until 4am.

Hartog's Ruysschtraat 56 (Amsterdam Oost) ☏020/665 1295. Fat-free, 100-percent-wholegrain breads, rolls and croissants. From 7am. Metro Wibautstraat.

't Goede Soet Keizersgracht/Herenstraat (Grachtengordel west) ☏020/420 8807. Chocolate lovers' paradise. Handmade bonbons and the best *hagelslag* (chocolate sprinkels) ever tasted.

Kwekkeboom Reguliersbreestraat 36 (Grachtengordel south) ☏020/623 1205. One of the city's most famous pastry shops, showered with awards. Not cheap, but you're paying for the chocolatier's equivalent of Gucci. Also at Ferdinand Bolstraat 119 and Linnaeusstraat 80.

Lanskroon Singel 385 (Grachtengordel west) ☏020/623 7743. Another famously good pastry shop, with a small area for on-the-spot consumption.

Mediterrané Haarlemmerdijk 184 (Jordaan and the Westerdok) ☏020/620 3550. Famous for their croissants; also North African pastries and French bread.

Paul Année Runstraat 25 (Grachtengordel west) ☏020/623 5322. The best wholegrain and sourdough breads in town, bar none – all made from organic grains.

Pompadour Chocolaterie Huidenstraat 12 (Grachtengordel west) ☏020/623 9554. Chocolates and lots of homemade pastries (usually smothered in or filled with chocolate).

Runneboom 1e van der Helstraat (De Pijp) ☏020/673 5941. Wonderful selection of breads from around the world – fitting, given its location in the multicultural Pijp district. Open from 7am.

Cheese

Arxhoek Damstraat 19 (Old Centre) ☏020/622 9118. Centrally situated general cheese shop.

Comestibles Kinders Westerstraat 189 (Jordaan and the Westerdok) ☏020/622 7983. Excellent selection of cheeses and other goodies.

De Kaaskamer Runstraat 7 (Grachtengordel west) ☏020/623 3483. Friendly shop, with tapas and olives too.

Robert & Abraham Kef Marnixstraat 192 (Jordaan and the Westerdok) ☏020/626 2210. A wide range of French cheeses – and facilities for tasting. Closed Mon & Tues.

Coffee and tea

The Coffee Company Leidsestraat 60 (Grachtengordel south) ☏020/622 1519. Other stores at Haarlemmerdijk (Jordaan and the Westerdok) and 2e Van Der Helstraat (De Pijp). More of an espresso bar, but with some whole and ground beans for sale as well.

Geels & Co. Warmoesstraat 67 (Old Centre) ☏020/624 0683. Oddly situated among Warmoesstraat's porn shops, this is one of the city's oldest and best-equipped specialists, with low prices on beans and utensils.

Levelt Prinsengracht 180 (Grachtengordel west) ☏020/624 0823. A specialist tea and coffee company has occupied this shop for over 150 years, and much of the original decor remains. Now also scattered over almost every part of the city, including Centraal Station, Huidenstraat, Ferdinand Bolstraat and Kinkerstraat. For sound advice go to Prinsengracht. Friendly service at all the shops.

Delis and imported foods

Eichholtz Leidsestraat 48 (Grachtengordel south) ☏020/622 0305. Specialists in imported foods from Britain and the US. The only place to find Oreo cookies, Pop

Tarts, Velveeta and Heinz beans.
Ithaka 1e Bloemdwarsstraat 18 (Jordaan and the Westerdok) ☎020/638 4665. Greek deli with snacks and takeaway meals, in the heart of the Jordaan. Open daily.
La Tienda 1e Sweelinckstraat 21 (De Pijp) ☎020/671 2519. Musty old Spanish deli, with chorizos, hams and cheeses galore. Also all kinds of Latin American spices.
Meidi-Ya Beethovenstraat 18 (Nieuw Zuid) ☎020/673 7410. Comprehensively stocked Japanese supermarket, with a takeaway section and sushi bar.
Olivaria Hazenstraat 2a (Jordaan and the Westerdok) ☎020/638 3552. Olive oil, and nothing but. Incredible range of oils, all self-imported from small- and medium-sized concerns around the world. Expert advice and a well-stocked tasting table.
Oriental Commodities Nieuwmarkt 27 (Old Centre) ☎020/626 2797. Warren-like Chinese supermarket. All sorts of stuff squirrelled away in corners – seaweed, water-chestnuts, spicy prawn crackers. Get there early for the handmade tofu.
Renzo Van Baerlestraat 67 (Museum Quarter and Vondelpark) ☎020/673 1673. Everything freshly made on the premises – from pastas to sandwiches and some exquisite desserts.

Fish and seafood

Although there are lots of fresh herring and seafood **stalls** dotted around the city at strategic locations, including one or two excellent ones in the Albert Cuyp market, perhaps the best is the award-winning Bloemberg, on Van Baerlestraat, on the corner of the Stedelijk Museum. Others worth trying are on the corner of Singel and Haarlemmerstraat, Singel and Raadhuisstraat, Utrechtsestraat and Keizersgracht, and at Muntplein. The following are good fish shops.

Viscenter Volendam Kinkerstraat 181 (Oud West) ☎020/618 7062. Out of the centre, but with consistently high-quality fresh and cured fish. Owned and run by a family from Volendam, a fishing village north of Amsterdam.
De Viswinkel Zeedijk 172 (Old Centre). Small fish shop with a nice window; good for herring too.
Volendammer Vis 1e van der Helststraat (De Pijp). Just at the corner of the Albert Cuypmarkt, with seats at the front to enjoy your herring or kibbeling.

Organic and natural food

De Aanzet Frans Halsstraat 27 (De Pijp) ☎020/673 3415. Organic supermarket co-operative, next to *De Waaghals* restaurant (see p.179) in the Pijp.
De Belly Nieuwe Leliestraat 174 (Jordaan and the Westerdok) ☎020/624 5281. Small and very friendly shop stocking all things organic.
Boerenmarkt See p.208. Weekly organic farmers' market.
Deshima See p.175. A little difficult to spot (it's in the basement), this is a macrobiotic food store with a small restaurant attached.
Gimsel Huidenstraat 19 (Grachtengordel west) ☎020/624 8087. Very central, with a good selection of fruit and vegetables and excellent bread.
De Groene Weg Huidenstraat 11 (Grachtengordel west) ☎020/627 9132. Organic butcher.
De Natuurwinkel See p.202. By far the best selection.
De Weegschaal Jodenbreestraat 20 (Old Jewish Quarter and the East) ☎020/624 1765. Small, friendly shop near the Waterlooplein flea market.

Music

The price of CDs in Amsterdam is higher than in Britain – and outrageous compared to the US. Where the city scores is in the selection available: there are lots of small, low-key shops specializing in one type of music, where you can turn up classic items unavailable elsewhere. If it's vinyl you're after, you've come to the wrong country. Some places still sell records, but it's very much taken for granted that music comes on CDs. However, the **Waterlooplein flea market** (see p.208) has stacks of old records (and CDs) on offer, and some shops – particularly jazz and reggae outlets – maintain sections devoted to used vinyl.

Most of these night shops (*avondwinkels*) open when everyone else is starting to think about closing up, and they stay open until well into the night – which sounds great, but you have to pay for the privilege: essentials can cost a barefaced three times the regular price. Most of them, too, are not immediately accessible from the centre of town, and may take a little looking for. There are more in the outskirts too – look in the *Gouden Gids* (Yellow Pages) under *"avondverkoop"*. Bear in mind, though, that Albert Heijn supermarkets are open until 10pm.

Big Bananas Leidsestraat 73 (Grachtengordel south) ☏020/627 7040. Well stocked and convenient, but absurdly expensive and not known for the kindly treatment of their customers. Mon–Fri & Sun 11am–1am, Sat 11am–2am.

Dolf's Willemsstraat 79 (Jordaan and the Westerdok) ☏020/625 9503. One of the better night shops: expensive, but reasonably central, tucked in a corner of the Jordaan. Mon–Sat 3pm–1am, Sun 10am–1am.

Sterk Waterlooplein 241 (Old Jewish Quarter and the East) ☏020/626 5097. Less a night shop than a city centre institution, with all kinds of fresh breads and pastries baked on the premises, a large fresh produce section, friendly staff – this place pulls something over on regular supermarkets; daily 9am–1am. Smaller, lower-key branch out west at De Clercqstraat 3 ☏020/618 1727; daily 8am–1am.

Back Beat Records Egelantiersstraat 19 (Jordaan and the Westerdok) ☏020/627 1657. Small specialist in soul, blues, jazz, funk, etc, with a helpful and enthusiastic owner.

Boudisque Haringpakkersteeg 10, in an alley off the top end of Damrak (Old Centre) ☏020/623 2603. Well known for its wide selection of rock, house and world music.

Broekmans & Van Poppel Van Baerlestraat 92 (Museum Quarter and Vondelpark) ☏020/679 6575, ⊕www.broekmans.com/en/. Specializes in classical music: historical recordings, small labels, opera, and sheet music.

Charles Weteringschans 193 (Grachtengordel south) ☏020/626 5538. Concentrates on classical and folk.

Concerto Utrechtsestraat 54 (Grachtengordel south) ☏020/623 5228. New and used records and CDs in all categories; equally good on baroque as on grunge. The best all-round selection in the city, with the option to listen before you buy.

Dance Tracks Nieuwe Nieuwstraat 69 (Old Centre) ☏020/639 0853. Imported dance music, hip-hop, jazz, dance, soul and house.

Distortion Records Westerstraat 72 (Jordaan and the Westerdok) ☏020/627 0004. Secondhand independent vinyl.

Fame Kalverstraat 2 (Old Centre) ☏020/638 2525. The only large music warehouse in town; predictable selection of CDs and tapes.

Forever Changes Bilderdijkstraat 148 (Oud West) ☏020/612 6378. New wave and collectors' items, secondhand and new.

Free Record Shop Kalverstraat 32 & 230 (Old Centre) ☏020/626 5808. Also at Leidsestraat 24 (Grachtengordel south), Centraal Station and Nieuwendijk 229 (both Old Centre). One of the better pop/rock chains. No records.

Get Records Utrechtsestraat 105 (Grachtengordel south) ☏020/622 3441. Sizeable selection of independent and alternative CDs, plus some vinyl. Check out also the deceptively small R&B section in the back of the shop.

Killa Cutz Nieuwe Nieuwstraat 19 (Old Centre) ☏020/428 4040. Specializes in all the latest techno and electronic music.

Kuijper Klassiek Ferdinand Bolstraat 6 (De Pijp) ☏020/679 4634, ⊕www.kuijperklassiek.nl. Classical music and Royal Concertgebouw recordings on CD and DVD.

Midtown Nieuwendijk 104 (Old Centre) ☏020/638 4252. House of all kinds from ambient to 200bpm. Also tickets and flyers.

Musiques du Monde Singel 281 (Grachtengordel west) ☏020/624 1354. As the name suggests, world music, both new and used. You can listen before you buy.

Outland Zeedijk 22 (Old Centre) ☏020/638 7576. Another good house selection, in a bright and breezily decorated environment.

Phantasio 2e Tuindwarssatraat 53 (Jordaan and the Westerdok) ☏020/421 7110. Friendly small shop with a good collection of mainstream alternative music.

Record Palace Weteringschans 33 (Grachtengordel south) ☎020/622 3904. Opposite the *Paradiso* (see p.182), a small shop specializing in records from the Fifties and Sixties.

The Sound of the Fifties Prinsengracht 669 (Grachtengordel south) ☎020/623 9745. Small

place near the Leidsegracht with stacks of Fifties and Sixties pop and jazz.

South Miami Plaza Albert Cuypstraat 116 (De Pijp) ☎020/662 2817. Large hall specializing in Caribbean music, but plenty of other styles too. Good atmosphere.

Staalplaat Staalkade 6 (Old Centre) ☎020/625 4176. Noise, avant-garde and obscure music. Good range of vinyl.

New Age and natural remedies

Dela Rosa Staalstraat 10 (Old Centre) ☎020/421 1201. One of the better shops for vitamins and dietary supplements, with friendly, expert advice.

Erica Centraal Station (Old Centre) ☎020/626 1842. Located in the unlikeliest of surroundings, this little shop is part of a chain selling a sizeable array of herbal remedies, teas, cosmetics and vitamins.

Himalaya Warmoesstraat 56 (Old Centre) ☎020/626 0899. Something of an oasis of calm in the midst of Warmoesstraat's porn shops, this cosy shop has a wide selection of books and magazines from around the world, with New Age music, tarot cards and bric-a-brac, as well as readings, a changing photo/art exhibit, and a marvellous café with a terrace and canal view out the back.

Jacob Hooij Kloveniersburgwal 10 (Old Centre) ☎020/624 3041. In business at this address

since 1778, and the shop and its stock are the same now as then. Homeopathic chemist with any amount of herbs and natural cosmetics, as well as a huge stock of *drop* (Dutch liquorice).

Kruiderij De Munt Vijzelstraat 1 (Grachtengordel south) ☎020/624 4533. A very wide range of herbal remedies, essential oils, teas and dietary supplements.

De Roos P.C. Hooftstraat 183 (Museum Quarter and Vondelpark) ☎020/689 0081, Ⓦwww.roos.nl. Delightful New Age centre, with a warm, intimate atmosphere. The bookshop has a wide selection of esoteric books, and the ground-floor café, with its own rambling garden, is the most peaceful in Amsterdam. A wide range of courses and workshops is available, including daily open sessions in yoga and meditation.

Ethnic shops

Baba Bazaar Nieuwe Hoogstraat 28 (Old Centre) ☎020/626 0542. Handcrafted textiles, statues and collectables sourced in India and Indonesia by the owner.

Baobab Elandsgracht 34 (Jordaan and the Westerdok) ☎020/626 8398. Textiles, jewellery and ceramics from Indonesia and the Far East.

D. Eberhardt Damstraat 16 (Old Centre) ☎020/624 0724. Chinese and southeast Asian crafts, ceramics, clothes and jewellery.

Fair Trade Heiligeweg 45 (Old Centre) ☎020/625 2245. Crafts from – and books about – the developing world.

't Japanse Winkeltje Nieuwezijds Voorburgwal 177 (Old Centre) ☎020/627 9523. Japanese arts and crafts.

Kawsara Fall Kerkstraat 143 (Grachtengordel south) ☎020/489 5134. The brothers Kane from Senegal have set up a shop with an enormous amount of drums, textiles and statues from West Africa.

Rarekiek Runstraat 31 (Grachtengordel west) ☎020/623 3591. Small tribal art shop with a focus on Asian and African jewellery, statues and books. Wed–Sat 1–6pm.

Santa Jet Prinsenstraat 7 (Grachtengordel west) ☎020/427 2070. Handmade Latin American items, from collectables to humorous knick-knacks, and plenty of religious icons. You can visit a palm-reader by appointment after the shop has closed.

Shalimar Utrechtsestraat 25 (Grachtengordel south) ☎020/639 2037. Tiny shop with a

Smart shops

Riding on the coat-tails of Amsterdam's liberal policy towards cannabis are a number of what have become known as "**smart shops**". Ostensibly established as outlets for "smart" drugs (memory enhancers, concentration aids, and so on), they do most of their business selling natural alternatives to hard drugs such as LSD, speed or ecstasy. These substitutes often have many or all of the effects of the real thing, but with greatly reduced health risks – and the added bonus of legality. A consistently popular alternative to LSD are psychotropic or "magic" mushrooms, which grow wild all over northern Europe, but when processed or dried are classified as hard drugs and thus illegal. Conscious Dreams was forced to fight a court case over its sale of magic mushrooms, but by reclassifying its business as a greengrocery it was permitted to continue its sale of fresh magic mushrooms (dried ones remain illegal). It also retains its role at the centre of a knowledgeable Amsterdam underground devoted to exploring altered states of consciousness.

Conscious Dreams Kokopelli Warmoestraat 12 (Old Centre) ☏020/421 7000, ⊕www.consciousdreams.nl. Everything you want to know about stimulants, with books, plants, aphrodisiacs etc. Very nicely set-up shop with Internet access and DJs on the weekend. Open till 10pm.

Dreamlounge Kerkstraat 93 (Grachtengordel south) ☏020/626 6907. A small smart shop, with Internet facilities.

The Magic Mushroom Gallery Spuistraat 249 (Old Centre) ☏020/427 5765; also at Singel 524 (Grachtengordel south). Mushroom mania.

Mushroom Galaxy Halve Maansteeg 12 (Grachtengordel south) ☏020/776 8121, ⊕www.mushroomgalaxy.nl. Small shop selling bongs & pipes, seeds, energizers and mushrooms.

When Nature Calls Leidsestraat corner Keizersgracht 508 (Grachtengordel south) ☏020/330 0700. Another shop selling cannabis products such as hemp chocolate and beer, plus seeds and, of course, mushrooms.

wonderful array of antique and modern Indian jewellery.

Tibet Shop Spuistraat 185a (Old Centre) ☏020/420 4538. Books, music, jewellery and more, all made by Tibetan refugees in Nepal and India. The Tibet Support Group (☏020/623 7699) can give travel advice, information on Tibetan restaurants in Holland, and on anything else concerned with Tibet.

Tikal Hartenstraat 2a (Grachtengordel west) ☏020/623 2147. Colourful textiles and jew-ellery from Mexico and Guatemala.

Tribal Design Nieuwe Spiegelstraat 52 (Grachtengordel south) ☏020/421 6695. Beautiful shop with some amazing feather necklaces and other tribal objects.

Willem Zwiep Kerkstraat 149 (Grachtengordel south) ☏020/320 759. An art dealer with a keen eye for spiritual masks, shields and tapestries mostly from Oceania and Asia, plus some from Africa. A good collection of books too.

Markets

Albert Cuypmarkt Albert Cuypstraat, between F. Bolstraat and Van Woustraat (De Pijp). The city's principal general goods and food market, with some great bargains to be had – including slick fashionwear and shoes. Amsterdammers in their natural habitat. Mon–Sat 9am–5pm.

Amstelveld Prinsengracht, near Utrechtsestraat (Grachtengordel south). Flowers and plants, but much less of a scrum than the Bloemenmarkt. Friendly advice on what to buy, and the location is a perfect spot to enjoy the canal. Mon 10am–3pm.

Antiekmarkt Nieuwmarkt (Old Centre). A low-key antiques market, with some good-quality books, furniture and objets d'art dotted in amongst the tat. May–Sept Sun 9am–5pm.

Bloemenmarkt Singel, between Koningsplein and Muntplein (Grachtengordel south). Flowers and plants, ostensibly for tourists, but regularly frequented by locals. Bulbs for export (with health certificate). Some stalls open on Sunday as well. Mon–Sat 9am–5pm.

Boekenmarkt Spui (Old Centre). Wonderful rambling collection of secondhand books, with many a priceless gem lurking in the unsorted boxes. Fri 10am–3pm.

Boerenmarkt Noordermarkt, next to the Noorderkerk (Jordaan and the Westerdok). Organic farmers' market selling all kinds of organically grown produce, plus amazing fresh breads, exotic fungi, fresh herbs and homemade mustards. Sat 9am–5pm.

Dapperstraat Dapperstraat, south of Mauritskade (Amsterdam Oost). Covers about the same ground as the Albert Cuyp, but with not a tourist in sight. Bags of atmosphere, exotic snacks on offer, and generally better prices. Mon–Sat 9am–5pm.

Kunstmarkt Spui (Old Centre) & Thorbeckeplein, south of Rembrandtplein (Grachtengordel south). Low-key but high-quality art market in two locations, with much lower prices than you'll find in the galleries; prints and occasional books as well. Neither operates during the winter. Sun 10am–3pm.

Lindengracht Lindengracht, south of Brouwersgracht (Jordaan and the Westerdok). Rowdy, raucous general household supplies market, a complete switch from the jollity of the neighbouring Boerenmarkt. Sat 8am–4pm.

Nieuwmarkt Nieuwmarkt (Old Centre). One of the last remnants of the Nieuwmarkt's ancient market history, and a rival to the more popular and better-stocked Boerenmarkt, with organic produce, breads, cheeses, and arts and crafts. Sat 9am–5pm.

Noordermarkt Noordermarkt, next to the Noorderkerk (Jordaan and the Westerdok). Junk-lover's goldmine, with a general market on Mondays full of all kinds of bargains, tucked away beneath piles of useless rubbish. Get there early. There's also a farmers' produce market, Boerenmarkt (see above) and a bird market (Sat 8am–1pm). Main market Mon 9am–1pm, Sat 8am–3pm.

Oudemanhuispoort Oudemanhuispoort, off O.Z. Achterburgwal (Old Centre). Charming little book market held in a university corridor since 1876, with new and used books of all kinds, many in Dutch but some in English. You can sit and read your purchases in the university hall, with a coffee and sandwich. Some stalls are closed on weekdays. Mon–Sat 10am–4pm.

Stamp and Coin Market N.Z. Voorburgwal, south of Dam square (Old Centre). For collectors of stamps, coins and related memorabilia, organized by the specialist shops crowded in the nearby alleys. Wed & Sat 11am–4pm.

Waterlooplein Waterlooplein, behind the Stadhuis (Old Jewish Quarter and the East). A real Amsterdam institution, and the city's best flea market by far. Sprawling and chaotic, it's the final resting place for many a pair of yellow corduroy flairs; but there are more wearable clothes to be found, and some wonderful antique/junk stalls to root through. Secondhand vinyl too. Mon–Sat 9am–5pm.

Westermarkt Westerstraat, from the Noorderkerk onwards (Jordaan and the Westerdok). Another general goods market, very popular with the Jordaan locals. Mon–Sat 9am–5pm.

Speciality shops

Perhaps more than any other place in Europe, Amsterdam is a great source of odd little shops devoted to one particular product or interest. What follows is a selection of favourites.

3-D Holograms Grimburgwal 2 (Old Centre) ☎020/624 7225. All kinds of holographic art, big and small.

1001 Kralen Rozengracht 54 (Jordaan and the Westerdok) ☎020/624 3681. "Kralen" means beads, and 1001 would seem a conservative estimate in this place, which sells nothing but.

Absolute Danny O.Z. Achterburgwal 78 (Old Centre) ☏ 020/421 0915. Bills itself as an "erotic lifestyle store", with everything that implies.

Akkerman Kalverstraat 149 (Old Centre) ☏ 020/623 1649. Vast array of pens, inks and writing implements.

Appenzeller Grimburgwal/Nes (Old Centre) ☏ 020/616 6865. State-of-the-art designer jewellery, watches and spectacles.

Art d'Eco Haarlemmerdijk 130 (Jordaan and the Westerdok) and Ferdinand Bolstraat 101 (De Pijp) ☏ 020/622 1210. Accessories, clothing and stationery made of recycled everyday materials.

De Beelden Winkel Berenstraat 39 (Grachtengordel west) ☏ 020/676 4903, ⊛ www.beeldenwinkel.nl. A lovely shop with small statues, models and artworks at affordable prices. Classic and contemporary.

Bragiotti Gallery Singel 242 (Grachtengordel west) ☏ 020/638 9654. Contemporary glass from new and established talents. Wed–Sat noon–6pm.

Condomerie Het Gulden Vlies Warmoesstraat 141 (Old Centre) ☏ 020/627 4174. Condoms of every shape, size and flavour imaginable. All in the best possible taste.

Demmenie Sports Marnixstraat 2 (Jordaan and the Westerdok) ☏ 020/624 3652. Sports shop selling everything you could need for hiking, camping and survival.

Donald E. Jongejans Noorderkerkstraat 18 (Jordaan and the Westerdok) ☏ 020/624 6888. Hundreds of old spectacle frames, all of them without a previous owner. They supplied the specs for Bertolucci's *The Last Emperor*.

Droog Design Rusland 3 (Old Centre) ☏ 020/626 9809, ⊛ www.droogdesign.nl. Founded in 1993, Droog Design has made a serious contribution to the international reinvention of design. Some of their products, such as their milk bottle chandelier, have ended up in museum collections – this is their gallery cum shop.

Gamekeeper Hartenstraat 14 (Grachtengordel west) ☏ 020/638 1579. The place to go if you're into games. All kinds of "fantasy" games from Games Workshop to role-play games, collectible cards, backgammon, magic accessories etc. Mainly for adults.

Gerda's Runstraat 16 (Grachtengordel west) ☏ 020/624 2912. Amsterdam is full of flower shops, but this one is the most imaginative and sensual. An aesthetic experience.

Gort Herenstraat 11 (Grachtengordel west) ☏ 020/620 6240. Pleasant goldsmith, with some beautiful designs and the opportunity to discuss your own. Closed Sun & Mon.

P.G.C. Hajenius Rokin 92 (Old Centre) ☏ 020/623 7494. Old, established tobacconist selling its own and other brands of cigars, tobacco, smoking accessories, and every make of cigarette you can think of.

The Head Shop Kloveniersburgwal 39 (Old Centre) ☏ 020/624 9061. Every dope-smoking accessory you could possibly need, along with assorted marijuana memorabilia.

Hera Candles Overtoom 402 (Museum Quarter and Vondelpark) ☏ 020/616 2886. A wonderful little all-wood shop selling nothing but handmade candles of all shapes, sizes and scents.

Joe's Vliegerwinkel Nieuwe Hoogstraat 19 (Old Centre) ☏ 020/625 0139. Kites, frisbees, boomerangs, diabolos, yo-yos, juggling balls and clubs.

Keck & Lisa Herenstraat 15 (Grachtengordel west) ☏ 020/624 4334. Designer giftshop with every imaginable gadget for the house.

Kitsch Kitchen 1e Bloemdwarsstraat 21 (Jordaan and the Westerdok) ☏ 020/622 8261. Crammed full of bowls, spoons and other kitchen stuff in Day-Glo colours.

't Klompenhuisje Nieuwe Hoogstraat 9a (Old Centre) ☏ 020/622 8100. Amsterdam's best and brightest array of clogs.

Knopenwinkel Wolvenstraat 14 (Grachtengordel west) ☏ 020/624 0479. Buttons in every conceivable shape and size.

Kramer and Pontifex Reestraat 20 (Grachtengordel west) ☏ 020/626 5274. On one side of the shop, Mr Kramer repairs old broken dolls and teddies; on the other, Pontifex sells all kinds of candles, oils and incense.

Mobilia Utrechtsestraat 62 (Grachtengordel south) ☏ 020/622 9075. Decorative studio with designer lamps, rubbish bins and sofas. Also a good range of cleverly designed small household items.

Nieuws Prinsengracht 297 (Grachtengordel west) ☏ 020/627 9540. Specialists in modern designer items for the home – projector clocks, remote control lamps, Philippe Starck vases, etc. Also round dice, chocolate body-paint and shark laundry pegs.

Nijntje Beethovenstraat 71 (Nieuw Zuid) ☏ 020/671 9707; Nieuwendijk 4 (Old Centre); and Schiphol. Created by Dick Bruna, the delightful Nijntje (Miffy) books have spawned a cult following and a range of merchandise.

Nostalgia Herenstraat 37 (Grachtengordel west) ☎020/622 2400. Beautiful small antiques and gifts including glasses, boxes, cutlery and picture frames.

Partyhouse Rozengracht 93b (Jordaan and the Westerdok) ☎020/624 7851. Every conceivable funny item – masks, rentable costumes and wigs, talking clocks, crazy feet, streamers and hats. You name it.

Pink Gravenstraat 19 (Old Centre) ☎020/330 1077. Shiny and brightly coloured glasses, vases, boxes, jewellery. A fantastic giftshop.

Peter Doeswijk Vijzelgracht 11 (Grachtengordel south) ☎020/420 3133. Phones – hundreds of identical, old rotary-dial phones, each painted with a different design (and they all work).

Posthumus Sint Luciensteeg 23 (Old Centre) ☎020/625 5812. Posh stationery, cards and, best of all, a choice of hundreds of rubber stamps. By appointment to Her Majesty.

Schaak en Go Het Paard Haarlemmerdijk 147 (Jordaan and the Westerdok) ☎020/624 1171. Many different – and very beautiful – types of chessboards and figures; also the Japanese game "Go". Books too.

A Space Oddity Prinsengracht 204 (Grachtengordel west) ☎020/427 4036 ⓦwww.spaceoddity.nl. Shop specializing in toys from TV and film, including a large collection of Star Wars paraphernalia, plus Toy Story, James Bond, and Spiderman.

Van Coevorden Leidsestraat 5 (Grachtengordel south) ☎020/624 5150. Wide variety of cigarettes and cigars.

Waterwinkel Roelof Hartstraat 10 (Oud Zuid) ☎020/675 5932. The only thing on offer here is water – over 100 different bottled mineral waters from all over the world. Try the wonderful German *Statl Fasching*.

't Winkeltje Prinsengracht 228 (Grachtengordel south) ☎020/625 1352. Jumble of cheap glassware and crockery, candlesticks, antique tin toys, kitsch souvenirs, old apothecaries' jars and flasks. Perfect for browsing.

Witte Tandenwinkel Runstraat 5 (Grachtengordel west) ☎020/623 3443. The "White Teeth Shop" sells wacky toothbrushes and just about every dental hygiene accoutrement you could ever need.

Yokoso Nieuwe Zijds Voorburgwal 334 (Old Centre) ☎020/489 1605. Hello Kitty emporium – very pink.

Gay and lesbian Amsterdam

n keeping with the Dutch reputation for tolerance, no other city in Europe accepts **gay people** as readily as Amsterdam. Here, more than perhaps anywhere else, it's possible to be openly gay and accepted by the straight community. Gays are prominent in business and the arts, the age of consent is 16 and, with the Dutch willingness to speak English, French and just about any other language, Amsterdam has become a magnet for the international gay scene – a city with a good network of advice centres, bars, clubs and cinemas. The COC (pronounced "say-oh-say"), the national gay and lesbian pressure group, celebrated its fiftieth birthday in 1996 – one of the longest-lived, and largest, groups of its kind in the world.

Homosexuality was decriminalized in the Netherlands as long ago as 1811; a century later – still sixty years ahead of the UK – the gay **age of consent** was reduced to 21, and in 1971 it was brought into line with that of heterosexuals at 16. The most recent legal development was in 2001, with the legalization of **same-sex marriages** with non-discriminatory adoption rights.

Gay couples have full legal rights, and it is maybe a mark of the level of acceptance of gay lifestyles in mainstream Dutch society that every year there is a party in Amsterdam for Holland's gay and lesbian civil servants. It also says much for the strength of the gay community that the arrival of **AIDS** was not accompanied by the homophobia seen in many other places. Rather than close down clubs and saunas, the city council funded education programmes, encouraged the use of condoms, and has generally conducted an open policy on the issue.

However, gay men in Amsterdam are much better catered for than **lesbians**. Although there is a sizeable lesbian community, there are no strictly women-only establishments in the city – even the *Saarein*, previously Amsterdam's solitary women-only café, has finally opened its doors to men. The lesbian scene is largely limited to a few women-only nights held in otherwise male or mixed clubs.

The city has four recognized gay areas: **Reguliersdwarsstraat** with its trendy bars and clubs is the best known and it attracts a young, lively and international crowd, while quieter **Kerkstraat** is populated as much by locals as visitors. The streets just north of **Rembrandtplein** and along the Amstel are a camp focus, as well as being home to a number of rent-boy bars, while **Warmoesstraat**, in the heart of the Red Light District, is cruisey and mainly leather- and denim-oriented.

Same-sex couples holding hands and kissing in the streets are no more worthy of comment than straight couples. **Cruising** is generally tolerated in places where it's not likely to cause offence, and many bars and clubs have **dark-rooms**, which are legally obliged to provide safe sex information and condoms.

If you want more information, get hold of a copy of the widely available **Columbia Fun Map** of Amsterdam produced by the *SAD-Schorerstichting* (see below), or visit ⓦ www.gaymap.ws. You could also invest in a copy of the *Best Guide to Amsterdam*, a comprehensive gay **guidebook** (in English) available from any of the shops listed on p.216 and most gay bookshops around the world. Among the many local gay **newspapers and magazines**, *Gay & Night* (ⓦ www.gay-night.nl), which appears monthly and costs €3 in newsagents, features interviews and news. The fortnightly *Gay Krant* (ⓦ www.gaykrant.nl) has all the details you could conceivably need, including up-to-the-minute listings, though it is in Dutch only. You can also pick up free brochures and maps in most of the gay bars and businesses. Finally, the *PS* magazine of *Het Parool* on Saturday has a Gay section included in its nightlife listings.

Resources and contacts

In addition to the organizations and centres listed below, two important sources of information on the gay and lesbian scenes are the **Gay and Lesbian Switchboard** (☏ 020/623 6565; ⓦ www.switchboard.nl; daily 2–10pm), an English-speaking service which provides help and advice, and **MVS Radio** (☏ 020/620 0247; ⓦ www.mvs.nl), Amsterdam's gay and lesbian radio station, which broadcasts daily from 6pm to 8pm on 106.8FM (or 88.1 via cable) – try and catch the English-language talk show *Aliens*, at 7pm on Friday and 6pm on Sunday. Radio 747AM also broadcasts *Het Roze Rijk* ("The Pink Empire") on Saturday from 6pm.

COC Rozenstraat 14 (Jordaan and the Westerdok) ☏ 020/626 3087, ⓦ www.cocamsterdam .nl. Amsterdam branch of the national gay and lesbian organization, offering advice, contacts and social activities (office Mon–Fri 10am–5pm), plus a meeting point (Sat 1–5pm) and a large noticeboard. The general COC café (Wed & Thurs 8pm–midnight, Fri 8pm–3am) is also the venue for more specific "themed" nights. One of the most popular women-only nights in Amsterdam, "Just Girls", is held regularly on Saturday in both the café (10pm–3am) and the nightclub (10pm–3am), under 24s only.

Gala Postbus 15815, 1001 NH Amsterdam ☏ 020/616 1979. Organization responsible for various Homomonument Festivals, including those on Queen's day and Liberation Day. Also features an information point at the Homomonument itself called the Pink Point of Presence, where you can get general info and flyers.

Homodok (The Documentation Centre for Lesbian and Gay Studies) Nieuwpoortkade 2a, 1055 RX Amsterdam ☏ 020/606 0712, ☏ 020/606 0713, ⓦ www.homodok-laa.nl. A major archive of all forms of literature, as well as videos

and photographs, relating to lesbian and gay studies, contemporary and historical. Prospective visitors should write several weeks ahead detailing areas of interest. See also the IIAV archive, p.235. Mon–Fri 10am–4pm.

Long Yang Club Postbus 1172, 1000 BD Amsterdam ☏ 020/538 4646, ⓦ www .longyangclub.nl. International organization for Asian gays, which holds regular parties in Amsterdam, as well as publishing a monthly magazine called *Oriental Express*.

SAD Schorerstichting P.C. Hooftstraat 5 (Museum Quarter and Vondelpark) ☏ 020/662 4206, ⓦ www.sadschorer.nl. Gay and lesbian counselling centre offering professional and politically conscious advice on identity, sexuality and lifestyle (Mon–Fri 10am–4pm). Its clinic, held at the Municipal Health Department, provides STD examinations and treatment.

Sjalhomo ("Shalom-o") Postbus 2536, 1000 CM Amsterdam ☏ 020/531 2318, ⓦ www .shalhomo.dds.nl. National organization for Jewish gays and lesbians.

Stichting Tijgertje Tijgertje 10521, 1001 EM Amsterdam ☏ 020/673 2458, ⓦ www.tijgertje.nl.

Gay and lesbian sports club.
Wildside COC Rozenstraat 14 (Jordaan and the Westerdok) ☏071/512 8632, ℮wildside@dds.nl.

A lesbian SM group which has regular open meetings at the COC (see p.212).

Accommodation

The city's **gay-friendly hotels** are reviewed below. There are no women-only hotels, although two unofficial, privately run bed-and-breakfasts – *Johanna's* (p.153) and *Liliane's Home* – cater for gay women, the latter exclusively so. *Hotel Quentin* is particularly popular with lesbians, though all the hotels listed below are lesbian-friendly. Note that it's illegal for a hotel to refuse entry to anyone on the grounds of sexual orientation.

Old Centre

Anco Oudezijds Voorburgwal 55, ☏020/624 1126, ℱ020/620 5275, ℮info@ancohotel.nl. Small and friendly hotel, with private bar catering exclusively to leather-wearing gay men; in the Red Light District. Three- and four-person dorms (€37) and studios with private bathroom and kitchenette. Booking advised; 10min from CS. ❸–❺
Centre Apartments Heintje Hoeksteeg 27, ☏020/627 2503, ℱ020/625 1108. Studios and apartments for rent in the middle of the Old Centre; Heintje Hoeksteeg is 5min from CS. ❹
Stablemaster Warmoesstraat 23, ☏020/625 0148, ℱ020/638 9074. Small, exclusively male gay hotel above a popular leather bar in the heart of the Red Light action; the bar is known for its wild theme parties. English-speaking staff; 5min from CS. ❺

Grachtengordel south

Aero Kerkstraat 45–49 ☏020/622 7728, ℱ020/638 8531. Friendly hotel linked to the *Camp Café*. Sixteen clean enough rooms, many with shower and/or toilet. Off-season discounts a possibility. No single rooms. Tram #1, #2 or #5 to Prinsengracht. ❸–❹
Amistad Kerkstraat 42 ☏020/624 8074, ℱ020/622 9997, ℗www.amistad.nl. Stylish gay hotel that's recently gone through a total revamp; conveniently located for the Kerkstraat area. Each room is equipped with soft lighting, and cosy duvets, TV, fridge and a safe. Standard rooms come without shower, deluxe rooms have shower (and in some cases bathtub) and stereo. Late breakfast 10am–2pm. Tram #1, #2 or #5 to Koningsplein. ❷–❺

Golden Bear Kerkstraat 37 ☏020/624 4785, ℱ020/627 0164, ℗www.goldenbear.nl. Solid, budget option, with a good range of clean, comfortable rooms, some en suite. Tram #1, #2 or #5 to Prinsengracht. Booking essential. ❷–❹
Greenwich Village Kerkstraat 25 ☏020/626 9746, ℱ020/625 4081. A well-kept, if slightly down-at-heel, gay-friendly hotel, situated next door to a karaoke bar. Rooms sleeping from one to six people, all €40 per person. Helpful and friendly staff. Free pool in the downstairs bar. Tram #1, #2 or #5 to Prinsengracht. ❷
ITC (International Travel Club) Prinsengracht 1051 ☏020/623 0230, ℱ020/624 5846, ℮office@itc-hotel.com. A little way out from the major gay areas, close to the Amstelveld on a tranquil section of canal, and perhaps the least expensive gay hotel of this quality. Five percent discount on cash payments. Women welcome. Tram #4 to Prinsengracht. ❷–❺
Orfeo Leidsekruisstraat 14 ☏020/623 1347, ℱ020/620 2348, ℗www.hotelorfeo.com. Very pleasant gay and lesbian hotel round the back of Leidseplein, with decent breakfasts served until midday. Rooms with shared shower starting from €75, some triples and quads available, plus more rooms planned in the future. Tram #1, #2 or #5 to Prinsengracht. ❷
Quentin Leidsekade 89. See p.152. ❸
Waterfront Singel 458 ☏ & ℱ020/421 6621, ℗www.waterfront.demon.nl. Smart, value-for-money hotel on a major canal, close to shopping and nightlife, with decent rooms and service. Tram #1, #2 or #5 to Koningsplein. ❹

Liliane's Home Sarphatistraat 119 ℡ 020/627 4006. A privately run B&B for women only, Liliane runs the place herself, and doesn't have many rooms, so call first. Plush singles €50, doubles from €80, with triples and quads available. She also rents out two nearby apartments. Metro Weesperplein. ➌

Sander Jacob Obrechtstraat 69 ℡ 020/662 7574, ℻ 020/679 6067, ⊛ www.xs4all.nl/~htlsandr. Right behind the Concertgebouw, a spacious, pleasant hotel, welcoming to gay men and women, and everyone else too. Tram #16 to Jacob Obrechtstraat. ➎

Nightlife and entertainment

The main nightlife areas in the Old Centre and Grachtengordel are dotted with numerous **gay bars and clubs**. Some venues have both gay only and mixed gay/straight nights, as noted. Gay men should also check out posters and flyers for the monthly Club Trash and Wasteland events, or get a copy of SHARK at the AUB at Leidseplein (see p.22). There are currently no clubs exclusively for lesbians, however lesbian–only nights are on the increase. At present, the most popular women–only night is "Just Girls" on Saturday at the COC. Further information on where to go for women in Amsterdam can be found from the Gay and Lesbian Switchboard (see p.212).

The only **cinema** left that shows **gay films** on a regular basis is the Filmhuis Cavia which, in conjunction with De Balie (see p.189), hosts an annual event in December called **De Roze Filmdagen** ("The Pink Film Days"), a mini–season of gay and lesbian movies. Call the Gay and Lesbian Switchboard (see p.212) for details of gay movies showing around town, or take a look at the AUB's *Uitlijst*.

Bars

Old Centre

Anco Oudezijds Voorburgwal 55. Late-night hotel leather bar with a large darkroom.

Argos Warmoesstraat 95. Europe's oldest leather bar, with two bars and a raunchy cellar. Not for the faint-hearted. From 10pm.

Casa Maria Warmoesstraat 60. Mixed gay bar in the heart of the Warmoesstraat scene. Over-25s only.

Club Jaecques Warmoesstraat 93. A meeting place for locals, but appropriate (leather- and denim-clad) visitors are made welcome.

Cuckoo's Nest Nieuwezijds Kolk 6. A cruisey leather bar with a long reputation, this is described as "the best place in town for chance encounters". Vast and infamous darkroom. From 1pm.

The Eagle Warmoesstraat 90. Long-established leather bar popular with men of all ages. Gets very busy after 1am.

Le Shako 's Gravelandseveer 2. Friendly bar in a quiet street on the Amstel. Look out for their Neatherbearparties; for hairy or

bearded men and their partners.

Stablemaster Warmoesstraat 23. A leather bar with hotel attached; English-speaking staff and a British following.

The Web St Jacobsstraat 6. Strict rubber, leather and denim bar with a dance floor, darkrooms and a pool table. Bear hug on Saturday. From 2pm.

Why Not Nieuwezijds Voorburgwal 28. Long-standing, intimate bar with a porno cinema above.

Grachtengordel south

April Reguliersdwarsstraat 37. On the itinerary of almost every gay visitor to Amsterdam. Lively and cosmopolitan, with a good selection of foreign newspapers, cakes and coffee, as well as booze.

ARC Reguliersdwarsstraat 44. Mixed club open for breakfast, lunch, dinner and dancing. Mon–Thurs & Sun 10am–1am, Fri & Sat 10am–3am.

Camp Café Kerkstraat 45. Pleasant mix of friendly regulars and foreign visitors. Worth a visit for the ceiling alone, which is covered with a collection of beer mugs from around the world.

Downtown Reguliersdwarsstraat 31. A favourite with visitors. Relaxed and friendly, with inexpensive meals.

Entre Nous Halvemaansteeg 14. Camp and often outrageous small bar. Can be packed at peak times, when everyone joins in the singalongs.

Gaiety Amstel 14. Small gay bar with a warm welcome. One of the most popular young gay haunts in Amsterdam.

Hot Spot Amstel 102. Saturday night Seventies and Eighties music. Occasional live performances and strippers.

Krokodil Amstelstraat 34. Amiable, noisy bar in between the discos and clubs.

Lellebel Utrechtsestraat 4. A gay-friendly café featuring drag acts, with a lively and cheerful atmosphere.

Mankind Weteringstraat 60. Quiet, non-scene bar with its own terrace and landing stage. Lovely in summer.

Mix Café Amstel 50. Dutch *gezellig*, and a pub-crawl on Thursday 8pm.

Montmartre de Paris Halvemaansteeg 17. A convivial brown café, with the emphasis on music and entertainment, recommended by the readers of the *Gaykrant*.

Rouge Amstel 60. Hotel bar, popular with both tourists and locals, especially on hot afternoons.

De Spijker Kerkstraat 4. Leather and jeans bar showing porn movies. Darkroom. Open from 1pm.

Clubs

April Reguliersdwarsstraat 37 (Grachtengordel south) ☏020/625 9572. An established gay bar opening at 2pm, with a happy hour at 6pm announced by flashing lights and a siren. Small dance floor in the back.

COC Rozenstraat 14 (Grachtengordel west) ☏020/626 3087, ⊛www.coc.nl. Successful women-only disco and café every Sat from 10pm called "Just Girls", popular with younger lesbians. Pumping on Friday nights too (mixed men/women).

Cockring Warmoesstraat 96 (Old Centre) ☏020/623 9604. Currently Amsterdam's most popular – and very cruisey – gay men's disco. Light show and bars on two levels. Get there early at the weekend to avoid queuing. Nightly; free.

Exit Reguliersdwarsstraat 42 (Grachtengordel south) ☏020/625 8788. A classic gay club in

the centre of town. Current sounds play nightly to an upbeat, cruisey crowd. Predominantly male, though women are admitted. Free.

Getto Girls Warmoesstraat 51 (Old Centre) ☏020/421 5151. Women-only night on Tuesdays at the *Getto* with plenty of music, plus a bar serving vegetarian food and cocktails. Transforms into a dance club later on in the evening.

Habiba At More See p.192. Monthly clubby women's night.

Habibi Ana Lange Leidsedwarsstraat 4 (Grachtengordel south) ☏020/620 1788. A Mediterranean gay bar with a small dance-floor, Arab music and belly-dance shows every weekend.

IT Amstelstraat 24 (Grachtengordel south) ☏020/625 0111, ⊛www.it.nl. Large disco with a superb sound system. Popular and glamorous gay club with a mixed gay/straight Friday night. Recently refurbished in a cool New York club style, but still attracting a dressed up, uninhibited crowd.

Oomph! At Mazzo See p.191. Every third Sunday in the month is girls' night with good alternative techno.

De Trut Bilderdijkstraat 165 (Jordaan and Westerdok). Housed in a former factory building, this squat venue holds a Sunday night, gay-only dance party: there's a large dance floor, cheap drinks, and non-commercial music. Very popular with both men and women – the doors are closed at midnight and if you arrive after 11pm you may not get in. Gets very hot as it's in a basement.

Vive la Vie Amstelstraat 7 (Old Centre) ☏020/624 0114. Café mainly for women, which shifts its tables at the weekend to make room for a dance space.

Vrankrijk See p.163. Every Monday is "Queersnight", in Amsterdam's most famous squat café.

The Web St Jacobsstraat 6 (Old Centre) ☏020/623 6758. Somewhat underground leather and denim club, held on the last Friday of the month; for both men and women.

You II Amstel 178 (Grachtengordel south) ☏020/421 0900, ⊛www.youii.nl. Amsterdam's first and long-awaited lesbian dance club, which opened its doors in the summer of 1999. Men are in fact welcome, as long as they're under female supervision.

Events

Three leading events in Amsterdam's gay calendar are **Remembrance Day** (May 4), the celebration of **Liberation Day** (May 5) and **World AIDS Day** (Dec 1). All of these prompt ceremonies and happenings around the Homomonument, the symbolic focus of the city's gay community (see p.65). In addition, **Queen's Day** (April 30), when the whole town has a knees-up, sees gay parties and drag acts hosted throughout the city, culminating with The Pink Wester festival at the Homomonument. Other events include **Coming Out Day** (Sept 5), and **Leather Pride** (ⓦwww.leatherpride.nl), held at the beginning of November with a number of organized fetish parties.

The first **Amsterdam Pride** took place in 1996, organized by the Gay Business Association (ⓣ020/620 8807), with street parties and performances, as well as a "Canal Pride" flotilla of boats parading along the Prinsengracht. If you're in the city in August, keep an eye out for parties around this annual event.

Finally, the old Amsterdam tradition of **Hartjesdag** ("Day of the Hearts"), which ceased to be observed just before World War II, was recently rediscovered and then popularized by a researcher in Gay and Lesbian Studies at the University of Amsterdam. At some time in August, it was once common for Amsterdammers to dress up in the clothes of the opposite sex and, although the majority of the population have hardly flocked to the cross-dressing banner, Amsterdam's nightclubs often have themed drag weekends in August.

Shops and services

Bookstores

American Book Center Kalverstraat 185 (Old Centre) ⓣ020/625 5537, ⓦwww.abc.nl. Large general bookstore, with a fine gay and lesbian section.

Intermale Spuistraat 251 (Old Centre) ⓣ020/625 0009, ⓦwww.intermale.nl. Well-stocked gay bookshop, with a wide selection of English, French, German and Dutch literature, as well as cards, newspapers and magazines. They have a worldwide mail order service.

Vrolijk Paleisstraat 135 (Old Centre) ⓣ020/623 5142, ⓦwww.vrolijk.nu. "The largest gay and lesbian bookstore on the continent", with a vast stock of new and secondhand books and magazines, as well as music and videos.

Xantippe Unlimited Prinsengracht 290 (Grachtengordel west) ⓣ020/623 5854, ⓦwww.xantippe.nl. An impressively wide range of books and resources by, for and about women, with a large lesbian section.

Leather, rubber and sex shops

Adonis Warmoesstraat 92 (Old Centre) ⓣ020/627 2959. Longstanding gay video and DVD cinema; also stocks toys, books and videos.

Black Body Lijnbaansgracht 292 (Grachtengordel west) ⓣ020/626 2553, ⓦwww.blackbody.nl. Huge selection of rubber and leather, new and secondhand, plus toys and much more.

Bronx Kerkstraat 53-55 (Grachtengordel south) ⓣ020/623 1548, ⓦwww.bronx.nl. Strictly porno books, magazines and videos for men.

Demask Zeedijk 64 (Old Centre) ⓣ020/620 5603, ⓦwww.demask.com. Expensive rubber and leather fetish store for men and women.

Drake's Damrak 61 (Old Centre) ⓣ020/627 9544. Gay porn cinema.

Female and Partners Spuistraat 100 (Old Centre) ⓣ020/620 9152, ⓦwww.femaleandpartners.nl. Shop selling lingerie plus plain and erotic sex toys for women, with probably the widest variety of vibrators in the city.

De Leertent Sarphatistraat 61 (Amsterdam Oost) ⓣ020/627 8090. Huge collection of leather and bikers' wear.

Mantalk Reguliersdwarsstraat 39 (Grachtengordel south) ⓣ020/627 2525. Small shop with an enormous choice in quality underwear and T-shirts, romantic and kinky.

Mister B Warmoesstraat 89 (Old Centre)
☎020/422 0003, ⊛www.mrb.nl. Rubber and leather clothing and sex toys, spread over three floors. Piercing and tattoos by appointment.

RoB Gallery Weteringschans 253 (Grachtengordel south) ☎020/625 4686, ⊛www.rob.nl; **ROB Accessories** Warmoesstraat 32 (Old Centre) ☎020/420 8548. Top-quality made-to-measure leather wear, with a worldwide mail order service.

Robin and Rik Runstraat 30 (Grachtengordel west) ☎020/627 8924. Handmade leather clothes and accessories.

Stout Berenstraat 9 (Grachtengordel west) ☎020/620 1676 ⊛www.stoutinternational.com. A wide range of erotica for women in a smart environment and with helpful (female) staff.

Saunas, beauty and fitness

Fenomeen 1e Schinkelstraat 14 (Amsterdam West) ☎020/671 6780. Laid-back, inexpensive sauna in an open-plan setting, with sunbeds, café and chill-out room, attracting a faithful lesbian clientele on Monday 1–11pm. Closed for six weeks during July and August. €6–8.

Sauna Damrak Damrak 54 (Old Centre) ☎020/622 6012. Centrally located gay men's sauna; €13, including towels. You can also get a private sauna for two for €30. Mon–Fri 10am–11pm, Sat & Sun noon–8pm. Women are also welcome on Saturday and Sunday.

Splash Looiersgracht 26 (Jordaan and the Westerdok) ☎020/624 8404. Gay-friendly gym. Daily 7am–midnight. See p.225.

Thermos Beauty Salon Raamdwarsstraat 5 (Jordaan and the Westerdok) ☎020/623 9158. Gay men's salon linked to the Thermos Day Sauna. Hairdressers, waxing and massage. Daily noon–8pm.

Thermos Day Sauna Raamstraat 33 (Jordaan and the Westerdok) ☎020/623 9158 ⊛www.thermos.nl. Modern gay men's sauna, with steam room, whirlpool, cinema and coffee bar spread out over five floors. Mon–Fri noon–11pm, Sat & Sun 11am–10pm; €17.50.

Thermos Night Sauna Kerkstraat 58–60 (Grachtengordel south) ☎020/623 4936 ⊛www.thermos.nl. Much the same facilities as the day sauna, with the addition of a Jacuzzi and dark steam room. Cruisey atmosphere. Nightly 11pm–8am; €17.50.

Travel agents

Beach Boy Holidays (Ticketlijn) Amstel 24 (Grachtengordel south) ☎020/428 1428, ✉ticketlijn@euronet.nl. Gay travel agent.

De Gay Krant Travel Service Kloveniersburgwal 40 (Old Centre) ☎020/421 0000, ✉travel@gaykrant.nl. Travel agent specializing in gay travel in Amsterdam and worldwide.

Kids' Amsterdam

With its canals, tiny cobbled alleys and – above all – trams, Amsterdam in itself can be entertaining enough for some kids. There's also a multitude of attractions specifically aimed at children, ranging from circuses, puppet theatres and urban farms to one of the best zoos in Europe, with a planetarium attached, as well as plenty of opportunities for play – practically all the city's parks and most patches of green have some form of playground, and the play area in the Vondelpark is heaven for kids and parents alike.

You'll find that most places are pretty child-friendly. If museums don't allow prams then they provide snugglies to carry small children in; most restaurants have highchairs and special children's menus (though they're not always that great); and bars don't seem to mind accompanied kids, as long as they're well under control. In short, it's rare that having a small child in your care will close doors to you.

Some hotels, however, don't welcome young children (they'll make this clear when you book), but many of those that do also provide a **babyminding** service. If yours doesn't, try contacting **Babysit Agency Kriterion** (℡020/624 5848; 6–8pm), a long-established agency with a good reputation.

Parks, playgrounds and farms

The city's most central park, the leafy and lawned **Vondelpark** (℡020/673 1499), has an excellent playground, as well as sandpits, paddling pools, ducks and even a couple of cafés where you can take a break. *De Vondeltuin*, a pancake house on the Amstelveen side of the park, rents out skates and is perfectly situated opposite the playground – see p.166. During the summer there's always some free entertainment put on for kids – mime, puppets, acrobats and the like.

Most other city parks offer something to keep children entertained, the best being the **Gaasperpark**, outside the centre (metro stop Gaasperplas; buses #60, #61, #157, #158, #174), which has a play area and paddling pools conveniently situated next to the campsite (see p.145). In the **Amsterdamse Bos** (see p.115) you'll find playgrounds, lakes, and herds of wild deer; you can also

One area where Amsterdammers fall flat on their face is in keeping **dog shit** off the streets and parks. They just don't seem able to do it, and the stuff is a major hazard, especially for kids. Although there are teams of street-cleaners armed with high-power hoses to regularly blast it off the pavement, wait another hour or two and there'll be more to replace it. Any patch of green space is obviously susceptible too, and unless an area is marked as being dog-free, you'd do well to keep one eye on your offspring and the other on your next step.

rent canoes to explore the waterways, or visit the Bosmuseum (see p.116) and the **Geitenhouderij Ridammerhoeve** (☎020/645 5034; March–Oct daily except Tues 10am–5pm; Nov–Feb also closed Mon), an entertaining mini-farm with a herd of goats and their kids.

There are also plenty of **urban farms** dotted around the city – look in the phone book under *Kinderboerderij* for a full list, but one of the best is the **Artis Zoo Children's Farm**, which can easily be visited as part of an Artis day out; see below for details of the zoo itself.

Canals and sporting activities

For older children, a good introduction to Amsterdam might be one of the **canal trips** that start from Centraal Station or Damrak. Much more fun, though, is a ride on a **canal bike**. This can get tiring, but jetties where boats can be picked up and dropped off are numerous, and it's quite safe; see p.26 for details. If your kids enjoy being on the water, you could also take them on a **free ferry ride** to Amsterdam North (only 5–10min away). The best ferry to take is the *Adelaarswegveer*, a small tug-like craft with a partly exposed deck, which leaves every 10min or so from Pier 8 behind Centraal Station (Mon–Sat 6.20am–8.50pm). On the other side, you can either come straight back, or walk a few hundred metres west along the riverfront and take the larger, closed-in *Buiksloterwegveer* back to Centraal Station. For more details on the city's **canal and bus tours**, see p.27.

For a panoramic **view** of the city, try a trek up the **towers** of the Oude Kerk or the Westerkerk (open summer only; see p.48 and p.63).

It's possible to take the kids along when you're **cycling** around the city, by renting either a bike with a child seat attached, or a tandem, depending on the size of the child. Bike City at Bloemgracht 70 (☎020/626 3721) rents both types and gives friendly advice too.

In the winter, there's **ice skating** at the Sporthal Jaap Eden (see p.226), which has indoor and outdoor rinks, open at different times. If the canals are frozen and you don't have any skates, just teeter along on the ice with everybody else.

The best **swimming pool** for kids is the indoor, tropical-style Mirandabad, De Mirandalaan 9 (☎020/644 6637), which has all sorts of gimmicks like wave machines, slides and whirlpools; there's also a separate toddlers' pool. In summer, the most popular outdoor pool is in the Flevopark; for details of this and other outdoor pools, see p.227.

The zoo and museums

A trip to the **Artis Zoo** is one of the best days out in the city. The ticket includes entry to the zoo and its gardens, the Zoological Museum, the Geological Museum, the Aquarium and the Planetarium. You can also combine an Artis day out with a canal cruise: the Artis Express runs daily 10am–5pm every 30min between Centraal Station and the zoo, including a little detour through the city (return €19 including zoo entry, 4- to 11-year-olds €16.75; information on ☎020/530 1090).

Artis Zoo Plantage Kerklaan 38–40 (Old Jewish Quarter and the East) ☎020/523 3400. **Tram #6, #9 or #14.** Opened in 1838, this is the oldest zoo in the country, and it's now one of the city's top tourist attractions, though thankfully its layout and refreshing lack of bars and cages mean that it never feels overcrowded. The huge aquariums are one of its main features. In addition to the usual creatures and creepy-crawlies, there is also a Children's Farm where kids can come nose-to-nose with sheep, calves, goats, etc. Feeding times – always popular – are as follows: 11am birds of prey; 11.30am and 3.45pm seals and sea lions; 2pm pelicans; 2.30pm crocodiles (Sun only); 3pm lions and tigers (not Fri); 3.30pm penguins. The on-site Planetarium has five or six shows daily, all in Dutch – you can pick up a leaflet with an English translation from the desk. Daily: April–Oct 9am–6pm; Oct–March 9am–5pm; adults €13.50, 4- to 11-year-olds €9.50; during September admission is reduced by thirty percent. Pushchairs can be rented for €1, and an English guidebook to the whole complex costs €4.

Kindermuseum In the Tropenmuseum, Linnaeusstraat 2 (Amsterdam Oost) ☎020/568 8233, 🖰www.kit.nl/kindermuseum. Tram #9, #10 or #14. Designed especially for children between the ages of 6 and 12, the Kindermuseum's aim is to promote international understanding through exhibitions on other cultures. It's nowhere near as dry as it sounds, and although the show is in Dutch only, this is more than compensated for by the lively exhibits, which are expertly presented, incorporating art and music and dance performances, all designed to fascinate children (which it does). There are lots of things for kids to get their hands on, but it's best to go on Sunday, when school groups aren't visiting. Exhibits tend to have a two-year run. Daily during school holidays, otherwise Wed afternoon, Sat & Sun

(3–4 shows, 1hr 30min; call to reserve). Adults €6.80, children €5.

Madame Tussaud's Dam 20 (Old Centre) ☎020/522 1010. Large waxworks collection with the usual smattering of famous people and rock stars, plus some Amsterdam peasants and merchants thrown in for local colour. Hardly the high point of anyone's trip to the city, but there are parts that might interest teenagers such as the Music Zone and TV Studio Backstage. Daily: mid-July to Aug 9.30am–7.30pm; Sept to mid-July 10am–5.30pm. Adults €17.50; 5- to 15-year-olds €10, over-65s €15; family tickets available.

Museum Tramlijn Amstelveenseweg 264 (Nieuw Zuid) ☎020/673 7538, 🖰www.trammuseum.demon.nl. Tram #6 or #16 (stop Haarlemmermeer Station). A set of working antique trams, which run down to the Amsterdamse Bos (see p.115). April–Oct Sun 11am–5pm, rides every 20min; May–Sept also Wed (1.45pm & 3.15pm only). Adults €3, 4- to 11-year-olds €1.50, under-4s free. No museumcards.

NEMO Oosterdok, near entrance to IJ tunnel (Old Jewish Quarter and the East) ☎0900/9191100 (€0.35 per min), 🖰www.e-nemo.nl. A 5min walk from CS, or bus #22 or #32. Well-conceived interactive "centre for human creativity" set out under four themes; Physics, Technology, Information Technology and Bio-science behaviour. Lots of hands-on activities for children, and a café. Daily during school holidays, July & August 10am–5pm, closed Monday the rest of the year; €9, under-4s free.

Theatres, circuses and funfairs

A number of **theatres** put on inexpensive (around €2.50) entertainment for children in the afternoon. Furthermore, a fair proportion get around the (English) language problem by being **mime**- or **puppet**-based: check the children's section ("Jeugdagenda") of the monthly *Uitkrant* (see p.180), and look for the words *mimegroep* and *poppentheater*. The Children's Theatre Phoneline (☎020/622 2999), has general information, but in Dutch only. Public holidays and the summer season bring touring **circuses** and the occasional mobile **funfair** (*kermis*) to the city, the latter usually setting up on Dam square and thus hard to miss. Lastly, check out the **festivals** listings in Chapter Fifteen: many of them, such as the Queen's Birthday celebrations, can be enjoyable for kids.

Carré Theatre Amstel 115–125 (Amsterdam Oost) ☎020/524 9494, 🖰www.theatercarre.nl. Occasionally books internationally famous

circuses.

Circustheater Elleboog Passeerdersgracht 32 (Jordaan and the Westerdok) ☎020/623 5326,

@www.elleboog.nl. For around €22 or so, kids aged 10 to 17 can spend the day learning how to juggle and unicycle, do conjuring tricks, be a clown, and practise face-painting. At the end of the day they put on a little show for the parents. Phone for full details of times and prices – some days are members-only sessions.

Deridas Hobbemakade 68 (Museum Quarter and Vondelpark) ☎020/662 1588. Excellent weekly puppet theatre, wonderful for the under-6s. The shows are every Saturday at 3pm (4- to 12-year-olds) and Sunday at 11am & noon (2- to 6-year-olds). Also the first Friday of the month 10.30am & 12.30pm (4- to 12-year-olds). Booking essential.

Kids go Paradiso Weteringsschans 6–8 (Grachtengordel south) ☎020/626 4521, @www.paradiso.nl. About three times a year the famous music venue *Paradiso* (see p.182) gives concerts for kids, with anything from bands playing high-tempo versions of nursery rhymes to chart music discos complete with make-up artists. Tickets from around €5.

De Krakeling Nieuwe Passeerdersstraat 1 (Jordaan and the Westerdok) ☎020/624 5123. Permanent children's theatre, with shows for youngsters up to the age of 18. The emphasis is often on full-scale audience participation. Phone for a schedule.

Restaurants

KinderKookKafé Oudezijds Achterburgwal 193 (Old Centre) ☎020/625 3257. A whole restaurant entirely run by children, from cooking to waitering to dishwashing (though there are adult staff on hand). The food is simple but well done, and the whole experience is worth it just for the novelty. Booking is essential, as the café is only open to the public for weekend dinners, while on weekdays the kids can attend cookery courses and hold birthday parties. Adults €8, 5- to 12-year-olds €5 (€10 if cooking), under-5s €2.50.

The Pancake Bakery Prinsengracht 191 (Grachtengordel west) ☎020/625 1333. Well-known busy pancake and omelette house that caters especially well for children. Delicious pancakes, and kids are kept entertained at the table with pens and paper and free novelty toys. Children's pancakes start at around €3.50 with toy, adult's pancakes start from €4.70 – no toy. Mon–Fri noon–9.30pm.

Shops

Abeltje Koningsstraat 2 (Old Centre) ☎020/420 7027. Kids' clothing outlet, with mainly top Dutch brands and friendly service.

Azzurro Kids P.C. Hooftstraat 122 (Museum Quarter and Vondelpark) ☎020/673 0457. Perhaps the city's chicest kids' clothes store, stocking Diesel, Replay, Armani and Tommy Hilfiger.

De Beestenwinkel Staalstraat 11 (Old Centre) ☎020/623 1805. Stuffed toy animals, in all shapes and sizes.

Berend Botje Zocherstraat 87 (Museum Quarter and Vondelpark) ☎020/618 3349. Secondhand clothes for children, near the Vondelpark, with everything from retro to designer labels.

De Bijenkorf Dam 1 (Old Centre) ☎020/552 1700. This department store has one of the best (and most reasonable) toy sections in town.

Broer & Zus 1e Bloemdwarsstraat 19 (Jordaan and the Westerdok) ☎020/422 9002. Small giftshop selling cute things for babies and toddlers.

Carla C Leliegracht 42 (Grachtengordel west) ☎020/620 6020, @www.carla-c.com. Stylish designer maternity wear, that also has outlets in London.

De Geboortewinkel Bosboom Toussaintstraat 22 (Oud West) ☎020/683 1806. Specialists in all kinds of stuff for new or expectant parents, from quality clothes to prams and bedding.

Intertoys Heiligeweg 26 (Old Centre) ☎020/638 3356. Amsterdam's largest toy shop, with branches throughout the city.

Kids Kitchen Rozengracht 183 (Jordaan and the Westerdok). Brightly coloured bags, hats, toys, etc.

De Kinderbrillenwinkel Nieuwezijds
Voorburgwal 129 (Old Centre) ☎020/626 4091.
Shop specializing in spectacles for children.
A selection of stylish frames for teenagers is
available next door at Marcel Barlag
Visuals.
Kleine Nicolaas Cornelis Schuytstraat 19 (Oud
Zuid) ☎020/676 9661. Handmade toys.

Mechanisch Speelgoed Westerstraat 67
(Jordaan and the Westerdok) ☎020/638 680.
Mechanical and wooden toys crammed into
a small shop. Closed Wed.
Tinkerbell Spiegelgracht 10 (Grachtengordel
south) ☎020/625 8830. A wonderful shop full
of old-fashioned toys, mobiles, models and
kids' books, with everything beautifully gift-
wrapped.

Sports and activities

Most visitors to Amsterdam tend to confine their exercise to walking around the major sights, but if you do get the urge to stretch your muscles, there's a wide range of sports to enjoy. In winter, skating on the frozen waterways is the most popular and enjoyable activity; other winter sports are mostly based in private, health or sports clubs, to which you can usually get a day pass, though many are well outside the city centre.

The chief spectator sport is football. Amsterdam is home to the legendary Ajax (pronounced "eye-axe") who play in their spanking new ArenA stadium out in the suburbs – though you'll be hard pressed to get a ticket. Less mainstream offerings include Holland's own *korfbal* and the weird spectacle of pole sitting. For up-to-the-minute details on all sporting activities in the city, call the Sport and Recreation information service on ℡020/552 2490, or consult ⓦwww.sport.amsterdam.nl, though this is mainly in Dutch.

Baseball (Honkbal)

The local team is the **Amsterdam Pirates**, based at Sportpark Jan van Galenstraat (℡020/616 2151; tram #13). Matches take place on Saturday and Sunday afternoons in the summer, and most matches are free, €3.50 being the most you'll pay to watch. The Pirates are in the top baseball division. To **play**, you need only wander into the Vondelpark on any summer afternoon – impromptu baseball games are commonplace.

Beaches

The Netherlands has some great **beaches**, although the weather is unreliable and the North Sea is pretty murky and often littered with stray jellyfish. For swimming or sunbathing, the nearest resort is **Zandvoort** (see p.129) a short train ride from Amsterdam – though be warned that it attracts large crowds in season. Otherwise, there are low-key resorts and long sandy beaches all the way up the dune-filled western coastline: Katwijk and Noordwijk, both of which can be reached by bus from Leiden, are probably the pick.

Bowling

The closest bowling alley to the city centre is Knijn Bowling Centre, Scheldeplein 3, opposite the RAI complex (℡020/664 2211; Mon–Fri

10am–1am, Sat noon–1am, Sun noon–midnight), with eighteen lanes and a bar. Lanes cost between €15 and €28.50 per hour, with a maximum of six people per lane. Reservations recommended. Fridays and Saturdays have "night bowling", accompanied by a DJ playing club music.

Bungee jumping

A new permanent **jump site** opened in 1996 behind Centraal Station. Here you can throw yourself from a height of 75m into the Amsterdam skies, and even request a masochistic dip in the River IJ to boot. The site is operated by Bungee Jump Holland, a member of the Dutch Federation of Bungee Jumping. The first jump costs €50, the second €40; you can also buy a ten-jump season ticket for a mere €250. Open April–Nov, but times vary – call Bungee Jump Centre Amsterdam ☎020/419 6005, or visit ⓦwww.bungy.nl for further details.

Chess and draughts

There are two **cafés** in Amsterdam where chess and draughts are played to the exclusion of (almost) everything else: *Gambit* at Bloemgracht 20 (see p.165), and *Het Hok* at Lange Leidsedwarsstraat 134 (see p.164). There's a small charge for a board. In addition, a number of cafés may have a board behind the bar if you ask – for instance, *The Jolly Joker* at Nieuwmarket 4A allows customers to play for free.

Football

It's a mark of the dominance of Amsterdam's **Ajax**, Rotterdam's **Feyenoord** and Eindhoven's **PSV** that most foreigners would be hard pushed to name any other Dutch football teams. More generally familiar perhaps is the Dutch style of play – based on secure passing with sudden, decisive breaks – which has made Dutch players highly sought-after all over Europe. Nevertheless, with the building of Ajax's extravagant all-seater ArenA stadium in the suburbs of Amsterdam, it's actually become more than a little difficult to get to see Ajax play. You can't buy a ticket without a "clubcard", and although these only cost €6 for two years, you must apply in advance (☎020/3111 6666) and wait up to five weeks for your application to be processed. Having done all that, ticket prices are between €15 and €47 – and it's more or less the same situation for Feyenoord and PSV, whose grounds are both within easy striking distance of Amsterdam by public transport. The football season runs from September to May, and matches are generally on Sunday at 2.30pm, with occasional games at 8pm on Wednesday. Your best bet is to catch a game on screen in a bar. Try the *Globe* at Oudezijds Voorburgwal 3.

Ajax Amsterdam ArenA Stadium, Bijlmer ☎020/3111 4444, ⓦwww.ajax.nl. Metro Bijlmer.
Feyenoord Rotterdam Olympiaweg 50, Rotterdam ☎010/292 3888,

ⓦwww.feyenoord.nl. Trains from Amsterdam stop near the ground.
PSV Eindhoven Frederiklaan 10a, Eindhoven ☎040/250 5505, ⓦwww.psv.nl.

Gyms, saunas and flotation

Deco Herengracht 115 (Grachtengordel west) ☎020/623 8215. In the running for Amsterdam's most stylish sauna and steam bath, with a magnificent Art Deco interior and a nice café. A great place to hang out for the day without a stitch on. Highly recommended. Entry costs €14.50. Mon–Sat noon–11pm, Sun 1–6pm.

Eastern Bathhouse Hammam Zaanstraat 88 (Amsterdam Noord) ☎020/681 4818. A unique and wonderful institution, for women only. Comprises hot and cold rooms and top-to-toe washing; full body scrub and massage available. Emerge feeling cleaner and more alive than you ever thought possible. Last admission 2.5hr before closing. Tues–Fri noon–10pm, Sat & Sun noon–8pm; closed Aug. €11.

Garden Gym Jodenbreestraat 158 (Old Jewish Quarter and the East) ☎020/626 8772, ⓦwww.thegarden.nl. Weight-training and dance-workout studio, with saunas, solarium, massage and self-defence classes. Mainly, but not exclusively, for women. A sauna costs €9; a day pass for all activities €11. Mon, Wed & Fri 9am–11pm, Tues & Thurs noon–11pm, Sat 11am–6pm, Sun 10am–7pm.

Koan Float Herengracht 321 (Grachtengordel west) ☎020/555 0333, ⓦwww.koan-float.com. The only place in Amsterdam currently offering flotation as a relaxation technique. The idea is to float in a large bath of warm water, to which magnesium and sodium salt have been added to aid muscular relaxation and provide buoyancy. Because the water is the same temperature as your body, the sensation is of floating freely, and you don't have to move to stay afloat, allowing your mind and body to release pent-up stress. There are three lockable individual floating cabins, each with its own shower; once you're inside, lights, music and clothing are optional. Advance reservations are essential. Current charges are €29 per 45min or €36 for an hour, and there are discounts for return visits. The centre also offers massage. Towels and bathrobes are provided. Daily 9.30am–11pm.

Sauna Damrak Damrak 54 (Old Centre) ☎020/622 6012. Centrally located gay sauna, though women are also welcome at weekends. See p.217.

Splash Looiersgracht 26 (Jordaan and the Westerdok) ☎020/624 8404. Very popular hi-tech fitness centre with sauna, tanning salon and Turkish bath. Daily aerobic classes and single-sex training rooms. Day pass €16 including towel and a drink; week pass €40. Daily 7am–midnight.

Sporthal De Stokerij 1e Rozendwarsstraat 8 (Jordaan and the Westerdok) ☎020/625 9417. Municipal fitness centre with facilities for football, tennis, volleyball, etc, plus a gym. €2 for a session, otherwise you must buy a month's pass for €28.50; you'll also need some ID. Daily 8am–10.30pm.

Horse riding

Amsterdamse Manege Nieuwe Kalfjeslaan, Amstelveen (Nieuw Zuid) ☎020/643 1342. The place for a ride in the Amsterdamse Bos – but only with supervision. You need your own boots and riding hat, and you must reserve ahead. An hour's lesson costs €18.50 for adults and €15 for children.

Hollandsche Manege Vondelstraat 140 (Museum Quarter and Vondelpark) ☎020/618 0942. Stables built in 1882 in neo-Renaissance style on the rim of the Vondelpark. Again, your own boots and hat are required; a lesson costs €17.50 for adults, €14.50 for 11- to 17-year-olds, and €12.50 for under-11s.

Ice skating

Whenever the city's canals and waterways freeze over, local **skaters** are spoiled for choice with almost every stretch of water utilized, providing an exhilarating way to whizz round the city – much more fun than a rink. Surprisingly, canal cruises continue even when the ice is solid, with the boats crunching their way up and down the Prinsengracht, but they leave the Keizersgracht well alone – to be occupied by bundled-up Amsterdammers, who take to the ice in droves. Most Amsterdammers have their own skates, and there are surprisingly few places where you can **rent** a pair. **Buying** a pair from a department store or sports shop will cost close to €70; one option is to look out for a second-hand pair often advertised on notice boards in bars.

Before you venture out on the ice, however, take note of a few **safety points**:

- If no one's on the ice, don't try skating – locals have a better idea of its thickness.
- To gain confidence, start off on the smaller ponds in the Vondelpark.
- Be careful under bridges, where the ice takes longest to freeze.
- If the ice gives way and you find yourself underneath, head for the darkest spot you can see in the ice above – that's the hole.

Probably the easiest and safest option is to head for **Sporthal Jaap Eden**, Radioweg 64 (☎020/694 9652; tram #9; €3), a large ice-skating complex, to the east of the city centre, with an indoor and outdoor rink. You can rent skates for €5 from Waterman Sport next door (☎020/694 9884), but you can only use them at Jaap Eden, and you must leave your passport or driving licence as a deposit. Outdoor rink Oct–March Mon–Fri 8.30am–4pm & 9–11pm, Sat 2–4pm, Sun 11am–4pm; indoor rink Mon–Fri 2–4pm & 9–11pm.

One of the great events in Holland's sporting calendar is the annual **Elfstedentocht**, a race across eleven towns and 200km of frozen waterways in Friesland, in the north of the Netherlands (see p.229). If you're around in January and the ice is good, you'll hear talk of little else.

In-line skating

If you're equipped with skates, or a skateboard, there is a free public ramp at the northeastern edge of Museumplein. For the more experienced skater there's also the free Friday Night Skate (🌐www.fridaynightskate.nl), a fifteen-kilometre tour around Amsterdam, which takes place – weather permitting – every week from the Vondelpark entrance. Two places to **rent** skates, gear and boards are: *De Vondeltuin* at the Amstelveen entrance in the Vondelpark (see p.107); and Rodolfo's, Sarphatistraat 59 (☎020/622 5488). If you're renting to skate around town – and many do – take care not to get stuck in the tram-tracks.

Korfbal

This is a home-grown sport, cobbled together from netball, basketball and volleyball, and played with mixed teams and a high basket. **Blauw Wit** play at the Sportpark Joos Banckersweg, off Jan van Galenstraat (☎020/616 0894), on Sunday at 2.30pm from September to June.

Pole sitting

Every year in July or early August, there's the chance to witness the offbeat spectator sport of pole sitting. In Noorderwijkerhout, just north of Scheveningen on the coast near The Hague, there's a **pole-sitting marathon** that lasts about five days. Although hardly a dynamic sport, it generates a fair amount of excitement as some fifteen braves sit it out on poles perched in the North Sea. The last one left is the winner.

Snooker and carambole

There are plenty of bars and cafés across the city where you can find a game of **pool**, although you may have to go to a hall to play **snooker.** A popular local variation on billiards (*biljart*) is **carambole**, played on a table without pockets. You score by making cannons, and the skill of some of the locals, often spinning the ball through impossible angles, is unbelievable in a misspent sort of way. You'll find tables in many cafés, and get plenty of advice on how to play if you so much as look at a ball.

Snooker and Pool Centre Bavaria Van Ostadestraat 97 (Oud Zuid). The first, third and fourth floors comprise the **pool centre** (Mon–Fri 2pm–1am, Sat & Sun 2pm–2am; ☎020/676 7903), with 26 tables costing a flat rate of €7.30 per hour plus drinks. The second floor is the **snooker centre** (Mon–Fri 1pm–1am, Sat & Sun 1pm–2am; ☎020/676 4059), which has seven tables at €7.80 per hour. There's also one carambole table, charged at €7.30 per hour.
Snooker Centre Rokin 28 (Old Centre)

☎020/620 4974, ⊛ www.snookerrokin.nl. Twelve tables at €8.75 per hour, plus €10 deposit. Pool costs €8.25 per hour. Mon–Thurs & Sun 11am–1am, Fri & Sat 11am–3am.
Snooker Centre de Keizer Keizersgracht 256 **(Grachtengordel west)** ☎020/623 1586. Eight high-quality tables in a seventeenth-century canal house. Charges for snooker are €5 per hour before 7pm, €8 after 7pm, pool costs €6 per hour; members pay a little less. Mon–Thurs noon–1am, Fri & Sat noon–2am, Sun 1pm–1am.

Swimming pools (Zwembaden)

Flevoparkbad Zeeburgerdijk 630 (Amsterdam Oost) ☎020/692 5030. Tram #3 or #10. The best outdoor pool in the city; gets very busy on sunny days. May to early Sept daily 10am–5.30pm, until 7pm on warm days.
Jan van Galenbad Jan van Galenstraat 315 (Amsterdam West) ☎020/612 8001. Outdoor pool in the west of the city. May–Sept.
Marnixbad Marnixplein 9 (Jordaan and the Westerdok) ☎020/625 4843. Central 25-metre indoor pool complete with whirlpools. €2.50, with discounts for repeat visits.
De Mirandabad De Mirandalaan 9 (Nieuwe Zuid) ☎020/546 4444. Superbly equipped

swimming centre (outdoor and indoor pools), with wave machine, whirlpools and slides. As with all the pools, you should call before you set out, since certain times are set aside for small children, family groups, etc. Admission €3.
Zuiderbad Hobbemastraat 26 (Museum Quarter and Vondelpark) ☎020/679 2217. Lovely old pool dating from the nineteenth century and refreshingly free of the gimmicks that clutter up the others. That said, they have a naturist hour on Sunday from 4.30 to 5.30pm. €2.70 adults, €2.40 under-12s.

Tennis and squash

Most outdoor **tennis** courts are for members only, and those that aren't need to be reserved well in advance. Your best bets for getting a game at short notice are either at the open-air tennis courts in the Vondelpark, or at one of the following.

Frans Otten Stadion Stadionstraat 10 (Nieuwe Zuid) ☎020/662 8767. Five indoor tennis

courts and twenty squash courts. Tennis courts €15.35–21.80 per hour before 5pm,

€24.30 after 5pm; squash courts €14–18.50 per hour. Racket rental €2.50. Call ahead to reserve a court in the evenings. Mon–Fri 9am–11pm, Sat & Sun 9am–8pm.

Gold Star Tennis Gustav Mahlerlaan 20 **(Nieuwe Zuid)** ℡ 020/644 5483. Near Vrije Universiteit, next to Station Zuid; Tram #5. Twelve indoor and 24 outdoor tennis courts, for €16–21 per hour. Racket rental €2.50. Indoor courts Mon–Fri 7am–11pm, Sat & Sun 7am–8pm. Outdoor courts 9am till dark.

Squash City Ketelmakerstraat 6 **(Jordaan and the Westerdok)** ℡ 020/626 7883. Fifteen squash courts at €6.30–9 per person for 45min; also includes use of the sauna and fitness area. Racket rental €2.50. Call ahead to reserve courts. Mon–Fri 8.30am–11pm, Sat & Sun 8.30am–9pm.

Festivals and events

M ost of Amsterdam's festivals are music and arts events, supplemented by a sprinkling of religious celebrations and, as you might expect, the majority take place in the summer. The **Queen's Birthday** celebration at the end of April is the city's most touted and exciting annual event, with a large portion of the city given over to an impromptu flea market and lots of street-partying. On a more cultural level, the art extravaganza, the **Holland Festival**, held throughout June, attracts a handful of big names. Check with the VVV (see p.22) for further details, and remember that many other interesting events, such as the Easter performance of Bach's *St Matthew Passion* in Grote Kerk Naarden and the North Sea Jazz Festival in The Hague (ⓦwww.northseajazz.nl*)*, are only a short train ride away.

January

Elfstedentocht (Eleven Cities' Journey)
Annual ice-skating marathon across eleven towns and frozen rivers, in Friesland, starting and finishing in Leeuwarden. Held, weather permitting, sometime in January. Though the race had to be suspended for twenty years, a recent spate of cold winters has meant a number of competitions and an increasing number of participants – 16,000 is now the maximum number. For more details, call the organizers, De Friese Elfsteden, in the town of Leeuwarden (Ⓣ058/215 5020 11am–2pm, ⓦwww .elfstedentocht.nl).

February

Chinese New Year First or second week.
Dragon dance and fireworks, held at Nieuwmarkt.

Commemoration of the February Strike
February 25. Speeches and wreath-laying at the Docker Statue on J.D. Meijerplein (see p.91).

March

Stille Omgang (Silent Procession) Sunday closest to March 15 Ⓣ023/524 6229.
Procession by local Catholics commemorating the Miracle of Amsterdam, starting and finishing at Spui and passing through the Red Light District.

"Head of the River" rowing competition Last week Ⓣ035/577 1308, ⓦwww .amsterdamscheroeibond.nl. Actually three races along the River Amstel starting at 10am from Oudekerk to the centre and back; the last race, at 4pm, finishes near the *Amstel Hotel*.

April

Vondelpark Open Air Theatre April–Aug
℡ 020/523 7790, ✆ www.openluchttheater.nl.
Free theatre, dance and music performances throughout the summer.

Nationaal Museumweekend Second week
℡ 020/670 1111, ✆ www.museumweekend.nl.
Free entrance to most of the museums in
the Netherlands.

Koninginnedag (the Queen's Birthday) April
30. This is one of the most popular dates in
the Dutch diary, a street event par excellence, which seems to grow annually and is
almost worth planning a visit around,
despite some claiming it has become too
commercialized over recent years.
Celebrations for Queen Beatrix take place
throughout the whole of Holland, though
festivities in Amsterdam tend to be somewhat wilder and larger in scale. Special club
nights and parties are held both the night
before and the night after; however, to gain
entry you'll need to book in advance either
from the club itself or from selected record
stores, such as Boudisque and Get Records
(see p.205). The next day sees the city's
streets and canals lined with people, most
of whom are dressed in ridiculous costumes
(not surprisingly, Queen's Day is one of the
most flamboyant events on the gay calendar
as well). Anything goes, especially if it's
orange – the Dutch national colour. A fair is
held on the Dam, and music blasts continu-
ously from huge sound systems set up
across most of the major squares. This is
also the one day of the year when anything
can be legally bought and sold to anyone by
anyone on the streets.

**World Press Photo Exhibition Annual com-
petition** ✆ www.worldpressphoto.nl. Open to
photographers from all over the world.
Judging and award days take place mid-
April, marking the beginning of the exhibition, which is held at the Oude Kerk until
the end of May.

May

Herdenkingsdag (Remembrance Day) May 4.
There's a wreath-laying ceremony and two-
minute silence at the National Monument in
Dam square, commemorating the Dutch
dead of World War II, as well as a smaller
event at the Homomonument in
Westermarkt in honour of the country's gay
soldiers who died.

Bevrijdingsdag (Liberation Day) May 5.
The country celebrates the 1945 liberation
from Nazi occupation with bands,
speeches and impromptu markets around
the city.

Oosterparkfestival First week. Held in the
large park near the Tropenmuseum, this
free festival celebrates the mix of cultures
living in the area, with live music and
numerous food stands.

World Wide Video Festival Mid-May to end
May ℡ 020/420 7729, ✆ www.wwvf.nl.
Celebrating small-screen culture with seminars on media art, screenings, exhibitions
and meet-the-artist programmes. Held at
the Passenger Terminal Amsterdam (PTA)
situated on the River IJ, with smaller pre-
sentations at the Melkweg and the Dutch
Institute for Media Art.

National Windmill Day Second Saturday
℡ 020/623 8703. Over half the country's
remaining windmills and watermills are
opened to the public. Contact Vereniging
De Hollandsche.

Drum Rhythm Festival Second or third week
✆ www.drumrhythm.com. Amsterdam's first
real summer event previously held over a
weekend at the Westergasfabriek and very
popular with locals. Famous musicians
from all over the world take part, from
Moby to Salif Keita. Sponsorship problems
mean that they have yet to reschedule
more dates, but check the website for the
latest information.

KunstRAI Third week ℡ 020/549 1212,
✆ www.kunstrai.nl. The annual mainstream
contemporary arts fair, held in the RAI
conference centre, south of the centre. A
less commercial alternative is the
Kunstvlaai at the Westergasfabriek,
always held the week before or after
KunstRAI.

June

Holland Festival Throughout June ☎020/530 7111, ⊛www.hollandfestival.nl. The largest music, dance and drama event in the Netherlands, aimed at making the dramatic arts more accessible. Showcasing around thirty productions, it features a mix of established and new talent. See "Entertainment and Nightlife" chapter (p.180) for more details.

July

Beachbop Throughout July and August ⊛www.beachbop.nl. Live percussion, dance acts and plenty of beach parties at the Bloemendaal beach (close to Zandvoort). Friendly, low-key atmosphere; weekends only.

Over het IJ Festival First one or two weeks ☎020/771 3000, ⊛www.overhetij.nl. Modern theatre and dance festival held at the NDSM (☎020/330 5480) in Amsterdam-Noord, across the river from the city centre. A festival boat runs there from behind Centraal Station.

Kwakoe Festival Weekends only from second week of July to second week of August ⊛www.kwakoe.nl. A Surinamese and Antillian festival held at a playground close to the Amsterdam ArenA in the southeastern suburbs, featuring lots of music, dance acts and stand-up comedy. There are also workshops, and even prayer services on Sunday morning. In the middle of the festival there's a football competition between several "tropical" teams. Caribbean delicacies such as *roti* and the Surinamese *bakabana*, baked banana with peanut sauce, are widely available from stalls around the festival.

August

Amsterdam Pride First or second weekend ⊛www.amsterdampride.nl. The city's gay community celebrates, with street parties and performances held along the Amstel, Warmoesstraat and Reguliersdwarsstraat, as well as a "Canal Pride" flotilla of boats cruising along the Prinsengracht.

Dance Valley First week ⊛www.dancevalley.nl. Huge international dance event held over a weekend at the natural amphitheatre in the hills of Spaarnwoude, just north of Haarlem, with all the techno, drum-and-bass, house and ambient DJs you could possibly wish for. Check the website for further music events held here throughout the year.

The Parade First two weeks ☎033/465 4577, ⊛www.mobilearts.nl. An excellent travelling theatrical fair with various short theatre performances given in or in front of the artists' tents (they all work independently). Held in the Martin Luther King Park, next to the River Amstel (from CS tram #25 to Hunzestraat), with a special kids' parade in the afternoons.

Uitmarkt Last week ⊛www.uitmarkt.nl. A weekend where every cultural organization in the city advertises itself with free preview performances either on Museumplein or by the Amstel.

Grachtenfestival Last week ⊛www .grachtenfestival.nl. International musicians perform classical music at twenty historical locations around the three main canals. Includes the Prinsengracht Concert, one of the world's most prestigious free open-air concerts, held opposite the *Pulitzer Hotel*.

September

Bloemencorso (Flower Parade) First week ⊛www.bloemencorsoaalsmeer.nl. The Aalsmeer–Amsterdam flower pageant in the city centre, celebrating every kind of flower except tulips, which are out of season. Each year has a different theme. Vijzelstraat is the best place to see things, since the events in Dam square are normally packed solid.

Chinatown Festival Second weekend. Tong and Soeng musicians, acrobatics, kung-fu and tai-chi demonstrations at the Nieuwmarkt.

The Jordaan Festival Second or third week ☎020/626 5587, ⊛www.jordaanfestival.nl. A street festival in the Jordaan, a friendly and fairly central neighbourhood. There's a commercial fair on Palmgracht, talent contests on Elandsgracht, a few street parties and a culinary fair on the Sunday afternoon at the Noordermarkt.

October

Amsterdam City Marathon Late October, usually the third weekend ⊛www.amsterdammarathon .nl. A 42-kilometre course around Amsterdam starting at and finishing inside the Olympic Stadium, passing through the old city centre along the way.

November

Crossing Border Usually first week ☎020/346 2355, ⊛www.crossingborder.nl. Festival centred around the Leidseplein area that explores and crosses artistic boundaries, with performances by over a hundred international acts presenting the spoken word in various forms, from rap to poetry.

Parade of Sint Nicolaas Second or third week. The traditional parade of *Sinterklaas* (Santa Claus) through the city on his white horse, starting from behind Centraal Station where he arrives by steam boat, before parading down the Damrak towards Rembrandtplein accompanied by his helpers the *Zwarte*

Pieten ("Black Peters") – so called because of their blackened faces – who hand out sweets and little presents. It all finishes in Leidseplein on the balcony of the Stadsschouwburg.

Cannabis Cup Late November ⊛www .hightimes.com. Five-day harvest festival organized by *High Times* magazine at the Melkweg (☎020/531 8181), with speeches, music and a competition to find the best cultivated seed. Judging is open to the general public, but the entrance fee is pricey.

December

Pakjesavond (Present Evening) Dec 5. Though it tends to be a private affair, Pakjesavond, rather than Christmas Day, is when Dutch kids receive their Christmas presents. If you're here on that day and have Dutch friends, it's worth knowing that it's traditional to give a present together with an amusing poem you have written caricaturing the recipient.

The Winter Parade Last two weeks ☎033/465 4577, ⊛www.mobilearts.nl. Winter version of the August Parade (see p.231), except this one is held at the Westergasfabriek.

New Year's Eve Dec 31. New Year's Eve is big in Amsterdam, with fireworks and celebrations everywhere. Most bars and discos stay open until morning – make sure you get tickets in advance. This might just qualify as the wildest and most reckless street partying in Europe, but a word of warning: Amsterdammers seem to love the idea of throwing lit fireworks around and won't hesitate to chuck one at you.

Directory

Addresses These are written as, for example, "Kerkstr. 79 II", which means the second-floor apartment at Kerkstraat 79. The ground floor is indicated by **hs** (*huis*, house) after the number; the basement is **sous** (*sousterrain*). In some cases, especially in the Jordaan, streets have the same name and to differentiate between them, **1e**, **2e**, **3e** and even occasionally **4e** are placed in front. These are abbreviations for *Eerste* (first), *Tweede* (second), *Derde* (third), and *Vierde* (fourth). Thus, "1e Vogelstraat 10" is a completely different address from "2e Vogelstraat 10". In addition, many **side streets** take the name of the main street they run off, with the addition of the word *dwars*, meaning "crossing"; for instance, Palmdwarsstraat is a side street off Palmstraat. Furthermore, and for no apparent reason, some dead-straight cross-streets change their name – so that, for example, in the space of about 300m, 1e Bloemdwarsstraat becomes 2e Leliedwarsstraat and then 3e Egelantiersdwarsstraat. As for boats, **T/O** (*tegenover*, or "opposite") in an address shows that the address is a boat: hence "Prinsengracht T/O 26" would indicate a boat to be found opposite Prinsengracht 26. Incidentally, the main Grachtengordel canals begin their **numbering** at Brouwersgracht and increase as they progress counterclockwise. By the time they reach the Amstel, Herengracht's house numbers are in the 600s, Keizersgracht's in the 800s and Prinsengracht's in the 900s.

Airlines All at Schiphol airport: Aer Lingus ☎020/517 4747; Alitalia ☎020/470 0118; British Airways ☎020/346 9559; British Midland ☎020/346 9211; Delta Airlines ☎020/201 3536; easyJet ☎023/568 4880; KLM ☎020/474 7747; United Airlines ☎020/201 3708.

Art galleries Amsterdam has over 200 commercial art galleries, showcasing art of every kind. In addition, groups of artists often combine to put on special shows. The best bet to find out what is going on is the gallery guide **Alert**, which is only in Dutch but is fairly easy to follow; it's available from some galleries themselves and from larger city-centre newsagents.

Bike rental You can rent bikes at the following outlets: Bike City, Bloemgracht 70 (Jordaan and the Westerdok) ☎020/626 3721; Damstraat Rent-a-Bike, Damstraat 20 (Old Centre) ☎020/625 5029; Holland Rent-a-Bike, Damrak 247 (Old Centre) ☎020/622 3207; Koenders Take-a-Bike, Stationsplein 12 (Old Centre) ☎020/624 8391; MacBike, Mr Visserplein 2 (Old Jewish Quarter and the East) ☎020/620 0985; Macbike Too, Marnixstraat 220 (Jordaan and the Westerdok) ☎020/626 6964.

Car parks The following are all 24-hour city-centre car parks: De Bijenkorf, Beursplein, off Damrak; Byzantium, Tesselschadestraat 1, near Leidseplein; De Kolk, Nieuwezijds Kolk 20; Muziektheater, Waterlooplein (under City Hall); Parking Plus Amsterdam Centraal, Prins Hendrikkade 20a, east of Centraal Station. Expect to pay €2–3 per hour with a maximum of €25–30 for 24hr.

Car rental Selected car rental agencies (*auto-verhuur*) all in the Oud West just north of the Vondelpark include: Avis, Nassaukade 380 ☎020/683 6061; Budget, Overtoom 121 ☎020/612 6066; Europcar, Overtoom 51 ☎020/683 2123; Hertz, Overtoom 333 ☎020/612 2441.

Concessions Concessionary rates are applied at every city sight and attraction as well as on the public transport system. Rates vary, but usually seniors (65+) get in free, as do children under 5. Concessionary cut-off points for children over 5 and under 18 vary; family tickets are common too. For details of visitors' passes and the museum-jaarkaart (museum year-card), see p.22.

Consulates UK, Koningslaan 44 (Museum Quarter and Vondelpark) ☎020/676 4343; USA, Museumplein 19 (Museum Quarter and Vondelpark) ☎020/575 5309.

Contraceptives Condoms are widely available from *drogists* or the Condomerie (see p.209). To get the pill you need a prescription.

Diamonds Refugee diamond workers from Antwerp founded Amsterdam's diamond industry in the late sixteenth century, but since World War II it has been dependent on tourists. Currently around twenty diamond firms operate in Amsterdam. All are working factories, but several open their doors to the public for viewing the cutting, polishing and sorting practices, and (most importantly) for buying. The best one to visit is Gassan Diamonds (see p.89).

Electric current 220v AC – effectively the same as British, although with round two- (or occasionally three-) pin plugs. British equipment will need either an adaptor or a new plug; American requires both a transformer and a new plug.

Emergencies For all emergencies (Police, Ambulance, Fire) dial ☎112.

Laundry (wassalons) The Clean Brothers, Kerkstraat 56 (Grachtengordel south; daily 7am–9pm), is the city's best self-service laundry, with a sizeable load currently €4 to wash, €1 per 30min in the drier and soap for €0.50; they also do service-washes, dry-cleaning, ironing, etc; there is also a branch at Jacob van Lennepkade 179 (Oud West). Other laundries are to be found at: Elandsgracht 59 (Jordaan and the Westerdok), Warmoesstraat 30 and Oude Doelenstraat 12 (Old Centre).

Left luggage Centraal Station has both coin-operated luggage lockers (daily 7am–11pm) and a staffed left-luggage office (daily 7am–11pm). Small coin-operated lockers cost €2.70, the larger ones €4.20 per 24 hours; left luggage costs €5.70 per item.

Libraries The main public library, Centrale Bibliotheek, is at Prinsengracht 587, just north of Leidsegracht (Mon 1–9pm, Tues–Thurs 10am–9pm, Fri & Sat

10am–5pm; Oct–March also Sun 1–5pm). There's no problem about using its books for reference purposes, but to borrow them you'll need to show proof of residence and pay €20 for a year's membership (less for under-18s & over-65s).

Lost property For items lost on the trams, buses or metro, contact GVB Head Office, Prins Hendrikkade 108–114 (Mon–Fri 9am–4pm; ☎020/460 5858). For property lost on a train, go to the Gevonden Voorwerpen office at the nearest station; Amsterdam's is at Centraal Station, near the left-luggage lockers (☎020/557 8544; 24hr). After three days all unclaimed property goes to the Central Lost Property Office at 2e Daalsedijk 4, Utrecht (☎030/235 3923), and costs €7 per item to pick up. If you lose something in the street or a park, try the police lost property at Stephensonstraat 18 (Mon–Fri noon–3.30pm; ☎020/559 3005). Schiphol airport's lost and found number is ☎020/601 2325 (Mon–Fri 7.30am–5.30pm, Sat & Sun 9am–5pm).

Moped rental Moped Rental Service, Willemsstraat 133 (Jordaan and the Westerdok) ☎020/422 0266.

Mosquitoes These thrive in Holland's watery environment and are at their worst, as you would expect, near any stagnant or slow-moving stretch of water. Muggenmelk, with DEET, is very powerful: a little smear will keep them well away for a good night's sleep. Other popular brands include the Autan range. For more sensitive skins, Prrrikweg contains pungent citronella oil. After the event, an antihistamine cream such as Phenergan helps. All these and more are available all over Amsterdam.

Public transport Information on ☎0900/9292.

Time One hour ahead of Britain, six hours ahead of New York, nine hours ahead of Los Angeles. Daylight-saving operates from the end of March to the end of October.

Tipping There's no necessity to tip, but a ten to fifteen percent tip is expected by taxi drivers and anticipated by many restaurant waiters.

Toilets Public toilets are invariably spotlessly clean and well maintained; many cost €0.25 or €0.50. For men, there are also free, al-fresco pissoirs located all over the city centre.

Women's contacts Amsterdam has an impressive feminist infrastructure: there are support groups, health centres and businesses run by and for women. A good starting point to find out what's going on is Het Vrouwenhuis, Nieuwe Herengracht 95 (☎020/625 2066, ⓦwww.vrouwenhuis.nl; Mon–Fri 11am–4pm), a centre which organizes women's activities and cultural events. IIAV at Obiplein 4 (☎665 0820, ⓦwww.iiav.nl; Tues–Fri 10am–5pm) houses the International Archives of the Women's Movement and has a wealth of literature of all kinds detailing the history of the feminist movement in the Netherlands.

Contexts

Contexts

A brief history of Amsterdam

To a large degree, a history of Amsterdam is a history of the whole of the Netherlands, which in turn was an integral part of the Low Countries – today's Belgium, Luxembourg and the Netherlands – until the late sixteenth century. It was then that the Dutch broke with their Habsburg masters and, ever since, Amsterdam has been at the centre of Dutch events. The city was the country's most glorious cultural and trading centre throughout its seventeenth-century heyday, the so-called Golden Age, and, after a brief downturn in the eighteenth century, picked itself up to emerge as a major metropolis in the nineteenth. In the 1960s Amsterdam was galvanized by its youth, who took to hippy culture with gusto; their legacy is a social progressiveness – most conspicuously over drugs and prostitution – that still underpins the city's international reputation, good and bad, today.

Medieval foundations

Amsterdam's earliest history is as murky as the marshes from which it arose. Legend asserts that two Frisian fishermen were the first inhabitants and, true or not, it is indeed likely that the city began as a fishing village at the mouth of the **River Amstel**. Previously, this area had been a stretch of peat bogs and marshes, but a modest fall in the sea level permitted settlement on the high ground along the riverside. The village was first given some significance when the local lord built a castle here around 1204, and then, some sixty years later, the Amstel was dammed – hence Amstelredam – and it received its municipal **charter** from a new feudal overlord, Count Floris V, in 1275. Designating the village a toll port for beer imported from Hamburg, the charter led to Amsterdam's flourishing as a trading centre from around 1300, when it also became an important transit port for Baltic grain, destined for the burgeoning cities of the Low Countries (modern-day Belgium and the Netherlands).

As Amsterdam grew, its **trade** diversified. In particular, it made a handsome profit from English wool: the wool was imported into the city, barged onto Leiden and Haarlem – where it was turned into cloth – and then much of it returned to Amsterdam to be exported. The cloth trade drew workers into the town to work along Warmoesstraat and the Amstel, and ships were able to sail right up to Dam square to pick up the finished work and drop off imported wood, fish, salt and spices.

Though the city's **population** rose steadily in the early sixteenth century, to around 12,000 souls, Amsterdam was still small compared to Antwerp or London: building on the waterlogged soil was difficult and slow, requiring timber piles to be driven into the firmer sand below. And with the extensive use of timber and thatch, fires were a frequent occurrence. A particularly disastrous blaze in 1452 resulted in such destruction that the city council made building with slate and stone obligatory – one of the few wooden houses that survived the fire still stands today in the Begijnhof (see p.67). In the mid-sixteenth century the city underwent its first major **expansion**, as burgeoning trade with the Hanseatic towns of the Baltic made the city second only to Antwerp as a marketplace and warehouse for northern and western Europe. The trade in cloth, grain and wine brought craftspeople to the city, and its merchant fleet grew: by the 1550s three-quarters of all grain cargo out of the Baltic was carried in Amsterdam vessels. The foundations were being laid for the wealth of the Golden Age.

The rise of Protestantism

At the beginning of the sixteenth century the superstition, corruption and elaborate ritual of the established **Church** found itself under attack throughout northern Europe. First, Erasmus of Rotterdam promoted ideas of reformation and then, in 1517, **Martin Luther** went one step – or rather, leap – further, producing his 95 theses against the Church practice of indulgences, a prelude to his more comprehensive assault on the entire institution. Furthermore, when Luther's works were disseminated his ideas gained a European following amongst a range of reforming groups branded as **Lutheran** by the Church, whilst other reformers were drawn to the doctrines of **John Calvin** (1509–64). Luther asserted that the Church's political power was subservient to that of the state; Calvin emphasized the importance of individual conscience and the need for redemption through the grace of Christ rather than the confessional. Luther's writings and Bible translations were printed in the Netherlands, but the doctrines of Calvin proved more popular in Amsterdam, setting the seal on the city's religious transformation. Calvin was insistent on the separation of church and state, but the lines were easily fudged in Amsterdam by the church's ruling council of ministers and annually elected elders. The council had little time for other (more egalitarian) Protestant sects and matters came to a head when, in 1535, one of the radical splinter groups, the **Anabaptists**, occupied Amsterdam's town hall, calling on passers-by to repent. Previously the town council had tolerated the Anabaptists but, prompted by the Calvinists, it acted swiftly when civic rule was challenged: the town hall was besieged and the leaders of the Anabaptists were executed on the Dam.

The revolt of the Netherlands

In 1555 the fanatically Catholic **Philip II** succeeded to the Spanish throne. Through a series of marriages the Spanish monarchy – and Habsburg family – had come to rule over the Low Countries, and Philip was determined to rid his empire of its heretics, regardless of whether they were Calvinists or Anabaptists. Philip promptly garrisoned the towns of the Low Countries with Spanish mercenaries, imported the **Inquisition** and passed a series of anti-Protestant edicts. However, other pressures on the Habsburg empire forced him into a tactical withdrawal and he transferred control to his sister **Margaret of Parma** in 1559. Based in Brussels, the equally resolute Margaret implemented the policies of her brother with gusto. In 1561 she reorganized the church and created fourteen new bishoprics, a move that was construed as a wresting of power from civil authority, and an attempt to destroy the local aristocracy's powers of religious patronage. Right across the Low Countries, Protestantism – and Protestant sympathies – spread to the nobility, who now formed the "League of the Nobility" to counter Habsburg policy. The League petitioned

Philip for moderation but were dismissed out of hand by one of Margaret's Walloon advisers, who called them "ces geux" (those beggars), an epithet that was to be enthusiastically adopted by the rebels. In 1565 a harvest failure caused a winter famine among the urban workers and, after years of repression, they struck back. In 1566 a Protestant sermon in the tiny Flemish textile town of Steenvoorde incited the congregation to purge the local church of its papist idolatry. The crowd smashed up the church's reliquaries and shrines, broke the stained-glass windows and terrorized the priests, thereby launching the **Iconoclastic Fury**. The rioting spread like wildfire and within ten days churches had been ransacked from one end of the Low Countries to the other, nowhere more so than in Amsterdam – hence the plain whitewashed interiors of many of the city's churches today.

The ferocity of this outbreak shocked the upper classes into renewed support for Spain, and Margaret regained the allegiance of most nobles – with the principal exception of the country's greatest landowner, Prince William of Orange-Nassau, known as **William the Silent**, who prudently slipped away to his estates in Germany. Meanwhile, Philip II was keen to capitalize on the increase in support for Margaret and, in 1567, he dispatched the **Duke of Albe**, with an army of ten thousand men, to the Low Countries to suppress his religious opponents absolutely. One of Albe's first acts was to set up the Commission of Civil Unrest, which was soon nicknamed the "**Council of Blood**", after its habit of executing those it examined. No fewer than 12,000 citizens were polished off, mostly for taking part in the Fury. Initially the repression worked: in 1568, when William attempted an invasion from Germany, the towns, including Amsterdam, offered no support. William waited and conceived other means of defeating Albe. In April 1572 a band of privateers entered Brielle on the Maas and captured it from the Spanish. This was one of several commando-style attacks by the so-called **Waterguezen** or sea-beggars, who were at first obliged to operate from England, although it was soon possible for them to secure bases in the Netherlands, whose citizens had grown to loathe Albe and his Spaniards.

After the success at Brielle, the revolt spread rapidly. By June the rebels controlled all of the province of Holland except for Amsterdam, which steadfastly refused to come off the fence. Albe and his son Frederick fought back, but William's superior naval power frustrated him and a mightily irritated Philip replaced Albe with **Luis de Resquesens**. Initially, Resquesens had some success in the south, where the Catholic majority were more willing to compromise with Spanish rule than their northern neighbours, but the tide of war was against him – most pointedly in William's triumphant relief of Leiden in 1574. Two years later, Resquesens died and the (unpaid) Habsburg garrison in Antwerp mutinied and attacked the town, slaughtering some eight thousand of its people in what was known as the **Spanish Fury**. Though the Habsburgs still held several towns, the massacre alienated the south and pushed its peoples – including the doubting Thomases of Amsterdam – into the arms of William, whose troops now swept into Brussels, the heart of imperial power. Momentarily, it seemed possible for the whole region to unite behind William and all signed the **Union of Brussels**, which demanded the departure of foreign troops as a condition for accepting a diluted Habsburg sovereignty.

Philip was, however, not inclined to compromise, especially when he realized that William's Calvinist sympathies were giving his newly found Walloon and Flemish allies the jitters. The king bided his time until 1578, when, with his enemies arguing amongst themselves, he sent another army from Spain to the Low Countries under the command of Alessandro Farnese, the **Duke of**

Parma. Events played into Parma's hands. In 1579, tiring of all the wrangling, seven northern provinces agreed to sign the **Union of Utrecht**, an alliance against Spain that was to be the first unification of the Netherlands as an identifiable country – the **United Provinces**. It was then that Amsterdam formally declared for the rebels and switched from Catholicism to Calvinism in what became known as the "Alteratie" of 1578. The rebels had conceded freedom of religious belief, but in Amsterdam as elsewhere this did not extend to freedom of worship. Nonetheless, a pragmatic compromise was reached in which a blind eye was turned to the celebration of Mass if it was done privately and inconspicuously. It was this ad hoc arrangement that gave rise to "clandestine" Catholic churches (*schuilkerken*) like that of the Amstelkring on Oudezijds Voorburgwal (see p.61).

The assembly of these United Provinces was known as the **States General**, and met at Den Haag (The Hague); it had no domestic legislative authority, and could only carry out foreign policy by unanimous decision, a formula designed to reassure the independent-minded merchants of every Dutch city. The role of **Stadholder** was the most important in each province, roughly equivalent to that of governor, though the same person could occupy this position in any number of provinces. Meanwhile, in the south – and also in 1579 – representatives of the southern provinces signed the **Union of Arras**, a Catholic-led agreement that declared loyalty to Philip II and counterbalanced the Union of Utrecht in the north. Thus, the Low Countries were, de facto, divided into two – the Spanish Netherlands and the United Provinces – beginning a separation that would lead, after many changes, to the creation of Belgium, Luxembourg and the Netherlands. With the return of more settled times, Amsterdam was now free to carry on with what it did best – trading and making money.

The Golden Age

The brilliance of Amsterdam's explosion onto the European scene is as difficult to underestimate as it is to detail. The size of its **merchant fleet** carrying Baltic grain into Europe had long been considerable. Even the Spaniards had been unable to undermine Dutch **maritime superiority** and, with the commercial demise of Antwerp, Amsterdam became the emporium for the products of northern and southern Europe as well as the East and West Indies. The city didn't prosper from its market alone, though, as Amsterdam ships also carried produce, a cargo trade that greatly increased the city's wealth. Dutch **banking and investment** brought further prosperity, and by the middle of the seventeenth century Amsterdam's wealth was spectacular. The Calvinist bourgeoisie indulged themselves in fine canal houses, and commissioned images of themselves in group portraits. Civic pride knew no bounds as great monuments to self-aggrandizement, such as the new **town hall** (now the Royal Palace), were hastily erected and, if some went hungry, few starved, as the poor were cared for in municipal almshouses.

The arts flourished and **religious tolerance** extended even to the traditional scapegoats, the Jews, and in particular the Sephardic Jews, who had been hounded from Spain by the Inquisition but were guaranteed freedom from religious persecution under the terms of the Union of Utrecht. By the end of the eighteenth century Jews accounted for ten percent of the city's population. Guilds and craft associations thrived, and in the first half of the seventeenth century Amsterdam's population quadrupled: the relatively high wages paid by the city's industries attracted agricultural workers from every part of the country and Protestant refugees arrived from every corner of Catholic Europe.

To accommodate its growing populace, Amsterdam **expanded** several times during the seventeenth century. The grandest and most elaborate plan to enlarge the city was begun in 1613, with the building of the western stretches of the Herengracht, Keizersgracht and Prinsengracht, the three great canals of the **Grachtengordel** that epitomized the wealth and self-confidence of the Golden Age. In 1663 this sweeping crescent was extended beyond the River Amstel, but by this time the population had begun to stabilize, and the stretch that would have completed the ring of canals around the city was left only partially developed – an area that would in time become the Jewish Quarter.

One organization that kept the city's coffers brimming throughout the Golden Age was the **East India Company**. Formed in 1602, this Amsterdam-controlled enterprise sent ships to Asia, Indonesia and as far away as China to bring back spices, wood and other assorted plunder. Given a trading monopoly in all lands east of the Cape of Good Hope, it also had unlimited military powers over the lands it controlled, and was effectively the occupying government in Malaya, Ceylon and Malacca. Twenty years later the **West Indies Company** was inaugurated to protect new Dutch interests in the Americas and Africa. It never achieved the success of the East India Company, expending its energies in waging war on Spanish and Portuguese colonies from a base in Surinam, but it did make handsome profits until the 1660s. The company was dismantled in 1674, ten years after its small colony of New Amsterdam had been ceded to the British – and renamed **New York**. Elsewhere, the Dutch held on to their colonies for as long as possible – Indonesia, its principal possession, only secured its independence in 1949.

Decline – 1660 to 1795

Although the economics of the Golden Age were dazzling, the **political climate** was dismal. The United Provinces were dogged by interminable wrangling between those who hankered for a central, unified government under the pre-eminent House of Orange-Nassau and those who championed provincial autonomy. Frederick Henry, the powerful head of the House of Orange-Nassau, died in 1647 and his successor, William II, lasted just three years before his death from smallpox. A week after William's death, his wife bore the son who would become William III of England, but in the meantime the leaders of the province of Holland, with the full support of Amsterdam, seized their opportunity. They forced measures through the States General abolishing the position of Stadholder, thereby reducing the powers of the Orangists and increasing those of the provinces, chiefly Holland itself. Holland's foremost figure in these years was **Johan de Witt**, Council Pensionary to the States General. He guided the country through wars with England and Sweden, concluding a triple alliance between the two countries and the United Provinces in 1668. There had been two Anglo-Dutch wars (1652–54 and 1665–67) and in the second of them **Admiral Michiel de Ruyter** had inflicted an embarrassing defeat on the English fleet when he sailed up the Thames and caught his enemies napping. This infuriated England's Charles II and, eager to exact revenge, he was quite willing to break with his new-found allies and join a French attack on the Provinces in 1672. The republic was in deep trouble – previous victories had been at sea, and the army, weak and disorganized, could not withstand the onslaught. In panic, the country turned to William III of Orange for leadership and Johan de Witt was brutally murdered by a mob of Orangist sympathizers in Den Haag. By 1678 William had defeated the French and made peace with the English – and was rewarded (along with his wife Mary) with the English crown ten years later.

Though King William had defeated the French, **Louis XIV** retained designs on the United Provinces and the pot was kept boiling in a long series of dynastic wars that ranged across northern Europe. In 1700 Charles II of Spain, the last of the Spanish Habsburgs, died childless, bequeathing the Spanish throne and control of the Spanish Netherlands to Philip of Anjou, Louis' grandson. Louis promptly forced Philip to cede the latter to France, which was, with every justification, construed as a threat to the balance of power by France's neighbours. The **War of the Spanish Succession** ensued, with the United Provinces, England and Austria forming the **Triple Alliance** to thwart the French king. The war itself was a haphazard, long-winded affair distinguished by the spectacular victories of the Duke of Marlborough at Blenheim, Ramillies and Malplaquet. It dragged on until the Treaty of Utrecht of 1713 in which France finally abandoned its claim to the Spanish Netherlands.

However, the fighting had drained the United Provinces' reserves and its slow economic and political decline began, accelerated by a reactive trend towards conservatism. This in turn reflected the development of an increasingly socially static society, with power and wealth concentrated within a small elite. Furthermore, with the threat of foreign conquest effectively removed, the Dutch ruling class divided into two main camps – the Orangists and the pro-French "Patriots" – whose interminable squabbling soon brought political life to a virtual standstill. The situation deteriorated even further in the latter half of the century and the last few years of the United Provinces present a sorry state of affairs.

French occupation

In 1795 the **French**, aided by the Patriots, invaded, setting up the **Batavian Republic** and dissolving the United Provinces – along with much of the control of the rich Dutch merchants. Effectively part of the Napoleonic empire, the Netherlands were obliged to wage unenthusiastic war with England, and in 1806 Napoleon appointed his brother **Louis** as their king in an attempt to create a commercial gulf between the country and England. **Louis** was installed in Amsterdam's town hall, giving it its title of Koninklijk Paleis (Royal Palace; see p.46). Louis, however, wasn't willing to allow the Netherlands to become a simple satellite of France; he ignored Napoleon's directives and after just four years of rule was forced to abdicate. The country was then formally incorporated into the French Empire, and for three gloomy years suffered occupation and heavy taxation to finance French military adventures.

Following Napoleon's disastrous retreat from Moscow, the **Orangist faction** surfaced to exploit weakening French control. In 1813 Frederick William, son of the exiled William V, returned to the country and eight months later, under the terms of the **Congress of Vienna**, was crowned King William I of the **United Kingdom of the Netherlands**, incorporating both the old United Provinces and the Spanish (Austrian) Netherlands. A strong-willed man, he spent much of the later part of his life trying to control his disparate kingdom, but he failed primarily because of the Protestant north's attempt – or perceived attempt – to dominate the Catholic south. The southern provinces revolted against his rule and in 1830 the separate Kingdom of Belgium was proclaimed. During the years of the United Kingdom, Amsterdam's status was dramatically reduced. Previously, the self-governing city, made bold by its wealth, could (and frequently did) act in its own self-interest, at the expense of the nation. From 1815, however, it was integrated within the country, with no more rights than any other city. The seat of government (and the centre for all decision-making) was Den Haag (The Hague), and so it remained after the southern provinces broke away.

The nineteenth century

In the first decades of the nineteenth century the erosion of Amsterdam's pre-eminent position among Dutch cities was largely camouflaged by its profitable colonial trade with the East Indies (Indonesia). This trade was however hampered by the character of the **Zuider Zee**, whose shallows and sandbanks presented real problems, given the increase in the size of merchant ships. The **Noordhollandskanaal** (North Holland Canal), completed in 1824 to bypass the Zuider Zee, made little difference, and it was Rotterdam, strategically placed on the Rhine inlets between the industries of the Ruhr and Britain, that prospered at Amsterdam's expense. Even the opening of the **Nordzeekanaal** (North Sea Canal) in 1876 failed to push Amsterdam's trade ahead of rival Rotterdam's, though the city did hold on to much of the country's **shipbuilding industry**, remnants of which can still be seen at the 't Kromhout shipyard (see p.97). The city council was also slow to catch on to the railway, but finally, in 1889, the opening of **Centraal Station** put the city back on the main transport routes. Nonetheless, Amsterdam was far from being a backwater: in the second half of the nineteenth century its industries boomed, attracting a new wave of migrants, who were settled outside of the centre in the vast tenements of De Pijp and the Oud Zuid (Old South). These same workers were soon to radicalize the city, supporting a veritable raft of Socialist and Communist politicians. One marker was a reforming **Housing Act** of 1901 that pushed the city council into a concerted effort to clear the city's slums. Even better, the new municipal housing was frequently designed to the highest specifications, no more so than under the guidance of the two leading architects of the (broadly Expressionist) **Amsterdam School**, Michael de Klerk (1884–1923) and Piet Kramer (1881–1961). The duo were responsible for the layout of much of the Nieuw Zuid (New South; see p.112).

Nationally, the outstanding political figure of the times, **Jan Rudolph Thorbecke**, formed three ruling cabinets (1849–53, 1862–66 and 1872, in the year of his death) and steered the Netherlands through a profound attitudinal change. The political parties of the late eighteenth century had wished to resurrect the power and prestige of the seventeenth-century Netherlands; Thorbecke and his liberal allies resigned themselves to the country's reduced status as a small power and eulogized its advantages. For the first time, from about 1850, liberty was seen as a luxury made possible by the country's very lack of power, and the malaise that had long disturbed public life gave way to a positive appreciation of the very narrowness of its national existence. One of the results of Thorbecke's liberalism was a gradual extension of the franchise, culminating in the **Act of Universal Suffrage** in 1917.

The war years

The Netherlands remained neutral during **World War I** and although it suffered privations from the Allied blockade of German war materials, this was offset by the profits many Dutch merchants made by trading with both sides. Similar attempts to remain neutral in **World War II**, however, failed: the Germans invaded on May 10, 1940, and the Netherlands was quickly overrun. Queen Wilhelmina fled to London to set up a government-in-exile, and members of the **NSB**, the Dutch fascist party, which had welcomed the invaders, were rewarded with positions of authority. Nevertheless, in the early months of the occupation, life for ordinary Amsterdammers went on pretty much as usual. Even when the first roundups of the Jews began in late 1940, many managed to turn a blind eye, though in February 1941 Amsterdam's newly outlawed Communist Party did organize a widely supported strike, spearheaded by the city's transport workers and dockers (see p.91). It was a gesture rather than a move to undermine German control, but an important one all the same. Interviewed after the war, one of the leaders summarized it thus: "If only one of Amsterdam's Jews did not feel forgotten and abandoned as he was packed off in a train, then the strike was well worth it."

As the war progressed, so the German grip got tighter and the Dutch **Resistance** stronger, its activities – primarily industrial and transportation sabotage – trumpeted by underground newspapers such as *Het Parool* (The Password), which survives in good form today. The Resistance paid a heavy price with some 23,000 of its fighters and sympathizers losing their lives, but the city's Jews (see box on p.88) took the worst punishment. In 1940 the city's Jewish population, swollen by refugees from Hitler's Germany, was around 140,000, but when the Allies liberated the city in May 1945 only a few thousand were left. The Old Jewish Quarter (see Chapter Four) lay deserted, a rare crumb of comfort being the survival of the diary of a young Jewish girl – **Anne Frank**.

Reconstruction – 1945 to 1960

The **postwar years** were spent patching up the damage of occupation, though at first progress was hindered by a desperate shortage of food, fuel and building materials. Indeed, things were in such short supply and the winter so cold that hundreds of Amsterdammers died of hunger and/or hypothermia, their black cardboard coffins being trundled to mass graves. Neither did it help that the retreating Germans had blown up all the dykes and sluices on the North Sea coast at Ijmuiden, at the mouth of the Nordzeekanaal. Nevertheless, Amsterdam had not received an aerial pounding of the likes dished out to Rotterdam and Arnhem and the reconstruction soon built up a head of steam. One feature of the reconstruction was the creation of giant suburbs like **Bijlmermeer**, to the southeast of the city, the last word in early 1960s large-scale residential planning, with low-cost modern housing, play areas and traffic-free foot and cycle paths.

Two events were, however, to mar Dutch reconstruction in the late 1940s and early 1950s. The former **Dutch colonies** of Java and Sumatra, taken by the Japanese at the outbreak of the war, were now ruled by a nationalist Republican government that refused to recognize Dutch sovereignty. Following the failure of talks between Den Haag and the islanders in 1947, the Dutch sent the troops in, a colonial enterprise that soon became a bloody debacle. International opposition was intense and, after much condemnation and pressure, the Dutch reluctantly surrendered their most important Asian colonies, which were ultimately incorporated as **Indonesia** in 1950. Back at home, tragedy struck on February 1, 1953 when an unusually high tide was pushed over Zeeland's sea defences by a westerly wind, flooding 160 square kilometres of land and drowning over 1800 people. The response was the **Delta Project**, which closed off the western part of the Scheldt and Maas estuaries with massive sea dykes, thereby ensuring the safety of cities to the south of Amsterdam, though Amsterdam itself had already been secured by the completion of the **Afsluitdijk** in 1932. This dyke closed off the Zuider Zee, turning it into the freshwater Ijsselmeer and Markermeer (see box on p.131).

The Provos and the 1960s

The radical and youthful mass movements that swept through the West in the 1960s transformed Amsterdam from a middling, rather conservative city into a turbocharged hotbed of **hippy action**. In 1963 one-time window cleaner and magician extraordinaire **Jasper Grootveld** won celebrity status by painting "K" – for *kanker* ("cancer") – on cigarette billboards throughout the city. Two years later he proclaimed the statue of the *Lieverdje* ("Loveable Rascal") on the Spui (see p.56) the symbol of "tomorrow's addicted consumer" – since it had been donated to the city by a cigarette manufacturer – and organized large-scale gatherings there once a week. His actions enthused others, most notably **Roel van Duyn**, a philosophy student at Amsterdam University, who assembled a Left-wing-cum-anarchist movement known as the **Provos** – short for *provocatie* ("provocation"). The Provos participated in Grootveld's meetings and then proceeded to organize their own street "happenings", which proved to be fantastically popular among young Amsterdammers. The number of Provos never exceeded about thirty, and the group had no coherent structure, but they did have one clear aim – to bring points of political or social conflict to public attention by spectacular means. More than anything, they were masters of publicity, and pursued their "games" with a spirit of fun rather than grim political fanaticism. The reaction of the police, however, was aggressive: the first two issues of the Provos' magazine were confiscated and, in July 1965, they intervened at a Saturday-night "happening", setting a pattern for future confrontations. The magazine itself contained the Provos' manifesto, a set of policies which later appeared under the title "**The White Plans**". These included the famously popular **white bicycle plan**, which proposed that the council ban all cars in the city centre and supply 20,000 bicycles (painted white) for general public use.

There were regular police-Provo confrontations throughout 1965, but it was the **wedding of Princess Beatrix** to Claus von Amsberg on March 10, 1966, that provoked the most serious unrest. Amsberg had served in the German army during World War II and many Netherlanders were deeply offended by the marriage. Consequently, when hundreds took to the streets to protest, pelting the wedding procession with smoke bombs, a huge swath of Dutch opinion supported them – to some degree or another. Amsberg himself got no more than he deserved when he was jeered with the refrain "Give us back the bikes", a reference to the commandeering of hundreds of bikes by the retreating German army in 1945. The wedding over, the next crisis came in June when, much to the horror of the authorities, it appeared that students, workers and Provos were about to combine. In panic, the Hague government ordered the dismissal of Amsterdam's police chief, but in the event the Provos had peaked and the workers proved far from revolutionary, settling for arbitration on their various complaints.

The final twist in the Provo tale was the formation of a splinter group called the **Kabouters**, named after a helpful gnome in Dutch folklore. Their manifesto described their form of socialism as "not of the clenched fist, but of the intertwined fingers, the erect penis, the escaping butterfly..." – appealing perhaps, but never massively popular.

The 1970s and 1980s – and the squatters

In 1967 the Provos formally dissolved their movement at a happening in the Vondelpark, but many of their supporters promptly moved on to **neighbourhood committees**, set up to oppose the more outlandish development plans of the city council. The most hated scheme by a long chalk was the plan to build a **metro line** through the Nieuwmarkt to the new suburb of Bijlmermeer as this involved both wholesale demolitions and compulsory relocations. For six months there were regular confrontations between the police and the protestors and, although the council eventually had its way, the scene was set for more trouble. In particular, the council seemed to many to be unwilling to tackle Amsterdam's acute **housing shortage**, neglecting the needs of its poorer citizens in favour of business interests. It was this perception that fuelled the **squatter movement**, which coalesced around a handful of symbolic squats. The first major incident came in March 1980 when several hundred police evicted squatters from premises on **Vondelstraat**. Afterwards, there was widespread rioting, but this was small beer in comparison with the protests of April 30, 1980 – the **coronation day** of Queen Beatrix – when a mixed bag of squatters and leftists vigorously protested both the lavishness of the proceedings and the expense of refurbishing Beatrix's palace in Den Haag. Once again there was widespread rioting and this time it spread to other Dutch cities, though the unrest was short-lived.

Now at its peak, Amsterdam's squatting movement boasted around ten thousand activists, many of whom were involved in two more major confrontations with the police – the first at the **Lucky Luyk** squat, on Jan Luykenstraat, the second at the **Wyers** building, when, in February 1984, the squatters were forcibly cleared to make way for a Holiday Inn, now the Crowne Plaza Hotel (see p.45). The final showdown – the **Stopera** campaign – came with the construction of the **Muziektheater/Stadhuis** complex on Waterlooplein (see p.89). Thereafter, the movement faded away, at least partly because of its repeated failure to stop the developers, who now claim, with some justification, to be more sensitive to community needs.

The present

The street protests and massive squats of Amsterdam's recent past now seem a distant memory, but some of the old ideas – and ideals – have been carried forward by the **Greens**, who attract a small but significant following in every municipal – and national – election. The much larger Labour Party – the Pvda – has picked up on some of these issues too, though it has a problem with **Schiphol airport**, which needs to be expanded, but is an environmental minefield. Politically, one of the problems is that the city's finely balanced system of **proportional representation** brings little rapid change and often mires in interminable compromise and debate. The same is true nationally, where politicking has long seemed a bland if necessary business conducted between the three main parties, the **Protestant-Catholic CDA** coalition, the **Liberal VVD** and the **Socialist Pvda**. However, the entire political class received a major jolt in the national elections of May 2002 when a brand-new Rightist grouping – **Leefbaar Neederlands** (Liveable Netherlands) – led by **Pim Fortuyn** swept to second place behind the CDA, securing seventeen percent of the national vote. Stylish and witty, openly gay and a former Marxist, Fortuyn managed to cover several popular bases at the same time, from the need for law and order through to tighter immigration controls. Most crucially, he also attacked the liberal establishment's espousal of multiculturalism even when the representatives of minority groups were deeply reactionary, anti-gay and sexist. Politically, it worked a treat, but a year later Fortuyn was assassinated and his party rapidly unravelled, losing almost all its seats in the general election of January 2003. Since then, normal political service seems to have been resumed, with the CDA, the Pvda and the VVD once again the largest parties, though Fortuyn's popularity is likely to push certain sorts of social debate, particularly on immigration, to the right both in Amsterdam and the country as a whole.

One of the reasons for Fortuyn's electoral success reflected the other shock to the Dutch system, which came with the publication of a damning report on the failure of the Dutch army to protect the Bosnian Muslims ensconced in the UN safe-haven of **Srebrenica** in 1995. Published in April 2002, the report told a tale of extraordinary incompetence: the UN's Dutch soldiers were inadequately armed, but still refused American assistance, and watched as Serb troops separated Muslim men and women in preparation for the mass executions, which the Dutch soldiers then did nothing to stop (though they were never involved). In a country that prides itself on its internationalism, the report was an especially hard blow and the whole of the Pvda-led government, under **Wim Kok**, resigned in April 2002.

National events aside, the majority of Amsterdammers have readily accepted the city council's recent attempt to recast the city as a dynamic, go-ahead metropolis with the drugs and the hippies as a byline. Redevelopment has become the name of the game, most importantly in the ultramodern 51,000-capacity Amsterdam ArenA, the new home of the Ajax football team. And yet, Amsterdam retains its idiosyncratic character, of houseboats and sky-rises, and its historic centre is now recognized as too valuable a tourist attraction to be placed under threat.

Dutch art

Designed to serve only as a quick reference, the following outline is the very briefest of introductions to a subject that has rightly filled volumes. Inevitably, it covers artists that lived and worked in both the Netherlands and Belgium, as these two countries have – along with Luxembourg – been bound together as the "Low Countries" for most of their history. For in-depth and academic studies, see the recommendations in "Books" on p.265. For a list of where to find some of the paintings mentioned here, turn to the box on p.262.

Beginnings – the Flemish Primitives

Throughout the medieval period, **Flanders**, in modern-day Belgium, was one of the most artistically productive parts of Europe and it was here that the solid realist base of later Dutch painting developed. Today the works of these early Flemish painters, the **Flemish Primitives**, are highly prized and although examples are fairly sparse in the Netherlands, all the leading museums – especially Amsterdam's Rijksmuseum and Den Haag's Mauritshuis – have a sample.

Jan van Eyck (1385–1441) is generally regarded as the first of the Flemish Primitives, and has even been credited with the invention of oil painting – though it seems more likely that he simply perfected a new technique by thinning his paint with (the newly discovered) turpentine, thus making it more flexible. His most famous work still in the Low Countries is the altarpiece in Ghent cathedral (debatably painted with the help of his lesser-known brother, Hubert), which was revolutionary in its realism, for the first time using elements of native landscape in depicting Biblical themes. Van Eyck's style and technique were to influence several generations of Low Countries artists.

Firmly in the Eyckian tradition were the **Master of Flemalle** (1387–1444) and **Rogier van der Weyden** (1400–64), one-time official painter to the city of Brussels. The Flemalle master is a shadowy figure: some believe he was the teacher of Van der Weyden, others that the two artists were in fact the same person. There are differences between the two, however: the Flemalle master's paintings are close to Van Eyck's, whereas Van der Weyden shows a greater degree of emotional intensity in his religious works. Van der Weyden also produced serene portraits of the bigwigs of his day that were much admired across a large swath of western Europe. His style, never mind his success, influenced many painters, with one of the most talented of these being **Dieric Bouts** (1415–75). Born in Haarlem but active in Leuven, Bouts is recognizable by his stiff, rather elongated figures and horrific subject matter, all set against carefully drawn landscapes. **Hugo van der Goes** (d. 1482) was the next Ghent master after Van Eyck, most famous for the Portinari altarpiece in Florence's Uffizi gallery. After a short painting career, he died insane, and his late works have strong hints of his impending madness in their subversive use of space and implicit acceptance of the viewer's presence.

Few doubt that **Hans Memling** (1440–94) was a pupil of Van der Weyden. Active in Bruges throughout his life, he is best remembered for the pastoral charm of his landscapes and the quality of his portraiture, much of which survives on the rescued side panels of triptychs. **Gerard David** (1460–1523) was a native of Oudewater, near Gouda, but he moved to Bruges in 1484, becoming the last of the great painters to work in that city, before it was outstripped by Antwerp, producing formal religious works of traditional bent. Strikingly different, but broadly contemporaneous, was **Hieronymus Bosch** (1450–1516), who lived for most of his life in Holland, though his style is linked to that of his Flemish contemporaries. His frequently reprinted religious allegories are filled with macabre visions of tortured people and grotesque beasts, and appear at first faintly unhinged, though it's now thought that these are visual representations of contemporary sayings, idioms and parables. While their interpretation is far from resolved, Bosch's paintings draw strongly on subconscious fears and archetypes, giving them a lasting, haunting fascination.

The sixteenth century

At the end of the fifteenth century, Flanders was in economic and political decline and the leading artists of the day were drawn instead to the booming port of Antwerp. The artists who worked here soon began to integrate the finely observed detail that characterized the Flemish tradition with the style of the Italian painters of the Renaissance. **Quentin Matsys** (1464–1530) introduced florid classical architectural details and intricate landscapes to his works, influenced perhaps by the work of Leonardo da Vinci. As well as religious works, he painted portraits and genre scenes, all of which have recognizably Italian facets – and paved the way for the Dutch genre painters of later years. **Jan Gossaert** (1478–1532) made the pilgrimage to Italy too, and his dynamic works are packed with detail, especially finely drawn classical architectural backdrops. He was the first Low Countries artist to introduce the subjects of classical mythology into his works, part of a steady trend through the period towards secular subject matter, which can also be seen in the work of **Joachim Patenier** (d.1524), who painted small landscapes of fantastical scenery.

The middle of the sixteenth century was dominated by the work of **Pieter Bruegel the Elder** (c.1525–69), whose gruesome allegories and innovative interpretations of religious subjects are firmly placed in Low Countries settings. Pieter also painted finely observed peasant scenes, though he himself was well-connected in court circles in Antwerp and, later, Brussels. **Pieter Aertsen** (1508–75) also worked in the peasant genre, adding aspects of still life: his paintings often show a detailed kitchen scene in the foreground, with a religious episode going on behind. Bruegel's two sons, **Pieter Bruegel the Younger** (1564–1638) and **Jan Bruegel** (1568–1625), were lesser painters: the former produced fairly insipid copies of his father's work, while Jan developed a style of his own – delicately rendered flower paintings and genre pieces that earned him the nickname "Velvet". Towards the latter half of the sixteenth century highly stylized Italianate portraits became the dominant fashion, with **Frans Pourbus the Younger** (1569–1622) the leading practitioner. Frans hobnobbed across Europe, working for the likes of the Habsburgs and the Medicis.

Meanwhile, there were artistic rumblings in Holland. Leading the charge was **Geertgen tot Sint Jans** (Little Gerard of the Brotherhood of St John; d. 1490), who worked in Haarlem, initiating – in a strangely naive style – an artistic vision that would come to dominate the seventeenth century. There was a tender melancholy in his work very different from the stylized paintings produced in Flanders and, most importantly, a new sensitivity to light – and lighting. **Jan Mostaert** (1475–1555) took over after Geertgen's death, developing similar themes, but the first painter to effect real changes in northern painting was **Lucas van Leyden** (1489–1533). Born in Leiden, his bright colours and narrative technique were refreshingly novel, and he introduced a new dynamism into what had become a rigidly formal treatment of devotional subjects. There was rivalry, of course. Eager to publicize Haarlem as the artistic capital of the northern Netherlands, Carel van Mander (see below) claimed Alkmaar native **Jan van Scorel** (1495–1562) as the better painter, complaining, too, of Van Leyden's dandyish ways. Certainly Van Scorel's influence should not be underestimated. Like many of his contemporaries, Van Scorel hotfooted it to Italy to view the works of the Renaissance, but in Rome his career went into overdrive when he found favour with Pope Hadrian VI, one-time bishop of Utrecht, who installed him as court painter in 1520. Van Scorel stayed in Rome for four years and when he returned to Utrecht, armed with all that papal prestige, he combined the ideas he had picked up in Italy with those underpinning Haarlem realism, thereby modifying what had previously been an independent artistic tradition once and for all. Amongst his several students, probably the most talented was **Maerten van Heemskerck** (1498–1574), who went off to Italy himself in 1532, staying there five years before returning to Haarlem.

The Golden Age

The seventeenth century begins with **Carel van Mander**, Haarlem painter, art impresario and one of the few contemporary chroniclers of the art of the Low Countries. His *Schilderboek* of 1604 put Flemish and Dutch traditions into context for the first time, and in addition specified the rules of fine painting. Examples of his own work are rare – though Haarlem's Frans Hals Museum (see p.125) weighs in with a couple – but his followers were many. Among them was **Cornelius Cornelisz van Haarlem** (1562–1638), who produced elegant renditions of biblical and mythical themes; and **Hendrik Goltzius** (1558–1616), who was a skilled engraver and an integral member of Van Mander's Haarlem academy. These painters' enthusiasm for Italian art, combined with the influence of a late revival of Gothicism, resulted in works that combined Mannerist and Classical elements. An interest in realism was also felt, and, for them, the subject became less important than the way in which it was depicted: biblical stories became merely a vehicle whereby artists could apply their skills in painting the human body, landscapes, or copious displays of food. All of this served to break religion's stranglehold on art, and make legitimate a whole range of everyday subjects for the painter.

In Holland (and this was where the north and the south finally diverged) this break with tradition was compounded by the **Reformation**: the austere Calvinism that had replaced the Catholic faith in the United (ie northern) Provinces had no use for images or symbols of devotion in its churches. Instead, painters catered to the burgeoning middle class, and no longer visited Italy to learn their craft. Indeed, the real giants of the seventeenth century – Hals, Rembrandt, Vermeer – stayed in the Netherlands all their lives. Another innovation was that painting split into more distinct categories – genre, portrait, landscape – and artists tended (with notable exceptions) to confine themselves to one field throughout their careers. So began the greatest age of Dutch art.

Historical and religious painting

The artistic influence of Renaissance Italy may have been in decline, but Italian painters still had clout with the Dutch, most notably **Caravaggio** (1571–1610), who was much admired for his new realism. Taking Caravaggio's cue, many artists – Rembrandt for one – continued to portray classical subjects, but in a way that was totally at odds with the Mannerists' stylish flights of imagination. The Utrecht artist **Abraham Bloemaert** (1564–1651), though a solid Mannerist throughout his career, encouraged these new ideas, and his students – **Gerard van Honthorst** (1590–1656), **Hendrik Terbrugghen** (1588–1629) and **Dirck van Baburen** (1590–1624) – formed the nucleus of the influential **Utrecht School**, which followed Caravaggio almost to the point of slavishness. Honthorst was perhaps the leading figure, learning his craft from Bloemaert and travelling to Rome, where he was nicknamed "Gerardo delle Notti" for his ingenious handling of light and shade. In his later paintings, however, this was to become more routine technique than inspired invention, and though a supremely competent artist, Honthorst is somewhat discredited among critics today. Terbrugghen's reputation seems to have aged rather better: he soon forgot Caravaggio and developed a more individual style, his later, lighter work having a great influence on the young Vermeer. After a jaunt to Rome, Baburen shared a studio with Terbrugghen and produced some fairly original work – work which also had some influence on Vermeer – but today he is the least studied member of the group and few of his paintings survive.

Above all others, **Rembrandt** (1606–1669) was the most original historical artist of the seventeenth century, also chipping in with religious paintings throughout his career. In the 1630s, the poet and statesman Constantijn Huygens procured for him his greatest commission – a series of five paintings of the Passion, beautifully composed and uncompromisingly realistic. Later, however, Rembrandt received fewer and fewer commissions, since his treatment of biblical and historical subjects was far less dramatic than that of his contemporaries and he ignored their smooth brushwork, preferring a rougher, darker and more disjointed style. It's significant that while the more conventional Jordaens, Honthorst and Van Everdingen were busy decorating the Huis ten Bosch near Den Haag for the Stadholder Frederick Henry, Rembrandt was having his monumental *Conspiracy of Julius Civilis* – painted for the new Amsterdam Town Hall – thrown out. The reasons for this rejection have been hotly debated, but it seems probable that Rembrandt's rendition was thought too pagan an interpretation of what was an important event in Dutch history – Julius had organized a revolt against the Romans, which had obvious resonance in a country just freed from the Habsburgs. Even worse, perhaps, Rembrandt had shown Julius to be blind in one eye, which was historically accurate but not at all what the city's burghers had in mind for a Dutch hero.

Finally, **Aert van Gelder** (1645–1727), Rembrandt's last pupil and probably the only one to concentrate on historical painting, followed the style of his master closely, producing shimmering biblical scenes well into the eighteenth century.

Genre painting

Often misunderstood, the term **genre painting** was initially applied to everything from animal paintings and still lifes through to historical works and landscapes, but later – from around the middle of the seventeenth century – came to be applied only to scenes of everyday life. Its target market was the region's burgeoning middle class, who had a penchant for non-idealized portrayals of common scenes, both with and without symbols – or subtly disguised details – making one moral point or another. One of its early practitioners was Antwerp's **Frans Snijders** (1579–1657), who took up still-life painting where Aertsen (see p.251) left off, amplifying his subject – food and drink – to even larger, more sumptuous canvases. Snijders also doubled up as a member of the Rubens art machine (see p.259), painting animals and still-life sections for the master's works. In the north, in Utrecht, Hendrik Terbrugghen and Gerard van Honthorst adapted the realism and strong chiaroscuro learned from Caravaggio to a number of tableaux of everyday life, though they were more concerned with religious works, whilst Haarlem's Frans Hals dabbled in genre too, but is better known as a portraitist. The opposite is true of one of Hal's pupils, **Adriaen Brouwer** (1605–38), whose riotous tavern scenes were well received in their day and collected by, among others, Rubens and Rembrandt. Brouwer spent only a couple of years in Haarlem under Hals before returning to his native Flanders, where he influenced the inventive **David Teniers the Younger** (1610–1690), who worked in Antwerp, and later in Brussels. Teniers' early paintings are Brouwer-like peasant scenes, although his later work is more delicate and diverse, including *kortegaardje* – guardroom scenes that show soldiers carousing. **Adriaen van Ostade** (1610–85), on the other hand, stayed in Haarlem most of his life, skilfully painting groups of peasants and tavern brawls – though his later acceptance by the establishment led him to water down the realism he had learnt from Brouwer. He was teacher to his brother **Isaak** (1621–49), who produced a large number of open-air peasant scenes, subtle combinations of genre and landscape work.

The English critic E.V. Lucas dubbed Teniers, Brouwer and Ostade "coarse and boorish" compared with **Jan Steen** (1625–79) who, along with Vermeer, is probably the most admired Dutch genre painter. You can see what he had in mind: Steen's paintings offer the same Rabelaisian peasantry in full fling, but they go their debauched ways in broad daylight, and nowhere do you see the filthy rogues in shadowy hovels favoured by Brouwer and Ostade. Steen offers more humour, too, as well as more moralizing, identifying with the hedonistic mob and reproaching them at the same time. Indeed, many of his pictures are illustrations of well-known proverbs of the time – popular epithets on the evils of drink or the transience of human existence that were supposed to teach as well as entertain.

Leiden's **Gerrit Dou** (1613–75) was one of Rembrandt's first pupils. It's difficult to detect any trace of the master's influence in his work, however, as Dou initiated a style of his own: tiny, minutely realized and beautifully finished views of a kind of ordinary life that was decidedly more genteel than Brouwer's – or even Steen's for that matter. He was admired, above all, for his painstaking attention to detail: and he would, it's said, sit in his studio for hours waiting for the dust to settle before starting work. Among his students, **Frans van Mieris** (1635–81) continued the highly finished portrayals of the Dutch bourgeoisie, as did **Gabriel Metsu** (1629–67) – perhaps Dou's most talented pupil – whose pictures often convey an overtly moral message. Another pupil of Rembrandt's, though a much later one, was **Nicholaes Maes** (1629–93), whose early works were almost entirely genre paintings, sensitively executed and again with an obvious didacticism. His later paintings show the influence of a more refined style of portrait, which he had picked up in France.

As a native of Zwolle, **Gerard ter Borch** (1619–81) found himself far from all these Leiden/Rembrandt connections; despite trips abroad to most of the artistic capitals of Europe, he remained very much a provincial painter. He depicted Holland's merchant class at play and became renowned for his curious doll-like figures and his enormous ability to capture the textures of different cloths. His domestic scenes were not unlike those of **Pieter de Hooch** (1629–after 1684), whose simple depictions of everyday life are deliberately unsentimental, and have little or no moral commentary. De Hooch's favourite trick was to paint darkened rooms with an open door leading through to a sunlit courtyard, a practice that, along with his trademark rusty red colour, makes his work easy to identify and, at its best, exquisite. That said, his later pictures reflect the encroaching decadence of the Dutch Republic: the rooms are more richly decorated, the arrangements more contrived and the subjects far less homely.

It was, however, **Jan Vermeer** (1632–75) who brought the most sophisticated methods to painting interiors, depicting the play of natural light on indoor surfaces with superlative skill – and the tranquil intimacy for which he is now famous the world over. Another recorder of the better-heeled Dutch households and, like De Hooch, without a moral tone, he is regarded (with Hals and Rembrandt) as one of the big three Dutch painters – though he was, it seems, a slow worker. As a result, only about forty paintings can be attributed to him with any certainty. Living all his life in Delft, Vermeer is perhaps the epitome of the seventeenth-century Dutch painter – rejecting the pomp and ostentation of the High Renaissance to record quietly his contemporaries at home, painting for a public that demanded no more than that – bourgeois art at its most complete.

Portraits – and Rembrandt

Predictably enough, the ruling bourgeoisie of Holland's flourishing mercantile society wanted to record and celebrate their success, and consequently portraiture was a reliable way for a young painter to make a living. **Michiel Jansz Miereveld** (1567–1641), court painter to Frederick Henry in Den Haag, was the first real portraitist of the Dutch Republic, but it wasn't long before his stiff and rather conservative figures were superseded by the more spontaneous renderings of **Frans Hals** (1585–1666). Hals is perhaps best known for his "corporation pictures" – portraits of the members of the Dutch civil guard regiments that were formed in most of the larger towns during the war with Spain, but subsequently becoming social clubs. These large group pieces demanded superlative technique, since the painter had to create a collection of individual portraits while retaining a sense of the group, and accord prominence based on the relative importance of the sitters and the size of the payment each had made. Hals was particularly good at this, using innovative lighting effects, arranging his sitters subtly, and putting all the elements together in a fluid and dynamic composition. He also painted many individual portraits, making the ability to capture fleeting and telling expressions his trademark; his pictures of children are particularly sensitive. Later in life, however, his work became darker and more akin to Rembrandt's, spurred – it's conjectured – by his penury.

Jan Cornelisz Verspronck (1597–1662) and **Bartholomeus van der Helst** (1613–70) were the other great Haarlem portraitists after Frans Hals – Verspronck recognizable by the smooth, shiny glow he always gave to his sitters' faces, Van der Helst by a competent but unadventurous style. Of the two, Van der Helst was the more popular, influencing a number of later painters and leaving Haarlem as a young man to begin a solidly successful career as portrait painter to Amsterdam's burghers.

△ Vermeer's mesmerizing *Girl in a Turban*

The reputation of **Rembrandt van Rijn** (1606–69) is still relatively recent – nineteenth-century connoisseurs preferred Gerard Dou – but he is now justly regarded as one of the greatest and most versatile painters of all time. Born in Leiden, the son of a miller, he was a boy apprentice to Jacob van Swanenburgh, a then quite important, though singularly uninventive, local artist. Rembrandt shared a studio with Jan Lievens, a promising painter and something of a rival, though now all but forgotten, before venturing forth to Amsterdam to study under the fashionable Pieter Lastman. Soon he was painting commissions for the city elite and became an accepted member of their circle. The poet and statesman Constantijn Huygens acted as his agent, pulling strings to obtain all of Rembrandt's more lucrative jobs, and in 1634 the artist married Saskia van Ulenborch, daughter of the burgomaster of Leeuwarden and quite a catch for a relatively humble artist. His self-portraits from this period show the confident face of security – on top of things and quite sure of where he's going.

Rembrandt would not always be the darling of the Amsterdam burghers, but his fall from grace was still some way off when he painted *The Night Watch*, a group portrait often – but inaccurately – associated with the artist's decline in popularity. Indeed, although Rembrandt's fluent arrangement of his subjects was totally original, there's no evidence that the military company who commissioned the painting was anything but pleased with the result. More likely culprits are the artist's later pieces, whose obscure lighting and psychological insights took the conservative Amsterdam merchants by surprise. His patrons were certainly not sufficiently enthusiastic about his work to support his taste for art collecting and his expensive house on Jodenbreestraat (see p.87), and in 1656 he was declared bankrupt. Rembrandt died thirteen years later, a broken and embittered old man – as his last self-portraits show. Throughout his career he maintained a large studio, and his influence pervaded the next generation of Dutch painters. Some – Dou and Maes – more famous for their genre work, have already been mentioned. Others turned to portraiture.

Govert Flinck (1615–60) was perhaps Rembrandt's most faithful follower, and he was, ironically enough, given the job of decorating Amsterdam's new Town Hall after his teacher had been passed over. Unluckily for him, Flinck died before he could execute his designs and Rembrandt took over, but although the latter's *Conspiracy of Julius Civilis* (see p.253) was installed in 1662, it was discarded a year later. The early work of **Ferdinand Bol** (1616–80) was so heavily influenced by Rembrandt that for centuries art historians couldn't tell the two apart, though his later paintings are readily distinguishable, blandly elegant portraits, which proved very popular with the well-heeled. At the age of 53, Bol married a wealthy widow and promptly stopped painting – perhaps because he knew how emotionally tacky his work had become. Most of the pitifully slim extant work of **Carel Fabritius** (1622–54) was portraiture, but he too died young, before he could properly realize his promise as perhaps the most gifted of all Rembrandt's students. Generally regarded as the teacher of Vermeer, he forms a link between the two masters, combining Rembrandt's technique with his own practice of painting figures against a dark background, prefiguring the lighting and colouring of the Delft painter.

Landscapes

Aside from **Pieter Bruegel the Elder** (see p.251), whose depictions of his native surroundings make him the first true Low Countries landscape painter, **Gillis van Coninxloo** (1544–1607) stands out as the earliest Dutch landscapist. He imbued his native scenery with elements of fantasy, painting the richly wooded views he had seen on his travels around Europe as backdrops to biblical scenes. In the early seventeenth century, **Hercules Seghers** (1590–1638), apprenticed to Coninxloo, carried on his mentor's style of depicting forested and mountainous landscapes, some real, others not: his work is scarce but is believed to have had considerable influence on the landscape work of Rembrandt. **Esaias van der Velde**'s (1591–1632) quaint and unpretentious scenes show the first real affinity with the Dutch countryside, but while his influence was likewise considerable, he was soon overshadowed by his pupil **Jan van Goyen** (1596–1656). A remarkable painter, who belongs to the so-called "tonal phase" of Dutch landscape painting, Van Goyen's early pictures were highly coloured and close to those of his teacher, but it didn't take him long to develop a marked touch of his own, using tones of green, brown and grey to lend everything a characteristic translucent haze. His paintings are, above all, of nature, and if he included figures it was just for the sake of scale. A long neglected artist, Van Goyen only received recognition with the arrival of the Impressionists, when his fluid and rapid brushwork was at last fully appreciated.

Another "tonal" painter, Haarlem's **Salomon van Ruisdael** (1600–70) was also directly affected by Esaias van der Velde, and his simple and atmospheric, though not terribly adventurous, landscapes were for a long time consistently confused with those of Van Goyen. More esteemed is his nephew, **Jacob van Ruysdael** (1628–82), generally considered the greatest of all Dutch landscapists, whose fastidiously observed views of quiet flatlands dominated by stormy skies were to influence European landscapists right up to the nineteenth century. Constable, certainly, acknowledged a debt to him. Ruysdael's foremost pupil was **Meindert Hobbema** (1638–1709), who followed the master faithfully, sometimes even painting the same views (his *Avenue at Middelharnis* may be familiar).

Nicholas Berchem (1620–83) and **Jan Both** (1618–52) were the "Italianizers" of Dutch landscapes. They studied in Rome and were influenced by the Frenchman Claude Lorraine, taking back to Holland rich, golden views of the world, full of steep gorges and hills, picturesque ruins and wandering shepherds. **Allart van Everdingen** (1621–75) had a similar approach, but his subject matter stemmed from travels in Norway, which, after his return to the Netherlands, he reproduced in all its mountainous glory. **Aelbert Cuyp** (1620–91), on the other hand, stayed in Dordrecht all his life, painting what was probably the favourite city skyline of Dutch landscapists. He inherited the warm tones of the Italianizers, and his pictures are always suffused with a deep, golden glow.

Of a number of specialist seventeenth-century painters who can be included here, **Paulus Potter** (1625–54) is rated as the best painter of **domestic animals**. He produced a surprisingly large number of paintings in his short life, the most reputed being his lovingly executed pictures of cows and horses. The accurate rendering of **architectural** features also became a specialized field, in which **Pieter Saenredam** (1597–1665), with his finely realized paintings of Dutch church interiors, is the most widely known exponent. **Emanuel de Witte** (1616–92) continued in the same vein, though his churches lack the spartan crispness of Saenredam's. **Gerrit Berckheyde** (1638–98) worked in Haarlem soon after, but he limited his views to the outside of buildings, producing variations on the same scenes around town. **Nautical scenes** in praise of the Dutch navy were, on the other hand, the speciality of **Willem van der Velde II** (1633–1707), whose melodramatic canvases, complete with their churning seas and chasing skies, are displayed to greatest advantage in the Nederlands Scheepvaartsmuseum in Amsterdam (see p.96).

A further thriving category of seventeenth-century painting was the **still life**, in which objects were gathered together to remind the viewer of the transience of human life and the meaninglessness of worldly pursuits. Thus, a skull would often be joined by a book, a pipe or a goblet, and some half-eaten food. Again, two Haarlem painters dominated this field: **Pieter Claesz** (1598–1660) and **Willem Heda** (1594–1680), who confined themselves almost entirely to these carefully arranged groups of objects.

Rubens and his followers

Back down to the south, in Antwerp, **Pieter Paul Rubens** (1577–1640) was easily the most important exponent of the Baroque in northern Europe. Born in Siegen, Westphalia, he was raised in Antwerp, where he entered the painters' Guild in 1598. He became court painter to the Duke of Mantua in 1600, and until 1608 travelled extensively in Italy, absorbing the art of the High Renaissance and classical architecture. By the time of his return to Antwerp in 1608 he had acquired an enormous artistic vocabulary: like his Dutch contemporaries (see p.254), the paintings of Caravaggio were to influence his work strongly. His first major success was *The Raising of the Cross*, painted in 1610 and displayed today in Antwerp cathedral. A large, dynamic work, it caused a sensation at the time, establishing Rubens' reputation and leading to a string of commissions that enabled him to set up his own studio.

The division of labour in Rubens' studio, and the talent of the artists working there (who included Anthony van Dyck and Jacob Jordaens – see below) ensured an extraordinary output of excellent work. The degree to which Rubens personally worked on a canvas would vary – and would determine its price. From the early 1620s onwards he turned his hand to a plethora of themes and subjects – religious works, portraits, tapestry designs, landscapes, mythological scenes, ceiling paintings – each of which was handled with supreme vitality and virtuosity. From his Flemish antecedents he inherited an acute sense of light, and used it not to dramatize his subjects (a technique favoured by Caravaggio and other Italian artists), but in association with colour and form. The drama in his works comes from the vigorous animation of his characters. His large-scale allegorical works, especially, are packed with heaving, writhing figures that appear to tumble out from the canvas.

The energy of Rubens' paintings was reflected in his private life. In addition to his career as an artist, he also undertook diplomatic missions to Spain and England, and used these opportunities to study the works of other artists and – as in the case of Velázquez – to meet them personally. In the 1630s gout began to hamper his activities, and from this time his painting became more domestic and meditative. Hélène Fourment, his second wife, was the subject of many portraits and served as a model for characters in his allegorical paintings, her figure epitomizing the buxom, well-rounded women found throughout his work.

Rubens' influence on the artists of the period was enormous. The huge output of his studio meant that his works were universally seen and also widely disseminated by the engravers he employed to copy his work. Chief among his followers was the portraitist **Anthony van Dyck** (1599–1641), who worked in Rubens' studio from 1618, often taking on the depiction of religious figures in his master's works that required particular sensitivity and pathos. Like Rubens, van Dyck was born in Antwerp and travelled widely in Italy, though his initial work was influenced less by the Italian artists than by Rubens himself. Eventually van Dyck developed his own distinct style and technique, establishing himself as court painter to Charles I in England, and creating portraits of a nervous elegance that would influence the genre there for the next hundred and fifty years. **Jacob Jordaens** (1593–1678) was also an Antwerp native who studied under Rubens. Although he was commissioned to complete several works left unfinished by Rubens at the time of his death, his robustly naturalistic works have an earthy – and sensuous – realism that is quite distinct in style and technique.

The eighteenth and nineteenth centuries

Accompanying Holland's economic decline was a gradual deterioration in the quality and originality of Dutch painting. The delicacy of some of the classical seventeenth-century painters was replaced by finicky still lifes and minute studies of flowers, or finely finished portraiture and religious scenes, as in the work of **Adrian van der Werff** (1659–1722). Of the era's big names, **Gerard de Lairesse** (1640–1711) spent most of his time decorating a rash of brand-new civic halls and mansions, but, like the buildings he worked on, his style and influences were French. **Jacob de Wit** (1695–1754) continued where Lairesse left off, painting burgher ceiling after ceiling in flashy style. He also benefited from a relaxation in the laws against Catholics, decorating several of their (newly legal) churches. The period's only painter of any true renown was **Cornelis Troost** (1697–1750) who, although he didn't produce anything really original, painted competent portraits and some neat, faintly satirical pieces that have since earned him the title of "The Dutch Hogarth". Cosy interiors also continued to prove popular and the Haarlem painter **Wybrand Hendriks** (1744–1831) satisfied demand with numerous proficient examples.

Johann Barthold Jongkind (1819–91) was the first important artist to emerge in the nineteenth century, painting landscapes and seascapes that were to influence Monet and the early Impressionists. He spent most of his life in France and his work was exhibited in Paris with the Barbizon painters, though he owed less to them than to Van Goyen and the seventeenth-century "tonal" artists. Jongkind's work was a logical precursor to the art of the **Hague School**. Based in and around Den Haag between 1870 and 1900, this prolific group of painters tried to re-establish a characteristically Dutch national school of painting. They produced atmospheric studies of the dunes and polders around Den Haag, nature pictures that are characterized by grey, rain-filled skies, windswept seas, and silvery, flat beaches – pictures that, for some, verge on the sentimental. **J.H. Weissenbruch** (1824–1903) was a founding member, a specialist in low, flat beach scenes dotted with stranded boats. The banker-turned-artist **H.W. Mesdag** (1831–1915) did the same but with more skill than imagination, while **Jacob Maris** (1837–99), one of three artist brothers, was perhaps the most typical with his rural and sea scenes heavily covered by grey, chasing skies. His brother **Matthijs** (1839–1917) was less predictable, ultimately tiring of his colleagues' interest in straight observation and going to London to design windows, while the youngest brother **Willem** (1844–1910) is best known for his small, unpretentious studies of nature.

Anton Mauve (1838–88) is better known, an exponent of soft, pastel land-scapes and an early teacher of Van Gogh. Profoundly influenced by the French Barbizon painters – Corot, Millet et al – he went to Hilversum in 1885 to set up his own group, which became known as the "Dutch Barbizon". **Jozef Israëls** (1826–1911) has often been likened to Millet, though it's generally agreed that he had more in common with the Impressionists, and his best pictures are his melancholy portraits and interiors. Lastly, **Johan Bosboom**'s (1817–91) church interiors may be said to sum up the romanticized nostalgia of the Hague School: shadowy and populated by figures in seventeenth-century dress, they seem to yearn for Holland's Golden Age.

Vincent van Gogh (1853–90), on the other hand, was one of the least "Dutch" of Dutch artists, and he lived out most of his relatively short painting career in France. After countless studies of peasant life in his native North Brabant – studies which culminated in the sombre *Potato Eaters* – he went to live in Paris with his art-dealer brother Theo. There, under the influence of the Impressionists, he lightened his palette, following the pointillist work of Seurat and "trying to render intense colour and not a grey harmony". Two years later he went south to Arles, the "land of blue tones and gay colours", and, struck by the brilliance of Mediterranean light, his characteristic style began to develop. A disastrous attempt to live with Gauguin, and the much-publicized episode when he cut off part of his ear and presented it to a local prostitute, led eventually to his committal in an asylum at St-Rémy. Here he produced some of his most famous, and most Expressionistic, canvases – strongly coloured and with the paint thickly, almost frantically, applied. Now one of the world's most popular – and popularized – painters, Van Gogh has his own museum in Amsterdam (see p.103).

Like Van Gogh, **Jan Toorop** (1858–1928) went through multiple artistic changes, though he did not need to travel to do so; he radically adapted his technique from a fairly conventional pointillism through a tired Expressionism to Symbolism with an Art Nouveau feel. Roughly contemporary, **George Hendrik Breitner** (1857–1923) was a better painter, and one who refined his style rather than changed it. His snapshot-like impressions of his beloved Amsterdam figure among his best work and offered a promising start to the new century.

The twentieth century

Each of the major modern art movements has had – or has – its followers in the Netherlands and each has been diluted or altered according to local taste. Of many lesser names, **Jan Sluyters** (1881–1957) stands out as the Dutch pioneer of Cubism, but this is small beer when compared with the one specifically Dutch movement – **De Stijl** (The Style). **Piet Mondriaan** (1872–1944) was De Stijl's leading figure, developing the realism he had learned from the Hague School painters – via Cubism, which he criticized for being too cowardly to depart totally from representation – into a complete abstraction of form which he called **Neo-Plasticism**. He was something of a mystic, and this was to some extent responsible for the direction that De Stijl – and his paintings – took: canvases painted with grids of lines and blocks made up of the three primary colours and white, black and grey. Mondriaan believed this freed the work of art from the vagaries of personal perception, making it possible to obtain what he called "a true vision of reality".

De Stijl took other forms too: there was a magazine of the same name, and the movement introduced new concepts into every aspect of design, from painting to interior design and architecture. But in all these media, lines were kept simple, colours bold and clear. **Theo van Doesburg** (1883–1931) was a De Stijl co-founder and major theorist. His work is similar to Mondriaan's except for the noticeable absence of thick, black borders and the diagonals that he introduced into his work, calling his paintings "contra-compositions" – which, he said, were both more dynamic and more in touch with twentieth-century life. **Bart van der Leck** (1876–1958) was the third member of the circle, identifiable by white canvases covered by seemingly randomly placed interlocking coloured triangles. Mondriaan split with De Stijl in 1925, going on to attain new artistic extremes of clarity and soberness before moving to New York in the 1940s and producing atypically exuberant works such as *Victory Boogie Woogie* – named for the artist's love of jazz.

During and after De Stijl, a number of other movements flourished, though their impact was not so great and their influence largely confined to the Netherlands. The Expressionist **Bergen School** was probably the most local-ized, its best-known exponent **Charley Toorop** (1891–1955), daughter of Jan, developing a distinctively glaring but strangely sensitive realism. **De Ploeg** (The Plough), centred in Groningen, was headed by **Jan Wiegers** (1893–1959) and influenced by Kirchner and the German Expressionists; the group's artists set out to capture the uninviting landscapes around their native town, and pro-duced violently coloured canvases that hark back to Van Gogh. Another group, known as the **Magic Realists**, surfaced in the 1930s, painting quasi-surrealis-tic scenes that, according to their leading light, **Carel Willink** (1900–83), revealed "a world stranger and more dreadful in its haughty impenetrability than the most terrifying nightmare."

Postwar Dutch art began with **CoBrA**: a loose grouping of like-minded painters from Denmark, Belgium and Holland, whose name derives from the initial letters of their respective capital cities. Their first exhibition at Amsterdam's Stedelijk Museum in 1949 provoked a huge uproar, at the centre of which was **Karel Appel** (b.1921), whose brutal Abstract Expressionist pieces, plastered with paint inches thick, were, he maintained, necessary for the era – indeed, inevitable reflections of it. "I paint like a barbarian in a barbarous age," he claimed. In the graphic arts the most famous twentieth-century Dutch figure was **Maurits Cornelis Escher** (1898–1972), whose Surrealistic illu-sions and allusions were underpinned by his fascination with mathematics.

Amsterdam galleries: a hit list

Of the galleries in **Amsterdam**, the **Rijksmuseum** (see p.98) gives the most com-plete overview of Dutch art up to the end of the nineteenth century, in particular the work of Rembrandt, Hals and the major artists of the Golden Age. The **Van Gogh Museum** (see p.103) is best for the Impressionists and, of course, Van Gogh; and for contemporary Dutch art, there's **De Appel** (see p.71). The **CoBrA Museum voor Moderne Kunst** (CoBrA Museum of Modern Art; Tues–Sun 11am–5pm; €6; ⊛www.cobra-museum.nl) is dedicated to the CoBrA art movement of the 1950s and 60s. It's located way out beyond the southern suburbs at Sandbergplein 1, in Amstelveen. To get there from Centraal Station, take tram #5 to Amstelveen bus sta-tion, Plein 1960. In addition, neighbouring **Haarlem** possesses the **Frans Hals Museum** (see p.125), which holds some of the best work of Hals, Mander and the Haarlem School.

As for today, there's as vibrant a contemporary art scene as there ever was, best exemplified in Amsterdam by the rotating exhibitions of De Appel (see p.71) and by the dozens of galleries and exhibition spaces dotted across the city. Among contemporary Dutch artists, look out for the abstract work of **Edgar Fernhout** and **Ad Dekkers**, the reliefs of **Jan Schoonhoven**, the multimedia productions of **Jan Dibbets**, the glowering realism of **Marlene Dumas**, the imprecisely coloured geometric designs of **Rob van Koningsbruggen**, the smeary Expressionism of **Toon Verhoef**, and the exuberant figures of **Rene Daniels** – to name just eight of the more important figures.

Books

M ost of the following books should be easily available in the UK, US, Australasia and Canada, though you may have a little more difficulty tracking down those few titles we mention which are currently out of print, signified o/p. Titles marked with the ⊡ symbol are especially recommended.

Travel and general

A. Burton et al *Smokers' Guide to Amsterdam.* Exactly what it says – a dope-smokers' guide to the city with no leaf unturned.

Richard Huijing (ed & trans.) *The Dedalus Book of Dutch Fantasy.* A fun and artfully selected collection of stories that contains contributions from some of the greats of Dutch literature, including a number whose work does not as yet appear in translation anywhere else.

Simon Kuper *Ajax, the Dutch, the War: Football in Europe in the Second World War.* A tad cumbersome in its execution, but some intriguing details.

Sir William Temple *Observations upon the United Provinces of The Netherlands.* An entertaining and evocative account of the country written by a seventeenth-century English diplomat.

Tim Webb *Good Beer Guide to Belgium & Holland.* Detailed and enthusiastic guide to the best bars, beers and breweries, including a strong showing for Amsterdam. A good read, and extremely well

informed to boot. Undoubtedly, the best book on its subject on the market. Published in 2002.

David Winner *Brilliant Orange – The Neurotic Genius of Dutch Football.* Great title; great cover and great idea – zeroing in on the fine Dutch footballers of the 1960s and 1970s, including super-talented Johan Cruyff, and the way they – and their style of play – reflect Dutch culture and history. The problem is that sometimes the inferences and conclusions seem too obtuse, or at least unconvincing.

⊡ **Manfred Wolf (ed)** *Amsterdam: A Traveler's Literary Companion.* Published by an independent American press, Whereabout Press, these anthologies aim to get to the heart of the modern cities they cover, and this well-chosen mixture of travel pieces, short fiction and reportage does exactly that, uncovering a low-life aspect to the city of Amsterdam that exists beyond the tourist brochures. A high-quality – and evocative – selection, and often the only chance you'll get to read some of this material in translation.

History and politics

J. C. H. Blom (ed) *History of the Low Countries.* Dutch history books are fairly thin on the round, so this heavyweight volume fills a few gaps, though it's hardly sun-lounge reading. A series of historians weigh in with their specialities, from Roman times

onwards. Taken as a whole, its forte is in picking out those cultural, political and economic themes that give the region its distinctive character.

Mike Dash *Tulipomania.* An examination of the introduction of the tulip into the Low Countries at the height of the Golden Age, and the extraordinarily inflated and speculative market in the many varieties of bulbs and flowers that ensued. There's a lot of padding and scene-setting, but it's an engaging enough read, and has nice detail on seventeenth-century Amsterdam, Leiden and Haarlem.

★ **Pieter Geyl** *The Revolt of The Netherlands 1555–1609*. Geyl presents a concise account of the Netherlands during its formative years, chronicling the uprising against the Spanish and the formation of the United Provinces. Without doubt the definitive book on the period.

Christopher Hibbert *Cities and Civilisation*. Includes a diverting chapter on Amsterdam in the age of Rembrandt. Hibbert, one of the UK's best historians, is always a pleasure to read.

★ **Carol Ann Lee** *Roses from the Earth: the Biography of Anne Frank*. Amongst a spate of recent publications trawling through and over the life of the young Jewish diarist, this is probably the best, written in a straightforward and insightful manner without sentimentality. Working the same mine is the same author's *The Hidden Life of Otto Frank* – clear, lucid and equally as interesting.

Geert Mak *Amsterdam: A Brief Life of the City*. Published in 2001, this is a readable and evocative social history of Amsterdam written by a leading Dutch journalist. It's light and accessible enough to read from cover to cover, but its index of places makes it useful to dip into as a supplement to this guide too.

★ **Geoffrey Parker** *The Dutch Revolt*. Compelling account of the struggle between the Netherlands and Spain. Quite the best thing you can read on the period. Also *The Army of Flanders and the Spanish Road 1567–1659*. The title may sound academic, but this book gives a fascinating insight into the Habsburg army which occupied the Low Countries for well over a hundred years – how it functioned, was fed and moved from Spain to the Low Countries along the so-called Spanish Road.

John Leslie Price *Culture and Society in the Dutch Republic in the 17th Century*. An accurate, intelligent account of the Golden Age.

Simon Schama *The Embarrassment of Riches: An Interpretation of Dutch Culture in the Golden Age*. Long before his reinvention on British TV, Schama had a reputation as a specialist in Dutch history and this chunky volume draws on a huge variety of archive sources. Also by Schama, *Patriots and Liberators: Revolution in the Netherlands 1780–1813* focuses on one of the less familiar periods of Dutch history and is particularly good on the Batavian Republic set up in the Netherlands under French auspices. Both are heavyweight tomes and leftists might well find Schama too reactionary by half. See also Schama's *Rembrandt's Eyes* (see p.266).

Andrew Wheatcroft *The Habsburgs*. Excellent and well-researched trawl through the family's history, from eleventh-century beginnings to its eclipse at the end of World War I. Enjoyable background reading.

Art and architecture

Svetlana Alpers *Rembrandt's Enterprise*. Intriguing 1988 study of

Rembrandt, positing the theory – in line with findings of the Leiden-based

Rembrandt Research Project – that many previously accepted Rembrandt paintings are not his at all, but merely the products of his studio. Bad news if you own one.

★ **Anthony Bailey** *A View of Delft*. Concise, startlingly well-researched book on Vermeer, complete with an accurate and well-considered exploration of his milieu.

★ **R.H. Fuchs** *Dutch Painting*. As complete an introduction to the subject – from Flemish origins to the present day – as you could wish for in just a couple of hundred pages.

R.H. Fuchs et al *Flemish and Dutch Painting (from Van Gogh, Ensor, Magritte and Mondrian to Contemporary)*. Excellent, lucid account giving an overview of the development of Flemish and Dutch painting.

Walter S. Gibson *Bosch* and *Bruegel*. Two wonderfully illustrated Thames & Hudson titles on these most famous allegorical painters. The former contains everything you wanted to know about Hieronymus Bosch, his paintings and his late fifteenth-century milieu, while the latter takes a detailed look at Pieter Bruegel the Elder's art, with nine well-argued chapters investigating its various components.

H.L.C. Jaffe *De Stijl: Visions of Utopia*. A good, informed introduction to the twentieth-century movement and its philosophical and social influences. Well illustrated too.

Melissa McQuillan *Van Gogh*. Extensive, in-depth look at Vincent's paintings, as well as his life and times. Superbly researched and illustrated.

★ **Simon Schama** *Rembrandt's Eyes*. Published in 1999, this erudite work received good reviews, but it's very long – and often very long-winded. Some judicious pruning would have helped.

Irving Stone *Lust for Life: the Life of Vincent van Gogh*. Everything you ever wanted to know about Van Gogh in a pop genius-is-pain biography.

Dirk de Vos *Rogier van der Weyden*. One of the most talented and influential of the Flemish Primitives, Weyden was the official city painter to Brussels in the middle of the fifteenth century. This 400-page volume details everything known about him and carries illustrations of all his works – but then no more than you would expect from such an expensive tome.

★ **Mariet Westerman** *The Art of the Dutch Republic 1585–1718*. This excellently written, well-illustrated and enthralling book tackles its subject thematically, from the marketing of works to an exploration of Dutch ideologies.

★ **Christopher White** *Rembrandt*. This is the most widely available – and wide-ranging – study of the painter and his work. Well illustrated, as you would expect of a Thames & Hudson publication, plus a wonderfully incisive and extremely detailed commentary. Also by White is *Peter Paul Rubens: Man and Artist* (o/p), a beautifully illustrated introduction to both Rubens' work and social milieu.

Literature

Tracey Chevalier *Girl with a Pearl Earring*. Chevalier's book is a fanciful piece of fiction, building a story around the subject of one of Vermeer's most enigmatic paintings. It's an absorbing read, if a tad too detailed and slow-moving for some tastes, and it paints a convincing picture of seventeenth-century Delft and Holland, exploring its social structures and values. Has proved a popular novel.

Anne Frank *The Diary of a Young Girl*. Lucid and moving, the most revealing thing you can read on the plight of Amsterdam's Jews during the war years.

⭐ **Nicolas Freeling** *Love in Amsterdam*; *Dwarf Kingdom*; *A City Solitary*; *Strike Out Where Not Applicable*; *A Long Silence*. Freeling writes detective novels, and his most famous creation is the rebel cop, Van der Valk. These are light, carefully crafted tales, with just the right amount of twists to make them classic cops 'n' robbers reading – and with good Amsterdam (and Dutch) locations. London-born, Freeling hasn't actually been resident in Amsterdam for years, but he still evokes Amsterdam (and Amsterdammers) as well as any writer ever has, subtly and unsentimentally using the city and its people as a vivid backdrop to his fast-moving action.

Etty Hillesum *An Interrupted Life: the Diaries and Letters of Etty Hillesum, 1941–1943*. The Germans transported Hillesum, a young Jewish woman, from her home in Amsterdam to Auschwitz, where she died. As with Anne Frank's more famous journal, penetratingly written – though on the whole much less readable.

⭐ **Arthur Japin** *The Two Hearts of Kwasi Boachi*. Inventive recreation of a true story in which the eponymous Ashanti prince was dispatched to the court of King William of the Netherlands in 1837. Kwasi and his companion Kwame were ostensibly sent to Den Haag to further their education, but there was a strong colonial subtext. Superb descriptions of Ashanti-land in its pre-colonial pomp.

Sylvie Matton *Rembrandt's Whore*. Taking its cue from Chevalier's *Girl with a Pearl Earring* (see p.266), this slim novel tries hard to conjure Rembrandt's life and times with some success. Matton certainly knows her Rembrandt onions – she worked for two years on a film of his life.

Margo Minco *The Fall*; *An Empty House*; *The Glass Bridge*; *Bitter Herbs: Vivid Memories of a Fugitive Jewish girl in Nazi-occupied Holland*. One of the best known of Amsterdam's modern writers, the prolific Margo Minco has written widely and well about the city's Jewish community, particularly during the German occupation. She herself was a Holocaust survivor, spending several years in hiding – unlike the rest of her family, who were dispatched to concentration camps where they all died. One of Minco's favourite hideaways was Kloveniersburgwal 49, which served as a safe house for various Dutch artists and later as the inspiration for *An Empty House*. Published in 1991, *Bitter Herbs* is her testament.

Deborah Moggach *Tulip Fever*. At first Deborah Moggach's novel seems no more than an attempt to build a story out of her favourite domestic Dutch interiors, genre scenes and still-life paintings. But ultimately the story is a basic one – of lust, greed, mistaken identity and tragedy. The Golden Age backdrop is well realized, but almost incidental.

Harry Mulisch *The Assault*. Set part in Haarlem, part in Amsterdam, this novel traces the story of a young boy who loses his family in a reprisal raid by the Nazis. A powerful tale, made into an excellent and effective film. Also, *The Discovery of Heaven,* a gripping yarn of adventure and happenstance, and 2002's offering, *The Procedure*, featuring a modern-day Dutch scientist investigating strange goings-on in sixteenth-century Prague.

Multatuli *Max Havelaar, or, The Coffee Auctions of the Dutch Trading Company.* Classic nineteenth-century Dutch satire of colonial life in the East Indies. Eloquent and intermittently amusing. If you have Dutch friends, they should be impressed (dumbstruck) if you have read it, especially as it's 352 pages long. For more on Multatuli, see p.62.

Cees Nooteboom *Rituals.* Cees Nooteboom is one of Holland's best-known writers. He published his first novel in 1955, but only really came to public attention after the publication of his third novel, *Rituals*, in 1980. The central theme of all his work is the phenomenon of time: *Rituals* in particular is about the passing of time and the different ways of controlling the process. Inni Wintrop, the main character, is an outsider, a well-heeled, antique-dabbling "dilettante" as he describes himself. The book is almost entirely set in Amsterdam, and although it describes the inner life of Inni himself, it also paints a strong picture of the decaying city. Bleak but absorbing. Born in Den Haag in 1933, Nooteboom lives by turn in Germany, Spain and the Netherlands.

Rudi van Dantzig *For a Lost Soldier.* Honest and convincing tale, largely autobiographical, that gives an insight into the confusion and loneliness of the approximately 50,000 Dutch children evacuated to foster families during the war. The novel's leading character is Jeroen, an 11-year-old boy from Amsterdam who is sent away to live with a family in Friesland. During the Liberation celebrations, he meets an American soldier, Walt, with whom he has a brief sexual encounter; Walt disappears a few days later. One of Holland's most famous choreographers, Van Dantzig was the artistic director of the Dutch National Ballet until 1991. This was his debut novel.

★ **Janwillem van de Wetering** *Hard Rain*; *Corpse on the Dyke*; *Outsider in Amsterdam*; *Amsterdam Cops – Collected Stories.* Off-beat detective tales set in Amsterdam and provincial Holland. Humane, quirky and humorous, Wetering's novels have inventive plots and feature unusual characters in interesting locations.

David Veronese *Jana.* A hip thriller set in the underworld of Amsterdam and London.

Jan Wolkers *Turkish Delight.* Wolkers is one of the Netherlands' best-known artists and writers, and this is one of his early novels, a close examination of the relationship between a bitter, working-class sculptor and his young, middle-class wife. A compelling work, at times misogynistic and even offensive, by a writer who seeks reaction above all. If you like it, try Wolkers' *Horrible Tango* – great title, good book.

Language

Language

LANGUAGE

Language

I t's unlikely that you'll need to speak anything other than English while you're in Amsterdam: the Dutch have a seemingly natural talent for languages, and your attempts at speaking theirs may be met with some bewilderment – though this can have as much to do with your pronunciation (Dutch is very difficult to get right) as their surprise that you're making an effort. Outside Amsterdam, people aren't quite as cosmopolitan, but even so the following Dutch words and phrases should be the most you'll need to get by. We've also included a basic food and drink glossary, though menus are nearly always multilingual and where they aren't, ask and one will almost invariably appear.

Dutch is a Germanic language – the word "Dutch" itself is a corruption of Deutsche, a label inaccurately given by English sailors in the seventeenth century. Though the Dutch are at pains to stress the differences between the two languages, if you know any German you'll spot many similarities. As for **phrasebooks**, the *Rough Guide's Dutch Dictionary and Phrasebook* has a perfectly adequate dictionary section and a menu reader; it also provides a useful introduction to grammar and pronunciation.

Pronunciation

Dutch is pronounced much the same as English. However, there are a few Dutch sounds that don't exist in English, which can be difficult to pronounce without practice.

Consonants

Double-consonant combinations generally keep their separate sounds in Dutch – **kn**, for example, is never like the English "knight". Note also the following consonants and consonant combinations:

v like the English f in **f**ar

w like the v in **v**at

j like the initial sound of **y**ellow

ch and **g** are considerably harder than in English, enunciated much further back in the throat; in Antwerp at least, where the pronunciation is particularly coarse, there's no real English equivalent. They become softer the further south you go, where they're more like the Scottish lo**ch**.

ng is as in bri**ng**

nj as in o**ni**on

Vowels and diphthongs

Doubling the letter lengthens the vowel sound.

a is like the English **a**pple
aa like c**a**rt
e like l**e**t
ee like l**a**te
o as in p**o**p
oo in p**o**pe
u is like the French t**u** if preceded by a consonant; it's like w**oo**d if followed by a consonant
uu the French t**u**
au and **ou** like h**ow**
ei and **ij** as in f**i**ne, though this varies strongly from region to region; sometimes it can sound more like l**a**ne
oe as in s**oo**n
eu is like the diphthong in the French l**eu**r
ui is the hardest Dutch diphthong of all, pronounced like h**ow** but much further forward in the mouth, with lips pursed (as if to say "oo")

Words and phrases

Basics and greetings

yes	ja	good evening	goedenavond
no	nee	goodbye	tot ziens
Please	alstublieft	see you later	tot straks
(no) thank you	(nee) dank u or bedankt	do you speak English?	spreekt u Engels?
		I don't understand	Ik begrijp het niet
hello	hallo or dag	women/men	vrouwen/mannen
good morning	goedemorgen	children	kinderen
good afternoon	goedemiddag	push/pull	duwen/trekken

Getting around

how do I get to... ?	hoe kom ik in... ?	left/right	links/rechts
where is... ?	waar is... ?	straight ahead	rechtuit gaan
how far is it to... ?	hoe ver is het naar... ?	platform	spoor or perron
when?	wanneer?	ticket office	loket
far/near	ver/dichtbij	here/there	hier/daar

Ordering, shopping and money

I want...	Ik wil...	cash desk	kassa
I don't want...	Ik wil niet... (+verb)	good/bad	goed/slecht
	Ik wil geen... (+noun)	big/small	groot/klein
how much is... ?	wat kost... ?	new/old	nieuw/oud
post office	postkantoor	cheap/expensive	goedkoop/duur
stamp(s)	postzegel(s)	hot/cold	heet or warm/koud
money exchange	geldwisselkantoor	with/without	met/zonder

Useful cycling terms

tyre	band	pedal	trapper
puncture	lek	pump	pomp
brake	rem	handlebars	stuur
chain	ketting	broken	kapot
wheel	wiel		

Signs and abbreviations

A.U.B.	*Alstublieft*: please (also shown as S.V.P., from French)	K	*kelder*: basement
		let op!	attention!
BG	*Begane grond*: ground floor	heren/dames	men's/women's toilets
		open	open
BTW	*Belasting Toegevoegde Waarde*: VAT	T/M	*Tot en met*: up to and including
		toegang	entrance
geen toegang	no entry	uitgang	exit
gesloten	closed	Z.O.Z.	please turn over (page, leaflet etc)
ingang	entrance		

Days of the week

Monday	Maandag	today	vandaag
Tuesday	Dinsdag	tomorrow	morgen
Wednesday	Woensdag	tomorrow morning	morgenochtend
Thursday	Donderdag	year	jaar
Friday	Vrijdag	month	maand
Saturday	Zaterdag	week	week
Sunday	Zondag	day	dag
yesterday	gisteren		

Months of the year

January	januari	July	juli
February	februari	August	augustus
March	maart	September	september
April	april	October	oktober
May	mei	November	november
June	juni	December	december

Time

hour	uur	it's...	het is...
minute	minuut	3.00	drie uur
what time is it?	hoe laat is het?	3.05	vijf over drie

273

3.10	tien over drie	3.45	kwart voor vier
3.15	kwart over drie	3.50	tien voor vier
3.20	tien voor half vier	3.55	vijf voor vier
3.25	vijf voor half vier	8am	acht uur 's ochtends
3.30	half vier	1pm	een uur 's middags
3.35	vijf over half vier	8pm	acht uur 's avonds
3.40	tien over half vier	1am	een uur 's nachts

Numbers

When saying a number, the Dutch generally transpose the last two digits: for example, €3.25 is *drie euros vijf en twintig*.

0	nul	10	tien	20	twintig	80	tachtig
1	een	11	elf	21	een en twintig	90	negentig
2	twee	12	twaalf			100	honderd
3	drie	13	dertien	22	twee en twintig	101	honderd een
4	vier	14	veertien			200	twee honderd
5	vijf	15	vijftien	30	dertig	201	twee honderd een
6	zes	16	zestien	40	veertig		
7	zeven	17	zeventien	50	vijftig	500	vijf honderd
8	acht	18	achttien	60	zestig	1000	duizend
9	negen	19	negentien	70	zeventig		

Food and drink terms

Basics

boter	butter	pindakaas	peanut butter
boterham/broodje	sandwich/roll	sla/salade	salad
brood	bread	smeerkaas	cheese spread
dranken	drinks	stokbrood	French bread
eieren	eggs	suiker	sugar
gerst	barley	vis	fish
groenten	vegetables	vlees	meat
honing	honey	voorgerechten	starters/hors d'oeuvres
hoofdgerechten	main courses		
kaas	cheese	vruchten	fruit
koud	cold	warm	hot
nagerechten	desserts	zout	salt
peper	pepper		

Starters and snacks

erwtensoep/snert	thick pea soup with bacon or sausage	huzarensalade	potato salad with pickles

Kkoffietafel	a light midday meal of cold meats, cheese, bread and perhaps soup	patates/frites	chips/French fries
		soep	soup
		uitsmijter	ham or cheese with eggs on bread

Meat and poultry

biefstuk (hollandse)	steak	karbonade	chop
biefstuk (duitse)	hamburger	kip	chicken
eend	duck	kroket	spiced veal or beef in hash, coated in breadcrumbs
fricandeau	roast pork		
fricandel	frankfurter-like sausage		
		lamsvlees	lamb
gehakt	minced meat	lever	liver
ham	ham	rookvlees	smoked beef
kalfsvlees	veal	spek	bacon
kalkoen	turkey	worst	sausages

Fish

forel	trout	oesters	oysters
garnalen	prawns	paling	eel
haring	herring	schelvis	haddock
haringsalade	herring salad	schol	plaice
kabeljauw	cod	tong	sole
makreel	mackerel	zalm	salmon
mosselen	mussels		

Vegetables

aardappelen	potatoes	rijst	rice
bloemkool	cauliflower	sla	salad, lettuce
bonen	beans	stampot andijvie	mashed potato and endive
champignons	mushrooms		
erwten	peas	stampot boerenkool	mashed potato and cabbage
hutspot	mashed potatoes and carrots		
		uien	onions
knoflook	garlic	wortelen	carrots
komkommer	cucumber	zuurkool	sauerkraut
prei	leek		

Cooking terms

belegd	filled or topped, as in *belegde broodjes* – bread rolls topped with cheese, etc	doorbakken	well-done
		gebakken	fried/baked
		gebraden	roasted

gegrild	grilled
gekookt	boiled
geraspt	grated
gerookt	smoked
gestoofd	stewed

half doorbakken	medium-done
hollandse saus	hollandaise (a milk and egg sauce)
rood	rare

Indonesian dishes and terms

ajam	chicken
bami	noodles with meat/chicken and vegetables
daging	beef
gado gado	vegetables in peanut sauce
goreng	fried
ikan	fish
katjang	peanut
kroepoek	prawn crackers
loempia	spring rolls
nasi	rice
nasi goreng	fried rice with meat/chicken and vegetables

nasi rames	rijsttafel on a single plate
pedis	hot and spicy
pisang	banana
rijsttafel	collection of different spicy dishes served with plain rice
sambal	hot, chilli-based sauce
satesaus	peanut sauce to accompany meat grilled on skewers
seroendeng	spicy shredded and fried coconut
tauge	bean sprouts

Sweets and desserts

appelgebak	apple tart or cake
drop	Dutch liquorice, available in *zoet* (sweet) or *zout* (salted) varieties – the latter an acquired taste
gebak	pastry
IJs	ice cream
koekjes	biscuits
oliebollen	doughnuts

pannekoeken	pancakes
pepernoten	Dutch ginger nuts
poffertjes	small pancakes, fritters
(slag)room	(whipped) cream
speculaas	spice and honey-flavoured biscuit
stroopwafels	waffles
taai-taai	Dutch honey cake
vla	custard

Fruits and nuts

aardbei	strawberry
amandel	almond
appel	apple
appelmoes	apple purée
citroen	lemon
druiven	grape
framboos	raspberry

hazelnoot	hazelnut
kers	cherry
kokosnoot	coconut
peer	pear
perzik	peach
pinda	peanut
pruim	plum/prune

Drinks

anijsmelk	anis`	melk	milk
appelsap	apple juice	met ijs	with ice
bessenjenever	blackcurrant gin	met slagroom	with whipped cream
chocomel	chocolate milk	pils	Dutch beer
citroenjenever	lemon gin	proost!	cheers!
droog	dry	sinaasappelsap	orange juice
frisdranken	soft drinks	thee	tea
jenever	Dutch gin	tomatensap	tomato juice
karnemelk	buttermilk	vruchtensap	fruit juice
koffie	coffee	wijn	wine
koffie verkeerd	coffee with warm milk	(wit/rood/rosé)	(white/red/rosé)
kopstoot	beer with a jenever chaser	vieux	Dutch brandy
		zoet	sweet

A glossary of Dutch words and terms

abdij abbey

amsterdammertje phallic-shaped objects placed alongside Amsterdam streets to keep drivers off pavements and out of the canals

beiaard carillon chimes

belfort belfry

begijnhof similar to a *hofje* but occupied by Catholic women (*begijns*) who lead semi-religious lives without taking full vows – also see box on p.57.

beurs stock exchange

botermarkt butter market

brug bridge

burgher member of the upper or mercantile classes of a town, usually with certain civic powers

fietspad bicycle path

gasthuis hospice for the sick or infirm

gemeente municipal, as in *Gemeentehuis* (town hall)

gerechtshof law courts

gevel gable

gezellig a hard term to translate – something like "cosy", "comfortable" and "inviting" in one – which is often said to lie at the heart of the Dutch psyche. A long, relaxed meal in a favourite restaurant with friends is *gezellig*; grabbing a quick snack is not. The best brown cafés ooze *gezelligheid*; Kalverstraat on a Saturday afternoon definitely doesn't

gilde guild

gracht canal

groentenmarkt vegetable market

grote kerk literally "big church" – the main church of a town or village

hal hall

hijsbalk pulley beam, often decorated, fixed to the top of a gable to lift goods, furniture etc – essential in canal houses whose staircases were narrow and steep, *hijsbalken* are still very much in use today

hof courtyard

hofje almshouse, usually for elderly women who could look after themselves but needed small charities such as food and fuel; usually a number of buildings centred around a small, enclosed courtyard

huis house

jeugdherberg youth hostel

kasteel castle

kerk church

koning king

koningin queen

koninklijk royal

kunst art

kursaal casino

lakenhal cloth hall – the building in medieval weaving towns where cloth would be weighed, graded and sold

luchthaven airport

markt central town square and the heart of most Dutch communities, normally still the site of weekly markets

mokum A Yiddish word meaning "city", originally used by the Jewish community to indicate Amsterdam; now in general usage as a nickname for the city

molen windmill

nederland the Netherlands

nederlands Dutch

noord north

ommegang procession

oost east

paleis palace

plein square or open space.

polder an area of land reclaimed from the sea

poort gate

raadhuis town hall

randstad literally "rim-town", this refers to the urban conurbation that makes up much of North and South Holland, stretching from Amsterdam in the north down to Rotterdam and Dordrecht in the south

rijk state

schepenzaal alderman's hall

schone kunsten fine arts

schouwburg theatre

sierkunst decorative arts

spionnetje small mirror on a canal house enabling the occupant to see who is at the door without descending the stairs.

spoor train station platform

stadhuis the most common word for a town hall

stedelijk civic, municipal

steeg alley

steen stone

stichting institute or foundation

straat street

toren tower

tuin garden

vleeshuis meat market

volkskunde folklore

VVV Dutch tourist information office

waag old public weighing-house, a common feature of most towns

weg way

west west

wijk district (of a city)

zuid south

An art and architecture glossary

ambulatory Covered passage around the outer edge of the choir of a church.

apse Semicircular protrusion (usually) at the east end of a church.

Art Deco Geometrical style of art and architecture popular in the 1930s.

Art Nouveau Style of art, architecture and design based on highly stylized vegetal forms. Especially popular in the early part of the twentieth century.

balustrade An ornamental rail, running, almost invariably, along the top of a building.

Baroque The art and architecture of the Counter-Reformation, dating from around 1600 onwards. Distinguished by extreme ornateness, exuberance and by the complex but harmonious spatial arrangement of interiors.

carillon A set of tuned church bells, either operated by an automatic mechanism or played by a keyboard.

caryatid A sculptured (female) figure used as a column.

chancel The eastern part of a church, often separated from the nave by a screen (see "rood screen" opposite). Contains the choir and ambulatory.

Classical Architectural style incorporating Greek and Roman elements – pillars, domes, colonnades, etc – at its height in the seventeenth century and revived, as Neoclassical, in the nineteenth century.

clerestory Upper storey of a church, incorporating the windows.

diptych Carved or painted work on two panels. Often used as an altarpiece – both static and, more occasionally, portable.

Expressionism Artistic style popular at the beginning of the twentieth century, characterized by the exaggeration of shape or colour; often accompanied by the extensive use of symbolism.

Flamboyant Florid form of Gothic.

fresco Wall painting – durable through application to wet plaster.

gable The triangular upper portion of a wall – decorative or supporting a roof – which is a feature of many Amsterdam canal houses. Initially fairly simple, they became more ostentatious in the late seventeenth century, before turning to a more restrained classicism in the eighteenth and nineteenth centuries.

genre painting In the seventeenth century the term "genre painting" applied to everything from animal paintings and still lifes through to historical works and landscapes. In the eighteenth century the term came only to be applied to scenes of everyday life.

Gothic Architectural style of the thirteenth to sixteenth centuries, characterized by pointed arches, rib vaulting, flying buttresses and a general emphasis on verticality.

grisaille A technique of monochrome painting in shades of grey.

misericord Ledge on choir stall on which occupant can be supported while standing; often carved with secular subjects (bottoms were not thought worthy of religious ones).

nave Main body of a church.

Neoclassical A style of classical architecture revived in the nineteenth century, popular in the Low Countries during and after French rule in the early nineteenth century.

Neo-Gothic Revived Gothic style of architecture popular between the late eighteenth and nineteenth centuries.

pediment Feature of a gable, usually triangular and often sporting a relief.

pilaster A shallow rectangular column projecting, but only slightly, from a wall.

Renaissance The period of European history marking the end of the medieval period and the rise of the modern world. Defined, amongst many criteria, by an increase in classical scholarship, geographical discovery, the rise of secular values and the growth of individualism. Began in Italy in the fourteenth century. Also the art and architecture of the period.

retable Altarpiece.

Rococo Highly florid, light and graceful eighteenth-century style of architecture, painting and interior design, forming the last phase of Baroque.

Romanesque Early medieval architecture distinguished by squat forms, rounded arches and naive sculpture.

rood screen Decorative screen separating the nave from the chancel. A rood loft is the gallery (or space) on top of it.

stucco Marble-based plaster used to embellish ceilings, etc.

transept Arms of a cross-shaped church, placed at ninety degrees to nave and chancel.

triptych Carved or painted work on three panels. Often used as an altarpiece.

tympanum Sculpted, usually recessed, panel above a door.

vault An arched ceiling or roof.

Index

and small print

Index

Map entries are in colour

Z

INDEX

Twenty Years of Rough Guides

In the summer of 1981, Mark Ellingham, Rough Guides' founder, knocked out the first guide on a typewriter, with a group of friends. Mark had been travelling in Greece after university, and couldn't find a guidebook that really answered his needs.There were heavyweight cultural guides on the one hand – good on museums and classical sites but not on beaches and tavernas – and on the other hand student manuals that were so caught up with how to save money that they lost sight of the country's significance beyond its role as a place for a cool vacation. None of the guides began to address Greece as a country, with its natural and human environment, its politics and its contemporary life.

Having no urgent reason to return home, Mark decided to write his own guide. It was a guide to Greece that tried to combine some erudition and insight with a thoroughly practical approach to travellers' needs. Scrupulously researched listings of places to stay, eat and drink were matched by careful attention to detail on everything from Homer to Greek music, from classical sites to national parks and from nude beaches to monasteries. Back in London, Mark and his friends got their Rough Guide accepted by a farsighted commissioning editor at the publisher Routledge and it came out in 1982.

The Rough Guide to Greece was a student scheme that became a publishing phenomenon. The immediate success of the book – shortlisted for the Thomas Cook award – spawned a series that rapidly covered dozens of countries. The Rough Guides found a ready market among backpackers and budget travellers, but soon acquired a much broader readership that included older and less impecunious visitors. Readers relished the guides' wit and inquisitiveness as much as the enthusiastic, critical approach that acknowledges everyone wants value for money – but not at any price.

Rough Guides soon began supplementing the "rougher" information – the hostel and low-budget listings – with the kind of detail that independent-minded travellers on any budget might expect. These days, the guides – distributed worldwide by the Penguin group – include recommendations spanning the range from shoestring to luxury, and cover more than 200 destinations around the globe. Our growing team of authors, many of whom come to Rough Guides initially as outstandingly good letter-writers telling us about their travels, are spread all over the world, particularly in Europe, the USA and Australia. As well as the travel guides, Rough Guides publishes a series of dictionary phrasebooks covering two dozen major languages, an acclaimed series of music guides running the gamut from Classical to World Music, a series of music CDs in association with World Music Network, and a range of reference books on topics as diverse as the Internet, Pregnancy and Unexplained Phenomena. Visit **www.roughguides.com** to see what's cooking.

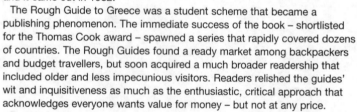

Rough Guide credits

Text editor: Jo Mead
Managing director: Kevin Fitzgerald
Series editor: Mark Ellingham
Editorial: Martin Dunford, Jonathan Buckley, Kate Berens, Ann-Marie Shaw, Helena Smith, Olivia Swift, Ruth Blackmore, Geoff Howard, Claire Saunders, Gavin Thomas, Alexander Mark Rogers, Polly Thomas, Joe Staines, Richard Lim, Duncan Clark, Peter Buckley, Lucy Ratcliffe, Clifton Wilkinson, Alison Murchie, Matthew Teller, Andrew Dickson, Fran Sandham, Sally Schafer, Matthew Milton, Karoline Densley (UK); Andrew Rosenberg, Yuki Takagaki, Richard Koss, Hunter Slaton (US)
Design & Layout: Link Hall, Helen Prior, Julia Bovis, Katie Pringle, Rachel Holmes, Andy Turner, Dan May, Tanya Hall, John McKay, Sophie Hewat (UK); Madhulita Mohapatra,

Umesh Aggarwal, Sunil Sharma (India)
Cartography: Maxine Repath, Ed Wright, Katie Lloyd-Jones (UK); Manish Chandra, Rajesh Chhibber, Jai Prakash Mishra (India)
Cover art direction: Louise Boulton
Picture research: Sharon Martins, Mark Thomas
Online: Kelly Martinez, Anja Mutic-Blessing, Jennifer Gold, Audra Epstein, Suzanne Welles, Cree Lawson (US); Manik Chauhan, Amarjyoti Dutta, Narender Kumar (India)
Finance: Gary Singh
Marketing & Publicity: Richard Trillo, Niki Smith, David Wearn, Chloë Roberts, Demelza Dallow, Claire Southern (UK); Geoff Colquitt, David Wechsler, Megan Kennedy (US)
Administration: Julie Sanderson
RG India: Punita Singh

Publishing information

This 7th edition published August 2003 by **Rough Guides Ltd**,
80 Strand, London WC2R 0RL.
345 Hudson St, 4th Floor,
New York, NY 10014, USA.
Distributed by the Penguin Group
Penguin Books Ltd,
80 Strand, London WC2R 0RL
Penguin Putnam, Inc.
375 Hudson Street, NY 10014, USA
Penguin Books Australia Ltd,
487 Maroondah Highway, PO Box 257,
Ringwood, Victoria 3134, Australia
Penguin Books Canada Ltd,
10 Alcorn Avenue, Toronto, Ontario,
Canada M4V 1E4
Penguin Books (NZ) Ltd,
182–190 Wairau Road, Auckland 10,
New Zealand
Typeset in Bembo and Helvetica to an original design by Henry Iles.
Printed in Italy by LegoPrint S.p.A

336pp includes index
A catalogue record for this book is available from the British Library

ISBN 1-85828-898-3

The publishers and authors have done their best to ensure the accuracy and currency of all the information in **The Rough Guide to Amsterdam**, however, they can accept no responsibility for any loss, injury, or inconvenience sustained by any traveller as a result of information or advice contained in the guide.

1   3   5   7   9   8   6   4   2

SMALL PRINT

Help us update

We've gone to a lot of effort to ensure that the 7th edition of **The Rough Guide to Amsterdam** is accurate and up-to-date. However, things change – places get "discovered", opening hours are notoriously fickle, restaurants and rooms raise prices or lower standards. If you feel we've got it wrong or left something out, we'd like to know, and if you can remember the address, the price, the time, the phone number, so much the better.

We'll credit all contributions, and send a copy of the next edition (or any other Rough

Guide if you prefer) for the best letters. Everyone who writes to us and isn't already a subscriber will receive a copy of our full-colour thrice-yearly newsletter. Please mark letters: **"Rough Guide Amsterdam Update"** and send to: Rough Guides, 80 Strand, London WC2R 0RL, or Rough Guides, 4th Floor, 345 Hudson St, New York, NY 10014. Or send an email to **mail@roughguides.com**
  Have your questions answered and tell others about your trip at
www.roughguides.atinfopop.com

Acknowledgements

Phil would like to extend a special thanks to Els Wamsteeker of the Amsterdam Tourist Board, and to Jo Mead, his efficient and well-organized editor. Thanks also to Stratigraphics for the maps, Dan May for typesetting, Joe Mee for picture research, Louise Boulton for the jacket and Jan Wiltshire for proofreading.

Martin would like to thank Andrew, Vanessa, Marianne and Mathilda – and of course Caroline.

Readers' letters

Thanks to all the following for their letters and emails:

Tim Adams, Joachim Allgaier, Birgit Arkesteijn, A.C. Berridge, Sian Beusch, Victor Blease, Christel de Boer, David Bradford, Adrian Brown, Craig Bryant, Andy Coates, Alan & Anita Cohen, John Connolly, Adam Cook, Maire Corbett, Kelly Cross, Paul Croy, Steve Doughtery, Peter Dudley, Paul Duggan, Peter Ellis, Bill Fitton, Colin Francis, John Gordon, Carol Hakins, Steven Goldberg, Patricia Griffin, Caroline Harmer, R. E. Havard, Yvonne Jeanneret, Tushar Jiwarajka, Alan Jolly, Peter de Koning, Joep Koperdraat, Jan Lameer, Pieter van Litsenburg, Wendy Lloyd, Reinhard Maarleveld, Margot McCarthy, David L. McDonagh, Constance Messer, Abby Miller, P. Moffat, Ronald Moor, Colm Murphy, Janey Napier, Judith Orford, Jill Pearson, Valentina Pennazio, Elizabeth Plummer, Peter da Real, Nick Reeves, Eleanor Renwick, Chris Roberts, Naomi Robinson, G. Rosebery, Amy Ryan, Sumitra Sankar, Karin Selter, Ela Serdaroglu, Johanna Sleeswijk, Phyllis Snyder, Jorge Solis, Douglas Smith, Keith Spanner, Dave Sutton, K Tan, Kiran Thomas, Charles Wass, David Wilson, Andrew White, David Wilson, J. Wood, Alison Wright, James Wright.

SMALL PRINT

Photo credits

Cover credits

Main front cover photo Canal houses © Robert Harding

Small front top picture Clogs © Louise Boulton

Small front lower picture Keizersgracht © Robert Harding

Back top picture © Robert Harding

Back lower picture Montelbaanstoren © Robert Harding

Introduction

Street performer at Centraal Station © Richard T. Nowitz/Corbis

Regulierbreestraat, lit up at night © Ronald Badkin/Travel Ink

Bicycle in a rack beside Centraal Station © Ian Cumming/Axiom

Illuminated bridges, Amsterdam © Netherlands Tourism

Tulip fields © Abbie Enock/Travel Ink

Row of gabled houses © A. Cassidy

Bunched tulips in an Amsterdam flower market © Annebicque Bernard/Corbis Sygma

Canal Museumplein, café, bicycles © Angela Hampton/Travel Ink

Magere Brugge with boat in foreground © C. Bowman/Axiom

Frozen canals, Keizersgracht © A. Cassidy

Things not to miss

Trams at night © Dominic Beddow

The foyer of the Tusschinski Theatre © Netherlands Tourism

Windmill at Haarlem © Dominic Beddow

Albert Cuyp Market © Dominic Beddow

Beginhof © A. Cassidy

Amsterdam's flea & antique markets © Abbie Enock/Travel Ink

The Golden Bend © Dominic Beddow

Queen's Day © Netherlands Tourism

Houseboats, Browersgracht © A. Cassidy

Dinner at the *Speciaal*, one of Amsterdam's

many Indonesian restaurants © Adam Woolfitt/Corbis

Self portrait by Vincent van Gogh © Archivo Iconografico, S.A./Corbis

Museum Amstelkring © Richard T. Nowitz/Corbis

Junk/Bric a brac shop "t'Winkeltje in the Jordaan district" © Barry Stacey/Travel Ink

De Wilderman "Brown Café" © Abbie Enock/Travel Ink

Patron at the Rijksmuseum © Adam Woolfitt/Corbis

Inside *Kadinsky* coffee shop © Ian Cumming/Axiom

Sitting-room at the Van Loon Museum © Christian Sarramon/Corbis

Vondelpark in the sunshine © A. Cassidy

Portuguese Synagogue © Dominic Beddow

Dutch gin nottles © A. Cassidy

Rembrandt House © Dominic Beddow

The Westerkerk Bell Tower and Canal © Jean-Pierre Lescourret/Corbis

Anne Frank House © Netherlands Tourism

Black and white

Condom shop, Condomerie Het Gulden Vlies an Warmosstraat © Abbie Enock/Travel Ink (p.50)

Bicycles on bridge on Herengracht canal © Abbie Enock/Travel Ink (p.66)

Cafés and bars in the Jordaan district © A. Cassidy (p.79)

Scheepvart Museum, in the Old Jewish Quarter © Dominic Beddow (p.93)

Exterior of the Rijksmuseum © Netherlands Tourism (p.104)

Windmills and boats on the Zaan at Zaanse Schans © Ronald Badkin/Travel Ink (p.124)

Restaurant terrace © Netherlands Tourism (p.160)

Old-fashioned grocery shop counter © Christian Sarramon/Corbis (p.200)

Girl in a Turban by Jan Vermeer © Francis G. Mayer/Corbis (p.256)

SMALL PRINT

Rough Guides publishes new books every month

Rough Guides music, reference & CDs

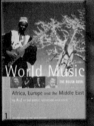

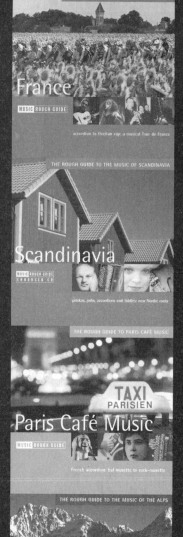

Amsterdam from £25*

Dam *that's good!*

ndon - Amsterdam

pool Street   **Centraal Station**

ny other Dutch station by train and fast ferry from **£25*** single

, sail & stay from **£117***

rail & sail **08704 00 67 60**

rail, sail & stay **0870 777 9195** quote RG1

www.amsterdamexpress.co.uk
ee your travel agent

Amsterdam Express

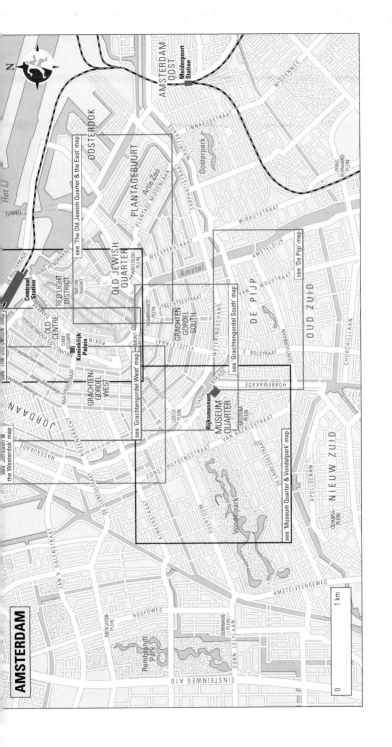

AMSTERDAM

N

Het IJ

TUNNEL

DE RUITERKADE

PRINS HENDRIKKADE

Centraal
Station

JORDAAN

see Jordaan &
the Westerdok map

NASSAUKADE

OLD
CENTRE

RED LIGHT
DISTRICT

NIEUW
MARKT

Koninklijk
Paleis

DAM
SQUARE

OLD JEWISH
QUARTER

WATERLOO-
PLEIN

OOSTERDOK

PLANTAGEBUURT

Artis Zoo

PLANTAGE MIDDENLAAN

see 'The Old Jewish Quarter & the East' map

LINNAEUSSTRAAT

AMSTERDAM
OOST

Muiderpoort
Station

MIDDENWEG

Oosterpark

SARPHATISTRAAT

WEESPERSTRAAT

Amstel

WIBAUTSTRAAT

PRINS
BERNHARD-
PLEIN

GRACHTEN-
GORDEL
WEST

ROKIN

RAADHUISSTRAAT

GRACHTEN
GORDEL
SOUTH

REMBRANDT-
PLEIN

UTRECHTSESTRAAT

VIJZELSTRAAT

MINT-
PLEIN

see 'Grachtengordel West' map

LEIDSE-
PLEIN

ROZENGRACHT

DE CLERCQSTRAAT

WETERINGSCHANS

STADHOUDERSKADE

HOBBEMAKADE

Rijksmuseum

MUSEUM
QUARTER

MUSEUM-
PLEIN

VAN BAERLESTRAAT

see 'Grachtengordel South map

CEINTUURBAAN

F. BOLSTRAAT

VAN WOUSTRAAT

AMSTELDIJK

DE PIJP

see 'De Pijp map

OUD ZUID

CHURCHILLLAAN

see 'Museum Quarter & Vondelpark' map

CONST HUYGENSSTRAAT

DE LAIRESSESTRAAT

Vondelpark

OVERTOOM

KINKERSTRAAT

JAN V GALENSTRAAT

MERCATOR-
PLEIN

Rembrandt
Park

HOOFDWEG

EINSTEINWEG A10

SURINAME-
PLEIN

CORN. LELYLAAN

NIEUW ZUID

APOLLOLAAN

OLYMPIA-
PLEIN

AMSTELVEENSEWEG

0   1 km

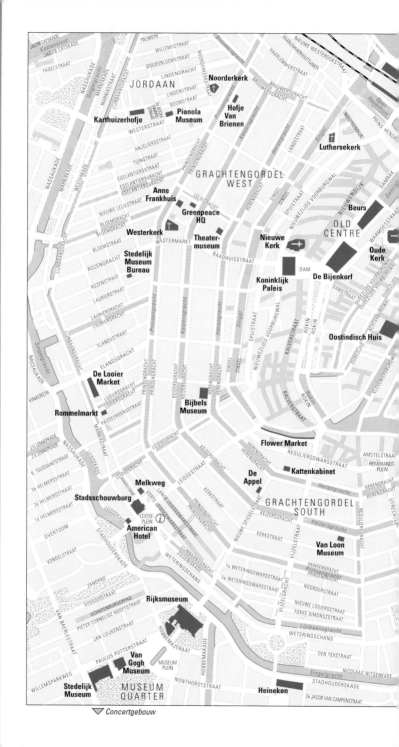

▽ Concertgebouw

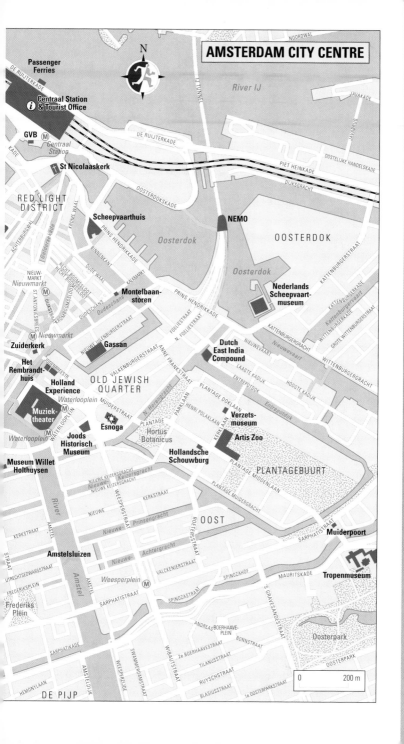

AMSTERDAM CITY CENTRE

N

NOORDWAL

River IJ

Passenger
Ferries

DE RUIJTERKADE

Centraal Station
i & Tourist Office

JAVAKADE

JAVABRUG

GVB Ⓜ
*Centraal
Station*

DE RUIJTERKADE

DOSTELIJKE HANDELSKADE

St Nicolaaskerk

OOSTERDOKSKADE

PIET HEINKADE

DIJKSGRACHT

RED LIGHT
DISTRICT

Scheepvaarthuis

NEMO

OOSTERDOK

PRINS HENDRIKKADE

Oosterdok

KATTENBURGERSTRAAT

NIEUW-
MARKT
Nieuwmarkt

Oosterdok

Montelbaan-
storen

PRINS HENDRIKKADE

Nederlands
Scheepvaart-
museum

KATTENBURGERKADE

KATTENBURGERGRACHT

ST ANTONIESBREE

Ⓜ *Nieuwmarkt*

FOELIESTRAAT

N. FOELIESTRAAT

KATTENBURGERGRACHT

Nieuwevaart

GROTE WITTENBURGERSTRAAT

Zuiderkerk

Gassan

NIEUWEVAART

WITTENBURGERGRACHT

Dutch
East India
Compound

Het
Rembrandt-
huis

OLD JEWISH
QUARTER

Holland
Experience

LAAGTE KADIJK

PLANTAGE DOKLAAN

ENTREPOTDOK

HOOGTE KADIJK

Waterlooplein

MUIDERSTRAAT

Verzets-
museum

Muziek-
theater

Ⓜ

Esnoga

PLANTAGE

Hortus
Botanicus

Artis Zoo

Waterlooplein

Ⓜ

Joods
Historisch
Museum

Hollandsche
Schouwburg

PLANTAGE MIDDENLAAN

PLANTAGEBUURT

Museum Willet
Holthuysen

NIEUWE KEIZERSGRACHT

Nieuwe   Keizersgracht

NIEUWE KEIZERSGRACHT

KERKSTRAAT

River

NIEUWE

Nieuwe   Prinsengracht

OOST

KERKSTRAAT

Amstel

Nieuwe   Achtergracht

ROETERSSTRAAT

SARPHATISTRAAT

Muiderpoort

STRAAT

Amstelsluizen

Amstel

VALCKENIERSTRAAT

MAURITSKADE

Tropenmuseum

UTRECHTSEDWARSSTRAAT

Weesperplein Ⓜ

SARPHATISTRAAT

SPINOZAHOF

FREDERIKSPLEIN

SPINOZASTRAAT

'S GRAVESANDESTRAAT

Frederiks
Plein

ANDREAS BOERHAAVE-
PLEIN

BONNSTRAAT

Oosterpark

SARPHATIKADE

2e BOERHAAVESTRAAT

TILANUSSTRAAT

AMSTELDIJK

WIBAUTSTRAAT

RUYSCHSTRAAT

OOSTERPARK

HEMONYLAAN

WEESPERZIJDE

SWAMMERDAMSTRAAT

BLASIUSSTRAAT

1e OOSTERPARKSTRAAT

DE PIJP

0   200 m

△ 1 2 & 3

BARS AND CAFÉS

Anco	33
Argos	28
Belgique	32
Bern	43
Blincker	64
De Brakke Grond	60
De Buurvrouw	57
Casa Maria	20
Club Jaecques	35
Cuckoo's Nest	10
Cul de Sac	41
Dante	90
Dantzig	31
De Drie Fleschjes	53
Droesem	36
Durty Nelly's	25
The Eagle	65
De Engelbewaarder	70
De Engelse Reet	85
Gaeper	71
't Gasthuis	62
Gollem	51
Hard Rock Café	76
Harry's American Bar	
Het Doktertje	74
Het Paleis	48
Hoppe	82
De Jaren	87
De Koningshut	68
Latei	39
Le Shako	89
Lokaal 't Loosje	45
Luxembourg	83
Mappa	61
Mercurius	4
't Nieuwe Kafé	37
Ot en Sien	1
De Pilserij	34
Scheltema	52
Schuim	50
Stablemaster	15
Tapvreugd	56
Vrankrijk	55
The Web	8
Why Not	7
Wilhelmina Dok	3
Wynand Fockink	44

RESTAURANTS

Bird	66
Centra	6
De Compagnon	11
Green Planet	72
Hemelse Modder	13
Het Begijntje	75
Het karbeel	19
Hoi Tin	38
In de Waag	30
Kantjil en de Tijger	5
De Klaes Compaen	24
Kopke Adega	23
Lana Thai	14
Luden	26
Pannekoekhuis	69
Upstairs	19
Sie Joe	38
De Silveren Spiegel	42
Stereo Sushi	78
Supperclub	54
Tolhuis	2
Tom Yam	86
Tonio	81
Top Thai	16
Van Beeren	46
Vasso	73
Kobe House	9
Werkendam	27

COFFEESHOPS

The Bulldog	47
Dampkring	88
Extase	58
Grasshopper	18
Homegrown Fantasy	22
Josephine Baker	59
Kadinsky	63
Rusland	67
Smoking Bull	21
De Tweede Kamer	79

TEAROOMS

Arnots	91
Cafeine	17
Café Esprit	80
Juicebar Tasty & Healthy	12
Puccini	84
Villa Zeezicht	29

River IJ

Passenger Ferries

DE RUIJTERKADE

PRINS HENDRIKKADE

Scheepvaarthuis

Centraal Station

STATIONS-PLEIN

Centraal Station Ⓜ

GVB

Open Havenfront

PRINS HENDRIKKADE

St Nicolaaskerk

Schreierstoren

OOSTERDOKSKADE

KROME WAAL

GELDERSEKADE

NIEUWE

In 't Aepjen

ZEEDIJK

Red Light District

Amstelkring

Spinhuis

ZEEDIJK

ACHTERBURGWAL

Prostitution Info Centre

Oude Kerk

Prostitution Information Centre

Condomerie Het Gulden Vlies

MARTELAARSGRACHT

Crowne Plaza Hotel

HEKELVELD

NIEUWEZIJDS ARMSTE

HARING PAKKERSSTEEG

KARNE MELKSTE

Damrak

Beurs

DAMRAK

De Bijenkorf

BEURSPLEIN

BEURS-PASSAGE

ZOUTSTEEG

NIEUWENDIJK

Lutherskerk

KATTENGAT

SINGEL

TEERKETEL STEEG

KORTE KOLKSTE

KORTE KORTE STEEG

Magna Plaza

SINGEL

HERENGRACHT

SINGEL

RAADHUISSTRAAT

Theater-museum

DRIEKONINGEN-STRAAT

Old Centre

Nieuwe Kerk

Koninklijk

N

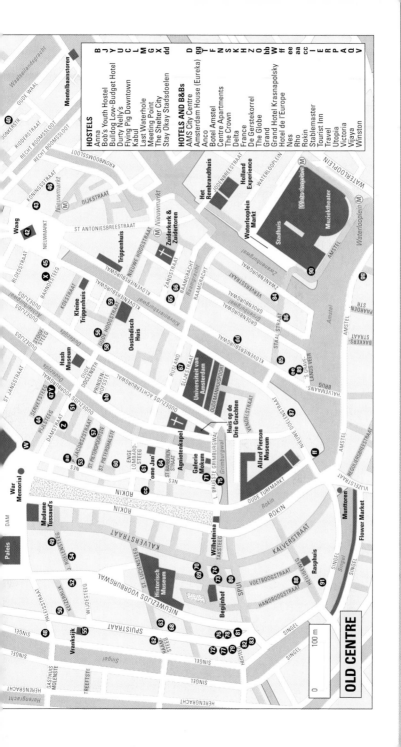

GRACHTENGORDEL WEST

RESTAURANTS	
Amigo	31
Bar5	11
Blakes	40
Bolhoed	7
Bordewijk	2
Chez Georges	17
Christophe	24
Cilubang	44
Damsteeg	33
De Voordeur	15
Intermezzo	14
Koh-I-Noor	30
Lieve	19
The Pancake Bakery	12
Prego	16
Puma	34
Rum Runners	27
D'Theeboom	32
Top Thai	13
Turquoise	37
De Twee Grieken	10
't Zwaantje	36

BARS AND CAFÉS	
Aas van Bokalen	42
De Admiraal	39
't Arendsnest	22
Belhamel	4
De Doffer	43
Hegeraad	1
De Klepel	9
Het Molenpad	46
De Prins	21
Sjaalman	29
't Smackzeyl	3
Spanjer & van Twist	23
Twee Prinsen	8
De Twee Zwaantjes	20
Van Puffelen	35

COFFEESHOPS	
Grey Area	28
La Tertulia	41
Siberië	6

TEAROOMS	
Baton Espresso Corner	18
Buffet van Odette & Yvette	38
Dialoog	26
Greenwood's	25
Lunchcafé Winkel	5
Pompadour Patisserie	45

HOTELS AND B&Bs
Ambassade N
Aspen I
Blakes O
Brian B
Canal House C
Clemens G
Estherea M
Galerij F
Hegra K
Hoksbergen L
't Hotel E
Keizersgracht A
Pax H
Pulitzer J
Toren D
Wiechmann P

0   100 m

De Bijenkorf
Magna Plaza
Koninklijk Paleis
DAM
War Memorial
Hash Museum
Oostindisch Huis
Madame Tussaud's
'Ome Jan'
Agnietenkapel
Drie Grachten
Galerie Mokum
Allard Pierson Museum
Vrankrijk
Historisch Museum
Begijnhof
Rasphuis
Flower Market
Stedelijk Museum Bureau
Woonbootmuseum
De Looier Market
Rommelmarkt
Felix Meritis Building
Bijbels Museum
Cromhouthuizen
No 380
No 386
No 394
Nos 361–369
Singel
Herengracht
Keizersgracht
Prinsengracht
Rokin
KALVERSTRAAT

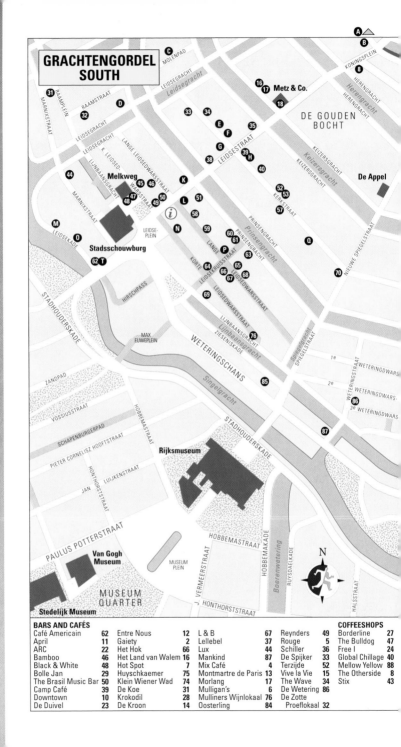

GRACHTENGORDEL SOUTH

BARS AND CAFÉS

Café Americain	62	Entre Nous	12	L & B	67
April	11	Gaiety	2	Lellebel	37
ARC	22	Het Hok	66	Lux	44
Bamboo	46	Het Land van Walem	16	Mankind	87
Black & White	48	Hot Spot	7	Mix Café	4
Bolle Jan	29	Huyschkaemer	75	Montmartre de Paris	13
The Brasil Music Bar	50	Klein Wiener Wad	74	Morlang	17
Camp Café	39	De Koe	31	Mulligan's	6
Downtown	10	De Kroon	14	Mulliners Wijnlokaal	76
De Duivel	23	Krokodil	28	Oosterling	84

Reynders	49	
Rouge	5	
Schiller	36	
De Spijker	33	
Terzijde	52	
Vive la Vie	15	
The Wave	34	
De Wetering	86	
De Zotte		
Proeflokaal	32	

COFFEESHOPS

Borderline	27			
The Bulldog	47			
Free I	24			
Global Chillage	40			
Mellow Yellow	88			
The Otherside	8			
Stix	43			

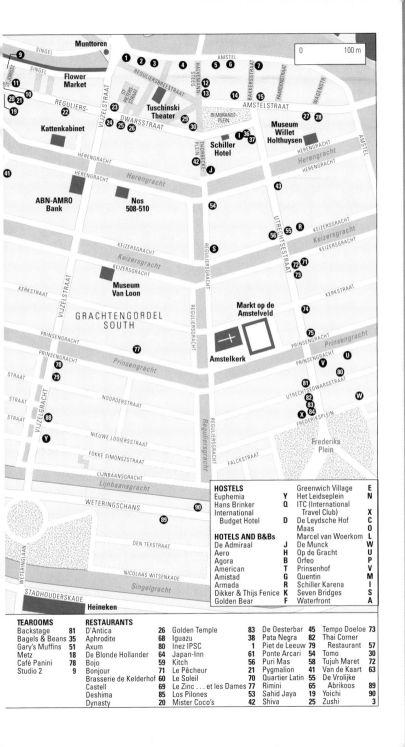

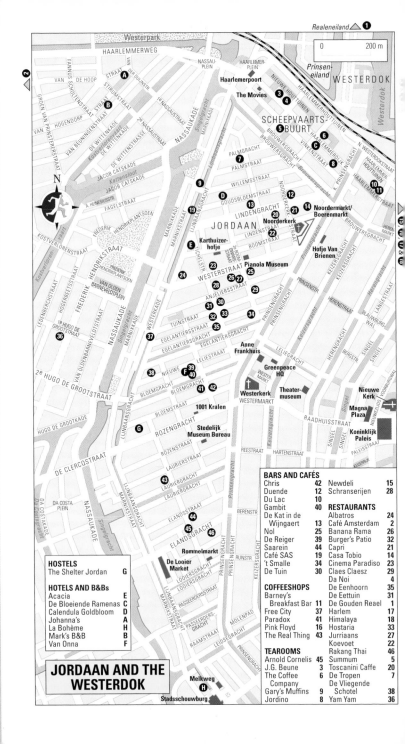

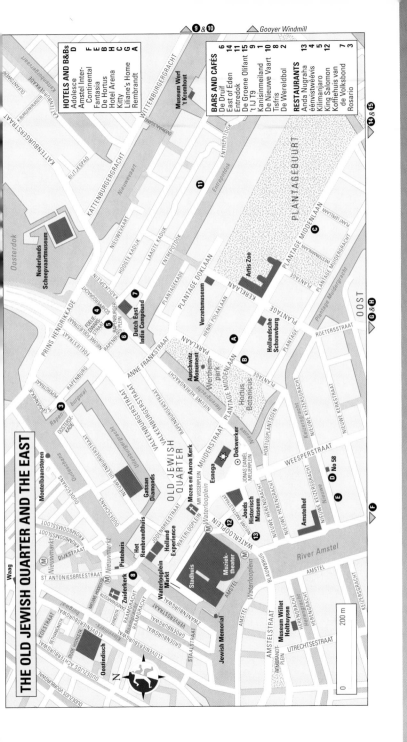

THE OLD JEWISH QUARTER AND THE EAST

HOTELS AND B&Bs

Adolesce	D
Amstel Inter-Continental	F
Fantasia	E
De Hortus	B
Hotel Arena	H
Kitty	C
Liliane's Home	G
Rembrandt	A

BARS AND CAFÉS

De Druif	6
East of Eden	14
Entredok	11
De Groene Olifant	15
't IJ T9	9
Kanisinmeiland	1
De Nieuwe Vaart	10
Tisfris	8
De Wereldbol	2

RESTAURANTS

Anda Nugraha	13
éénvistwéévis	4
Kilimanjaro	5
King Salomon	12
Koffiehuis van de Volksbond	7
Rosario	3

△ & ⑨ & ⑩

△ Gooyer Windmill

0   200 m

N

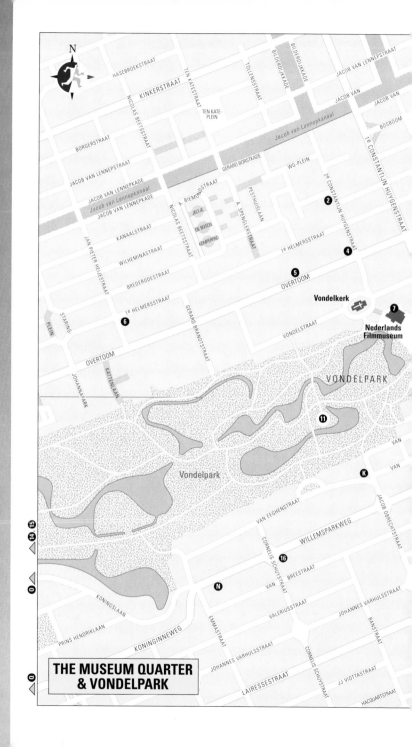

THE MUSEUM QUARTER
& VONDELPARK

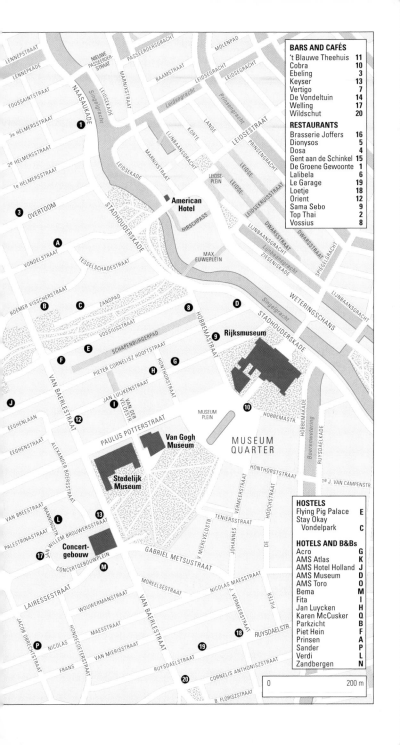

American Hotel

Rijksmuseum

MUSEUM QUARTER

Van Gogh Museum

Stedelijk Museum

Concert-gebouw

MUSEUM PLEIN

0	200 m

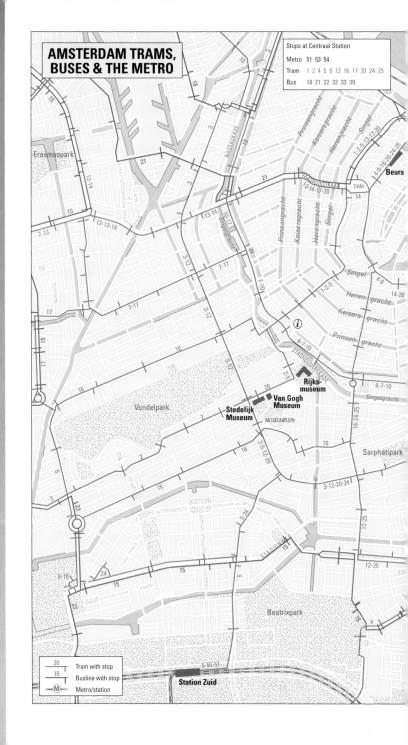

AMSTERDAM TRAMS, BUSES & THE METRO

Stops at Centraal Station
Metro 51 53 54
Tram 1 2 4 5 9 13 16 17 20 24 25
Bus   18 21 22 32 33 39

Erasmuspark

Beurs

DAM

Vondelpark

Rijks-museum

Van Gogh Museum

Stedelijk Museum

MUSEUMPLEIN

Sarphatipark

Beatrixpark

Station Zuid

20 Tram with stop
15 Busline with stop
Ⓜ Metro/station

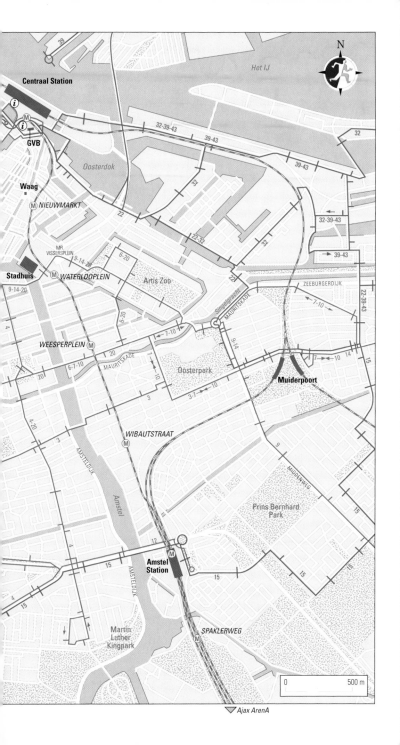

N

Het IJ

Centraal Station

Oosterdok

GVB

Waag

NIEUWMARKT

MR. VISSERSPLEIN

Stadhuis

WATERLOOPLEIN

Artis Zoo

ZEEBURGERDIJK

Singelgracht

MAURITSKADE

WEESPERPLEIN

MAURITSKADE

Oosterpark

Muiderpoort

WIBAUTSTRAAT

AMSTELDIJK

Amstel

MAGDENWEG

Prins Bernhard Park

Amstel Station

AMSTELDIJK

Martin Luther Kingpark

SPAKLERWEG

0   500 m

▽ Ajax ArenA

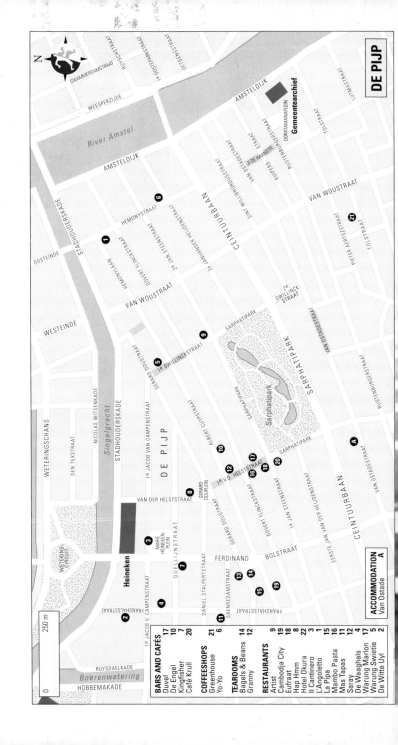

DE PIJP

BARS AND CAFÉS	
Duvel	17
De Engel	10
Kingfisher	7
Café Krull	20

COFFEESHOPS	
Greenhouse	21
Yo-Yo	6

TEAROOMS	
Bagels & Beans	14
Granny	12

RESTAURANTS	
Artist	9
Cambodja City	19
Eufraat	18
Hap Hmm	8
Hotel Okura	22
Il Cantinero	3
L'Angoletto	1
La Pipa	15
Mambo Pasta	16
Mas Tapas	11
Saray	12
De Waaghals	4
Warung Marlon	17
Warung Swietie	5
De Witte Uyl	2

ACCOMMODATION	A
Van Ostade	